D0761006

DOCTOR'S ORDERS

DOCTOR'S ORDERS

Goethe and Enlightenment Thought

Robert D. Tobin

Lewisburg
Bucknell University Press
London: Associated University Presses

Associated University Presses
440 Forsgate Drive
Cranbury, NJ 08512

Associated University Presses
16 Barter Street
London WC1A 2AH, England

Associated University Presses
P.O. Box 338, Port Credit
Mississauga, Ontario
Canada L5G 4L8

The paper used in this publication meets the requirements of the American National Standard for Permanence of Paper for Printed Library Materials Z39.48-1984.

Library of Congress Cataloging-in-Publication Data

Tobin, Robert Deam.
    Doctor's orders : Goethe and Enlightenment thought / Robert D. Tobin.
        p.   cm.
    Includes bibliographical references and index.
    ISBN 0-8387-5466-X (alk. paper)
    1. Goethe, Johann Wolfgang von, 1749–1832. Wilhelm Meisters Lehrjahre. 2. Goethe, Johann Wolfgang von, 1749–1832—Knowledge—Medicine. 3. Medicine in Literature. 4. Literature and medicine—Germany—History—18th century. 5. Medicine—Germany—History—18th century. 6. Enlightenment—Germany. 7. Germany—Intellectual ife—18th century. I. Title.
PT1982.A43 T63 2001
833'.6—dc21

00-068069

PRINTED IN THE UNITED STATES OF AMERICA

Contents

Preface

The doctor's orders are some of the most powerful and absolute in modern western society. Who would be so foolhardy as to disregard his or her doctor's orders? Physicians have an almost unchallenged right to distinguish between good and bad behavior, as the general acceptance of their recommendations about smoking, drinking, diet, and exercise has shown. While some may in fact occasionally ignore the advice of the medical establishment, such transgressions always have the slightly moral flavor of doing something "bad." Indeed, in broad swaths of modern western society, this medical morality applies more deeply and more generally than religious morality.

Part of the reason for the success of the medical model may lie in its claim to access a scientific truth that is less mystical and ambiguous than traditional religious truths. Even if one chooses to smoke, who but the most outrageous of tobacco company executives denies that cigarettes are "bad" for smokers? The medical community may send out conflicting reports about behavior: Is red wine really good for you? What about coffee? And what's the final word on eggs? Nonetheless, few doubt that eventually the truth of these behaviors will come out.

The absolute nature of medical opinions has been strengthened over the years, as scientific discoveries have uncovered bacteria, viruses, chemical imbalances, and the means to combat these problems. But while medicine now frequently has recourse to tests that claim to determine absolutely the status of health, the field was originally much more interpretative in nature. Prior to the nineteenth century, physicians had to *read* body and mind in order to discover the meaning of a particular ailment. Without the knowledge of such phenomena as infectious diseases and genetics, healing was an interpretative art.

Medical power is therefore a historical phenomenon. The rise of medicine in fact coincides with the rise of the bourgeoisie. It is still probably the paramount bourgeois profession, according its practitioners good salaries, a certain (if diminishing) amount of autonomy, and an honorable reputation in civil society. Anyone who teaches at the college level can confirm that a large number of the best and brightest students still aspire to become physicians, even though more experienced doctors chafe at the increasing restrictions on their freedom.

In literature also, the physician often represents the bourgeois perspective. In such plays by Molière as *The Hypochondriac*, physicians and their health-oriented clients play the emergent bourgeois figures, who are mocked in the aristocratic world of seventeenth-century France, but whose descendents will soon achieve great power. Gustave Flaubert's Emma Bovary, who arguably represents the fate of the bourgeoisie once it has achieved preeminence, is married unhappily to a doctor and thus linked to the medical field.[1] In George Eliot's *Middlemarch*, the physician represents hope, sincerity, and progress. The medical mind stands in for the bourgeois worldview, and is then evaluated according to the opinions that authors and readers have of that worldview.

Somewhere between the bumbling doctors of Molière, who primarily provide amusement for the court audiences, and the tragic figures of *Madame Bovary* and *Middlemarch*, which allow middle-class society to contemplate its hopes and failings, the doctor comes into his own. Between these works lies the eighteenth century, in whose literature one finds an increasing fascination with the medical profession. The Age of Enlightenment, with its belief in science and its dreams for improving humanity, provided a comfortable home for the physician.

Germany, whose literature in many ways came of age in the eighteenth century, provides a particularly clear view of these medical developments. While Germany has of course a splendid medieval literary tradition, its Renaissance and baroque literature has not attained the kind of worldwide renown that the literature from those time periods in Spain, England, France, or Italy has. In the United States, at least, many German departments begin their surveys of German literature with the eighteenth century.[2] The birth of German literature is thus constructed as taking place simultaneously with the rise of the bourgeoisie and the rise of medicine. In the German tradition, the literary depiction of the rise of the physician stands out with particular clarity.

An exceedingly acute chronicle of the emerging bourgeoisie and its medical mind-set can be found in Goethe's *Wilhelm Meister's Apprenticeship*. It is to be feared that in the United States Goethe's name remains better known than his works, but it goes without saying that in Germany he is one of the foundations of the national literary tradition. The *Apprenticeship* is not at all well known in the United States, but is probably the most important novel in German literary history. Its appearance sparked the coinage of a name for a new genre, the "bildungsroman," which has since come to be a meaningful term in Anglo-Saxon literary studies as well as in German ones.

A culture saw itself flatteringly reflected in the story of young Wilhelm Meister, who goes from middle-class origins through a bohemian phase on the stage to a life as landed gentry with wife and children. As would be expected, given Goethe's own wealthy but nonaristocratic background, the reflection of German culture has a bourgeois inflection. Wilhelm Meister periodically thematizes his class status, and in the end the novel can be seen as a triumph of the bourgeois worldview, supported by reformist aristocrats.

Medicine plays an integral part of this bourgeois and reformist tradition in the *Apprenticeship*. Wilhelm Meister himself represents the unity of the bourgeois and the medical perspectives when he chooses, in *Wilhelm Meister's Journeyman Years*, the sequel to the *Apprenticeship*, to become a physician. In retrospect, the choice makes perfect sense, for the organization forming and developing Wilhelm Meister, the so-called Tower Society, consistently promotes the progressive medical view. Wilhelm is seen as wounded and in need of a cure, which the Society provides. The Society surrounds itself with progressive medical figures and uses the most modern medicine of its day to take care of Wilhelm and other characters.

The Society's members are successful with Wilhelm, but less so with the other characters, who are written off as medical losses. These medical losses reveal the darker side of the rise of the bourgeoisie—a triumph of economy and rationality that leaves casualties in its wake. Goethe's novel, published as the eighteenth century turned into the nineteenth and as the bourgeoisie and its medical model rose to power, nonjudgmentally records the positive and the negative sides of these developments. A triumphant nationalist bourgeoisie in the nineteenth century chose to emphasize the positive aspects of Wilhelm's development. Many twentieth-century readers reviewed the novel with more critical eyes. But however one evaluates the *Apprenticeship* and the events it relates, it is clear that it documents the rise of the bourgeoisie and a medical model.

This study hopes to demonstrate the significance of medicine in the *Apprenticeship* and show how entwined the medical worldview is with that of the bourgeoisie. In so doing, it will shed light from a new perspective on this novel, which originated the genre of the bildungsroman and which has been so important for the German tradition. It is to be hoped that this analysis will introduce some readers to this important literary work. Because of the novel's importance in the German-speaking world, this study should also afford insight into German culture.

Most importantly, this research will allow for an investigation of medicine, which should reveal the origins of its claims to truth. Although there are important moments of cultural specificity in the differing medical traditions, overall it can be said that the bourgeois medical model is as important (if not more important) throughout the West in the twenty-first century as it was in Germany at the end of the eighteenth century. Thus a careful analysis of the history of this medical worldview will allow readers to appreciate both its benefits and its shortcomings. In this way, Goethe's late-eighteenth-century classic can still provide a service of inestimable value to twenty-first-century readers.

Acknowledgments

This book has been a long time in the making, and a great many people have helped me considerably as I worked on it. My interests in eighteenth-century literature and medicine were aroused in seminars taught by Stanley Corngold and Theodore Ziolkowski. As my dissertation advisor, Stanley Corngold gave me invaluable feedback on this project. Ruth Klüger's passion for Goethe's novels inspired me while I was in graduate school as well. My research in Germany was aided by Professors Wolfram Mauser and Friedrich Kittler. In the United States, many scholars have encouraged me in the study of eighteenth-century medicine and Goethe, including Jane and Marshall Brown, Todd Kontje, W. Daniel Wilson, Alice Kuzniar, Sander Gilman, and Laurence Rickels. Much of the initial research for this book was funded first by the DAAD and then through a position as research assistant with Professor Mauser. Whitman College funded a sabbatical, during which this book took its present form, and has generally been extraordinarily generous in supporting my research.

I dedicate the book to Joachim Pfeiffer and all the friends in Freiburg who made life there such a joy.

I have quoted extensively from *Wilhelm Meister's Apprenticeship,* translated by Eric A. Blackall, in cooperation with Victor Lange. This is volume 9 of Johann Wolfgang Goethe, *The Collected Works,* edited by Victor Lange, Eric A. Blackall, and Cyrus Hamlin (New York: Suhrkamp, 1989). Both Suhrkamp Verlag and Princeton University Press, which now holds the license for this edition in the United States, have generously given their permission for me to use this translation.

Goethe, Johann Wolfgang; *The Collected Works,* vol. 9. Copyright 1989 by PUP. Reprinted by permission of Princeton University Press.

Note on Goethe Editions
and Abbreviations

References to Goethe will be included parenthetically within the text, unless the reference intrudes on the flow of the reading too much. Given Goethe's canonical status, there are many editions of Goethe's works, each with its own problems. In this book, the following system is used:

Wherever possible, Goethe's works are cited from the most widely available Goethe edition, the Hamburger Ausgabe (HA): *Goethes Werke. Hamburger Ausgabe in 14 Bänden*, ed. Erich Trunz, 8th ed. (Munich: Beck, 1981).

Works not included in the Hamburger Ausgabe, including diary entries and letters, are cited from the most complete Goethe edition, the Weimarer Ausgabe (WA): *Goethes Werke. Herausgegeben im Auftrage der Großherzogin Sophie von Sachsen*, 143 vols. (1887–1919; reprint, Munich: DTV, 1987).

The conversations are cited from the Artemis Ausgabe (AA): *Johann Wolfgang Goethe, Gedenkausgabe der Werke, Briefe, und Gespräche*, ed. Ernst Beutler, 25 vols. (Zürich: Artemis, 1949).

Occasional references are made to the commentary in the Münchner Ausgabe (MA): *Johann Wolfgang von Goethe. Sämtliche Werke nach Epochen seines Schaffens. Münchner Ausgabe*, ed. Karl Richter, 20 vols. (Munich: Hanser, 1985–91).

For the convenience of the reader, wherever possible, English translations are taken from the Suhrkamp Edition (SE): *Goethe's Collected Works*, ed. Victor Lange, Eric A. Blackall, and Cyrus Hamlin, 12 vols. (Boston: Suhrkamp, 1982). Other translations are my own.

In addition, I use the following abbreviation:

MzE: *Gnothi Sauton oder Magazin zur Erfahrungseelenkunde* (Magazine of experiential psychology) (1782–92) . It is cited from the first ten volumes in Karl Philipp Moritz, *Die Schriften in dreissig Bänden*, ed. Petra and Uwe Nettelbeck (Nördlingen: Greno, 1986). It is also available, but with different pagination, in a facsimile edition, ed. Anke Bennholdt-Thomsen and Alfredo Guzzoni (Lindau: Antiqua, 1979).

DOCTOR'S ORDERS

1

Medicine in Goethe's Time, Life, and Works

At the end of the eighteenth century, Johann Wolfgang von Goethe (1749–1832) published one of his most famous novels, *Wilhelm Meister's Apprenticeship (Wilhelm Meisters Lehrjahre*, 1795–96). This novel is said to have founded the genre of the bildungsroman, the portrayal of a protagonist's discovery of him- or herself and of his or her position in the community. More than two centuries later, the novel retains a timely relevance that still attracts readers and elicits criticism and commentary. The *Apprenticeship* maintains its edge because its description of self-discovery is extraordinarily sensitive to societal, familial, and personal developments that were quite new in the late eighteenth century and remain powerful in the twentieth-first century.

One such development is the rise of medicine as an institution structuring the self and society. The controlling force behind the *Apprenticeship*, the Tower Society, embraces the medical attitudes arising in the eighteenth century, and recategorizes as pathological a number of characteristics, from a mania for theater to religious devotion, transvestism, and homosexuality. It uses the progressive medicine of its era to heal the characters of the novel. Whether this cure is entirely and exclusively positive remains in doubt. But it remains clear that *Wilhelm Meister's Apprenticeship* carefully depicts the new and modern medicine of its day and shows how this nascent institution of modern medicine prescribes the image of humanity at the center of the bildungsroman.

MEDICINE IN THE EIGHTEENTH CENTURY

Foucault argues provocatively that "before the end of the eighteenth century, man did not exist."[1] Following in Foucault's footsteps, others have discovered in the late eighteenth century the emergence of the modern conception of the body as well as of the sexes.[2] Like Foucault, who argues that an epistemic shift between the classical and the modern took place "at the outer limits" between 1775 and 1825 and more specifically between 1795 and 1800,[3] these scholars are quite specific about the time period in which this change took place: Londa Schiebinger, for instance, sees the development of the "two-sex system," the understanding of male and female as fundamentally different and complementary, as largely completed by the 1790s.[4] This new sense of humanity reconstructed the family, too, giving birth to the "first" children.[5] Children's literature and toys solidified the boundaries of childhood. It has been argued that the institution of adolescence appeared in the eighteenth century.[6] Although accounts of origins are always suspect, the eighteenth century can make a claim to offer the first Black writing within the Euro-American tradition (Phillis Wheatley),[7] the first feminist (Mary Wollstonecraft), and the first modern homosexual subcultures.[8] For these and many other reasons, Donna Haraway situates in the eighteenth century the beginnings of the embedding of "the great historical constructions of gender, race, and class . . . in the organically naked bodies of woman, the colonized or enslaved, and the worker."[9] Thus, the eighteenth century provides an excellent starting point for the study of linguistically and socially constructed aspects of reality.

Medicine was intimately involved with all of these constructions in the eighteenth century. One historian of medicine has noted that it was particularly interested in demographic patterns at this time, as it moved from an interest in private to public health and cataloged the medical status of demographic groups like Blacks, prisoners, and military men.[10] While the rising status of the physician made him a prototypical bourgeois, the ailments of the emerging bourgeoisie—hypochondria and melancholy—helped found the era's new medicine. Research into women's health issues—particularly those having to do with menstruation and the reproductive system—changed the way both medicine and gender were perceived. This was also the era when the intense medical interest in masturbation began the process of pathologizing sexuality. Medicine was, after all, in this era one of the few discourses (along with classics and religion) that could legitimately discuss sexuality. At this time, medicine was also particularly interested in the colonial effort: European nations expressly directed the explorers they sent out to make medical discoveries and, on the home front, physicians like Zimmermann avidly read the anthropological reports sent home by the explorers.[11] Especially in the eighteenth century, medicine tried to determine the medical criteria of body and mind that produced race.[12] A medical man, Samuel Thomas von Soemmerring (1755–1830), not only completed one of the first studies of the skeleton demonstrating that sex differences could be found at the level of the bone, but also contributed an important two-volume work on the medicine of race: *On the Physical Difference of the Negro from the European.*[13] Indeed in this era, medicine let loose the notion—one that admittedly only came into its own in the nineteenth century—that race, in particular the Jewish race, might be a disease.[14] This brief overview shows that not only is medicine in general implicated in the construction of race, sexuality, and ethnicity, but also eighteenth-century medicine has an important role to play in the development of these materialized discursive objects.

Not coincidentally, along with all these other constructions, "literature," in its modern sense, also appears at the end of the eighteenth century.[15] Ian Watt is famous for observing that the modern novel rises in this era.[16] Medicine was involved with this literary development, too. At the same time that modern literature appeared, the case study, the narrative of sickness, developed significantly. To begin with, autobiographical accounts of those afflicted by mental and physical illnesses became part of the tradition of modern storytelling, as such first-person memoirs as Diaetophilus's *Physical and Psychological History of His Seven-year Epilepsy* show.[17] Julia Epstein, who reports that "the first specific calls for a systematic record keeping came" in the first half of the eighteenth century under the influence of such reforming physicians as Boerhaave, suggests that the "full shift into placing diagnostic importance on a record of the body's *story* occurred by the later eighteenth century," placing it in the context of the rise of periodical journalism and the novel.[18] Duden confirms that detailed medical histories of patients were emerging in the early eighteenth century in Germany.[19]

Karl Philipp Moritz is an especially important figure in the interrelated development of literature and medicine. His own novel, *Anton Reiser: A Psychological Novel* (1785), is filled with insight into psychology, as its subtitle suggests. In addition, he urged the ill (especially the mentally ill) to write about their conditions; he published many of these first-person accounts of illness in his *Magazine of Experiential Psychology*, which was one of the first psychological journals anywhere.[20] His awareness of the linguistic nature of psychological illness manifests itself in the many articles in the *Magazine* that concentrate on the psychological ramifications of such phenomena as impersonal verbs, the psychology of the deaf and dumb, the acquisition of language, the conjugation of the verb *sein* (to be), and the origins of language.[21]

In this era, when literature and medicine worked together in such close harmony,[22] it is not surprising that many of the writers of fiction could be called "medicinal novelists" because of their medical knowledge and training. In England, the novelist Tobias Smollett (1721–71) and the poet

Erasmus Darwin (1731–1802), grandfather of the famous scientist Charles Darwin, both had medical training. Besides Karl Philipp Moritz (1756–93), there were others in the German-speaking world as well. The poet Albrecht Haller (1708–77) will show up repeatedly in this study because of his innovative medical work, especially regarding the nervous system. Gotthold Ephraim Lessing (1729–81) studied some medicine. The novelist Johann Heinrich Jung-Stilling (1740–1817) was an ophthalmologist by profession. The philosopher Johann Gottfried Herder (1744–1803) studied surgery before turning to philosophy and always emphasized the usefulness of medicine for psychological studies; indeed, Simon Richter finds medical discourses to be central to his aesthetics.[23] Another of the era's medical writers was Friedrich Schiller (1759–1805), who read Moritz's *Magazine* and completed two dissertations on medicine.[24]

Corresponding to the "medicinal novelist," the "philosophical physician," the scientifically trained doctor who can draw metaphysical conclusions from the hard facts he encounters in his patients, became an increasingly popular ideal in the eighteenth century. The term comes from Melchior Adam Weickard (1742–1803), the physician who popularized medicine in Germany and Russia, where he was court physician to Catherine the Great. The title of his book, *The Philosophical Physician* (*Der philosophische Arzt*, 2d ed., 1782), captured the spirit of his era's medical professionals. Like Weickard, physicians began to write in the vernacular in this century, and even the most technical of their writings was accessible to the reading public. The details of their teachings will be discussed later, but for now it suffices to say that medicine and literature were probably never so intertwined as in the eighteenth century.

PHYSICIANS IN GOETHE'S LIFE

In Goethe's writings there is ample evidence of a fascination with medicine.[25] A look at this evidence will shed light not only on Goethe but also on the eighteenth-century medical world in Germany—in other words, a review of Goethe's knowledge of his era's medicine can also serve as an introduction to the primary figures of that medicine.

Goethe did not study and publish on medicine as intensively as his friends and acquaintances, such as Lessing, Herder, Jung-Stilling, Moritz, and Schiller. Indeed, there are indications that he had a more distanced attitude toward medicine than many of his contemporaries. Nonetheless, his diary entries and other evidence show that he was well-informed and conversant on the subject. Goethe's friendship with physicians began while he was still a student. In Leipzig, he regularly ate lunch with a professor of medicine, Christian Gottlieb Ludwig (1709–73), at whose home he met a large circle of medical students, physicians, and scientists: "Now in this house I only heard conversation about medicine or natural history."[26] Although Goethe goes on to say that he was not exclusively interested in such subjects, he nonetheless continued to cultivate the acquaintance of medical students at Strassburg when, sometime later, he transferred to the university there: "Most of my table companions were medical students . . . thus at the table I heard therefore nothing but medical discussions" (SE 4:269; HA 9:361). As a young man conversing with Lavater, Goethe reportedly found medical case studies immensely useful: "Writing *historiam morbi* without any moral a, b, c, d given below is a thousand times more useful than the most splendid moral doctrine, represented historically or poetically."[27]

If Goethe's interest in medicine began while he was a student, it flourished in the 1780s.[28] At Weimar, Goethe continued learning from and socializing with members of the medical community. His own physician for many years was Christian Wilhelm Hufeland (1762–1836), who had studied with the famous scientist Georg Christoph Lichtenberg and went on to become the author of numerous important texts on medical and psychological subjects. Subsequently Hufeland became a professor of medicine at the nearby University of Jena before moving on to Berlin. As Goethe interacted with him frequently, Hufeland's name appears regularly in Goethe's diaries, often directly before or after a reference to work on *Wilhelm Meister*, "the novel."[29] Schiller's personal physician, Johann Christian Stark (1753–1811), figures extremely prominently in Goethe's diaries also, especially in the 1790s.[30]

Goethe was particularly interested in human anatomy, which he regarded as subordinate to medicine (SE 12:118; HA 13:171). The importance of anatomy for medicine actually shows up in *Wilhelm Meister's Journeyman Years*, when Wilhelm begins his study of surgery with lessons in anatomy (SE 10:322; HA 8:322). Throughout the 1780s and 1790s, Goethe attended lectures on anatomy by the physician Justus Christian Loder (1753–1832): "We [Goethe and the brothers Humboldt], along with our friend Meyer, walked mornings in deepest snow to see in an almost empty anatomical auditorium these important connections demonstrated most clearly according to the most exact preparations."[31] This pattern continued in 1795, as Goethe continued to work on *Wilhelm Meister:* "I almost never lost sight of anatomy and physiology in this year. With the clarity that distinguishes him, Counsellor Loder demonstrated the human brain to a small circle of friends, in the traditional way, starting at the top and moving by layers inward."[32] Others corroborated Goethe's story—David Veit wrote to Rahel Levin on 4 June 1795 that Goethe "comes every time to our clinic and inquires about every detail. He has mastered the theoretical parts completely."[33]

As early as 1786, Goethe's anatomical work with Loder resulted in his famous discovery in humans of the intermaxillary bone *(Zwischenkiefer-knochen)*, a jawbone that some eighteenth-century anatomists had attributed exclusively to animals (SE 12:111–16; HA 13:184–96, 593–94). References in the diaries to Goethe's teacher in anatomy, Loder, are almost too numerous to remark. He is one of the first physicians to merit mention, appearing as early as the 1780s;[34] like Hufeland, Loder appears again and again in connection with the final preparations of *Wilhelm Meister.*[35]

In 1795, after a reference to Loder's anatomical studies, Goethe mentions Soemmerring, the physician whose anatomical studies especially emphasized the medical particularity of Blacks and women. Goethe, incidentally, had complimented Soemmerring on his book about Africans (6 March 1785; WA 4.7:21). Between 1791 and 1797, Goethe and Soemmerring corresponded extensively and Soemmerring's name appears frequently throughout the 1790s, both in the *Campaign in France (Campagne in Frankreich)* and in the shorter autobiographical writings of the era. In addition to Soemmerring's work on anatomy, his attempt to find an organ of the soul in the body—that is to say, empirical proof of the unity of mind and body—attracted Goethe's particular, if somewhat skeptical, interest (Goethe to Soemmerring, 28 August 1796; WA 4.11:174–78). As the most intense phase of Goethe's friendship with Soemmerring took place in the first half of the 1790s, it was intricately interwoven with the birth of the novel. Goethe sent Soemmerring copies of the novel as it came out (12 January 1795, 25 May 1795; WA 4.10:229, 264, see also WA 1.35:278). Soemmerring enjoyed the novel and attempted to apply his medical and anatomical skills to it: "You will not be surprised," he wrote to Goethe, "that I am trying to anatomize, unravel, and decipher much in it."[36]

Elsewhere in his autobiographical works Goethe gives further indication of his taste in medical scholarship. He especially praises the aphorisms of the highly influential physician Hermann Boerhaave (1668–1738), who was the most famous physician of his day, an author of widely read medical textbooks and an important early-eighteenth-century medical reformer.[37] In both *Poetry and Truth (Dichtung und Wahrheit,* 1811–14) and the *Campaign in France* he also lauds the metaphysical observations of the Genevan professor Charles Bonnet (1720–93).[38] Later in life, Goethe wrote a review of *A Psychology in Clarification of Phenomena from the Soul (Psychologie zur Erklärung der Seelenerscheinungen,* 1824) by the Berlin professor Ernst R. Stiedenroth (1794–1858), maintaining that the controversies in the realm of psychology about "higher" and "lower" faculties of the soul had always been of interest to him (SE 12:45–46; HA 13:42).

In *Poetry and Truth,* Goethe attributes a leading role in eighteenth-century German intellectual development to the physicians: "Following the lead of a foreigner, Tissot, the physicians also began making a diligent effort to affect the general development of culture. Haller, Unzer, and Zimmermann exerted a very great influence . . ." (SE 4:210).[39] That physicians had an effect on the general *Bildung* of the culture is a fact that should enter into more discussions of that paradigmatic bildungsroman, *Wilhelm Meister.*

As mentioned, Goethe's interest in medicine was especially intense in the 1780s and 1790s, as he was completing *Wilhelm Meister's Apprenticeship.* Indeed, on a single day in July of 1795, a year before the completion of the novel, Goethe listed six medical authors whose works he presumably read: "Hufeland lifeforce, Brandis, Darvin, Broun. Weickert Jacob's empirical psychology. Reil."[40] In the course of this analysis, we will become familiar with these and many other eighteenth-century physicians who helped construct the image of humanity central to the project of the bildungsroman.

PATIENTS IN GOETHE'S LIFE

Although his spoofs and lampoons show that he always maintained a certain ironic detachment from the medical field, Goethe clearly knew quite a bit about his era's medicine. Indeed, Goethe was sufficiently interested in psychological medicine to dabble in psychological cures himself, especially from the 1770s through the 1790s. Considering himself a "moral physician" *(moralischer Leibarzt)*[41] Goethe had ample opportunity at the court of Weimar to exercise his psychological ingenuity. A subject of Duke Carl August of Sachsen-Weimar-Eisenach (1757–1828) provided one such occasion: "An old sickness is ruining the Einsiedel family, the state of the house, politics and morals have had such an effect on the father that he has undertaken actions that are near madness, insane, or at least difficult to explain."[42] In a letter to Charlotte von Stein (1742–1827) on 5 September 1785, Goethe humorously related another example of his psychological expertise, this time practiced upon Herder's wife, Marie Caroline (1750–1809):

Yesterday evening I performed a truly psychological trick [*ein recht Psychologisches Kunststück*]. Mrs. Herder was still most hypochondriacally tense [*auf das hypochondrischte gespannt*] about everything unpleasant that had happened to her in Carlsbad. Especially about her housemate. I had her tell me everything and confess the poor manners of others and her own mistakes, with the smallest details and consequences, and at the end I absolved her and with this phrase jocularly made her understand that these things were now done with and thrown into the depths of the ocean. She herself became merry about that and is now truly cured.[43]

The indirect and seemingly casual approach to Herder's hypochondria, the staged confession, and the idea of relieving mental tensions by acting them out are, as will become clear, characteristic features of eighteenth-century medicine.

Goethe gave more serious help to Friedrich V. L. Plessing (1749–1806), who wrote to him twice in 1777 requesting help in his battle with hypochondria and melancholia. Goethe did not answer directly but traveled incognito to Wernigerode in the Harz Mountains, where Plessing lived. Without ever revealing his identity, he advised the young man to avoid excessive introspection and get involved with nature and the outside world: "[O]ne can save and liberate oneself from a painful, self-torturing, gloomy state of the soul only by observation of nature and cordial participation in the external world."[44] Goethe was dissatisfied with his efforts in this instance, for he felt that Plessing remained eccentric and lonely, though he later became a successful academician.

Goethe persisted in his charitable work, and later took on the case of a man called Johann Friedrich Krafft. "Krafft" is only a pseudonym, and little is known about this man, except that he was a well-educated and well-traveled civil servant who, apparently because of a mishap on the job, lost his opportunity for a good position in Weimar. In 1778, plagued by hypochondria, he turned to Goethe for help. Goethe took on Krafft's case with a remarkable sense of devotion, hoping to restore his sense of well-being: "Were that I were in the position to brighten your gloomy state and give you a steady cheerfulness."[45] By this point, Goethe had acquired an understanding of the complexities involved in curing the mentally ill and no longer hoped for quick solutions. His metaphorical description of Krafft's situation is as sober as it is beautiful: "At this pond, which an angel only rarely disturbs, hundreds have waited many years, only a few can recover, and I am not the man suddenly to say: stand and go forth."[46] This general skepticism of rapid cures for the mentally ill manifests itself in Goethe's acknowledgment that individual hypochondriac fears (in this case about the city of Jena) could not be dismissed by mere reason: "I know that a person's imaginations are real to him. Therefore, although the image that you make for yourself of Jena is wrong, I know that nothing can be reasoned away less easily than such a hypochondriac anxiety."[47] Goethe's treatment of Krafft began with the assumption of fairly autocratic control over his life, combined with the assurance of financial support. He then encouraged Krafft to do such things as lead an active life, write an autobiography, and take charge of the education of a child. In the next chapters, it will be seen that all of this was much in the manner of eighteenth-century physicians.[48]

MEDICINE IN GOETHE'S WRITINGS

By now, admittedly, the list of physicians and patients Goethe mentions has become very long. Hopefully the names will become more familiar in the course of this investigation. What is important at this point is the link that Goethe draws between the medical trends of the time and societal changes in general. As Goethe himself notes in *Poetry and Truth*, "physicians" at large, not just one or two, affect the "general development." Public health policy, information on health in both journals and best-selling books, new medical technologies such as vaccinations, reforms in the education of physicians and in the structure of clinics and insane asylums—these are just some examples of the broad eighteenth-century medical discursive formation that could easily appear in a novel without the conscious effort of its author. Indeed, because such changes can affect a literary work in ways that transcend the individual author, the actual biographical connections between Goethe and specific physicians represent only one route bridging medical discourse and Goethe's writings. A novel like *Wilhelm Meister* might include a vast amount of medical discourse, mediated consciously or unconsciously by the author himself or even more generally by society at large.

However it got into his works, it is certainly true that medicine plays a large role in many of Goethe's writings. One turn-of-the-century scholar humorously tallies up the list of mentally ill patients in Goethe's works, labeling them "crazy Werther," "hysterical Lila," "paranoid Orestes," "mentally ill Tasso," "insane Harper," "fully degenerate Mignon," the "feeble-minded count," "the Beautiful Soul suffering from religious delusions," the "pathologically tense Aurelie," the "completely pathological Ottilie," "bizarre Makarie," "the decidedly abnormal deranged pilgrim," "the maniacal Cellini," "poor acutely confused Gretchen," and "the megalomaniac Faust."[49]

Although Gerber had his tongue in his cheek as he described these characters with the relatively new medical terminology available to him, some of these characters do merit attention. Goethe's early popular success, *The Sufferings of Young Werther* (*Die Leiden des jungen Werthers*, first version 1777), is about a suicide that one could term pathological, and indeed the novel directly addresses the question of whether the emotions and passions are sicknesses (SE 11:23; HA 6:33).[50] To emphasize the point, the novel also has a certifiably mad character who, like Werther, loved Lotte and whose madness apparently developed out of that love (SE 11:62–64; HA 6:88–91).[51] Diener has pointed out how another early work, *Lila* (first version 1777), dramatically depicts the madness of a character named Lila and her cure by a wise physician. *Faust* is also full of sickness and healing. Margarete's delusions are one obvious example of madness, but Faust himself can also be seen as a melancholic.[52] At the same time, Nager notes that *Faust* presents a veritable panoply of physician figures, consisting of Chiron, "the mythological hero"; Mephisto, "the charlatan"; Faust, "the human-all-too-human doctor"; and Wagner, "the technician."[53]

MEDICINE IN *WILHELM MEISTER'S APPRENTICESHIP*

As Gerber's list of sick characters in Goethe's oeuvre suggests, questions of sickness, healing, and health certainly play a major role in *Wilhelm Meister's Apprenticeship*. Mignon has heart pains, the Harper needs medical treatment for his insanity. Aurelie has headaches, Barbara toothaches. Therese's mother is infertile and Frau Melina has a stillborn child. The account of the stroke suffered by Therese's father, complete with right-side paralysis and language difficulties, is said to be clinically perfect.[54] According to Natalie, the Beautiful Soul suffers from "delicate health" (SE 9:317; HA 7:517), as does the physician for the Society of the Tower (SE 9:210; HA 7:347). As Theodore Ziolkowski has noted, madness permeates the entire novel, from the classic hysteria, melancholy, and hypochondria of Ophelia, the count, and the countess, to the sexual repression of the Beautiful Soul and the pathologies of Augustin, Sperata, and Mignon.[55] Alongside this panoply of sick characters stand representatives of health such as physicians and surgeons. The relatively high incidence of illness in a work by an author who allegedly declared that people should ignore sickness and that only health merited comment[56] suggests that a look at the medicine that Goethe studied throughout his life, especially when completing the *Apprenticeship*, could reveal much about the novel.

These medicinal revelations might help answer questions that the novel has presented to its readers for two centuries now. Indeed, even its author struggled with the novel. Goethe thought about and worked on *Wilhelm Meister* for most of his adult life. He began writing it in the 1770s, fresh from the successes of *Götz* and *Werther* and excited by the energy of the Storm and Stress; the novel receives its first mention in his diary entry of 16 February 1777 (WA 3.1:34). By 1782, Goethe referred to the novel as *Wilhelm Meister's Theatrical Mission*, which he worked on in the 1780s.[57] In this version, the young protagonist emerges from a dysfunctional bourgeois family. His parents are estranged from each other and distant from their child, who must turn to his grandmother for support. Eventually he embraces a bohemian life in the theatrical milieu. Perhaps Goethe planned to have Wilhelm Meister develop a version of the national theater for which so many Germans yearned in the late eighteenth century. Unwilling or unable to conclude Wilhelm's "theatrical mission," however, he abandoned the project when traveling to Italy in 1786, and devoted himself to various obligations related to the publication of the first edition of his collected works. The amusing and highly readable two-hundred-page fragment was lost for over a century, until a copy made by Barbara Schultheß and her daughter appeared in 1910.

By the time Goethe returned to the Wilhelm Meister story in 1794, he had evolved from the foremost *Genie* of the Storm and Stress to the most powerful bureaucrat in the administration of the duchy of Weimar.[58] Reflecting that transition, Wilhelm's theatrical ambitions in the new version are no longer a mission awaiting fulfillment, but rather merely a fruitful detour on the road to productive membership in society. The title of the novel, finally published in 1795–96,[59] became *Wilhelm Meister's Apprenticeship*. Wilhelm's formerly dysfunctional family emerges from the rewriting as an idealized bourgeois unit consisting of hardworking father, loving mother, and playful child, without interference of relatives or servants. While many of Wilhelm's theatrical adventures remain the same, Goethe adds the Tower Society *(Turmgesellschaft),* an association of liberal bourgeois and reform-minded nobility somewhat similar to the Illuminati and the Masons,[60] who oversee the protagonist's development. Through various mysterious machinations they lead him through his encounter with the arts and the theatrical world back into the world of business and the bourgeois family. Significantly, issues of medicine and sickness become more important in the *Apprenticeship*, with the Tower Society assuming the mantle of health, in opposition to the many sickly characters whom Wilhelm encounters early on in his adventures.[61]

The *Apprenticeship* ends with Wilhelm's assumption of bourgeois responsibility, as he marries Natalie, acknowledges the son he and Mariane begat, and joins the Tower Society. How Wilhelm concretely fulfills his obligations remains left to the reader's imagination. In the last three decades of his life, therefore, Goethe attempted to flesh out this vision of a productive life in society in *Wilhelm Meister's Journeyman Years (Wilhelm Meisters Wanderjahre)*. Goethe began to write many of the novel's inserted novellas in the decade immediately following the publication of the *Apprenticeship*. The *Journeyman Years* were first published in 1821; Goethe, however, completely revised them for a second edition published in 1829. This astonishing collage of novellas, aphorisms, letters, poems, and diaries relates Wilhelm Meister's further adventures, along with one interesting flashback to the protagonist's youth, providing the reader with a clearer example of a productive life in society than was present in the *Apprenticeship*.

Family continues to play a central role in the novel: Although his wife has moved to America while he remains in Europe as a journeyman, he does find time to develop his relationship with his son. Sickness also remains an issue: The old matriarch of the family, Makarie, for instance suffers from a mysterious condition that has at least the appearance of illness (SE 10:183, 410; HA 8:127, 450). Importantly, Wilhelm becomes a surgeon. In the course of the novel, Wilhelm and the Tower Society attempt to come to terms with specific psychological, aesthetic, pedagogical, medical, and economic developments of the early nineteenth century.[62]

CRITICAL RESPONSES TO WILHELM MEISTER'S APPRENTICESHIP

If Goethe spent most of his adult life working on versions of the Wilhelm Meister story,[63] it is no wonder that the novel has perplexed literary critics since its appearance. They have asked what the novel says about the relationship between art and life, and what proposals it offers for leading a healthy life in society. These are questions that can be described as medical: medicine also asks about the relationship between art and life, signifiers and signifieds, or symptoms and diseases. Similarly, medicine also looks for cures that enable people to lead lives that promote health. It is therefore to be hoped that a study of the medical side of the *Apprenticeship* will shed light on some of the issues that have bedeviled critics for two centuries.

From the beginning, one interpretative approach has regarded the novel as edifying or curative in a very direct way. In letters written as the final version of the novel appeared, Friedrich Schiller praised Goethe's accurate and instructive portrayal of Wilhelm Meister's development from his initially vague dreams as an immature youth to concrete, specific actions as a productive member of society.[64] Only a year after its appearance, Daniel Jenisch (1762–1804) emphasized the novel's didactic value in his book-length treatment, *On the Most Conspicuous Peculiarities of Meister's Apprenticeship (Ueber die hervorstechendesten Eigenthümlichkeiten von Meisters Lehrjahren),* which appeared in Berlin in 1797. In the nineteenth century, the novel came to be seen as a guidebook for the young bourgeois.[65]

Such didactic interpretations gave rise to an entirely new genre, the bildungsroman, which the Wilhelm Meister novels were credited with having founded. As early as 1813, Karl Morgenstern (1770–1852) called the *Apprenticeship* a bildungsroman because it depicted the education of its protagonist and, in so doing, also educated its reader. Wilhelm Dilthey (1833–1911) structured the term in a more sophisticated way, but, satisfied with Wilhelm Meister as his prime example, he remained true to the idea that a bildungsroman depicted a young man's development from a dreamy, self-centered childhood to a practical participation in the world.[66] After Dilthey, a host of critics perpetuated the term bildungsroman and continued to extol *Wilhelm Meister* as an edifying portrayal of exemplary development. In the twentieth century, Max Wundt, Melitta Gerhart, and, in their wake, Erich Trunz, editor of the most widely used and influential edition of Goethe's works, have continued to read and describe the *Apprenticeship* as a strong example of an uplifting bildungsroman.[67]

Viewing the novel as itself curative adds an additional twist to the study of medicine and literature. Perhaps the novel not only represents the healing of its character (and in so doing depicts the ways in which medicine constructs social realities) but also in fact heals its readers and gives them insight into the construction of the realities that surround them. But if the novel is a medicine, it is in Derrida's sense a *pharmakon,* a poison as well as a cure: Many critics have found the novel to be dangerous for its readers, while others have argued that its message is too ambiguous to be of much use in healing anyone.

For many critics, the inconclusive nature of the novel's end precluded any convincing interpretation of edification. Even Schiller wished that Goethe had spelled out more clearly his conception of Wilhelm Meister's ideal development.[68] The most dedicated defenders of the novel's didactic nature had to admit that Wilhelm Meister's much-vaunted active participation in society at the end of the *Apprenticeship* remains a prediction for the future, not a demonstrated reality.[69] Such critics liked the idea of a bildungsroman but felt that *Wilhelm Meister* did not carry through with that idea.

A related school of thought postulated that Wilhelm Meister's inconclusive development revealed the irony surrounding the novel. In his famous essay, Friedrich Schlegel (1772–1829) argued that the novel educated its reader, and even the other characters, better than its protagonist.[70] Typically, he does not reject the idea of *Bildung* entirely; he remains committed to the idea that the novel is in some way educational. Even today, critics who emphasize the novel's irony do not usually argue that the novel radically undercuts the ideology of *Bildung,* but that it surrounds that ideology in a cloud of ambiguity, putting forth while putting into question the concept of development and edification.[71] Benjamin Bennett is one commentator who sees a "radical irony" in much eighteenth-century writing, including Goethe's works, although he does not concentrate on the *Apprenticeship.*[72]

A third group of critics dissenting from uplifting interpretations of the novel did not merely find the ideals of *Bildung* inadequately achieved or playfully ironized, but regarded them as downright dangerous. To put it another way, they did not find the pharmakon of *Bildung* merely ambiguous, but actually poisonous. In particular, this school of thought attacked the Tower Society vehemently. Novalis (Friedrich von Hardenberg, 1772-1801) objected vituperatively to the Tower Society's economic machinations, Wilhelm's turn away from the theater, and the death of such artistic characters as Mignon and the Harper.[73] Such criticism came back with a vengeance in Karl Schlechta's account of the triumph of a machinating, deceptive, totalitarian, and antipoetic world over the world of the "original" Wilhelm, Philine, Mignon, and the Harper, a world in which life and art had been one.[74]

Just as the tradition of reading *Wilhelm Meister* as an edifying bildungsroman has survived for two centuries, so have variations of all three of the critical dissents. After two centuries, the face-off between those who read the novel as a didactic bildungsroman and those who do not has resulted in an impasse quite similar to the stalemate in the debate on the merits of medicine. In a sense, the novel, like the institution of medicine, reads its critics, rather than vice versa: it rapidly becomes apparent whether a particular Goethe scholar approves of eighteenth-century bourgeois culture (in which case the novel has a positive instructive function) or whether he or she dislikes that culture (in which case it stands as a dire warning).

MEDICAL SEMIOTICS AND *WILHELM MEISTER* CRITICISM

In order to avoid this standoff, some critics in recent decades deconstruct the binary oppositions dividing those for and against *Bildung*. Friedrich Kittler's pioneering study berates the naive utopian thinking of those who, like Novalis and Schlechta, found Wilhelm's eventual "embourgeoisement" too horrible to bear, insisting that the world of the "original" Wilhelm lacked true unity and life as much as the world of the Tower Society did.[75] Kittler's title, with its reference to "Socialization" instead of *Bildung,* reveals his interest in sidestepping these battles by arguing that the novel gives an anthropological depiction of the coming-of-age of bourgeois man.[76] Like Kittler, Hannelore Schlaffer takes off from Schlechta's perspective, but she also undermines the distinction between a "good" original Wilhelm and a "bad" Tower Society by looking for allusions to myth in the Society, allusions that reveal it to be more than prosaic.[77] Todd Kontje also sees the classical bildungsroman anthropologically, as a process of "self-fashioning" for private individuals in the newly formed public sphere.[78]

Much of this criticism pivots on issues of linguistics. Kittler's study concludes with Wilhelm Meister entering the archival, discursive system of the Tower.[79] According to Kontje, the bildungsroman is "metafiction," because the self-fashioning described in a novel like *Wilhelm Meister* inherently involves the creation of a fiction, making it a story about a story. For Jochen Hörisch, the novel is about leaving the maternal world of oral communication and entering the paternal world of the written signifier.[80] Dennis Mahoney adds a Schlegelian twist to this line of reasoning by seeing the novel in terms of teaching the reader, not the protagonist, to read.[81]

Where there is linguistics, medicine feels at home as well.[82] Like the above-mentioned critics, Helmut Ammerlahn argues that Wilhelm Meister becomes a writer, or at least an artist, but he sees this development in terms of a medical cure.[83] Indeed, many of the critics interested in overcoming the impasse surrounding the question of *Bildung* turn to eighteenth-century medical discourses, Goethe's knowledge of those discourses, and their relationship to *Wilhelm Meister*. Hannelore Schlaffer researches, among other figures, the role of Minerva, the goddess of medicine, in *Wilhelm Meister*.[84] Hans-Jürgen Schings[85] and Gloria Flaherty[86] have written numerous articles on the linkage between eighteenth-century medical history and *Wilhelm Meister's Apprenticeship*, working from the perspective of Wilhelm Meister's *Bildung* as a *Heilung,* or cure. In so doing, these critics hope to escape the ideological consequences of *Bildung* while still positing some sort of development for Wilhelm.

Psychoanalytic studies of the last decades parallel this movement toward interpreting Wilhelm Meister's *Bildung* as *Heilung* in that they see the main character going through a number of psychological stages as he approaches maturity. David Roberts tries to reconcile Eissler's very biographical psychoanalysis with more conventional approaches to literary texts by excluding the author's psyche from his analyses and by analyzing only the psychic structures within the novel itself. Wilhelm Meister successfully resolves his oedipal complex when his father dies, when he plays the role of Prince Hamlet (whose father of course also dies), and when he assumes the role of fatherhood.[87] While Roberts works with the oedipal crisis, Hörisch emphasizes the mirror stage. With Lacan's assistance, Wilhelm Meister's *Bildung* becomes the advance from a maternally oriented, narcissistic, imaginary phase, in which Wilhelm is particularly attracted to women who look like himself, to a paternal symbolic phase, in which Wilhelm assumes his position in the society of men and is able to relate to women as something other than mere images of himself.[88] Significantly, this psychoanalytic story of healing becomes, under Lacan's guidance, also a story of learning to manipulate signs. Health and language come together again.

As Kontje points out, however, such analyses can end up merely duplicating "the affirmative interpretation of the novel in clinical terminology."[89] In order to avoid that trap, history and semiotics must remain part of any discussion of the cure. Within a historical context, it is possible to see "cures" and medicine in general as beneficial for individuals, while at the same time resulting in institutional changes that deprive members of society of liberties in entirely new ways. Such a medico-literary analysis might suggest that Wilhelm's development or *Bildung,* for instance, has many positive aspects, but that the forces represented by the Tower Society reflect structural and institutional changes that go hand in hand with that development, aspects of which require close scrutiny. In other words, Wilhelm's *Bildung* is not exactly "curative," but, more precisely, "pharmaceutical"— it consists of drugs, medications with side effects.

The notion of historicizing and thus relativizing the concept of "cure" indicates that a study of the medical discourse of Goethe's age not only sheds light on Wilhelm's development, but also places the entire debate concerning *Bildung* in a larger context, specifically the context of signification. If *Bildung* is a problematic cure, then perhaps the problems lie in the nature of pharmakons, drugs, and cures. Particularly if the bildungsroman is a novel about entering discursivities or learning to manipulate language, then it will be worthwhile to investigate Goethe's use of medical imagery in *Wilhelm Meister*, to determine whether Goethe's novel also presents this use of language as a drug that can both cure and kill. The conception of *Bildung* as a drug or a cure for the reader would by its very linguistic or rhetorical nature then have an ambivalence that could explain the diverging critical reaction to *Wilhelm Meister*. *Bildung,* like medicine, can be interpreted in fundamentally opposing ways because it, like the pharmakon, is hermeneutically unmoored.

A study of medicine and literature therefore goes to the heart of *Wilhelm Meister's Apprenticeship.* The fundamental questions surrounding the bildungsroman—what is the role of art in the life of a character like Wilhelm Meister? how should a novel like *Wilhelm Meister* affect its readers?—are questions about the role of signifiers in the world. As such, medicine, which, with all of its materialized discursive objects, has always played at the intersection of signifiers and signifieds, can shed light on the bildungsroman. A study of the medicine of Goethe's age is not merely appropriate for a more thorough knowledge of the *Apprenticeship*, given Goethe's interest in medicine and the presence of medical issues in Goethe's writings—it is imperative, because such an analysis can explain the fundamental divisions in the reception of *Wilhelm Meister*, divisions that have to do with the basic ambiguity of medicine, cures, and all forms of signification and discursivity. Looking at *Bildung* medicinally, one looks at it semiotically, which is to say, one looks at it as a system of signs that are classified as sicknesses and cures. Looking at *Bildung* semiotically, one looks at it pharmaceutically, where every antitoxin is also toxic.

2

The Mind-Body Problem

The mind-body problem is fundamental to the semiotics of medicine and literature, in part because it asks whether the world of the mind, a world of abstractions and signifiers, can affect the concrete world of the signified body.[1] When Goethe conceived and wrote *Wilhelm Meister's Apprenticeship*, fundamental changes were taking place in German medicine, particularly with regard to the mind-body problem. These changes are reflected in the novel: Whereas many of the more sickly characters, such as Mignon and the Beautiful Soul, adhere to an older dualistic view, the Tower Society, a group that includes and hires such medical personnel as physicians and surgeons, adopts the (for its era) more progressive semiological belief in the unity of mind and body.

CARTESIAN DUALISM

The Tower Society's espousal of the medicinal belief in the unity of mind and body breaks with the traditional philosophy of the eighteenth century. Although philosophies advocating the separation of mind and body are at least as old as antiquity,[2] eighteenth-century physicians often took René Descartes (1596–1650) as the starting point of their discussions of the mind-body problem.[3] The philosophical orthodoxy had followed Descartes in positing a strict separation between *res cogitans,* the immaterial soul, and *res extensa,* the body.[4] According to Descartes's doctrine of occasional causes, empirically observed connections between the mind and the body resulted from frequent divine intervention that ensured that mind and body remain more or less balanced, rather than from psychological influence on the body or somatic influence on the mind. Descartes actually did permit a vague sort of interaction between body and soul in the "conarion" (pineal gland).[5] The thinkers who followed in his tracks, however,

33

regarded Descartes's discussion of the pineal gland as an unimportant slip and stressed only his division of body and soul.[6]

Although Gottfried Wilhelm Leibniz (1646–1716) attempted to overcome philosophically unpalatable aspects of Cartesian dualism—especially with his doctrines of monadism—some of his documents actually seem to perfect, rather than reject, the Cartesian system. In a number of places, he retains and even intensifies Descartes's strict division of body and soul:[7] "[T]he souls follow their laws . . . and the bodies follow theirs."[8] At the same time, he provided a more convincing philosophical explanation for this division. The Cartesian reliance on divine intervention to explain the empirically observed unity of mind and body was unsatisfactory for a philosophy trying to liberate itself from theology. Leibniz therefore departed from Descartes and used the doctrine of monads to explain the apparent parallelism of the two parts of the human being. He argued that the single monad of the soul and the aggregation of monads in the body were designed to coexist with each other harmoniously, just as all monads in the universe were designed to exist together in harmony.[9] Although Leibniz himself attempted to overcome Descartes's separation of mind and body with his theory of monads, progressive eighteenth-century physicians came to regard his doctrine of preordained harmony as nothing but a more sophisticated version of Cartesian dualism.

Ignoring any of Leibniz's subtleties on the mind-body problem, the systematizer and popularizer Christian Wolff (1679–1754) refined and elaborated this doctrine of preordained harmony, writing that "one sees easily that the soul does its part for itself and the body similarly has its changes for itself."[10] He rejects the notion of "the soul affecting the body, or the body the soul," as well as the Cartesian theory of "God arranging anything through his immediate intervention."[11] Nonetheless, he believes that "the sensations and desires of the soul are in agreement with the changes and movements of the body."[12] Thus he turns to and accepts "the explanation which Mr. Leibniz has given of the community of the body with the soul, and called the pre-ordained harmony or agreement."[13] The basic structures of philosophical thought on the mind-body problem in the eighteenth century stand out in relief in Wolff's work. On the one hand, the Cartesian doctrine of the separation of mind and body remained a cornerstone of Wolff's philosophy. On the other hand, Descartes's theory of occasional causes gave way to Leibniz's theory of preordained harmony. After the appearance of Wolff's *Reasonable Thoughts* (*Vernünftige Gedanken*, first edition, 1723), the doctrine of a preordained harmony between body and soul became the accepted theory in mainstream philosophy of the eighteenth century.[14]

It is said that Descartes believed that the means to the perfectibility of humanity lay in medicine.[15] Clearly, these Cartesian, Leibnizian, and Wolffian doctrines had important implications for medicine. They suggested that medicine was a mechanistic institution. Throughout the seventeenth and well into the eighteenth century, physicians and philosophers used Descartes to prove that medicine belonged to the natural sciences. Johann Georg Sulzer (1720–79) was only one of many to classify medicine as a subcategory of the mechanistic physics.[16] Leibniz tirelessly called for a more rigorous application of sciences like anatomy, physics, and chemistry to the field of medicine. His suggestions concerning regular temperature checks, yearly medical checkups, and physicians paid by the state were all aimed at a more positivistic attitude toward medicine.[17] At the same time, the strict division of mind and body in Cartesian philosophy implied that the physician had no say in psychological, emotional, and mental problems. For the Cartesians, faulty reasoning or sinful behavior caused true mental illness, which had nothing to do with the body. It was therefore treated by philosophers or priests, and not by physicians.[18]

Mechanistic physicians accepted these premises and concentrated exclusively on the body. Helped along by Harvey's discovery of the circulatory system in 1628, such mechanistic thinking became more and more popular throughout the seventeenth century as physicians found increasingly sophisticated ways to explain the chemical and physical workings of the body. They came up with theories bearing names like *Iatro-Physik, Iatro-Chemie,* and *Iatro-Mechanik,* which attempted to provide materialistic explanations for matters concerning health and sickness.[19]

Hermann Boerhaave, the influential professor of medicine and author of famous handbooks, developed a cohesive mechanistic view of humanity.[20] Although he rejected the godlessness he thought inherent in Descartes, his beliefs were based on mind-body dualism.[21] According to Boerhaave, the human body was a machine requiring maintenance like any other machine.[22] Since the physician's sole responsibility was the maintenance and repair of the human machine, he had nothing to do with psychology itself.[23]

Other physicians followed Boerhaave's example. The eminent physician and professor of medicine at Halle, Friedrich Hoffmann (1660–1742), a good friend of Leibniz, also endorsed the belief in the strict separation of mechanistic body and immaterial soul. Asserting that "our body is like a machine or automaton," he continued: "Life is achieved by causes that are wholly mechanical. The mind does not bring life to the body, nor is life oriented to mind, but rather to body."[24] As one historian explains, for Hoffmann "the body was solely of a material order and its dysfunctions were to be explained in material terms."[25] Another scholar adds that for Hoffmann "the body is a machine, with its columns, levers, springs, wedges, pulleys, bellows, sieves and presses." The science of pathology becomes a matter of being alert for breakdowns in the machine.[26] Like Boerhaave, Hoffmann distanced himself from the possibility of atheism in Descartes, but he saw a mechanistic interpretation of the human body as a demonstration of God's omnipotent wisdom. He believed that "the anatomical structure 'works' by God's eternal laws."[27]

Again, the boundary between body and soul is not always obvious to the modern reader. Although Hoffmann made sweeping statements about the body's mechanical nature, he actually devoted considerable attention to emotional disorders. He asserted at one point that "the soul is the first principle of motion in the body," anticipating Stahl's animism by a decade.[28] Arguing that emotions such as anger, fright, sadness, and love could affect the bodily fluids, he concluded: "Nothing shortens life or increases disease more than distorted emotions."[29] He also admitted that patients could "create a poison" in their own bodies "by excessive emotional activity" and that "terror of a particular disease may readily induce a similar disease in the body."[30] It is striking that even in a physician generally reputed to be a mechanist, medical thought attempts to overcome the barrier between mind and body.

Hoffmann's mechanism reasserted itself, though, in his therapy. In all of his treatments of emotional disorders, he relied on physical and chemical interventions. Whereas physicians later in the eighteenth century might propose mental or emotional cures for problems of the soul or psyche, Hoffmann assumed that only those illnesses that responded to medication or bloodletting were in his domain.

Both Boerhaave and Hoffmann took pains to emphasize the piety of their mechanism. In his notorious book *Man the Machine*,[31] Julian Offray de La Mettrie (1709–51) took no such pains as he demonstrated that the human being operated on purely mechanistic principles, concluding with the inflammatory thesis that the human being was nothing but a machine: "As now, however, all functions of the soul are so dependent on the corresponding organization of the brain and the entire body that they are apparently nothing other than this organization itself, we are clearly dealing with a machine."[32] The category of soul was eliminated: "'Soul' is therefore only an empty word, of which no one has any meaningful conception."[33] The furor caused by this book was extraordinary. Banned in Holland and France, it appeared in Latin, by the permission of Frederick the Great, in Prussia. Scholars pounced upon it in horror: "Haller expressed a by no means private opinion when he attacked Lamettrie," writes Wolfgang Promies.[34] But while the orthodox philosophers would shudder to hear such a statement, La Mettrie's theories were clearly the perverse offspring of a philosophical discourse that attempted to establish such a distinction between the psyche and the body that physicians who dealt with corporeal problems could come to ignore the psyche.

THE MEDICAL RESPONSE

Despite the predominance of Descartes, Leibniz, and Wolff in philosophy, despite the success of Boerhaave and Hoffmann and the notoriety of La Mettrie, many physicians were troubled by rationalist, dualist answers to the mind-body problem. As mentioned, even the "mechanist" Hoffmann had difficulties with dualism, as his extensive attention to psychological disorders suggests. At least five medical dissertations on the subject were written in the early 1720s in Tübingen alone;[35] a veritable avalanche of medical treatises appeared on the subject in the following years, mostly critical of the philosophical division of mind and body. Although the dualist philosophers all insisted that they were not atheists, much of the medical anxiety concerning the mind-body problem had religious, and specifically pietist, sources.[36] In contrast to the dualists, many physicians attempted to bring the soul or the psyche into the medical discourse.

Much of this early medicinal theorizing on the mind-body problem began with Hoffmann's colleague at Halle, Georg Ernst Stahl (1660–1734).[37] Very quickly Stahl came to be seen as the premier opponent of the mechanism championed by Boerhaave and Hoffmann. A history of medicine published in the same year as *Wilhelm Meister's Apprenticeship* refers to the preceding "era that Boerhaave and Stahl ruled with shared influence."[38] Kant also saw the history of eighteenth-century medicine in terms of an opposition between Stahl on the one hand and Hoffmann and Boerhaave on the other.[39] This view has not changed in the ensuing centuries: "It is possible to view all the later eighteenth-century medical system as adhering either to that of Hoffmann or to that of Stahl, according to their acceptance or rejection of the mechanistic philosophy."[40]

Originally an iatrochemist, Stahl's most important contribution to chemistry was his theory of the "phlogiston," defined in the *Oxford English Dictionary* as a "substance . . . supposed to exist in combination in all combustible bodies, and to be disengaged in the process of combustion." This theory remained important in chemistry for much of the eighteenth century.[41] Despite his interest in chemistry, Stahl rejected Cartesian dualism, and insisted on distancing medicine from the fields of chemistry, physics, and anatomy. In his seminal work *Theoria medica vera* (Halle, 1708), he established the fundamental concepts of eighteenth-century vitalist thought and mounted a powerful attack on dualistic answers to the mind-body problem.[42] Although teaching at the same university as Wolff and Hoffmann,

Stahl rejected a purely mechanistic biology and posited an "anima," a life-giving force that filled—indeed, created—the entire human body and distinguished it from a mere mechanism. According to Stahl, the anima or soul was directly responsible for the movement in the body as well as for the characteristics more commonly associated with the soul, like thought and volition.[43] In this theory, the soul was the motivating force of the body, and yet it was one with the living body.[44]

This vitalist doctrine had immediate applications in medical practice, since it made the soul directly responsible for most developments in the body, including pathological ones: "One concludes correctly, therefore, that it is the soul that immediately causes all these movements, be they orderly or unorderly, vital or animal, whether they contribute to the preservation of the body or to its destruction, whether rightly or wrongly guided."[45] At the same time, physical wounds could cause psychological illnesses: "Psychological suffering that stems from the wounding of the body often has serious and lasting consequences. Yet it can be eliminated through the cure of the bodily harm."[46] In a word, Stahl called for the inclusion of the psychological component in medical practice: "In vain is a medicine that does not take into account the constitution of the soul or that does not understand the world of feeling."[47]

Apparently Stahl's dismissal of the distinction between body and soul was attractive to physicians of the era, because his school gained increasingly in importance throughout the eighteenth century. Many physicians, including Ernst Anton Nicolai, Johann Gottlieb Krüger and Johann August Unzer, were followers of Stahl.[48] Some of these physicians were among the most important in establishing the eighteenth-century medical consciousness. Johann August Unzer (1727–99), whom Goethe mentions in *Poetry and Truth,* published *The Physician (Der Arzt),* one of a number of eighteenth-century periodicals devoted to improving the general health of the populace. As the above-mentioned eighteenth-century understanding of the opposition between Stahl and mechanists like Hoffmann and Boerhaave indicates, Stahl's importance was recognized in the eighteenth century. Simon-André Tissot (1728–97), the Swiss physician who wrote many popular monographs on such subjects as the dangers of masturbation and the health hazards to which academics were exposed, wrote of "Stahl, whose new ideas made history in medicine," that his philosophy relied on the dismissal of dualistic thinking: "This famous physician . . . maintained as a pillar of his system the doctrine of the immediate effect of the soul on all parts of the body." [49] Notably, it was Stahl's opinion on the mind-body problem that assured his renown.

One who agreed with Stahl was Andreas Rüdiger (1673–1731), professor both of medicine and philosophy at Halle. He was so troubled by the mind-body problem that he brought out a special edition of Wolff's *Reasonable Thoughts*, heavily annotated with his own critical remarks. He began his observations by noting that Cartesian categories preclude the interaction of mind and body: "[I]nsofar as the essence of the *corporis* is supposed to consist in *extensione* and the soul is supposed to be a *substantia non extensa*, . . . one understands that it would be impossible for them to affect each other."[50] He explained that, in order to get around this problem, Descartes and his disciples had argued that "the soul did not move the body, but rather God the Lord did, indeed immediately, but such that he followed the thought and will of the soul."[51] While this theory was inadequate, Leibniz's notion of the preordained harmony was even worse, "because far greater *dubia* could be raised against this *hypothesin* than against the Cartesian one."[52] Rüdiger's belief that the philosophers were going from bad to worse in their understanding of the mind-body problem led him to call for a new understanding, an understanding based on the empirical observations of physicians and natural scientists.

Another physician, Johann Gottlob Krüger (1715–59),[53] vehemently rejected mechanistic interpretations of the body and specifically mocked theories that reduced the human being to a mass of tubes filled with fluids: "Those physicians who cry the loudest about the mechanical movements of the human body tell us in big books a thousand times that the human body consists exclusively of little tubes in which fluids circulate. . . ."[54] A follower of Stahl, Krüger was interested in finding the source of the energy that powered this human machine, and he mordantly criticized those who did not share his interest: "It scarcely occurs to them, however, that no machine can move itself if there is no moving power. It is the first concern of the miller who builds a mill whether he also has water for it and that he only after that thinks about how he would like to position the mill. It pleases our mechanical physicians to reverse this and only to observe the mill, without considering the water."[55] If affects powered the human machine, then psychological forces controlled the body. Krüger concludes, like so many of his contemporary colleagues, that the soul maintains "the most exact association with the body."[56] Krüger's belief in the major tenet of vitalism—the unity of bodily machine and emotive energy—implied that he had to attend to both sides of the human in order to be a good physician.

The poet, theologian, and physician Albrecht von Haller also took part in the project of reevaluating the soul by seeking to set the limits between the soul and the body. A student of the mechanistic Boerhaave, Haller was attracted to Stahl's vitalist theories. He was not sure if he could accept Stahl's belief that the thinking, feeling, and moving forces in the body were all one and the same, because, although a pious Christian who wanted to believe in the sovereignty of the soul over the body, he was unable to see how anything like the soul could steer the movements of, for instance, a headless chicken.[57] An eighteenth-century historian of medicine summarized Haller's quandary: "Are the independent and at the same time unconscious life movements the work of the soul? or elasticity? . . . Haller found Boerhaave's explanation too mechanical and Stahl's theory too metaphysical. . . ."[58] In a series of famous, if gruesome, experiments on animals,[59] Haller produced a solution to the mind-body problem that distinguished between sensibility *(Empfindlichkeit)* and irritability *(Reizbarkeit)*, phenomena that today might be called, respectively, nerve impulse and contraction.[60] A conscious reaction to a physical stimulant implied sensibility and a connection to the soul, while an exclusively physical reaction meant irritability and hence pure mechanism.[61] Because Haller's system, despite initial dualistic assumptions, concluded that parts of the body were in close contact with the soul, it appealed to his contemporaries. As the eighteenth-century medical community rapidly accepted Haller's resolution of the mind-body problem, his conclusions on the subject set the stage for the biology of the Age of Goethe, "according to which everything was interrelated and alive, striving to unfold the potentials dormant in the womb of nature."[62]

Haller's meticulous distinction between soul (sensibility) and bodily energy (irritability) was perhaps a high point in the medical discussion of the mind-body problem. Subsequent medical thinkers did not dabble in the philosophical debate on the subject, even though they firmly believed in the unity of mind and body. Weickard, for instance, no longer researched the exact nature of the soul but continued to operate with assumptions based on the unity of mind and body.[63] Weickard's stance was typical of that of physicians in the final quarter of the eighteenth century. Most physicians admitted that they could not provide an exact philosophical explanation of the relationship between the two sides of the human being, but they still remained adamantly opposed to what they understood as dualism, and they abhorred anything that was tainted by mechanism. Practically every eighteenth-century physician emphasized the importance of overcoming mechanistic thinking and the dualism of orthodox philosophy. Jerome Gaub (1705–80), for instance, rejected dualistic theories in favor of the unity of mind and body.[64] Similarly, Ernst Anton Nicolai (1722–1802), a follower of Stahl, wrote in 1751: "Body and soul stand in the most exact harmony and a sickness in the body leads every time . . . to a sickness of the soul and this in turn to a sickness of the body."[65] Zimmermann, who specialized in the interplay between body and mind, explicitly underscored the interrelatedness of psychic and physical illnesses: "If sickness can be alleviated through means that directly act upon the soul, it is also true that there are cases in which the soul can change the body . . . we know how much damage to the body the soul of intelligent and emotional people can do."[66] On the one hand, the physical causes of mental disorders like melancholia, which was "an undeniable sign of ruined organs"[67] and caused by hard, dried-out brains, interested him.[68] On the other hand, he devoted a great deal of time to the effects of psychic phenomena like joy, anger, fear, shame, sadness, indignation, homesickness, unrequited love, and intellectual strain on the body.[69] Thomas Arnold, the English physician who specialized in cases of insanity and whose works on the subject were translated into German in the 1780s, declined to speculate on the theoretical details of the relationship between body and soul but nonetheless insisted that the relationship existed.[70] Although many of these writers refused to engage in extensive metaphysical speculations on the nature of the soul or its unity with the body, they still upheld that unity.

FURTHER REPERCUSSIONS

Many of the theories that flourished on the margins of medicine in the eighteenth century show the influence of monistic thinking. The physiognomic speculations of Johann Caspar Lavater (1741–1801) took for granted a link between appearance and psyche, body and soul. His works give a negative answer to his rhetorical question, "Shall it be affirmed that mind does not influence body, or that the body does not influence the mind?"[71] Franz Anton Mesmer's (1734–1815) attempt to explain both corporeal and psychic energy with the same laws that governed magnetism assumed that there was considerable interplay between mind and body.[72] Similarly, Luigi Galvani's (1737–98) arguments that electricity produced both bodily and mental energy—a theory that resulted in the first forms of electroshock therapy[73]—also implied the unity of mind and body. A contemporary took for granted that both Mesmer and Galvani assumed the interaction between physical and spiritual aspects of the human being: "And then both procedures [galvanizing and magnetizing] affect an agent generally present in the animal body, the life-giving fluid (life spirit, sensorial power, *aura vitalis*, life fluid, or however it is named!)."[74] Mesmerism and Galvanism, both reliant on the interaction between the "animal body" and the "life fluid," joined physiognomy in accepting the possibility of such interaction. Although the medical establishment rejected some aspects of these teachings, it did agree with the basic tenet that mind and body exerted an influence on each other.

The ancient doctrine of the four humors, based on theories put forth by Hippocrates and Galen, also survived throughout the eighteenth century, lending support to and receiving it from the belief in the unity of mind and body. At the beginning of the eighteenth century, Boerhaave explained melancholia as the product of black gall, one of the four bodily humors: "This sickness arises from that diseased constitution of the blood and the humors which the ancients called the black gall."[75] Starobinski asserts that Anne-Charles Lorry (1726–83) was the last to construct an active medical system based on humoral pathology,[76] but apparently Carl Rokitansky (1804–78) attempted to keep a modified humoral system going in conservative nineteenth-century Vienna.[77] In any case, fragments of this doctrine show up throughout the rest of the century and even into the nineteenth. Weickard, for instance, still used the humors—and the notion of mind-body unity—to explain human emotions and passions: "It is because of a physical condition that the choleric tends toward ambition and wrath, while the melancholic toward depressed pensiveness and greed."[78] This way of thinking was still intact at the end of the eighteenth century when the anthropologist Adolf Knigge (1759–90) asserted: "[A]s a rule one distinguishes between four primary types of temperament and declares that a person is either choleric, phlegmatic, sanguine, or melancholy."[79] The mechanist La Mettrie and the anthropologist Johann Carl Wezel (1747–1819) are examples of other thinkers of the era who maintained that humoral temperament determined character.[80] The desire of the era's physicians to see a connection between emotion, temperament, and the body certainly aided the survival of the doctrine of the four humors in the face of increasing evidence that the humors were outdated as means of understanding physiology.

The eighteenth-century medical resurgence of a belief in the unity of mind and body aroused more excitement about psychology than about physiology, which was, after all, old hat for most physicians. The era's adaptations of the doctrine of humoral pathology show this. While early physicians like Boerhaave had attempted to use physical means to improve faulty fluids or humors, later physicians concentrated on the psychological temperaments of their patients. According to Rather, Gaub provides a good example: "[A]lthough Gaub regards the temperaments as corporeal phenomena, he has little to say regarding their anatomical or physiological basis and limits himself to a description of their corresponding psychological traits."[81] This change in emphasis results in a "spiritualization"[82] of the doctrine of humoral pathology, with the emphasis more on, for example, the melancholy temperament than on the pathogenic black gall.[83]

The changes in the humors also reflect the move from the mechanistic medicine of, say, Hoffmann, who acknowledged some mental illness but treated it only with physical and pharmaceutical means, to the truly psychological medicine of the philosophical physicians, who were willing to use mental cures. The new medicine allowed not only for the influence of bodily fluids on the psychic state but also permitted—indeed, almost celebrated—the influence of the soul on the body. The bilateral, reciprocal influence of body and mind on each other permitted a much more intimate commerce between the two and allowed the doctrine of humoral pathology to be used for organic, rather than mechanistic, ideologies.

Although genetics was in its infancy in the eighteenth century, Hoffmann was already aware that "many severe diseases result from a hereditary disposition."[84] Johann Storch (1681–1751), the mid-eighteenth-century self-professed Stahlian physician whose practice in Eisenach and Gotha Barbara Duden has studied, believed in hereditary habits and propensities.[85] Moritz speculated that "the sicknesses of the soul can perhaps, just like the somatic ones, be hereditary in whole families, or transmitted from parents to children."[86] At the end of the century, physicians like Arnold used admittedly somewhat circular logic to prove that madness too could be hereditary: "Madness must so frequently be derived from parents . . . that I . . . do not refrain in the least from maintaining that madness is often propagated from parents to children. . . ."[87] The increasingly widely accepted notion that a person can inherit tendencies toward certain behaviors, particularly toward madness, is another indication of the expanding general supposition of the unity of mind (or soul) and body.[88]

This vitalistic denial of the separation of mind and body defined the new discipline of anthropology, as Ernst Platner (1744–1818) explained in the preface to his famous *Anthropology for Doctors and the Worldly*. He rejected "anatomy and physiology" as the study of the "machine alone" and "logic, aesthetics and a large part of moral philosophy" as the exclusive study of the soul; instead, he favored "anthropology," the study of "body and soul in their reciprocal connections, restrictions, and relationships."[89] Other anthropologists followed in Platner's footsteps. At the beginning of his book, Wezel conceded that "our insights have achieved much by cutting the human in two great halves, handing over the physical part to the anatomists and the physiologists, and giving the spiritual half to the philosopher as his part."[90] But he railed against those who forgot that the two categories represented one unified being: "But people seem in the end completely to have forgotten that both parts are one whole and must therefore stand in the most exact connection with each other."[91] The understanding of the division between the mind and the body as a heuristic device of limited usefulness characterized the thinking of the anthropologists. In its rejection of the mechanistic traditions of physiology and anatomy and the Cartesian metaphysical traditions of logic, aesthetics, and ethics, the anthropology of the eighteenth century institutionalized the era's organic thinking by organizing it into a discipline.

As Liliane Weissberg points out, an old philosophical tradition had seen literature as anthropological in the eighteenth-century sense. While philosophy was supposed to be pure mind, literature engaged the emotions, excited sexuality, and therefore also involved the body. Thus, Weissberg concludes, the arrival of anthropology as a discipline corresponds with the increasingly strict separation of philosophy from literature in the eighteenth century.[92] It is no surprise therefore that the anthropological attitudes of the physicians appealed to figures from the literary world. Medical concepts permeate the works of rococo and Enlightenment authors like Uz, Geßner, Brockes, and Gleim.[93] Christoph Martin Wieland (1733–1813), in the course of his friendship and correspondence with Zimmermann, moved from a Cartesian belief in the autonomy of the soul from the body to an anthropological belief in the unity of the two categories.[94]

The youthful Schiller also made this move. The first thesis he wrote while a medical student at school, *Philosophy of Physiology (Philosophie der Physiologie)*, still held to Cartesian theories of the separation of body and soul and was not accepted. The title of his second thesis, which was accepted—"Essay on the Connection between the Animal Nature of Humanity and the Spiritual Nature" (1789)—indicated that, under the influence of his teacher Abel, a student of Haller, he had begun to embrace his era's characteristic belief in the unity of soul and body. In this treatise he asserted that body and soul were intimately connected: "[P]eople are not souls and bodies, people are the most intimate mixtures of both substances."[95] Schiller, like his contemporaries in both literary and medical circles, proclaimed that humans were not amalgamations of metaphysical souls and mechanistic bodies, but unified wholes. In the same year that *Wilhelm Meister* began appearing, Ludwig Tieck's *William Lovell* (1795) was published, featuring a character named Balder with an inherited tendency toward madness.[96]

Simon Richter has brilliantly demonstrated how in the eighteenth century the fields of aesthetics and medicine overlapped on the issue of mind-body unity. Not only did most of the prominent German aesthetic thinkers, like Winckelmann, Lessing, Herder, and Moritz, in addition to Goethe, study medicine to some degree,[97] but eighteenth-century aesthetics was interested in phenomena about which medicine had a lot to say: the body's expression of emotional experiences like pain.

By the end of the century, even the philosophers had taken up this organicist view. Immanuel Kant (1724–1807), an avid reader of Haller,[98] was instrumental in carrying out this movement. As an author of an anthropology himself, he sided against the dualists, although he denied physicians sole competence in matters of insanity.[99] Although he admittedly asserts the priority of philosophy over all other disciplines, including medicine, in his *Battle of the Faculties (Streit der Fakultäten*, 1798) he singles out mechanistic medicine again and again as the misguided branch of medicine. He did not object so strongly to philosophical medicine, as his work with Hufeland indicates.[100] In one of his earliest works, "Thoughts on the True Estimation of the Living Powers and Evaluation of the Proofs of Which Mr. Leibniz and Other Mechanists Have Made Use . . ." (1747), he attacked Leibniz, Wolff, and others on a matter related to the mind-body problem.[101] In another precritical essay, he unambiguously took Stahl's side in the medical debates of the era: "At the same time I am convinced that Stahl, who liked to explain the animal changes organically, often was closer to the truth than Hofmann [sic], Boerhaave, etc."[102] An attack on mechanism also appears in his *Critiques:* "An organized being is not merely a machine, for a machine has only *moving* energy, but rather it possesses a self-*developing* energy . . . a self-reproducing developing energy, which cannot be explained only through the ability to move (mechanism)."[103] Thus, a century after the physicians began to reject the Cartesian and Leibnizian theories concerning the mind-body problem, the philosophers modified their opinions, revealing the persuasiveness of the medicinal worldviews.

The gradual acceptance by everyone in the eighteenth century of the medical belief in mind-body unity is related to the more general slow transfer of power in eighteenth-century Germany from the aristocracy to the bourgeoisie. Goethe considered Descartes the consummate aristocrat (HA 14:109–10), perhaps because Cartesian dualism is at home in a world order characterized by ceremony, formality, and artifice. Gerhard Sauder has argued that a powerful critique of the aristocracy emerged from much of the new psychology.[104]

Much of the bourgeoisie's sense of authenticity came from its belief in its religious superiority to the aristocracy. The eighteenth-century German middle class regarded itself as striving for a unity of essence and appearance, a unity that the aristocracy had long lost. The bourgeois religious experience was highly colored by the same pietist movement that heavily influenced the new physicians. Medicine's semiology of mind-body unity is therefore inextricably bound up with class and religion. It remains to be seen what linkages Goethe drew between medicine, mind-body unity, and societal structures.

THE SOCIETY OF THE TOWER

Given Goethe's knowledge of his era's medicine, it is not surprising to discover that Goethe followed the debate on the mind-body problem. From personal experience, he told his confidant Eckermann that "it is unbelievable how much the mind can do for the preservation of the body."[105] As a writer, he would have his own interest in showing the power of the signifier in a world of signifieds and thus generally favor the reasoning of the physicians and philosophers who propounded mind-body unity. Nonetheless, he remained, as will be seen in the course of this study, constantly attuned to the dangers of a belief in mind-body unity.

His characterization of Descartes as the ultimate aristocrat suggests a certain distancing from his own position as the (admittedly subsequently ennobled) scion of a bourgeois family. Leibniz's doctrine of preordained harmony is delicately lampooned in the "Xenien": "Zweierlei Dinge lass' ich passieren, die Welt und die Seele, Keins weiß vom anderen, und doch deuten sie beide auf Eins" [Two things I will allow, the world and the soul. Neither knows of the other, and yet they both point to one].[106] While Goethe may not be specifically targeting Leibniz's philosophy concerning body and soul with this distich, he mocks the general notion underlying the doctrine of preordained harmony, the idea that the soul and the physical world move along in harmony without interrelating. Atheistic mechanistic explanations of the human body are anathema to him, particularly those of a "fool called Lamettrie."[107] Otherwise, Goethe mentions the mechanists relatively infrequently, and then negatively. Wolff's "scholastic philosophy" is said to have made its objects of study "alien, unenjoyable, and, in the end, dispensable" (SE 4:207).[108] Goethe's great admiration for Boerhaave is directed most of all at his chemical expertise, rather than his theorizing on the mind-body problem.

While always maintaining a certain ironic distance, Goethe mentions many supporters of mind-body unity positively. Although he gently mocks Stahl in his "Xenien" (# 170; WA 1.5.1:229), the derision is directed at the physician's chemical theories of the "phlogiston," rather than at his medical opinions. The paralipomena to the *Farbenlehre* show that he knew of Krüger (WA 2.5.2:6,303), while a letter to Friedrich Heinrich Jacobi (1743–1819) demonstrates a knowledge of Gaub's medical writings (WA 4.10:107). Goethe writes that Soemmerring's work on the seat of the soul in the body provoked much observation, reflection, and testing, pointing to an interest in the corporeality of the soul (WA 1.35:61). Even Zimmermann, whose personality comes under some critical scrutiny in Goethe's writings, is nonetheless considered a great doctor, whose books merit praise. Goethe reserves the most laudations for Haller, who is described as "immortal" and "beatific" (WA 2.6:49, 1.53:442). Whenever Goethe describes the importance of medical thinking for the general intellectual atmosphere, he mentions Haller, the physician who had most carefully examined and demonstrated the unity of mind and body (SE 4:210, 482; HA 9:277, 10:67).

More important than Goethe's opinions of his contemporaries are his own writings and research, which reveal a sympathy for and thorough engagement with the eighteenth-century medical attempt to reestablish the unity of mind and body. The thrust of his research on the intermaxillary bone is the similarity between humans and animals, and is indicative of the kind of thinking that attempts to break down the distinction between the spiritual, intellectual, and the bestial. Speaking of "the spiritual as well as the physical human" in his essay *On Laokoon*, Goethe refuses to separate the two categories: "Far be it from me to dispute the unity of mind and body" (SE 3:20).[109] In *The Sorrows of Young Werther*, similarly, all parties agree that the body can influence mood and that medicine has a role to play in the psyche:

"Wir haben aber unser Gemüt nicht in unserer Gewalt"; versetzte die Pfarrerin. "Wie viel hängt von Körper ab! Wenn einem nicht wohl ist, ist's einem überall nicht recht." — Ich gestand ihr das ein. "Wir wollen es also," fuhr ich fort, "als eine Krankheit ansehen und fragen, ob dafür kein Mittel ist?" – "Das läßt sich hören," sagte Lotte. . . .

["But," observed the vicar's wife, "we cannot always control our tempers, so much depends on our nature; when the body suffers, the mind is ill at ease." "I admit that," I continued, "but let us regard it as a disease, and ask whether there is no remedy for it." "That sounds plausible," said Charlotte. . . .][110]

This assertion that the body can influence the emotions and that a physician should therefore treat the emotions runs contrary to a strict dualistic division between body and mind.

In *Wilhelm Meister's Apprenticeship*, this anthropological belief in the unity of body and mind also appears. Quite naturally, it comes from the organization that makes most use of the modern medicine of its time, the Society of the Tower. Throughout the novel, mind and body interact consistently. On the one hand, psychological changes almost invariably accompany physical ailments. While recovering from a gun wound, Lothario, for instance, reports that a bodily affliction has a positive effect on his mental state, above all on his memory:

Mein körperliches Leiden muß mich mürber gemacht haben, als ich selbst glaubte; ich fühlte mich weich und bei wieder auflebenden Kräften wie neugeboren. Alle Gegenstände erschienen mir in eben dem Lichte, wie ich sie in früheren Jahren gesehen hatte, alle so lieblich, so anmutig, so reizend, wie sie mir lange nicht erschienen sind. (HA 7:464)

[My bodily sickness must have mellowed me more than I thought; I felt soft but, as my strength revived, I felt born anew. Every object around me appeared in the same light as they had in former years, so pleasant, so delightful, so charming—such as they had not seemed to me for a long time.] (SE 9:284)

Lothario's gunshot wound causes somatic suffering, which has a significant impact on his psyche, suggesting that the body can influence the mind.

Even more characters experience psychological developments that have physical effects. When Frau Melina's child is stillborn after the attack on the theater troupe (SE 9:137; HA 7:232), she experiences what eighteenth-century medicine considered to be reality: that fright was a prime cause of disease in general and miscarriages in particular.[111] Werner's hypochondria causes or at least accompanies his hair loss and the changes in the shape of his face and chest (SE 9:304–5; HA 7:498–99). Emotion plays a significant role in the development of Aurelie's illness, which leads to her death. At the end of the fifth book, she has "a kind of intermittent fever" (SE 9:211; HA 7:349). Typically, the "condition of her body and the state of her mind" interest the physician (SE 9:212; HA 7:349). Like any eighteenth-century physician, he expressly warns her to stay away from excessive emotional feelings: "[N]othing is more detrimental to the health of such people than intentional revival of passionate feelings" (SE 9:212; HA 7:349). While rehearsing the role of Orsina in *Emilie Galotti*, Aurelie seemingly follows his advice and feigns relative indifference to the role, but during the performance she gives her emotional problems free reign: "[B]ei der Aufführung selbst aber zog sie, möchte man sagen, alle Schleusen ihres individuellen Kummers auf, und es ward dadurch eine Darstellung, wie sie sich kein Dichter in dem ersten Feuer der Empfindung hätte denken können" (HA 7:353–54) [{I}n the performance she opened up all the floodgates of her personal sorrow, and the result was a performance such as no poet could have imagined in the first heat of his invention" (SE 9:214)]. These emotions, intentionally aroused against the doctor's orders, have an immediate effect on her body—after the show she lies "half lifeless in a chair" (SE 9:214; HA 7:354). Moreover, her emotions are connected with her urge to go running in the cold without her coat, which induces the hoarseness, stiffness, muteness, and fever that lead to her death.

Frequently, the novel bolsters the age-old metaphorical connection between blood and emotion with the new medical theories of the era. Even Harvey's seventeenth-century work on the circulation of the blood emerges from an already highly structured semantic field around blood and the heart.[112] As belief in mind-body unity increased, the importance of blood as a mediator between the two poles also increased. This connection between an improperly functioning circulatory system and emotions went hand in hand with traditional literary tropes about love and the heart, passion and hot blood. Goethe picked up on this entire complex of medical and poetic discourse on blood. As early as 6 January 1782, he reports studying the heart with Loder (WA 3.1:134). Not surprisingly, therefore, *Wilhelm Meister's Apprenticeship* includes medical language in its references to the heart.

The novel makes clear the scientific basis of its blood imagery. Natalie's report illustrates the complicated interplay between the body, specifically the circulatory system, and the soul; this interplay, according to the Tower Society, causes Mignon's sickness. In her account, Natalie assumes that deep emotions accompany heart cramps and that unanticipated excitement can cause the heart to stop beating. The novel reports:

> Sie erzählte ihm . . . daß das Kind von wenigen tiefen Empfindungen nach und nach aufgezehrt werde, daß es bei seiner großen Reizbarkeit, die es verberge, von einem Krampf an seinem armen Herzen oft heftig und gefährlich leide, daß dieses erste Organ des Lebens bei unvermuteten Gemütsbewegungen manchmal plötzlich stille stehe, und keine Spur der heilsamen Lebensregung in dem Busen des guten Kindes gefühlt werden könne. (HA 7:513)

> [the girl was becoming more and more the prey of strong emotions, and, highly sensitive as always, concealed the fact that she often suffered from violent cramps around the heart, but so dangerously severe that sometimes this prime organ of life stopped beating suddenly when she was unexpectedly excited, and there seemed to be no sign of life in the dear child's body.] (SE 9:314–15)

Moreover, she assumes that a wild pulse can produce states of anxiety: "Sei dieser ängstliche Krampf vorbei, so äußere sich die Kraft der Natur wieder in gewaltsamen Pulsen und ängstige das Kind nunmehr durch Übermaß, wie es vorher durch Mangel gelitten habe" (HA 7:513–14) [Once this frightening convulsion had passed, the strength of her nature returned in strong pulse beats which now frightened the child by the intensity of what before had been completely lacking] (SE 9:315). All of these symptoms involve a crossing of the boundary between mind and body at the circulatory system.

The "emotions" *(Empfindungen)* and "sensitivity" *(Reizbarkeit)* that cause Mignon such problems might even refer specifically to Haller's essays on the mind-body problem, in which he had distinguished between sensibility *(Empfindlichkeit)* and irritability *(Reizbarkeit)*.[113] In that case, *Empfindungen* would be physical feelings that have connections to the soul, reinforcing the idea of unity between mind and body. These *Empfindungen* are preying on her, according to Natalie, while her *Reizbarkeit* merely refers to her corporeal constitution that sets the stage for the mind-body interreaction. Even if there is no direct reference to Haller's theories in this statement, however, the novel uses a clearly medical vocabulary to explain the linkage between emotional phenomena and the heart.

In addition to linking Mignon's emotional condition with the physical state of her heart, the Tower Society also implies that Mignon's "bad blood," in a genetic sense, is responsible for her illness. The Tower Society carefully includes exhaustive reports on the madness of both of Mignon's parents, as well as their incestuous relationship with each other, in order to make Mignon's diagnosis as mentally ill more convincing, scientifically and medically.[114]

Mignon herself yearns for a spiritual existence as a transfigured body in another, nonphysical world,[115] as she makes clear in one of her poems:

> So laßt mich scheinen, bis ich werde,
> Zieht mir das weiße Kleid nicht aus!
> Ich eile von der schönen Erde
> Hinab in jenes feste Haus.
>
> . . . .
>
> Ich lasse dann die reine Hülle,
> Den Gürtel und den Kranz zurück.
>
> Und jene himmlischen Gestalten,
> Sie fragen nicht nach Mann und Weib,
> Und keine Kleider, keine Falten
> Umgeben den verklärten Leib.
>
> (HA 7:515–16)
>
> [So let me seem till I become:
> Take not this garment white from me!
> I hasten from the joys of earth
> Down to that house so fast and firm.
>
> . . . .
>
> Then I will cast my dress aside
> Leaving both wreath and girdle there.
>
> For all those glorious heavenly forms,
> They do not ask for man or wife.
> No garments long or draperies fine
> Surround the body now transformed.]
>
> (SE 9:316)

Mignon uses clothes to refer to the things she would like to leave behind, a category that also includes the nontransfigured (i.e., sexual) body and the earth. Her wish to leave her body behind is understandable, since it is both the cause of physical pain and the source of disquieting sexual urges. On the one hand, an apparently physical ailment causes a seizure at the end of the second book[116] and a fatal heart attack in the eighth book (SE 9:333;

HA 7:544). On the other hand, her physical desires for Wilhelm thrust her into humiliating scenes in which she suffers unbearable rejections. Therefore, she quite understandably yearns for a transfigured, nonsexual, and nonphysical existence.

Mignon's belief that the heavenly figures are not concerned about the categories of male and female perhaps alludes to Paul's statement in the New Testament that only those who do not marry are worthy of heaven. But it also reflects the notion that the soul had no sex. Such thinking grew out of a strict Cartesian separation of the mind and body and was common among those intellectual women of the seventeenth and eighteenth centuries who were seeking to improve the lot of women. If the soul was sexless and women had souls, then limitations placed on the intellectual development of women were spurious and arbitrary, went the argument.[117] This belief was quickly rejected by those who saw a unity of mind and body and thus believed that the categories of male and female pervaded not only the entire body but also the soul.

The members of the Society of the Tower, certainly, will have nothing of Mignon's dualism. They emphasize the intimate interconnections between her psyche and her body, especially between her emotions and her heart. When Natalie sees Mignon writhing in pain in front of her, she tries to remember and use all of the "best means she knew of dealing with such a state of mind and body" (SE 9:321; HA 7:524). After Wilhelm's arrival, the physician insists that "they all try to restore her physical and mental equilibrium [sowohl körperlich als geistig im Gleichgewicht erhalten]" (SE 9:322; HA 7:525). As always, the physician is certain of his competence in prescribing measures both for her physical and her spiritual well-being.

With this self-granted competence in psychological matters, the physician looks to her mind and regards her desires as sickness. He emphasizes her homesickness and her lovesickness to the point of neglecting the physical ailment, telling Wilhelm that Mignon's earthly parts consist of almost nothing else but "the longing to see her motherland [Vaterland] again, and a longing, my friend, for you" (SE 9:320; HA 7:522). Wilhelm grasps the importance of this psychological component, too. When he tries to get out of visiting Mignon, he takes for granted that this emotional desire is just as responsible for her poor health as any physical deficiency: "Sind Sie als Arzt überzeugt, daß jene doppelte Sehnsucht ihre Natur so weit untergraben hat, daß sie sich vom Leben abzuscheiden droht, warum soll ich durch meine Gegenwart ihre Schmerzen erneuern und vielleicht ihr Ende beschleunigen?" (HA 7:525) [Are you convinced, as a doctor, that the twofold yearning you have described has so undermined her nature that she is in danger of dying? If that is the case, why should I aggravate her misery by my presence and perhaps bring on her death?] (SE 9:321). Although the physician and Wilhelm disagree on how to treat Mignon's problems, they both refuse to accept Mignon's belief that her healthy soul needs to escape her diseased body. Both view her psyche as something very much a part of her body and her desire for a division between the two categories as illness.

Besides Mignon, the "Beautiful Soul" also resists the Tower Society's belief in mind-body unity.[118] She pleads movingly for an absolute separation of body and soul:

> Es war, als wenn meine Seele ohne Gesellschaft des Körpers dächte; sie sah den Körper selbst als ein ihr fremdes Wesen an, wie man etwa ein Kleid ansieht. . . . der Körper wird wie ein Kleid zerreißen, aber Ich, das wohlbekannte Ich, Ich bin." (HA 7:415)

> [It was as if my soul were thinking without my body, looking on the body as something apart from itself, like some garment or other. . . . the body will be rent like a garment, but I, the well-known I, I am.] (SE 9:252–53)

The Beautiful Soul prefers an autonomous, Cartesian ego to her body because—like Mignon—her body is (a) sick throughout her life and (b) the source of upsetting erotic desires. As a twelve-year-old, she develops an attraction to a boy of her own age, based on his bodily sickness (SE 9:219; HA 7:362), while at the same time loving her French tutor so much that she awaits him with a pounding heart: "I loved him so dearly that I always awaited his arrival with heartthrobs [*Herzklopfen*]" (SE 9:219; HA 7:361). While sexuality and the body move in close tandem in both of these relationships, the connection becomes clearest in her affair with Narcissus. At their first encounter, he develops a nosebleed (SE 9:222; HA 7:365). They fall in love when she tends his wounded body because, as the blood from this wound covers her, she learns to appreciate her body: "[I]ch darf nicht verschweigen, daß ich, da man sein Blut von meinem Körper abwusch, zum erstenmal zufällig im Spiegel gewahr wurde, daß ich mich auch ohne Hülle für schön halten durfte" (HA 7:368) [I cannot fail to admit that when I first happened to see myself in the mirror while they were washing his blood off me, I thought I could consider myself beautiful, even without my clothes] (SE 9:223). In this affair particularly, the Beautiful Soul's appreciation of her body clearly grows with her erotic love of others. As these relationships fail, as she devotes herself increasingly to "the well-known I," her isolated individual soul, she loses interest in her body.[119]

The Beautiful Soul is very much a classical figure, reminiscent of Madame de Lafayette's Princess of Cleves in her desire to live in a world of signifiers, unsullied by physicalities. She has no problem with a medical system of signs consisting of signifier and signified, as long as it is applied to the body—her objection is to the application of this system to the mind.

She is willing, indeed happy, to control her material experiences by naming them, but she wants to avoid verbalizing her spiritual experiences—as indicated in her belief that the Supreme Being is ineffable (SE 10:277; HA 7:374).

The physician does not stand by idly as the Beautiful Soul retreats from the erotic love of others and rejects her body. When he informs himself about the constitution of her body and mind (SE 9:253; HA 7:415), he typifies the new physicians who are interested in both faculties. He warns her that dualistic thoughts are in fact threats to her health:

> Diesem großen, erhabnen und tröstlichen Gefühle so wenig als nur möglich nachzuhängen, lehrte mich . . . der Arzt, . . . er zeigte mir, wie sehr diese Empfindungen, wenn wir sie unabhängig von äußern Gegenständen in uns nähern, uns gewissermaßen aushöhlen und den Grund unseres Daseins untergraben. (HA 7:415)

> [I was persuaded . . . not to yield too much to . . . this lofty thought. . . . the physician . . . explained to me that such feelings, if nurtured without reference to external things, will drain us dry and undermine our existence.] (SE 9:253).

In so doing, he contradicts her implicit linkage of body, desire, and sickness, arguing instead that her thinking or her mind needs help. When she wants to abandon her sickly, sexual body and retreat exclusively to her soul, he views such dualism as wrong and perhaps even itself a sickness. In the tradition of eighteenth-century medicine, he attempts to cure her obsession with the afterlife by directing her attention to the gardens (SE 9:253; HA 7:416) and her relatives (SE 9:253; HA 7:417), rather than by arguing rationally with her.[120]

The case of Mignon and the Beautiful Soul show that older concepts of mind-body dualism still remain important in the novel, but that the Tower Society has fully embraced the nondualistic attitudes prevalent in eighteenth-century German medicine. In so doing, the Tower Society can submit those emotional, psychological, and spiritual aspects of the human experience to their medical semiotics, interpreting the symptoms of (in the case of Mignon and the Beautiful Soul) poetry and religion in a way hitherto inaccessible to secular society. The consequences of the Tower Society's acceptance of progressive eighteenth-century German medicine and its semiotics include an entirely new medicinal structure, which the *Apprenticeship* carefully documents.

3

Surgical, Internal, and Psychological Medicine in *Wilhelm Meister's Apprenticeship*

In the eighteenth century, in addition to changing its attitude toward the mind-body problem, medicine was also undergoing more practical transformations and establishing new professional boundaries. Johann Storch (1681–1751) provides a good indication of the many healers fighting for recognition in this era when he complains about "selfish apothecaries, know-it-all surgeons, barber-surgeons, midwives, greedy druggists and confectioners, depraved pedlars, ragged and seedy craftsmen."[1] By the end of the eighteenth century, the physicians had come out on top; in the nineteenth century, the surgeons were gradually rehabilitated. In the *Wilhelm Meister* novels, Goethe documents these developments. Dividing medicine, as was usual for the time, into surgical, internal, and psychological medicine,[2] Goethe portrays each of these fields, especially the final one, with great accuracy.

SURGERY

In contrast to the surgeon of today, the *Wundarzt* or *Chirurg* of eighteenth-century Germany was a skilled manual worker who, besides practicing surgery, also treated external wounds and abrasions. Heynatz's dictionary of synonyms of 1795 defines the duties of the practitioners of this profession: "A surgeon [*Wundarzt*] is a man who heals wounds and external disorders, bleeds veins, cuts limbs up and out, and so forth. Using a Greek word which means a man who undertakes clever things with his hand, such a doctor [*Wundarzt*] is also called a surgeon [*Chirurg*]."[3] In addition, the surgeon sometimes also performed other duties having to do

54

with the care of the human body, because the distinction was not always clear between the surgeon's profession and other "professions (shaver, barber, bather), who also took upon themselves a portion of the surgical duties."[4]

Surgeons attempted to improve the social status of their profession by distinguishing themselves from these other, lower-class professions involved with the body. In France and England, surgeons cut their ties with barbers in 1743 and 1745, respectively.[5] As early as 1748, Tobias Smollett's *Adventures of Roderick Random* depicts a relatively gentlemanly would-be surgeon accompanied by a more humble and common barber. In Germany, however, things were apparently different. As late as 1795, barbers and surgeons remained hard to distinguish from each other, much to the dismay of Heynatz: "Frequently in common life, one uses 'barber' for surgeon because in Germany the surgeons usually . . . let their apprentices and journeymen practice [barbering], whereas in other lands the barber's profession and wig making are more appropriately performed by one and the same person. 'Send for a barber!' people often say to those who have a wound or other external disorder."[6] Heynatz's reference to the apprentices and trainees of the surgeons is important, for the surgeons, as skilled laborers, received their education through the old-fashioned guild system. His dismay about the confusion between surgeons and barbers points to the chronic difficulties that surgeons had gaining respect.

The low social status of the surgeon explains the surprise of early readers of the *Journeyman Years:* "Now it might seem trivial to the superficial onlooker that Wilhelm selects the field of surgery, that after a prolonged schooling for which half the world was spent he became a mere surgeon."[7] Despite the lack of respect that many of Goethe's contemporary readers had for the surgical profession, Goethe was, particularly later in life, generally positively disposed to the surgical profession. In *The Nervous (Die Aufgeregten*, 1817), Breme, who is admittedly prejudiced because he is a surgeon himself, strongly defends the honor of his profession: "I tell you, my child, a surgeon [*Chirurgus*] is the most honorable man in the whole world" (HA 5:173–74). He quickly dismisses physicians: "[T]he physician [*Medikus*] cures one sickness away and brings another on, and you can never really know if he helped or hurt you" (HA 5:173–74). In contrast, however, surgeons help immediately and clearly: "[T]he surgeon [*Chirurgus*] however frees you from a real injury that you have drawn upon yourself or that has afflicted you coincidentally and innocently; he helps you, hurts no one, and you can convince yourself incontestably that his cure has been successful" (HA 5:174).

Very similar attitudes concerning the usefulness of surgeons appear in *Wilhelm Meister's Journeyman Years*, too. When Felix takes a fall from a

horse, Hersilie calls a surgeon, remarking: "[F]or general physicians
[*Leibärzte*] there is seldom need, but there is for surgeons [*Wundärzte*]
every moment" (SE 10:143; HA 8:72). Somewhat later in the novel, Jarno
suggests that surgeons maintain the health of the healthy who have been
injured, a skill "that nothing was more worth learning or achieving" (SE
10:293; HA 8:281). Wilhelm's decision in the *Journeyman Years* to become a surgeon also implies that Goethe considered the profession honorable. In all of these late works, one detects traces of the increasing skepticism toward the great taxonomical systems of eighteenth-century medicine and the concomitant turn inward to facts and bodies.

Although Goethe's later works reflect his growing admiration for surgeons as honest workers, the *Apprenticeship* provides a fairly sober depiction of the profession. The surgeons of the eighteenth century did not use
anesthetics, of course, for which reason J. Z. Platner counseled the aspiring
surgeon to be "merciless" [*unbarmherzig*]: "In all cases he should act as
though he was not at all moved by the whining of the patient . . . because
surgical cures are often very painful. . . ."[8] The absence of anesthetics provides an additional reason for surgery's relative lack of importance in eighteenth-century medicine: operations were clearly an option to be used only
in the last resort.[9]

In *Wilhelm Meister's Apprenticeship*, there are several allusions to this
painful aspect of the profession. Wilhelm loses consciousness after the surgeon extracts a bullet from him (SE 9:135; HA 7:228). In the marchese's
story about Augustin and Sperata, the metaphorical comparison of the con-
fessor with a surgeon is also to be understood in this light: "But this worthy
man soon persuaded us with a surgeon's reasoning [*mit den Gründen des
Wundarztes*] that our sympathy for the poor sick man was fatal."[10] The
surgeon's job in the marchese's story and elsewhere in the *Apprenticeship*
is painful and unpleasant.

Nor does the novel idealize the social status of surgeons, who clearly
belonged to a lower class than the physicians.[11] Natalie's surgeon's manners are "brusque rather than ingratiating" (SE 9:134; HA 7:227). Like
surgeons of the eighteenth century, the surgeons of the novel are uneducated. The surgeon who continues Wilhelm's treatment after Natalie leaves
is ignorant: "[T]he surgeon, not very knowledgeable but not unskilled [*der
Chirurgus, ein unwissender, aber nicht ungeschickter Mensch*], let nature
take its course, and the patient was soon on his way to recovery" (SE 9:139;
HA 7:235). The fact that this not very knowledgeable surgeon is able to
perform his duties skillfully underscores the difference between a university educated physician (with "knowledge") and a trained surgeon (with
"skills").

Moreover, the surgeon who replaces Natalie's surgeon has the bad habit of lying. Although he actually inherited his tool kit, he tells Wilhelm that he purchased it at an auction, prompting Jarno to exclaim: "If only that young fellow would speak the truth!" (SE 9:262; HA 7:429). Later the surgeon's prediction of a speedy recovery for Lothario makes Jarno fear that the situation is dangerous: "His condition is serious—I gather that from the politeness and encouragement of the surgeon" (SE 9:266; HA 7:435). The depiction of the painfulness of the surgical operations, the rough, uneducated manner of the surgeons, and their habit of prevaricating shows a realistic but sober and even distanced attitude toward this branch of the medical profession.

INTERNAL MEDICINE

In the Age of Goethe and before, the physician *(Leibarzt* or *Medikus)* stood in opposition to the surgeon *(Wundarzt):* "Even in early documents, field doctor (surgeon, physician for external ailments with a craftperson's training) stands next to or in opposition to physician (medicus, physician for internal sicknesses with an academic education ...)."[12] As noted previously, while surgeons in Germany underwent a training as specialized craftworkers, physicians received an academic education at a university. While other European countries saw the rise of separate medical schools for training physicians in the eighteenth century, the German universities remained responsible for teaching medicine, which preserved the academic, theoretical tradition of the German medical system.[13] Traditionally, the physician used his[14] schooling to identify diseases, perform nonsurgical cures having to do with internal medicine, prescribe drugs, and make general recommendations about living habits.

Much to the chagrin of the progressive physicians, the physician's primary activity in the minds of many patients was the prescription of drugs. In earlier days, the drug-manufacturing physician often specialized in alchemy. The alchemistic origins of the production of drugs become clear in Faust's description of his father's preparations of potions.[15]

Wilhelm Meister's Apprenticeship describes this kind of chemical medicine quite accurately, as shown by one case in point. When the suspicion arises that Felix is suffering from opium poisoning, the physician calls for vinegar (SE 9:368; HA 7:601). This was standard procedure for opium poisoning. Johann August Unzer, whom Goethe mentioned in *Poetry and Truth*, wrote that sour liquids were good against "swallowed narcotic, opiatic poisons": "For the actual potion, only sour things may be used. For example, sour milk, vinegar water, lukewarm water sweetened with vinegar mead; lemonade, barley brew made sour with vinegar or lemon juice or cream of tartar."[16] In a work published shortly after the *Apprenticeship*, Hufeland also prescribed vinegar, admittedly applied only externally, for a child who was suffering from opium poisoning.[17] In another book, Hufeland argued for the use of milk and oil, not vinegar, against poisoning in general,[18] but enough signs indicate that vinegar was used in one way or another specifically against opium poisoning to make clear that Goethe's reference to vinegar in Felix's case is well grounded in the medical thought of his day.

Although Felix's treatment is accurate, it is also ironized. What poisons him, after all, is a chemical drug, one that was greatly in vogue in the 1790s, particularly among those physicians like Weickard who followed the Brunonian system.[19] Thus, if drugs like opium did not exist, there would be no need for this treatment to counteract the poison they create. The superfluity of this realistic treatment of Felix, who is not in fact poisoned, further deepens the situation's irony.

Indeed, prescribed medicine proves either unnecessary or inadequate throughout the novel. The Beautiful Soul receives medications after all the excitement caused by the wounding of Narcissus: "Man gab dem Töchterchen Arznei ein und legte es zu Bett" (HA 7:369) [My parents gave their young daughter medication and put her to bed] (SE 9:224). In the German, the Beautiful Soul's use of the diminutive *Töchterchen* (young daughter) indicates her skepticism about this prescription. After the turbulence caused by the many events at the end of the novel, Wilhelm Meister, in a fit of desperation, also has medications prescribed for himself: "Fortunately the doctor helped Wilhelm out of his quandary, by declaring that he was sick and giving him medicine" (SE 9:370; HA 7:605). Friedrich does not believe in this sickness at all, and the reader should presumably also be skeptical, at least about the adequacy of these eighteenth-century equivalents of modern-day tranquilizers. The Beautiful Soul may indeed truly be upset, and Wilhelm Meister is certainly in bad shape a few pages before the end of the novel, but the vinegar, opium, and other medications that eighteenth-century physicians prescribed cannot solve their problems.

Elsewhere in Goethe's works, the same skepticism toward chemical medicine emerges. Faust continues describing his father's medicine with a bitter critique of the results of his alchemical concoctions:

> Hier war die Arzenei, die Patienten starben
> Und niemand fragte: wer genas?
> So haben wir mit höllischen Latwergen
> In diesen Tälern, diesen Bergen
> Weit schlimmer als die Pest getobt.
> Ich habe selbst den Gift an Tausende gegeben,

Sie welkten hin, ich muß erleben,
Daß man die frechen Mörder lobt.
                    (*Faust I*, "Vor dem Tor," 1048ff.; HA 3:39)

[That was our medicine—the patients died,
and no one thought to ask if anyone was healed.
And so, with diabolical electuaries,
we ravaged in these hills and valleys
with greater fury than the plague.
I have myself dosed thousands with the poison;
they wasted away—and I must live to hear
the brazen murders adulated.]
                    (*Faust I*, "Outside the City Gate," 1048ff.; SE 2:29)

Perhaps the mechanistic assumptions of chemical medicine provoke this critique. Although the apothecary in *Hermann and Dorothea*, composed in 1796 and 1797, immediately after *Wilhelm Meister's Apprenticeship*, is a positive figure, he denies the union of body and soul in the sixth canto (SE 8:284, lines 1250–52; HA 2:489, lines 299–301). In any case, this critique of drugs, and by extension of traditional physicians, also recurs in the *Apprenticeship*.

This critique is another indication of the proximity of the medicine of *Wilhelm Meister's Apprenticeship* to that of the Age of Goethe, for it corresponds to the objections, increasingly frequent among progressive physicians of the late eighteenth century, to pharmaceuticals. In his book *The Philosophical Physician*, Weickard referred scornfully to physicians who relied heavily on medications to treat their patients: "Many a physician even believes that the world could be brought back into order with pills."[20] Weickard perhaps contradicted himself by prescribing with gusto hard liquor and opium, but in theory at least he supported psychic over somatic treatments of mental disorders. Nicolai bluntly denied the efficacy of physiological medicinal treatments for melancholia: "Give a person who has become melancholy out of sadness the best medications and leave his or her passions untouched, and everything will be in vain."[21] Krüger concurred that excessive reliance on medication was useless: "I will be allowed here to make the observation that a physician who wishes to be successful must know something more than how to manufacture pills, powders and drops."[22] Krüger's belief that the physician "must be able to arouse and diminish affects, as these are the stream which moves the machine for which he has taken over the care"[23] points in the direction of a new kind of medicine.

At the root of these statements was a shift away from somatic to psychological medicine. Late-eighteenth-century physicians began to grow dissatisfied with their role as druggists, particularly since the pharmaceutical products of the era were not very effective. They were also involved in an increasingly bitter turf war with the apothecaries, druggists, and medicinal cooks (often women with folk remedies); the medical world attempted to disparage these healers and assert its own absolute authority in the field of medicine.[24] In casting a skeptical glance at traditional pharmaceutical medicine, then, *Wilhelm Meister's Apprenticeship* concurs with many of its epoch's more progressive physicians.

PSYCHOLOGICAL MEDICINE

With psychiatry soon to emerge as an important force, the physician of the soul *(Seelenarzt)* came to stand in contrast to the general physician *(Leibarzt)* and the surgeon *(Wundarzt)*.[25] This third category of physician included all those people who called themselves "philosophical," "moral," or "psychological physicians," and who performed functions similar to those of the modern-day psychologist, psychoanalyst, or psychiatrist. Although they did not actually restrict their practices to mental and psychological cases, feeling equally competent in somatic as well as psychic medicine, they were distinct from those old-fashioned physicians who insisted on treating the body alone. Although accurately portrayed, surgeons and internal physicians play minor and somewhat negative roles in *Wilhelm Meister's Apprenticeship*. Physicians who specialize in psychological problems and cares, however, are quite prominent in Goethe's works, including *Wilhelm Meister's Apprenticeship*.

The psychological physicians put forth theses that many eighteenth-century readers found engaging and exciting. Particularly the 1770s and 1780s witnessed an explosion of writings on the subject of mental disorders.[26] These physicians published thousands of articles on the psyche, nervous disorders, or the soul in the newly founded German-language psychological journals of the day, like *The Magazine of Experiential Psychology (Gnothi Sauton oder das Magazin zur Erfahrungsseelenkunde)*, edited primarily by Moritz, or its successors, *The General Repertory for Empirical Psychology and Related Sciences (Allgemeines Repertorium für empirische Psychologie und verwandte Wissenschaften)*, and *The Psychological Magazine (Psychologisches Magazin)*.

The era was so attuned to mental and emotional disorders that, in his short history of human health, Hufeland referred to it as the "nervous period," characterized by "general nervous ailments, hypochondria, hysteria, and cramps."[27] Earlier in the century, Johann Daniel Metzger (1739–1805) also complained about the increasingly large number of "insane, whose numbers are becoming too large for the space which is set aside for them."[28]

An increased interest in the care of the mentally ill, which led to the establishment of new insane asylums in Frankfurt and Vienna, accompanied the increase in the diagnosis of insanity.[29] In response to all this attention to the mentally ill, the first modern psychiatric hospital *(Psychische Heilanstalt für Geisteskranke)* was founded in 1805 in Bayreuth by Johann Gottfried Langermann, on principles established by Johann Christian Reil (1759–1813).[30] Reil, who coined the word *Psychiatrie* in 1808,[31] reported that throughout the latter part of the eighteenth century the increased capacity of insane asylums could not keep pace with the increased incidence of the disease: "Langermann says that in 1772 the places for the insane in the public houses in Torgen and Waldheim were doubled and only twenty years later space is already lacking to accept all the mad pouring out of Saxony."[32] The eighteenth-century fascination with the psyche, its constitution, and its disorders also manifests itself in the notorious practice of using insane asylums as tourist attractions.[33]

These philosophical physicians had a host of new therapeutic approaches for restoring and preserving the mental, spiritual, and psychological health of their patients.[34] These approaches fell into two large categories that reflected different assumptions concerning the origins of insanity. If the mental disorder was thought to stem from a poor relationship with society, the therapies emphasized improving that relationship. If it was thought to originate in a fixed idea, the physicians tried to divert the attention of the patient, sometimes even employing so-called pious frauds to trick him or her into a new way of thinking.

Moral Management: The Individual and Society

Therapies that emphasized improving relationships with society were founded on the thesis that sickness in general resulted from an aberrant or infelicitous relationship between the patient and his or her environment. As one historian of medicine writes, the physicians viewed "sickness as a disturbance in the equilibrium between the individual and the world."[35] Insanity, for these practitioners of medicine, was a variant of the general category of sickness, in which the individual and his or her society were no longer in a proper equilibrium. They therefore attempted to manage the morale of their patients by bringing them back into society.

These attempts at resocializing were subsumed under the motto of "moral management." Relying on physicians like J. C. Bolton, author of *Thoughts on Psychical Cures* (*Gedancken von psychischen Kuren,* 1751) and William Battie, author of the immensely influential *Treatise on Madness* (1758), the English developed a system of therapy for the insane that became

well known throughout Europe, especially after Francis Willis successfully used it to cure King George III of his madness, which had become
apparent in 1765 and was particularly virulent in 1788 and 1789.[36] In 1792,
William Tuke, a Quaker tea merchant, set up "The Retreat" near York,
which became the prime example of such an asylum run on the principles
of moral management.[37] The attractive natural setting, the system of authority and work, and the imposition of rules of etiquette were supposed
to lead to the acquisition of self-restraint, self-esteem, and sanity.[38]

Such systems usually began by establishing the authority of the physician. Moritz's *Magazine of Experiential Psychology* reprinted an article
from the *Mercure de France* in which Willis's use of "fear" to tame the
mad king of England is emphasized.[39] Willis supposedly always greeted
his patients with a fearsome and stern expression on his face in order to
make them obedient. As Foucault writes, "[F]ear appears as an essential
presence in the asylum."[40] At the same time, most progressive medical thinkers did want to improve conditions for the patients and decrease brutality
in the asylums. Knigge was typical when he argued that harsh treatment of
patients almost always backfired: "Finally, I have noted that incarceration
and every severe procedure almost always makes the ailment worse."[41]

After the inculcation of obedience in the patients, the physicians could
accustom them to a habitual schedule. Work was a particularly important
part of this schedule, as mechanical occupations were considered excellent
ways to heal illness; "The Retreat," for instance, generally provided its
inmates with jobs. Zur Hellen, a contributor to the *Magazine of Experiential Psychology*, argued that only hard work in isolation from the rest of
society could help a man of almost incorrigibly bad character: "A workhouse, more a house of improvement than one of discipline, where such a
person had to work several years quietly and industriously without any
society, would be the best cure and at the same time a charity for the state.
Working in society, such a person would certainly remain the same. . . ."[42]
Although, in this case, labor also served the purpose of protecting the patient from the bad influences of society, a bourgeois glorification of the
work ethic was another resonant subtext of this step of the cure.

Zur Hellen's remark that incarceration in a workhouse was a charity
for the state probably did not mean that the state planned to make a profit
on the labor of the insane. Although these institutions were clearly bourgeois
in emphasizing the importance of the work ethic, their founders were not
capitalistic in the sense of wanting to earn money from inmates' work. Reil
insisted that "insane asylums, like theaters, are not suitable for profit making."[43] Criticizing his predecessors who abused their patients in order to
earn money (like the notorious physician who yoked his patients to the
plow without feeding them),[44] Reil instead advocated government subsidies.

The psychologists of the eighteenth century attempted to bring their patients into harmony with the bourgeois world in other ways, too, aside from the work ethic. "The Retreat" stressed rules of etiquette, such as proper behavior at tea parties.[45] Daily newspaper reading was encouraged.[46] All of these techniques designed to force the patients to accept authority, follow a regular schedule, enjoy working, and adopt a bourgeois lifestyle show the middle-class bias of the psychological thinking in the second half of the eighteenth century. Thus, the psychology of this era attempted to rectify the relationship between individual and society by making the individual conform to bourgeois standards.

Fixed Ideas and Pious Frauds

In other eighteenth-century diagnoses, the source of mental illness was a specific fixed idea. As early as Boerhaave, an obsession with a particular fantasy or idea was seen as a symptom for melancholia: "Physicians call those sicknesses melancholia in which the patient stubbornly rages without fever and constantly nourishes one and the same obsession."[47] Hoffmann, too, knew about fixed ideas: "The signs of melancholia are sadness and fear without cause, mental anxiety, thoughts strongly fixed on some particular thing, and scanty, restless sleep. These signs are worse in overcast weather."[48] A century later, Knigge still agreed that a fixed idea was often the cause of mental illness: "In order to heal these unfortunates gradually, one often has to work on only one point, needs only carefully to destroy or modify one fixed idea in them."[49] But whereas the mechanists Boerhaave and Hoffmann had employed somatic means to cure their melancholy patients, the anthropological Knigge belonged to a new generation that wanted psychological cures. In the case of the fixed idea, the new physicians pursued a set of options different from those of the mechanists or of the moral managers. In addition to looking for ways of socially readjusting their melancholic, raging, hypochondriac, or hysterical patients, they resorted to a surprising number of tricks to get at that "single point," to modify or destroy that one dominant misconception.

Universally, the philosophical physicians discounted the importance of rational argumentation, knowing that the obsessions of the insane operated on a different level: "[G]eneral experience agrees that insanity never, or rather only in highly unusual cases and in special circumstances, can be healed through attempting to convince the patient [to act sanely]."[50] Instead, the medicine of the era relied on a number of creative, nonrational cures to awaken sanity in the soul.

The rejection of rational argumentation resulted in a turn to the imagination, which the physicians hoped to manipulate in order to dislodge fixed ideas: "As the understanding cannot be worked upon, if insanity is to be healed, . . . nothing else remains except to attempt to transfer the imagination from the hitherto dominant images to other ideas."[51] The physicians attempted to use the imagination with stories, drama, and other creative therapies.[52]

A reader of the *Magazine of Experiential Psychology* argued that narrations, for instance, effectively cured fixed ideas. For him, these fixed ideas consisted primarily in exaggerated desires for love and fame. When one of the two desires was clearly stronger than the other, the physician was to strengthen the weak desire at the cost of the stronger desire, playing the two drives off each other. For the case in which both desires were equally strong, the reader proposed a number of psychic cures that were typical for this branch of eighteenth-century psychology, including continuous activity and contact with varied people. Above all, storytelling was important: the writer stressed the narration of humorous stories about funny incidents in order to bring the soul into motion, as well as the narration of stories about charitable and praiseworthy instances in order to soften the soul, all with the intention of multiplying the thoughts of the patients.[53] As Moritz pointed out, the letter encapsulated remarkably well eighteenth-century theory about obsessions and how to overcome them.[54] Mauchart's concurrent recommendation shows how widespread the idea of using narrative to soothe the brain was: "The narration of interesting stories that occupy the imagination or stretch expectations is in general one of the best methods."[55]

Because of their rejection of the rational, these cures also emphasized indirection as well as creativity. When a cure consisted of introducing the patient to a new idea, the physician presented it in a casual, unfamiliar way. A letter from Ernestine Christiane Reiske, a classicist from the vicinity of Braunschweig, contained a report of such a cure, which was considered exemplary throughout the eighteenth century.[56] Her maid tortured herself with unfounded accusations of adultery. After many attempts to convince her maid that these self-reproaches were groundless, Reiske finally exclaimed: "If we couldn't commit any sins, then we wouldn't need a Savior."[57] Moritz compared this therapy admiringly to a well-chosen medication: "As false and dangerous as this perspective might be in other respects, here it has an excellent effect toward saving the spiritually ill from desperation. —These words took effect upon her like a well-chosen medication and from that time on she began to be calmer, worked industriously, and was completely recovered."[58] The thinking of the time found it completely understandable that rational discussion of the subject had failed, but that tricking the patient into seeing something had worked. Along the same indirect lines, another correspondent of the *Magazine* insisted that every move of the physician had to be hidden: "[T]he physician may not allow even the appearance of a physician to be observed in himself."[59]

Because the philosophical physicians often tried to catch their patients unawares, they called their therapies pious frauds *(fromme Betrüge)*. When Moritz mentioned the dangers inherent in Reiske's idea that humanity needed to sin in order to be saved, he put his finger on the interesting tendency of the era's medicine to use emotions, feelings, or even beliefs regarded by the era as unhealthy in order to restore mental health. Moritz himself was treated by such a psychic cure that relied on deception. While ill with tuberculosis, Moritz suffered from a severe attack of melancholia and was so depressed about the prospect of his impending death that he ignored the orders of his physician, thus making his condition worse. His physician, Markus Herz (1747–1803), finally lied to Moritz, telling him that his illness was indeed fatal, and that they could only hope to provide for a less painful death.[60] This had the proper effect. Moritz stopped brooding about the possibility of death and followed the orders of his physicians, with the result that his condition improved.[61] This therapy shows the willingness of the philosophical physicians to use untruths and even accept mad propositions in their struggle against insanity. In this case, for instance, the fixed idea itself—Moritz's belief in his impending death—provided the basis for a therapy that improved his attitude and health.

In summary, these pious frauds, which were meant to rid patients of their fixed ideas, consisted of artistic therapies that brought nonrational forces into play. The physicians of the era tried to surprise and even dupe their patients into new ways of thinking. At times, they were able to fight fire with fire by using their patients' mad ideas to cure their insanity.

PHILOSOPHICAL PHYSICIANS IN GOETHE'S WRITINGS:
THE TREATMENT OF MIGNON AND THE HARPER

The heated interest in psychological medicine that the last decade of the eighteenth century witnessed manifested itself in literature as well. Mad characters populate much of late-eighteenth-century German literature.[62] If the 1770s and 1780s had been especially rich in medical literature on the psyche and its abnormalities, the 1790s produced a bumper crop of fictive accounts of madness. As Theodore Ziolkowski has noted, in the same years that *Wilhelm Meister's Apprenticeship* appeared, 1795–96, two other highly successful novels with powerful depictions of madness were published in Germany: the popular *Biographies of the Insane (Biographien der Wahnsinnigen),* by Christian Heinrich Spieß (1755–99), and *William Lovell,* by Ludwig Tieck (1773–1853).[63]

Philosophical physicians, their patients, and the brand of medicine they use to heal such patients also make frequent appearances in Goethe's writings. The psychic cure in *Lila* is one obvious example, thoroughly studied by Diener. In this play, the main character, Lila, suffers from melancholia, based on the obsessive and mistaken idea that her husband, Sternthal, is trapped in the realm of evil spirits. A psychological physician appears and convinces the others to disguise themselves as spirits. When Sternthal acts as though he were entrapped, Lila gets the opportunity to fight her way through the realm of evil spirits and liberate her husband with the help of the good spirits. Only then does she believe he is alive and only then is she herself able, once again, to lead a happy life.

Carrying on in Diener's tradition, Reuchlein demonstrates that Orestes, in *Iphigenie auf Tauris*, also undergoes a cure that seamlessly conforms with the medical thinking of the late eighteenth century in Germany. Orestes suffers, according to Reuchlein, from obsessive guilt feelings. Pylades and Iphigenia know, being the products of an eighteenth-century German writer, that direct argumentation is of little avail in such cases; instead they patiently accept Orestes on his own terms, waiting for a crisis to come. In this crisis Orestes has a vision that has the same effect upon him that the theater has upon Lila. This vision—actually a hallucination—is a serious symptom of illness. But, in the tradition of eighteenth-century medicine, this madness functions to purge Orestes of some of his guilt. Afterward Orestes no longer feels guilty, but is in a new state of insanity in which he believes himself dead. Massages and discussions cure this second state of insanity.[64] In an essay of *The General Repertory*, Mauchart also discusses Orestes as a patient.[65] Passages like Mauchart's show the correctness of Reuchlein's assumption that eighteenth-century thinkers viewed Greek myth psychologically. Reuchlein's study shows that traces of eighteenth-century psychological medicine make their way even into a work set in another time period and without any overt references to medical figures like physicians. *Wilhelm Meister's Apprenticeship*, which is set in the eighteenth century and includes physicians and surgeons among its characters, contains even more references to the psychological medicine of its time.

As the previous chapter has shown, the physician's classification of Mignon's desires for mind-body unity as illnesses uses the rhetoric of the eighteenth century. His clinical description of her case as a consuming desire for Wilhelm and her homeland, indicating a diagnosis of homesickness and lovesickness, is well within the confines of the medicine of its time, which has a great deal to say about both illnesses. "The lively feeling that the common man calls homesickness"[66] was the subject of much medical attention. Similarly, lovesickness was a serious issue for eighteenth-century physicians. For Arnold, "Every example of extravagant and absurd action, of which the passion of love has many, can be seen as a degree of madness."[67] Most physicians of the era, however, agree with Zimmermann and treat as ill only victims of unrequited love.[68] Mignon's chief symptom—her seizures—are, according to the psychology of the time, typical products of excessively strong emotions.[69] The physician operates well within the eighteenth-century tradition when he assumes that Mignon's traumatic experience of observing her beloved Wilhelm in bed with Philine sets off a new bout of her illness. The Society's diagnosis of Mignon's homesickness, lovesickness, and jealousy as diseases is therefore characteristic for the eighteenth century.

The attempts of the Society to cure Mignon of her obsession with the soul also conform to the medicine of the time. Natalie's decision to allow Mignon to wear angel's clothes is an incipient psychic cure, allowing the young girl to live out her delusions in order to heal her. The winter play that provides the occasion itself operates on the same principles as the pious frauds of the psychological cures. The dramatization of an angel distributing gifts is intended to destroy the children's illusions about mythical figures (like angels, "Knecht Ruprecht," and Christ) who supposedly appear at certain times in person and reward good children and punish bad ones: "Sie hatten eine Vermutung, daß es verkleidete Personen sein müßten, worin ich sie dann auch bestärkte und, ohne mich viel auf Deutung einzulassen, mir vornahm, ihnen bei der ersten Gelegenheit ein solches Schauspiel zu geben" (HA 7:514) [The girls suspected that these were real persons dressed up; I encouraged them in this belief and, without offering any explanation, decided to organize such a spectacle on the first appropriate occasion] (SE 9:315). Here, Natalie, true to the principle of the Tower Society, does not directly confront error with correction, but lets error reveal itself, a strategy that allows the students to learn actively.

In addition to its didactic function, this drama also gives Mignon a chance to express important ideas about herself and to live out some of her wishes for a sexless, androgynous, transcendent body. Natalie seems to view this as at least an ameliorating step toward a cure: "'I decided immediately,' Natalie went on, 'to let her keep the dress, and had others made that were similar'" (SE 9:316; HA 7:516). Natalie's ploy shares with eighteenth-century medicine a willingness to indulge the fantasies of the patient. She allows Mignon to live out her irrational fantasies of being an angel, separate from the world, without a coarse human body, presumably in the hope of finding out more about her and bringing her back to her senses.

Eventually, Natalie obtains enough information about Mignon to construct a hypothesis concerning the immediate cause of Mignon's condition. She then commits the mistake of confronting Mignon directly with her situation. Although scared, she forces out of Mignon the story of the night in Wilhelm's room:

> Das gute Geschöpf . . . war kaum auf diesem Punkt seiner Erzählung oder vielmehr seiner Antworten auf meine steigenden Fragen, als es auf einmal vor mir niederstürzte und mit der Hand am Busen über den wiederkehrenden Schmerz jener schrecklichen Nacht sich beklagte. Es wand sich wie ein Wurm an der Erde. . . . (HA 7:524)

> [{W}hen the girl reached this point in her story, she suddenly fell down at my feet, clasped her breast and complained that the pain of that terrible night had come back again. She rolled about on the ground. . . .] (SE 9:321)

Besides attesting to the strength of the renewed eighteenth-century belief in the ability of mental phenomena such as memory to affect the body, this scene also demonstrates why the psychologists of the era preferred to avoid direct questioning. Natalie regrets having drawn the story out of the child: "In fact she reproached herself for eliciting by her questions these confidences and so cruelly reviving the memory of all that the dear child had suffered" (SE 9:321; HA 7:524). Although Natalie departs from the medical tradition of the era in questioning Mignon directly about her problems, she otherwise observes the conventions of her day when she talks with her patient and assumes that social and psychological phenomena, like love, can influence health.

At this point, the physician steps in with a therapy that is again characteristic for its time. He does not undertake anything against Mignon's homesickness, because, according to the medicine of the time, only a return home could cure that ailment: "If [homesickness] becomes full-blown, then a return to the motherland is the most certain, often the only means of cure."[70] Nor does he prescribe any medications against her lovesickness. He does, however, request that Wilhelm spend a large amount of time with her:

> "Mein Freund," versetzte der Arzt, "wo wir nicht helfen können, sind wir doch schuldig zu lindern, und wie sehr die Gegenwart eines geliebten Gegenstandes der Einbildungskraft ihre zerstörende Gewalt nimmt und die Sehnsucht in ein ruhiges Schauen verwandelt, davon habe ich die wichtigsten Beispiele." (HA 7:525)

> ["My dear friend!" the doctor replied, "even if we cannot help, we have an obligation to appease. And I know of several notable instances where the physical presence of what one loves can relieve the imagination of its destructive tendencies and transform longing into calm contemplation."] (SE 9:321)

In prescribing Wilhelm's presence, the physician performs the same sort of psychic cure to which Goethe referred when he described the treatment of Lila as a "cure, in which one allows madness to enter in order to cure madness."[71] Just as Natalie allows Mignon to assume the identity of an angel here on earth, the physician allows her to be near the object of her desire in order to cool that desire. In both cases, the same drug or pharmakon causes and cures her illness.

The cures seem to be partially successful. Like the physicians of his era, he knows that no medicine is foolproof and that his therapy could backfire: "Alles mit Maß und Ziel!" (HA 7:525) [Everything should be undertaken with moderation and purpose.] (SE 9:321). Despite this caveat, the cure seems to have a positive effect, although it does not, in the long run, save Mignon's life: "The tranquility with which Mignon greeted Wilhelm was a source of great satisfaction to the rest of the company" (SE 9:322; HA 7:525). This therapy demonstrates the willingness of eighteenth-century physicians to communicate with their patients, determine what they desire, and incorporate their desires into the cure, even when the desires themselves cause the illness.

Augustin, the Harper, further exemplifies the accuracy with which the novel reduplicates eighteenth-century psychological medicine.[72] One of Augustin's problems is a poor socialization that the novel analyzes in great detail. Augustin probably inherits a proclivity for a poor relationship with society from his father, who, because of his exceptionally high standards, cannot find his place in the world: "The older he became, the more cut off he felt from all society" (SE 9:355; HA 7:580). By the end of his life, the father has only one friend, who never contradicts him. Augustin goes from this unhealthy environment to the monastery, a "state of unnatural isolation" (SE 9:357; HA 7:582), which causes an alternating enthusiasm and melancholia:

Indessen hatte Bruder Augustin im Kloster seine Jahre in dem sonderbarsten Zustande zugebracht; er überließ sich ganz dem Genuß einer heiligen Schwärmerei, jenen halb geistigen, halb physischen Empfindungen, die, wie sie ihn eine Zeitlang in den dritten Himmel erhuben, bald darauf in einen Abgrund von Ohnmacht und leeres Elend versinken ließen. (HA 7:581)

[Meanwhile, my brother Augustin was spending his time at the monastery in the most peculiar way: he gave himself over to indulgence in ecstasies of both spiritual and physical nature, which at times transported him into a seventh heaven, but at others plunged him into depths of weakness and a void of misery.] (SE 9:356)

Throughout his childhood and youth, then, Augustin leads a solitary life that prevents him from having a proper relationship with society and makes him mentally ill.

The novel adheres to the theories of its era when it places much of the blame for Augustin's unstable mental health on life in a religious institution. According to eighteenth-century medicine, religious extremism frequently produced such wild swings of mood from deep depression to ecstatic euphoria, and monks were among the most susceptible, because of the unhealthy isolation of their lives. Zimmermann, for instance, vehemently attacked the monasteries and castigated the Catholic religious orders for hundreds of pages because of their insistence on celibacy and solitude. One chapter title of *On Solitude* is especially informative on the subject: "Disadvantageous Effects of Solitude on the Passions, Particularly in Hermits and Monks."[73] The enforced solitude and celibacy of the monastery purportedly caused a wide array of "mad" perversions, including self-mutilation, lecherousness, unnatural emissions during communion, self-castration, insanity, and pederasty.[74] The lesbian nun in Diderot's "La Religieuse" demonstrates how commonplace accusations of homosexuality were in anti-Catholic circles. *Wilhelm Meister's Apprenticeship* also makes use of this tradition of thinking when it links Augustin's religious fanaticism or *Schwärmerei*, the monastery, his incestuous relationship with his sister, and his insanity.

The second part of the Harper's insanity is his obsessive fear of death at the hands of an innocent youth: "His strongest delusion is that he brings misfortune wherever he goes and that he will die at the hands of an innocent boy" (SE 9:268; HA 7:437). The Harper's religious background accords well with eighteenth-century thought on his condition, for the *Magazine of Experiential Psychology* reports on pastors who abuse children and who obsess on death.[75] His attempt at killing Felix parallels the story of the child murderer who is driven by his own dissatisfaction with life.[76] As mentioned earlier, the eighteenth-century physician regarded the fixed idea or obsession as a central cause of melancholia. In this respect, too, then, the *Apprenticeship* works within the eighteenth-century medical tradition.

Augustin's insanity manifests itself most clearly in acts of violence that might not seem to conform to the image of the melancholy poet that other parts of the novel evoke. Mignon informs Wilhelm that the Harper is going into a rage and attempting to murder Felix: "Meister! Rette deinen Felix! Der Alte ist rasend! der Alte bringt ihn um!" (HA 7:330) [Master! Save your Felix! The old man has gone mad! He's killing him!] (SE 9:200). Wilhelm supposes that the Harper sets the fire at the end of the fifth book (SE 9:202; HA 7:334). When Felix is in danger at the end of the novel, Augustin rushes to inform the others. His wild appearance causes them to fear that his insanity has returned:

Eines Tages waren sie ... heiterer als gewöhnlich, als Augustin auf einmal zur Türe, die er aufriß, mit gräßlicher Gebärde hereinstürzte; sein Angesicht war blaß, sein Auge wild, er schien reden zu wollen, die Sprache versagte ihm. Die Gesellschaft entsetzte sich, Lothario und Jarno, die eine Rückkehr des Wahnsinns vermuteten, sprangen auf ihn los und hielten ihn fest. (HA 7:600–601)

[One day when they were amusing themselves and merrier than usual, Augustin appeared at the door, tore it open, and rushed in. His whole appearance was frightening—his face deathly pale, his eyes wild, his attempts to speak, fruitless. They were all alarmed: Lothario and Jarno, suspecting a recurrence of his madness, grabbed him and held him fast.] (SE 9:367)

The eighteenth century was as aware of the close connection between melancholy and mania as the twenty-first century is of the existence of manic-depressive states. Particularly the German physicians emphasized that manic behavior was merely an intensification of melancholy. Boerhaave, for example, wrote that the melancholy patient began raving when his brain fluids moved too turbulently: "When melancholia advances so far that such a violent movement of the cranial fluids arises that the patient falls into a cruel rage, it is called mania. Which is only different in degree from gloomy melancholia. . . ."[77] Hoffmann is another example: "Mania can easily pass over into melancholy and conversely, melancholy into mania."[78] Thus, the allusions to Augustin's manic attacks of violence are not unbelievable ornamentations on a sensationalist picture of insanity, but thoroughly credible aspects of a severe case of melancholy.

The attempts to cure the Harper are as typical for the Age of Goethe as the descriptions and diagnoses of his illness. Since the Harper's illness stems from both main causes of eighteenth-century madness—that is, a poor relationship with society and a fixed idea—his cure also contains elements from both traditions of eighteenth-century therapy. Parts of the therapy are highly reminiscent of systems like the "moral management" for readjusting patients to society, while other parts of the therapy involve psychic cures designed to shake Augustin out of his obsessions.

Augustin's treatment begins when the clergyman attempts on his estate to bring the Harper back into touch with society. The cooperation between the physician and the clergyman is itself typical for this era, in which medicine was encroaching upon turf that was formerly exclusively religious. Hufeland even wrote an article calling for a greater exploitation of country clergymen as a health resource.[79]

The details of Augustin's cure, which one reader calls a "monument to 'moral management,'"[80] also closely resemble those of actual eighteenth-century therapies. The conditions of the clergyman's estate are similar to those at Willis's institution where moral management was practiced. Like Willis's estate, the clergyman's establishment is in a "peaceful and pleasant" area (SE 9:210; HA 7:346). Although no tastelessly direct mention of authority is made, the patients must get accustomed to "order" (SE 9:210; HA 7:346). Typically for the time, however, the clergyman de-emphasizes the role of authority and proceeds quickly to the cure. The first step of this cure involves good work habits and a regular schedule: "Ich habe des alten Mannes Stunden eingeteilt, er unterrichtet einige Kinder auf der Harfe, er hilft im Garten arbeiten und ist schon viel heiterer" (HA 7:347) [I have organized the old man's day so that he gives lessons on the harp, and helps in the garden. As a result he is much brighter in spirits] (SE 9:210). It is characteristic for the psychology of the eighteenth century that the clergyman does not confront Augustin's insanity directly but encourages him to work: "Als Geistlicher suchte ich ihm über seine wunderbaren Skrupel nur wenig zu sagen, aber ein tätiges Leben führt so viele Ereignisse herbei, daß er bald fühlen muß, daß jede Art von Zweifel nur durch Wirksamkeit gehoben werden kann" (HA 7:347) [As a pastor I have not said much to him about his strange fears, but an active life brings with it so much occupation that he will soon feel that his doubts can only be overcome by activity] (SE 9:210). The activities the clergyman promotes consist of harp instruction and gardening. Instruction is also an important part of Goethe's therapy for Krafft, and work with nature is part of his advice for Plessing. Both are important: Harp instruction alone would probably be too sedentary, which would be dangerous, since excessive sitting was regarded as a primary cause of hypochondria and melancholia among artisans in the eighteenth century.[81] The clergyman's program gives Augustin both the physical and the mental activity that the eighteenth century regarded as vital for healthy development.

As usual with "moral management," the therapy intends to bring Augustin into conformity with bourgeois society. The clergyman hopes to convince Augustin to abandon his beard and religious habit: "[W]enn ich ihm aber noch seinen Bart und seine Kutte wegnehmen kann, so habe ich viel gewonnen, denn es bringt uns nichts näher dem Wahnsinn, als wenn wir uns vor andern auszeichnen, und nichts erhält so sehr den gemeinen Verstand, als im allgemeinen Sinne mit vielen Menschen zu leben" (HA 7:347) [{I}f I can get rid of his beard and his cowl, I will have achieved a lot; for nothing brings us closer to madness than distinguishing ourselves from others, and nothing maintains common sense more than living in a normal way with many people] (SE 9:210). The beard, significantly, is what makes people think the Harper is Jewish (SE 9:142; HA 7:239). While the clergyman encourages the Harper to wear normal, Christian, bourgeois clothes, the physician advocates newspaper reading: "'Es geht langsam vorwärts', versetzte der Arzt, 'aber doch nicht zurück. Seine bestimmten Beschäftigungen treibt er fort, und wir haben ihn gewöhnt, die Zeitungen zu lesen, die er jetzt immer mit großer Begierde erwartet'" (HA 7:438) ["Things are developing slowly, but not backwards," the doctor replied. "He continues in his specific occupations, and we have accustomed him to reading newspapers, which he now looks forward to with great eagerness"] (SE 9:268). The doctor's language, incidentally, is strikingly reminiscent of the Beautiful Soul's. Shortly after she has had her discussions with the physician and shortly before he makes his remarks about the Harper, she says: "I am always moving forward and never backward" (SE 9:255; HA 7:420). Possibly her discussions with him have induced her to speak about her progress in this linear fashion; perhaps the similarity simply shows how related the new medicine and the Beautiful Soul's pietistic religious tradition were. In any case, the physician and the clergyman establish order and normalcy in the life of the Harper through a dietetic regime, in a way typical for the eighteenth century.

This part of the therapy seems to be successful. When the Harper returns at the end of the eighth book, he is almost unrecognizable because he wears normal clothes and behaves reasonably in society: "Er war in der gewöhnlichen Tracht eines Reisenden, reinlich und anständig gekleidet, sein Bart war verschwunden, seinen Locken sah man einige Kunst an . . . er . . . betrug sich sehr vernünftig . . ." (HA 7:595–96) [He was dressed like a normal traveler, clean and tidy, the beard was gone, his hair was cared for. . . . His behavior was completely rational . . .] (SE 9:364). The clergyman and the physician are doing everything in the power of eighteenth-century medicine to readjust Augustin to Christian, bourgeois society.

Although this initial phase has some success, Augustin still nourishes several obsessions that require treatment. The physician of the *Apprenticeship* attempts several "psychic cures" that bear strong resemblances to cures prevalent in late-eighteenth-century Germany. Typically, he refuses out of principle to confront Augustin's fixed ideas directly: "Nur durch Mutmaßungen können wir seinem Schicksal näherkommen; ihn unmittelbar zu fragen, würde gegen unsere Grundsätze sein" (HA 7:437) [We have only been able to make surmises about his life story: direct questioning would be against our principles] (SE 9:267). In order to give the Harper a chance to explain himself indirectly, the physician tries a dramatic situation, a sort of pious fraud, by giving Augustin a chance to go to confession: "Da wir wohl merken, daß er katholisch erzogen ist, haben wir geglaubt, ihm durch eine Beichte Linderung zu verschaffen" (HA 7:437) [Since we have observed that he had a Catholic upbringing, we thought we might gain some relief for him by suggesting he go to confession] (SE 9:267). Reil mentioned that religious men and priestly accouterments were often necessary for the successful treatment of those who suffered from religious mania[82] and specifically suggested staged absolutions to heal those plagued by guilt complexes.[83] Even though Augustin refuses to submit to this therapy and always slips away when he is brought to a priest (SE 9:267; HA 7:437), the attempt to cure him is firmly rooted in the medical tradition of its era.

A second attempt at a pious fraud does succeed in improving Augustin's health. The physician reports that, although the Harper's adjustment to society is successful up to a certain point, his obsessive fear of death remains intact:

> Wir hatten ihn lange nach unserer Überzeugung moralisch und physisch behandelt, es ging auch bis auf einen gewissen Grad ganz gut, allein die Todesfurcht war noch immer groß bei ihm, und seinen Bart und sein langes Kleid wollte er uns nicht aufopfern. Übrigens nahm er mehr teil an den weltlichen Dingen, und seine Gesänge schienen wie seine Vorstellungsart wieder dem Leben zu nähern. (HA 7:596)

> [For a long time we had been treating him morally and physically as we thought fit, things were going pretty well, but his fear of death was still intense, and he would not give up his beard or his long cloak. Otherwise, he was taking more interest in the things of this world, and his songs as well as his mental reactions seemed to indicate that he was drawing closer to life again.] (SE 9:364–65)

The Harper can overcome, in part at least, this stubbornly insistent fear of death and the accompanying quirky clothing when he comes into possession of a flask of opium. The possibility of taking his own life frightens him into acting responsibly. He counsels his caretakers: "Sorgt nicht, . . . daß ich Gebrauch davon mache, sondern entschließt euch, als Kenner des menschlichen Herzens, mich, indem ihr mir die Unabhängigkeit vom Leben zugesteht, erst vom Leben recht abhängig zu machen" (HA 7:597) [Do not be concerned that I shall make use of it. . . . Satisfy yourself, as persons with knowledge of the human heart, that you have made me attached to life by allowing me the means of detaching myself from it] (SE 9:365). When Augustin calls the physician and his friends knowledgeable about "the human heart" and imputes to them the belief that accepting a patient's analysis may allow the patient to see the errors in that analysis, he categorizes them as philosophical physicians. In any case, as Reuchlein convincingly argues, their adaption of this policy concerning the Harper's death wish is certainly the sort of psychological cure favored by philosophical physicians.[84] Allowing the Harper to keep his opium gives him the possibility of actually carrying out his insane idea, and this confrontation with the reality of his obsession brings him to his senses.

After this psychological cure, Augustin sheds his eccentric garments and becomes a presentable and functional member of society. He is, however, not entirely cured, because of his persistent, obsessive fear of Felix, the youth he fears will kill him: "Augustin had never overcome his fear of Felix, and was therefore glad to see the boy depart as soon as possible" (SE 9:365; HA 7:597). Since the fixed idea is the central node of melancholia according to eighteenth-century thinking, the physician cures only the symptoms of Augustin's disease and not the cause.[85]

Even the failure of this cure contains possible references to the medical discourse of the time. Augustin's suicide with a razor blade had a specific meaning in eighteenth-century medicine. One of the more frequently discussed aspects of moral management was the assurance with which its clients—notably King George III—were allowed to keep their razor blades. Since patients supposedly had almost complete freedom, they had every right to keep potentially dangerous objects.[86] It was a sign of the success of the method that patients did not inflict any damage upon themselves or others. It is therefore perhaps not coincidental that the Tower Society provides the Harper with a razor blade, with which he, not as healthy as the king of England and other patients of The Retreat, in fact does commit suicide (SE 9:369; HA 7:604). Thus, although the Harper's treatment is not successful, it is authentic for the eighteenth century, and even the final proof of its failure is historically appropriate.

Augustin and Mignon are just two of many characters in the *Apprenticeship* who exhibit and are treated for mental problems. The other characters will be studied in other contexts later; the cases of these two suffice to show that the novel records the most minute details of eighteenth-century psychological medicine. This painstaking reduplication of the work of the philosophical physicians, along with the brief but accurate portrayal of surgery and internal medicine, reveals that Goethe used his knowledge of eighteenth-century medicine in writing the novel. As the Tower Society is the organization that frequently plays the role of philosophical physician in the Wilhelm Meister story, it is now time to see how it employs this new medicine.

4

The Physician's Power

In the course of the eighteenth century physicians like Stahl, Krüger, Haller, Zimmermann, and Weickard promoted a belief in the unity of mind and body that changed both the conception of the human being and medical practice. As they professionalized their practice, they strengthened and redrew boundaries separating them from other medical healers such as midwives, medicinal cooks, barbers, druggists, and apothecaries. At the same time, physicians were fighting other battles with specialists outside the field of medicine—philosophers, priests, and artists. The new medical assertion of competence in the mental and spiritual spheres as well as in the physical arena stands out as one of the many important implications of this new outlook. In *Wilhelm Meister's Apprenticeship*, the inclusion of this vitalistic, organicist philosophy gives the Society of the Tower an institutional tool—medicine—for treating a vast range of mental and psychological problems that had formerly been under the jurisdiction of philosophy and religion. As medicine expanded the realm of its competence, physicians began to interpret more and more areas of human experience. The semiotic fields in which they operated expanded from the body to include philosophy, religion, and art.

PHILOSOPHY

When philosophers like Locke began borrowing concepts like semiotics from medicine, they established a precedent for medical intervention in philosophy that lasted throughout the eighteenth century. From the very beginning a belief in the unity of mind and body permitted the physicians to increase their participation in philosophical debates about the psyche. Initially, philosophers like Wolff and Sulzer had divided "Psychology," "the science of the human soul," into two parts: an empirical branch and a rational branch. *Psychologia empirica* relied on practical experience with phenomena

76

like visions, dreams, and mental disorders. Sulzer called this field a sort of "experimental physics of the soul," and indicated that it belonged to medicine in the realm of the physical sciences. Rational analytic psychology *(psychologia rationalis)* was interested in more metaphysical questions. Its task was the discovery of "the essence and basic characteristics of the soul,"[1] and it belonged to the realm of philosophy. The philosophers therefore had always ceded a certain portion of psychology to the physicians but had retained for themselves analytic psychology, which they considered more important and rewarding. Their contemporaries, however, began to distrust *psychologia rationalis* on the grounds that physicians knew more about the psyche than anyone else.

The physicians made a two-pronged attack on philosophy. To begin with, physicians like Markus Herz insisted that metaphysics had little business with medicine: "[T]he subtler principles of metaphysics that are so far removed from perceptible recognition will therefore still be able to be of only very limited use in the field of medicine."[2] This was because "we in the field of medicine have not yet reached that point where we could deduce its principles a priori from pure conceptions of reason";[3] instead medicine should rely on "observation and experience."[4] Herz's patient Moritz agreed on the importance of empirical facts: "[E]xperience should of course be led by reflection, but reflection must also be reciprocally corrected by experience."[5]

While the physicians rejected the claim of philosophers to competence in the field of medicine, they put forward their own claim to knowledge on the formerly philosophical topic of the soul. According to Gaub, the philosophers had in fact always relied on physicians for the facts and insights needed to ground their interpretations: "[I]f they [the philosophers] see anything clearly in the darkness, it would hardly be discernible but for the light borne in front by physicians."[6] La Mettrie also spurned the argumentations of philosophers not schooled in medicine and insisted that psychology needed the practical experience of a physician: "Experience and observation alone may direct us in this area. One finds them sufficiently documented in the annals of the philosophically thinking physicians—and not at all in those of the nonmedical philosophers."[7] Although more insolent than most, La Mettrie was by no means an anomaly. Zimmermann made the same demand for medical observation and experience over metaphysical speculation about the soul.[8]

The new psychological press agreed that the physicians knew more about the mind than the philosophers. The editors of the *Magazine of Experiential Psychology*, for instance, clearly supported the physicians and their approach to the mind-body problem. The very title of the magazine underscored its interest in empirical studies of the psyche. Moritz, the primary force behind the magazine, was in complete agreement with the attack on philosophy. In a footnote, Moritz acknowledged his debt to Herz and posited a firm link between psychology and medicine: "Because of the remarkable similarity that psychological medicine has with medicine in general, the medical encyclopedia of Dr. Markus Herz has been of great use to me in my observations on the field of psychological pathology."[9] In the introductory preface to the *General Repertory for Empirical Psychology and Related Sciences*, I. D. Mauchart also made clear that the title of his journal reflected a conscious decision to work with empirical (and thereby medical) as opposed to rational (or metaphysical) psychology.[10]

Other thinkers and even some philosophers soon joined the physicians and granted medicine priority in psychology. Johann Gottfried Herder (1744–1803) insisted that psychology had to have a physiological fundament: "In my humble opinion, no psychology that is not in every step physiology is possible."[11] His reference to physiology contained an implicit rejection of the purely mental *psychologia rationalis* in favor of the somatic *psychologia empirica*. Only those who knew the body, like physicians, along with poets[12] and biographers, could provide relevant information about the soul: "Life descriptions, the remarks of physicians and their friends, the oracles of poets—these alone can provide the material of a true psychology!"[13] Whereas the philosophical physicians and their allies were confronting extreme mechanism among the orthodox physicians and therefore had to convince them that they should pay attention to the mind as well as the body, this new medical school was contesting extreme dualism among the philosophers and had to convince them to pay attention to the body as well as to the mind.

Although the established philosophy of the Leibnizian and Wolffian schools resisted monistic theories on the mind-body problem, a rejuvenated philosophy at the end of the century was not so stubborn. Once the new philosophy accepted that the vitalists had vanquished the mechanists in medicine, it attempted an alliance with the victors. Kant's preference for Stahl over Hoffmann and Boerhaave clearly signaled a willingness to cede a much greater role in psychology to the physicians.[14] Philosophers and, indeed, thinkers from all conceivable disciplines joined in granting the physicians the title of "philosophical physicians," extending the boundaries of medicine to include psychology, which once belonged at least in part to philosophy.

THEOLOGY

The dispute with the philosophers over the soul or the psyche was also a dispute with the theologians. When medicine decided to treat problems of the soul, it naturally came into contact, not to say conflict, with religion.

Religion had, so to speak, been there first. Words like *Seelenheilkunde* (literally, "knowledge of the healing the soul") made clear that medicine was interested in spiritual matters: as one historian of the late eighteenth century notes, specific terms of religion and the church were transferred to the medical field and used by physicians without any qualms.[15] Religious figures therefore entered the medical debate without any compunction. Wrote George Berkeley, the bishop of Clone in Ireland who often treated patients: "If physicians think they have a right to treat of religious matters, I think I have an equal right to treat of medicine!"[16] Nor was he alone: the founder of Methodism, John Wesley, was also the author of an incredibly popular medical handbook, *Primitive Physick* (1747), which went through twenty-three editions in his own lifetime.

Eighteenth-century physicians were themselves aware of the closeness of this relationship, as shown by the homage Tissot pays to religion at the beginning of one of his treatises: "It would please me greatly to declare here publicly how many important things medicine has borrowed from religion."[17] Stahl was typical of these physicians of the psyche in that he came from a pietist background and had strong religious motivations: Haller, Krüger, and others also made the seriousness of their commitment to religion evident while they discussed the unity of mind and body.

From the beginning, the fields overlapped. The attempts of physicians to treat vices showed their interest in handling the same people whom the priests treated. Zur Hellen wrote in the *Magazine of Experiential Psychology* that he was convinced that sinfulness was a disease of the soul: "I am also of the opinion that every sinful person has a sick soul. . . ."[18] Such thinking persisted at the beginning of the nineteenth century, as well. Johann Christian Heinroth (1773–1842), to whom Goethe occasionally referred (SE 12:39; HA 13:37, 573), made the same identification of sinfulness and sickness, this time reversing zur Hellen's equation by saying that psychological illnesses were sinful: "The cessation of the life of the soul must be regarded as sin."[19] A commentator explains that for Heinroth sickness was sin becoming visible.[20] The physicians were also aware of the similarities between the therapies used by these two systems. The religious confession consisted, according to Moritz, of remorse for sins committed, penance, and a breakthrough to health, a procedure that corresponded to a psychic cure.[21]

While physicians had initially cooperated with religious authors, in the latter half of the eighteenth century they grew increasingly skeptical of religion and began to treat certain religious attitudes as illnesses. *Schwärmerei*, or religious fanaticism, became a widespread and dangerous disease.[22] Carl Friedrich Pockels thundered against the dangers of religion, using the *Magazine of Experiential Psychology*, when it was under his control in 1786, for a broadside against "religious fanaticism." According to Pockels, one of the causes of religious fanaticism was the unheard-of luxury and excessive, nerve-weakening lifestyle of the upper classes.[23] Arnold also saw religious fanaticism as a major cause of insanity and argued that "reasonable conceptions of God and religion, free of superstition, enthusiasm, and desperation," were necessary for the preservation of mental health.[24] Weickard warned against the dangers of excessive devotions.[25] Zimmermann spent a large part of his career proving that religious fanaticism was a mental illness. For him, the mystical saints were "all in the highest degree hypochondriac, hysterical, at times catatonic and often crazy."[26] In a typical case, a woman's insanity was blamed on religiously inspired guilt feelings after an abortion: "[O]ppressive concern, combined with fanatical and eccentric religious beliefs may have been the first source of her melancholy, her madness, and finally her mania."[27] Thus even physicians like Tissot, who viewed themselves as religious, emphasized the dangers of exaggerated religious feelings: "Exaggerated devotion very often causes the total destruction of health . . . it throws the soul into the nonsense of religious fanaticism and the body into exhaustion."[28]

Because of these dangerous side effects, physicians sought to put strict controls on religion. Although he conceded the priests had done psychological work in the past, Moritz cautioned in his "Suggestion for a Magazine on Experiential Psychology" that religious leaders could not adequately perform the tasks of psychologists because their outlook was tainted too heavily by superstition. Goethe revealed that he was aware of the transition between superstitious religion and scientific medicine when he cited a historian of medicine who wrote: "Medicine, long exclusive property of the priests, especially the Aesclepians in Thessalonia, began gradually to give up her tight connection to religious superstition."[29] While Goethe sets this transition in ancient Greece, his pairing in *Hermann and Dorothea* of the apothecary and the pastor shows that he knew that the same thing was going on in his own eighteenth century, which, after all, considered itself a revival of ancient Greece. While physicians did use religion for some cases, they reserved the right to make judgment on the validity of various religious beliefs. Even though physicians like Hufeland called for the use of country vicars as medical assistants, they denied priests and ministers the competence to heal the ill on their own. The physicians were therefore happy to take over the spiritual disorders that the priests had formerly handled and to accept the title of "moral physicians."[30]

THE PHYSICIAN AS ARTIST

A relativistic attitude toward cures and medications turned the physician's profession into a creative one as well as a philosophical and religious one. Novalis saw "higher medicine" as art—which is to say, he meant that art is a kind of medicine.[31] Kant reversed the relationship, arguing that, with some limitations, "the physician is an artist."[32] While Novalis and Kant, like Goethe, remained somewhat distanced from the actual practitioners of their era's medicine, other thinkers of the time wholeheartedly endorsed the idea that doctors are artists.

Art brings the discussion back to the pharmakon. The "artistry" of medical work stemmed from the late-eighteenth-century medical denial of the existence of wonder drugs. In a lecture on medicine, Johann Daniel Metzger held that, just as all poisonous substances could become medicines, every beneficial drug could also become a toxin: "[I]t is also certain that there is no medication that, given at the wrong time, could become useless or even a poison."[33] The patient Diaetophilus also agreed with Metzger that the medical profession could not rely on formulaic responses to illnesses.[34]

Because one and the same drug could both kill and cure, the physician had to be a sort of artist who intuitively shaped individual therapies based on general principles. He became a master of the pharmakon. The very vocabulary of the era underscored this connection between artistry and medicine when it called dental physicians "dental artists": "Skilled dentists are better called dental artists."[35] Many physicians made a point of distinguishing between the "science" of medical knowledge and the "art" of medical practice.[36]

For Zimmermann, physicians, along with politicians and military commanders, belonged to the same category as the artist, because they needed "genius" and the ability to sense, understand, and make connections quickly.[37] Goethe, of course, admired Zimmermann's book on experience, where he treated the subject of medical genius. It is therefore possible that Goethe explicitly drew from his era's medical writings an analogy between works of the poetic and the medical genius.

With the prerogatives of a writer, the physician achieved the rights of interpretation in an increasing number of semiotic fields. The accession of the physician to the rank of artist and his assumption of duties that formerly belonged to religion and philosophical thinkers comprised part of a tendency to grant more and more importance to medicine, a tendency that accompanied the resurgence of the belief in the unity of body and soul. The insistence on this unity strengthened the role of the physicians and increased the stature of medicine by allowing physicians and medicine—formerly restricted to the care of the body—to make claims on spiritual matters. The increasingly medicalized world of the eighteenth century eagerly accepted the claims of the physicians and gave them a place of honor in its society.

THE IMPORTANCE OF PHYSICIANS IN
WILHELM MEISTER'S APPRENTICESHIP

The Society of the Tower takes part in the eighteenth-century semiotic enhancement of medicine by casting a wide range of phenomena in terms of health and sickness, and thus granting physicians interpretative competence in a variety of philosophical, aesthetic, and moral areas.

The imagination was one of the categories that eighteenth-century medicine appropriated for its own use.[38] As early as Hoffmann, it became one of the primary links between body and soul.[39] Nicolai argued that physicians could use it to affect the emotions, which in turn affected the body.[40] Just as frequently, physicians of the era emphasized the dangers, rather than the therapeutic possibilities, of the imagination: "[I]n this respect therefore, madness consists of an extreme, unnatural exaltation of the imagination out of proportion with the other faculties of the soul."[41] Arnold was one of many who insisted on strictly limiting the freedom of the imagination. His dietary recommendations instructed the reader to "pay attention to the effects of the imagination; restrain its tendency to all-too-great activity."[42] The imagination had to be tamed in order for the individual to recognize reality: "In a word, the imagination must be repressed and held under a yoke so that the soul is able to pay attention to the reality and nature of things and not be led down erroneous paths by the imagination."[43] Zimmermann blamed the religious excesses of Near Eastern monks on an hyperactive imagination.[44] The German word for hypochondriac was *eingebildeter Kranker* (imagined sick), suggesting that a faulty imagination was characteristic of this widespread illnesses. Thus, physicians of the eighteenth century began to find both positive and negative medical side effects of the imagination, something that formerly had not concerned them at all.[45]

Traces of this belief in the medical aspects of the imagination also appear in Goethe's writings. After viewing the prince of Pallagonia's grotesque gardens in southern Italy, he faulted an imagination run out of control for the "pathological" creations: "There it became quite apparent how necessary it was in education, not to remove but to regulate the imagination, to give it through noble images shown early a taste for the beautiful, a need for the excellent. What does it help to tame sensuality, to build understanding, to secure reason its rule? The imagination lies in wait as the most powerful enemy: it has from nature an irresistible drive to the absurd."[46] Characteristic of Goethe's analysis is the attempt to regulate the imagination and a refusal to stamp it out. In his works, physicians frequently try to point the imagination of their patients in healthier directions.

The physician and other members of the Tower Society also implicate imagination in the mental illness of the characters they treat. The sickness of the countess develops because "she imagines that this will end in cancer."[47] Particularly in the German original, variations of the word *Einbildung* (imagination) come up frequently in Aurelie's speech (SE 9:153–54; HA 7:258–59), suggesting that, in accordance with eighteenth-century thinking on this disease, a problem with her imagination causes her mental disorder. An imagination unchecked by memory causes the count to lose touch with reality: "The old gentleman had once had an excellent memory, and was always proud at being able to recall the most insignificant details of his youth. But now he confidently imposed the stamp of truth on the wildest combinations of fancy that his imagination created out of failing memory" (SE 9:367; HA 7:600). Sperata's case progresses as a physician of the eighteenth-century[48] would have expected: First her imagination affects her emotions: "Her imagination awakened and intensified the desire of her heart" (SE 9:360; HA 7:588); subsequently this emotional stress wears out her body. When the Harper defiantly tells his brothers that the fires of hell can only singe "morbid imaginations" (SE 9:357; HA 7:583), he is actually pointing to the weak link in his own health. The physician's attempt to cure Mignon's lovesickness assumes that Wilhelm's presence will "relieve the imagination of its destructive tendencies . . ." (SE 9:321; HA 7:525). In a wide range of cases, then, the Tower Society uses the new medicine of its era to demonstrate a link between the imagination of its patients and their illnesses.[49]

Foolishness and, by extension, wit were additional categories that began to interest medicine in the eighteenth century. Originally, an old tradition of respect for the fool had existed, a tradition emphasizing that the condition of foolishness required a certain amount of intelligence. Lichtenberg gave voice to this tradition: "There is an old proverb in English that says: he is too dumb to be a fool. Much fine observation is contained therein."[50] Above all, Lichtenberg appreciated the surprising and unusual connections that the fool was able to draw; for him, foolishness "can designate the unexpected and the strange in the union of ideas, the leaping that one finds in great amounts in foolish people."[51] Lichtenberg thereby classified foolishness as a kind of unexpected and peculiar wit. By the end of the century, however, foolishness had lost this positive evaluation, and foolishness or *Narrheit* had become a major disease. At the beginning of the nineteenth century, after the new medicine had become orthodoxy, Reil defined the fool as someone who made too many rapid connections, which led to a chaotic and unstable way of thinking: "In their faculty of representation, a series of ideas too fast for their powers rules; adventurous notions flood them, flash and then disappear just as quickly.

. . . Hence their generally great chattiness about things that have neither sense nor continuity. They talk in a single breath about sabers and tooth-picks, of children and hats, of broken pots and demasted ships. . . . Just as tumultuous and incoherent are their feelings and emotional swings."[52] The only difference between this attitude and the earlier one typified by Lichtenberg was that foolishness had become a sickness.

Court society and consequently the theater valued foolishness and wit particularly highly. There the fool had the privilege of expressing other-wise unutterable truths. As society changed, however, and the bourgeoisie replaced the aristocracy as the dominant class, the fool lost this role. Wolfgang Promies has shown how the rising bourgeoisie banned the fool, the jester, and the *Hanswurst* from the house and theaters and consigned them to the hospital; this was the fate of all who exhibited an untamed imagination. In the middle of the eighteenth century, the theater was no longer a showplace for the fool, but an instrument with which to cure fool-ishness. If it failed in its attempt to cure, then the fool belonged in an insti-tution: "Admittedly, a fool who is completely a fool will not be improved in comedies or satires; for such a one actually belongs under the whips of the insane asylum guard."[53] Thus, in the course of the eighteenth century, the witty aperçus of the fool had become symptoms of mental illness, and the fool himself had been relegated to the asylum.

Friedrich is the fool in *Wilhelm Meister's Apprenticeship*. The word occurs several times in connection with him: He calls his claim to paternity "ein recht närrischer Streich" (HA 7:559) [a crazy trick] (SE 9:342), and Philine, his partner, refers to herself at another point as "die Erznärrin" (HA 7:249) [a silly fool] (SE 9:148). As Trunz's commentary indicates, Friedrich is frequently associated with the baroque (HA 7:805), which sug-gests that his humor predates the bourgeois expulsion and medicalization of the fool. Friedrich sees his condition in old-fashioned literary terms, while the Society of the Tower views it medically.

In many ways, Friedrich acts like a fool in the old literary, Lichtenberg-ian sense of the word. He can make unusual comparisons and surprising connections—the very ability that Lichtenberg had ascribed to the fool. When he uses grammatical terminology to describe his reaction to Jarno's decision to marry Lydia, he exhibits a typically witty way of thinking: "'Old man,' said Friedrich, 'you are embarking on something that, as a substan-tive, invites various adjectives, and as a subject all sorts of predicates'" (SE 9:347; HA 7:566). The game he and Philine play of alternately reading arbitrarily selected passages from a baroque library produces the kind of literally sophomoric, learnedly foolish, effect known from the sixteenth century (SE 9:342; HA 7:558). Such witty foolishness is entertaining, charm-ing, and, moreover, vital for the plot. If Friedrich lacked the ability to see the connection between the painting of the lovesick prince and Wilhelm Meister's situation and the courage to speak about the matter, the happy end of the novel would never take place.

Friedrich has no compunctions about using his gifts. His extravagant quotes, his complicated riddles, his unabashed willingness to breach convention and tell the truth are all typical of the literary fool. A passage from the end of the novel shows that Friedrich enjoys privileges that are thoroughly comparable with those of the Shakespearean fool: "Friedrich, that uninhibited fellow who usually drank more wine than he should have, monopolized the conversation, making them laugh in his usual way with hosts of quotations and waggish allusions, but often disconcerting them by his habit of saying exactly what he thought" (SE 9:370; HA 7:605). Friedrich, therefore, seems to have a baroque understanding of his foolish condition and its usefulness.

Despite the wit and usefulness of foolishness, the Society of the Tower has a medical understanding of Friedrich's condition. Wilhelm Meister and the Tower Society view Friedrich's foolishness in the medical terms of the eighteenth-century German bourgeoisie. Both Wilhelm Meister and Lothario have a name for this illness which seems to befall Friedrich: madness. Wilhelm describes the way Friedrich and Philine study as "crazy" (SE 9:342; HA 7:558); Lothario refers to Friedrich as his "crazy brother" (SE 9:372; HA 7:608). Natalie responds to Friedrich's nonsense as Johann Christoph Gottsched and F. K. Neuber reacted to the *Hanswurst*: "Seine Art von Lustigkeit tut mir wehe; ich wollte wetten, daß ihm dabei nicht wohl ist" (HA 7:556) ["His brand of merriment makes me uncomfortable," said Natalie quietly to Therese. "I bet he is not so happy as he pretends to be"] (SE 9:341). The German allows for greater latitude in interpreting Natalie's remark along specifically medical lines. Although Friedrich resists this interpretation and counterattacks by delivering "a ridiculous encomium on medicine" (SE 9:371; HA 7:606), the narrator's description of his eulogium as "ridiculous" indicates that Natalie's treatment of his condition as illness, typical for the Tower Society, is dominant at the end of the novel.

Once medicine had taken an interest in imagination and wit, it was only a matter of time before it began to look at literature, traditionally a home for these two faculties, as a source of information about psychological disorders. Moritz, for instance, called for a study of characters and sentiments from "good novels and dramatic plays such as Shakespeare's."[54] Medicine was one of the major forces endorsing the rise of psychological realism and discussion of the emotions in literature. As Weissberg has noted, medicine and literature shared a common interest in the mind-body unity that orthodox philosophy resisted.[55]

Characters in and about the Society of the Tower also adopt a clinical approach to literature. As the Stranger, an emissary from the Tower Society, looks on, Wilhelm and his acting friends enjoy testing their wit *(Witz)* and imagination *(Einbildungskraft)* with impromptu acting. The Stranger's approval indicates that he and the Society view drama as an important tool for strengthening the health of the mental faculties. Later, Aurelie and Wilhelm dispute which songs and poems more accurately express Ophelia's mental state. While Aurelie would prefer "parts of some sad ballads" (SE 9:152; HA 7:255), Wilhelm insists that Ophelia's bawdy songs reveal her secret, otherwise inexpressible wishes: "Lustful tones resound throughout her mind and, like an imprudent nurse, she may well have tried more than once to sing her senses to sleep with ballads that merely keep them more awake. And when she has lost all control over herself and when her heart is on her tongue, this tongue betrays her . . ." (SE 9:152; HA 7:255). Both Wilhelm and Aurelie operate on the assumption that the songs or poems characters utter must have some relationship to their psyche. Wilhelm, moreover, assumes that the tongue can betray the rational mind, revealing something like an irrational, highly sexed unconscious.[56]

While all the characters share some of these assumptions about the power of poetry and songs to reveal unspoken and perhaps even unknown aspects of the mind, the Tower Society carries this assumption to a scientific extreme. The physician reports that Natalie uses the hermeneutic ability of a modern psychoanalyst to find clues about Mignon's history from seemingly unimportant statements, slips of the tongue, and poems: "What I have been telling you, was not something she conveyed in so many words to Natalie, but what Natalie has pieced together from occasional remarks, from songs and childish indiscretions which revealed what they intended to keep secret" (SE 9:320; HA 7:522). The Tower Society uses Mignon's songs—including, presumably, the poems printed in the novel—to come up with a convincing case history of the singer. This clinical, psychological approach to songs, poems, and words results from an anthropological approach to the mind-body problem, which allows physicians to pursue an interest in the mind and its faculties.

Finally, the Tower Society's diagnosis and treatment of religious fanatics demonstrates once again its use of medicine to handle problems that formerly had not belonged to the medical realm. When the physician relates the history of the count's religious fanaticism, he asserts that the case almost falls into the jurisdiction of the clergyman: "[T]he case almost belongs in your territory, my dear pastor."[57] The important word remains "almost," however, for the acknowledgment of the similarities between religion and medicine does not hinder the physician from keeping the case to himself. Like the physicians of the Age of Goethe, the physician in the novel insists on treating the religious fanatic. Again and again, the physician and others in the Society of the Tower assert the priority of medicine over religion.

The overlap between the two fields becomes clear in cases other than that of the count, as well. The etiology of the Harper's madness also includes *Schwärmerei* in a monastery (SE 9:356; HA 7:581). The physician draws upon the clergyman to bring about his cure of the Harper, and, as previously mentioned, the two of them attempt to use a fake confession as part of their treatment (SE 9:267; HA 7:437). The Beautiful Soul's case, which will be studied in more depth in the next chapter, abounds with material of interest both to theologians and psychologists. She herself begins to read the writings of Count Zinzendorf, leader of a religious group called the "Moravians," "if only in order to acquaint myself with a particular psychological phenomenon" (SE 9:241; HA 7:397). While her physician tells her that her religiously inspired dualistic way of thinking can damage her health (SE 9:253; HA 7:415), he himself is described as one of the "Penates" (household religious figures) and refuses to hide his interest in her religious behavior: "The doctor did not conceal the fact, either then or in our later discussions, that it was his interest in religious sentiments that made him seek me out" (SE 9:249; HA 7:409). In addition, the Beautiful Soul uses medical rhetoric to describe her religious progress. After she realizes that she has a potential to do evil, she expresses her wish to be healed: "my only desire being to be freed of this sickness and this whole disposition toward sickness. I was sure that the Great Physician would not refuse me help in this" (SE 9:239; HA 7:392–93). The idea of God as a great physician became popular among pietists as well as physicians in the late eighteenth century.[58] Goethe himself referred to "the heavenly physician" in a letter written in the 1770s, when he was also corresponding with Susanne Katharina von Klettenberg, the pietist model for the Beautiful Soul.[59] The metaphor gained strength in the context of late-eighteenth-century medicine, which began to view a predisposition to heinous acts as a medical as well as a religious problem. The Beautiful Soul's story, as well as those of the count and the Harper, shows that the novel mirrors this conflation of the theological concept of the soul and the medical one of the psyche in the latter part of the eighteenth century.

Sperata's case also shows how the novel records the ultimate triumph of medicine over theology in the eighteenth century. In her story, the dangers of a priestly treatment stand in contrast to the relative success of modern psychological treatments. The Tower Society, which carefully files this document, uses it as additional evidence for the importance of medicine.

In particular, the first intervention of the religious man comes across as an anticure. After Mignon's birth, Sperata is "happy to be the mother of the little creature" (SE 9:358; HA 7:586). The priest decides to change this situation by initiating a "therapy." It begins with a "pious fraud": "The priest thought he owed a nursing mother some pious deception . . ." (SE 9:358; HA 7:586). Pious deception *(frommer Betrug),* one of the key phrases in the terminology of late-eighteenth-century psychiatric medicine, suggests from the outset that the priest's work qualifies as a type of psychological cure. Unlike the physicians of the era, this man piously betrays his patient in a traditionally religious way, however, by telling Sperata that Augustin recommended that she place herself fully under the control of religion. Once he has her in that situation, the priest begins his psychomanipulation: "[H]e had the strange idea of making her repentance like to that she would have felt if she had known the true nature of her transgression" (SE 9:359; HA 7:586). This therapy resembles the psychic cures of the Enlightenment in its indirectness and in its assumption of authority over the patient. Moreover, typical for the era, it strives to achieve a certain appropriate affective response in the patient without the usual cause. Normally, the physician tries to make a patient, say, enjoy life, by tricking him or her out of an obsession; in this case the priest attempts to trick the patient into repenting. The thinking of the priest is so modern that he acknowledges the unity of soul and body and waits until her body has enough strength to bear an attack on the psyche: "As soon as the child was weaned, and she had regained sufficient bodily strength, the priest began . . ." (SE 9:359; HA 7:586). The difference between this cure and a medicinal one lies primarily in its effect. Whereas she is previously happy and pleased with her child, after this treatment, she is, if not insane, at least dazed: "[T]he priest's treatment had so confused her that, without being mad, she found herself in the strangest state of mind."[60] The use of the word *Behandlung* (treatment) supports the thesis that this story depicts a maleficent psychic cure.

Sperata's madness qualifies as a sort of religious fanaticism, in which she sees Mignon as a sort of new savior. After the death of her child, she develops the fantasy that Mignon, like a new savior, has died, but will come back and then redeem her sinful parents (SE 9:360; HA 7:588–89). The priest manages to pass this madness off as rapture: "Influenced by him, people in the neighborhood began to consider her as someone in a state of religious rapture, not someone out of her mind" (SE 9:360; HA 7:589). He, however, cannot do anything more than ensure that Sperata is well treated by her servants and the population at large.

In contrast to the priest, Sperata's relatives feel that her condition is a debilitating illness: "Meantime our poor sister seemed to be steadily more and more worn down by her single preoccupation and her limited activity" (SE 9:361; HA 7:590). They therefore call in a physician, who proposes a new pious fraud. Since Sperata believes that her child will come back to life if all its bones are collected, he proposes "that the bones of a child's skeleton should gradually be intermingled with those she already had, to increase her hopes" (SE 9:361; HA 7:590). The physician hopes to divert her from the constant searching and distract her from this fixed idea. This attempt succeeds only in part: "[A] great joy spread over the poor woman's face when the parts gradually fitted together . . ." (SE 9:361; HA 7:590); the final completion of the skeleton delights her: "From this time on, her whole soul was filled with joyful prospects" (SE 9:362; HA 7:591). Indeed, she is so happy that she loses interest in the world and passes away: "She no longer paid attention to earthly things, took little food, and her spirit gradually freed itself from the weight of the body" (SE 9:362; HA 7:591). Admittedly, in the final analysis, the medical treatment of Sperata scarcely betters the religious one. Nonetheless, the Tower Society, which chronicles this story and puts it into its archives, tries to put as good a face as possible on the matter by asserting that the physician can at least make Sperata happier, allowing her to attain a certain *Glückseligkeit* ("blissfulness," with an emphasis on the "blessedness" of *Seligkeit*), if not actual *Glück* (happiness) before she dies.

This brief survey shows the astonishing variety of aspects of life that the Tower Society can translate into medical terms. The Society supports the claim of the progressive medicine of its time to semiotic competence in matters concerning the imagination, wit, poetry, and religious ecstasy. In so doing, it takes part in the general expansion of medicine into philosophy, ethics, and aesthetics. By accepting the psychological physician with his medical belief in the unity of mind and body into their ranks, the Tower Society acquires an ally with expertise in a broad range of subjects.

5

Rapture and Melancholy,
Hypochondria and Hysteria:
The Cult of the Self

The extraordinary range of phenomena that fall under medical jurisdiction given the assumption of the unity of mind and body makes clear why the Tower Society embraces the progressive medicine of its era: in order to educate—or manipulate—the other characters more successfully. And while the Tower Society has an interest in the wit, imagination, religious beliefs, and even the physical health of the characters, it is most intrigued by the thought of overseeing their development into productive members of a re-structured society.[1] Medicine therefore becomes an important part of the effort at *Bildung* in Goethe's *Wilhelm Meister*, just as it was in his account, in *Poetry and Truth*, of the cultural development of Germany. The Tower Society has more interest in medically treating the relationship between the individual and society than any other phenomenon. The belief of the new physicians in the unity of mind and body allows the Tower to diagnose certain relationships between individuals and society as sicknesses and to promote others as healthy.

Specifically, the Tower Society equates asociability, narcissism, and excessive introspection with sickness. In so doing, it remains in the medical tradition of its era. It has already been mentioned that the moral managers and other philosophical physicians saw mental illness as the product of a poor relationship with society and of idiosyncratic fixed ideas that isolated the mad from the sane. Johann Georg Zimmermann devoted two books, one of them four volumes long, to the medical consequences of solitude—how much sociability was healthy? how much was deleterious? The conviction that madness implies social isolation and vice versa comes to the fore in *Wilhelm Meister's Apprenticeship*, too, in which, above all, rapturous religious fanaticism, melancholy, hypochondria, and hysteria inevitably point to asociability, introspection, and narcissism.[2]

RELIGIOUS FANATICISM AND MELANCHOLY

A study of the novel's portrayal of religious fanaticism and its claim that this religious fanaticism subsequently causes melancholia helps clarify the relationship between psychological disorders and socialization. Amplifying the general medical suspicion of religion that caused physicians to treat fanaticism as an illness, the novel strongly links it with excessive introspection.

Personal opinion grounded Goethe's linkage of religious extremism and introspection. Reviewing his own youthful religious experiences, Goethe concluded that "our religion, complicated by various dogmas and based on Bible passages that allowed for many interpretations" produced in "thoughtful people" "hypochondriac circumstances," which were eventually aggravated "to their highest peak, to fixed ideas" (SE 4:222; HA 9:293).[3] Fixed ideas, as has been seen, were thought to cause melancholy.

Early in life, Goethe developed the suspicion that narcissism motivated the ecstatic Christianity of friends like Lavater. According to Goethe, Lavater's Christ was a crystal vase that could hold the most intoxicating and deluding potions. Lavater, said Goethe, poured an idealized version of himself into his vision of Christ: "[F]rom the olden days one image remains for us in which you can transfer everything you have and, mirroring yourself in him, can worship yourself."[4] Goethe's analysis contains supportive as well as critical elements. He admired the strength and the energy that Lavater derived from his narcissistic religion. Nonetheless, he insisted that Lavater's religious beliefs stemmed from a need to find himself.

Such mirroring also stands behind the faith of the religious characters in *Wilhelm Meister's Apprenticeship*. And while Lavater's religious beliefs actually motivated him to undertake a great deal of social work, the characters in the novel who verge on being ecstatics remain mired in introspection. In other words, religion keeps characters like the count, the Harper, Mignon, and the Beautiful Soul chained within themselves rather than granting them true *ek-stasis*. Consistently, the religious beliefs of these characters keep them isolated from society and subvert what interpersonal relationships they have into narcissistic mirrorings.

The count is the first in the chain of characters who reveal the connections between religion and excessive introspection. The count's belief in omens and faith healing is reminiscent of numerous cases in the psychological annals of the eighteenth century. His obsession with death and subsequent melancholia are also typical of religious fanatics.[5] Nor is it surprising that the count, of noble and wealthy origin, should fall victim to this disease, given the theory of Pockels and others that the wealthy were particularly prone to religious extremism.[6]

The novel's portrayal of the count's illness links his turn to fanaticism with narcissism. At the beginning of the novel, the frequent recurrence of the leitmotif *in sich gekehrt* (turned inward) alerts the reader to the count's introspection.[7] In the physician's report, an attack of melancholy immediately follows the count's discovery of an image of himself: "The husband returns unexpectedly, goes to his room, thinks he sees himself, and thereupon falls into a state of melancholy, convinced that he is soon to die" (SE 9:211; HA 7:348). Thus an apparent confrontation with himself, which could be seen as a kind of pathological narcissism, initiates the psychological illness.

The count never learns that Wilhelm is responsible for the appearance of his vision. His ignorance concerning this one point conforms to a pattern of more serious misunderstandings, including his belief that Wilhelm Meister is an English gentleman (SE 9:366; HA 7:598) and that Felix recovers from the opium poisoning because of his own faith healing (SE 9:370; HA 7:604). The count's Anglophilia is perhaps also a sign of madness, because the English were considered particularly prone to mental illness.[8] These errors demonstrate his inability to understand the "real world," an inability that, in the end, forces the count to resort to the religious group known as Moravians to find happiness and a sense of community: "He consorts with persons who cajole him with religious ideas, and I don't see how he is to be prevented from joining the Moravians with his wife, and depriving his relatives (he has no children) of the greater part of his fortune" (SE 9:211; HA 7:348). The count's decision to associate with the Moravians, who, according to the Tower Society, flatter him, rather than to interact with society, reveals the powerful hold that narcissism has upon him. His melancholy, his hypochondriacal fear of death, and his religious fanaticism are all part of a general trend inward, which results in a loss of contact with the outside world and the count's retreat into the religious community.[9]

The madness of the Harper, which began in the monastery when he succumbed to religious ecstasies or *Schwärmerei* (SE 9:356; HA 7:581), also points to an excessively introspective and overly distant relationship with society. The physician reports that Augustin has been obsessively concerned with himself for years: "For many years now he has not taken the slightest interest in anything outside of himself, even to the point of not noticing much at all. Completely shut up in himself, all he looked at was his own hollow and empty self, which was a bottomless pit for him" (SE 9:267; HA 7:436). This all-consuming introspection prevents him from taking notice of the world and causes him to believe that nothing exists. "I see nothing before me, and nothing behind me," the physician quotes him as saying, "nothing but the endless night of loneliness in which I find myself" (SE 9:267; HA 7:436). Augustin's skepticism about the existence of the world leads him to reject the notion of change and time: "When something happens that compels him for a moment to realize that time has passed, he seems astonished at this, but then rejects whatever change has occurred as simply one more phantom" (SE 9:267; HA 7:437).

Such a disbelief in the existence of the world was typical for melancholic patients, according to the psychology of the time. Moritz's *Magazine* reports of several *Schwärmer*, or rapturous religious ecstatics, who are so dissociated that they have lost their belief in reality.[10] Zimmermann linked this condition with religion in describing a case of someone who had lost touch with reality when he discovered that masturbation was a sin: "He doubted the existence of everything that he saw, everything that stood before him, everything that he grasped with his hands."[11] Zimmermann does not make explicit whether the patient had lost his belief in that particular thing he was grasping with his hands, but presumably there is some connection between the sinful act and the object of that act.

The connection with masturbation is particularly important because onanism was regarded as a sin connected to solitude. Augustin's desire to remain isolated from the world causes him to spurn offers of friendship and love, because they alone could tempt him to abandon his isolation (SE 9:267; HA 7:436). This rejection of contact with society or people makes him a very lonely man, as even Mignon recognizes when she exclaims, "Send me to the old Harper. The poor old man is so much alone" (SE 9:299; HA 7:489). The Harper himself thematizes his isolation in the poem that begins tautologically and thus solipsistically:

> Wer sich der Einsamkeit ergibt,
> Ach! der ist bald allein.
>
> (HA 7:137)

> [He who turns to solitude
> is soon, alas! alone.]
>
> (SE 9:78)[12]

Zimmermann, the expert on solitude, recognizes such loneliness as a clear symptom of melancholy: "Nothing is so inseparable from every sort of melancholy as the desire to cut oneself off from people, to rip oneself free from all connections with them, to speak with no one, to see no one, to write to no one, to receive letters from no one. In this psychological state, one wants to be alone as much as possible. . . ."[13] The novel thus carefully documents connections between insanity, alienation from society, and introspection.

When Augustin does associate with other characters, he does so in a narcissistic way that allows him to find only himself. When he meets Sperata,

for instance, he believes, as he reports to his brothers, that he has abandoned his cloistered isolation: (SE 9:357; HA 7:582). Because it was often
used in conjunction with religious fanatics, the word "ecstatically" *(mit
Entzücken)* should alert the reader to the suspicious nature of this claim. In
fact, the true source of Augustin's bliss is not his entry into "real life" but
the fulfillment of his narcissistic fantasies. He betrays his narcissism in the
next clause of the sentence just cited, when he reveals that a part of Sperata's
attraction is the similarity between her temperament and voice (they meet
through music) and his: "He then ecstatically described . . . how their minds
had joined like two throats in harmony" (SE 9:357; HA 7:582). Augustin's
love for a woman whose voice matches his own fits into the novel's pattern
of echoing relationships motivated by narcissism.[14] When Augustin's brothers threaten him with the fires of hell if he does not break off the incestuous
relationship, Augustin intimates that the important effect of his love for
Sperata, the real reason for his jubilation, is that she restores his sense of
his own being (SE 9:357; HA 7:583). Augustin's relationship with Sperata
stems, therefore, not from his desire to communicate with another person
but from his need to affirm his own existence.

Once his brothers convince him that Sperata is indeed his sister, he
becomes more openly narcissistic, using the metaphor of the lily to defend
his relationship: "Seht die Lilie an: entspringt nicht Gatte und Gattin auf
einem Stengel?" (HA 7:584) [Consider the lilies: Do not husband and wife
grow on one and the same stem?] (SE 9:357). Augustin's emphasis (in the
original the word *einem*, one, is stressed) on the fact that there is only one
stem, as well as his use of the singular, rather than plural, form of *entspringen*
(to grow), hints that the analogy is a defense of narcissism, not incest: the
lily, after all, fertilizes itself.[15] *The Metamorphosis of Plants (Die Meta-
morphose der Pflanzen*, 1790), written shortly before the *Apprenticeship*,
makes clear that Goethe regarded the reproduction of plants as something
akin to narcissism, because the male and female reproductive organs are
practically identical: "Since both are produced by spiral vessels, we can
see plainly that the female part is no more a separate organ than the male
part. When our observation has given us a clearer picture of the precise
relationship between the female and male parts, we will find that the idea
of calling their union an anastomosis becomes even more appropriate and
instructive" (SE 12:87; HA 13:84).[16] Because the lily's "anastomosis" is a
union of similar entities, it does not merit the designation *Begattung*, that is
to say "union," or more explicitly, copulation.[17] Similarly, Augustin's lily
metaphor reveals that his relationship with his sister is not a traditional
love affair, which involves interaction with another person, but an affair
with his better half, a being who is part of him.

When Augustin first appears in the novel, he has long since lost Sperata.

Although the fulfillment of his mirror fantasies is a thing of the past, the "Harper," as he is now called, eloquently expresses typically narcissistic wishes. His desire for a unified self expresses itself in the first songs that he sings: "He sang of harmony [*Einheit*] and grace in limpid, mellifluous phrases" (SE 9:72; HA 7:129). He then describes the breakdown of this unity; his belief that union with Sperata would bring about a return to unity expresses itself in the harmonious conclusion:

> Auf einmal ward sein Gesang trocken, rauh und verworren, als er . . . gefährliche Zwiespalt bedauerte, und gern warf jede Seele diese unbequeme Fesseln ab, als er, auf den Fittichen einer vordringenden Melodie getragen, die Friedenstifter pries und das Glück der Seelen, die sich wiederfinden, sang. (HA 7:129)

> [{B}ut, suddenly, the music became harsh, discordant and troubled when he expressed his disapproval of . . . the dangers of strife—shackles of the mind that everyone listening was all too ready to cast off as the melody of his song soared upwards into praise of all peacemakers and of men's joys at rediscovering each other.] (SE 9:72)

The English translation, "men's joys at rediscovering each other," loses the ambiguity of the "sich" in the German phrase "das Glück der Seelen, die sich wiederfinden." The Harper's prehistory suggests that the "sich" is truly reflexive and not reciprocal: it is best translated as "themselves" and not as "each other," because the Harper is probably singing of the joy of finding himself in Sperata, not of the reciprocal joy of two lovers finding each other. Augustin's love affair reveals therefore the excessive introspection that results from his religious madness.[18]

As far as the Tower is concerned, Mignon's illness, too, has elements of religious fanaticism. Like the Harper, she is Roman Catholic. When Wilhelm meets her, she goes to church every day to say the rosary (SE 9:61; HA 7:110). According to the abbé, her piety even survives the rational care of the Tower Society (SE 9:353; HA 7:577). Mignon's passionate attachment to her angelic garb further indicates her devotion.

All of this suggests to the northern German philosophical physician that she has a predisposition for mental problems. Zimmermann ranted at length about the illnesses affecting primarily the Roman Catholic clergy.[19] A book review in Mauchart's *General Repertory* included the remark that "one admires . . . Vogt's intellect all the more when one considers that he was Catholic."[20] In Schiller's story *The Ghost-Seer* (*Der Geisterseher*, 1786–89), the possible conversion of the prince to Catholicism is a sign of his pathology.[21] Conversely, the romantics rehabilitate Catholicism, just as they rehabilitate illness and madness.

Pious belief alone, even if it was Catholic, was of course not usually enough to merit medical treatment. In Mignon's case, however, this religious fervor leads to mental illness when she is under extreme pressure and poorly treated by her captors; as the physician explains: "The poor creature was overcome by utter despair, in the midst of which the Mother of God appeared to her and promised to take care of her" (SE 9:320; HA 7:522). For eighteenth-century medicine, such religious hallucinations clearly signal pathological religious fanaticism. Significantly, Mignon's religious extremism stems from a threatening social situation, when kidnappers have just torn her from her family and community. Moreover, it leads to a worsening of that asociability, in that she vows neither to trust nor speak with others (SE 9:320; HA 7:522). Mignon's religious fanaticism is therefore also tied to her poisoned relationship with society.

Like the other religious fanatics, Mignon cannot escape her isolation because of her tendency toward narcissistic projection. Critics have noted that a desire to imitate Wilhelm motivates the characterization of Mignon, who undergoes significant changes to keep up with Wilhelm's developing psyche: in the first book, Mignon suffers from a heart disorder when Wilhelm is heartbroken after the loss of Marianne; in the third book, she becomes a poetic genius when he is discovering the joys of the theater; in the fourth book, she pines for a lover when he yearns for the Beautiful Amazon.[22] When Wilhelm almost absentmindedly promises Mignon a new outfit, she energetically expresses her wish to wear his colors (SE 9:65; HA 7:116). This little request reveals her desire to find an identity in Wilhelm.

The details surrounding the famous poem that begins "Kennst du das Land" (HA 7:145) [Know you the land] (SE 9:83) remove all doubt that Mignon finds a confirming echo in Wilhelm Meister. This poem, often ascribed to Mignon, is actually the product of a cooperative effort, as the narrator explains: "[H]e wrote it [the poem] down and translated it into German. He found, however, that he could not even approximate the originality of the phrases, and the childlike innocence of the style was lost when the broken language was smoothed over and the disconnectedness removed" (SE 9:83; HA 7:145–46).[23] Mignon finds her coherent verbal identity in Wilhelm's revisions of her songs, making this poem an aural realization of a narcissistic fantasy: Mignon sings and the echo that comes back transforms her broken and discontinuous language into something harmonious and unified.

Like the Harper after his loss of Sperata, Mignon suffers from a severe case of melancholy when this mirror image shatters. Her mirror cracks when she finds Wilhelm in bed with Philine after the opening-night banquet. Immediately afterwards, her appearance changes drastically for the worse and she begins to pine. Near the end of her life, her doctor reports that she is wasting away, hopelessly yearning for Wilhelm Meister and her homeland (SE 9:320; HA 7:522). The combination of the two desires supports the theory that a lost mirror image causes Mignon's sufferings. The desire for her homeland is a reminiscence of the moment of bliss when she and Wilhelm together expressed her desire for Italy; the desire for him is the desire for the mirror that grants her a unified and powerful reflection of her self. Since such yearning for an identity-creating mirror image subverts Mignon's attempt to enter society, her madness—like that of the count and the Harper—accompanies a failed socialization.

The Beautiful Soul provides another example of the introspection and asociability that accompany religious madness. Within both the novel itself and the secondary literature about the novel, there are frequent allusions to the Beautiful Soul's tendency toward self-involvement. Natalie suggests that "perhaps too much concern about her self" (SE 9:317; HA 7:517) prevents her aunt from developing more fully. The Beautiful Soul makes her desire to understand and know herself clear when she bemoans the difficulty of separating one's true essence from extraneous details: "But who can so early reach a state of complete blissful absorption in his own self without reference to external forms and systems?" (SE 9:236; HA 7:388). She admits that her search for herself makes an aesthetic, disinterested appreciation of art impossible: "I was too accustomed to occupying myself with the affairs of my own heart and soul and talking about these with like-minded persons to pay much attention to a work of art without soon withdrawing again into myself" (SE 9:250; HA 7:411). Goethe revered both the Beautiful Soul and her real-life model, Susanna von Klettenberg, but, ever since he referred to her *Confessions* as the most delicate "confusion of the subjective and the objective,"[24] critics have concurred that she leads a life that privileges the subject, that is self-centered, and that is primarily directed toward the interior.[25] While one could also interpret the Beautiful Soul as a strong female figure[26] who was able to exert remarkable and laudable control over her life in an era in which not so many women could, the standard critical view is also that of the Tower Society, which believes that introspection informs her relationships both with others and with God.

To begin with, narcissism structures the Beautiful Soul's love affairs. After her relationship with her father—and psychoanalysis suggests that the relationship with the parent is often a specular love affair[27]—her first serious relationship is with a man nicknamed, appropriately enough, Narcissus. Even the Beautiful Soul quickly recognizes that her love for Narcissus causes increasing isolation from the real world: "Except for Narcissus

everything else in the world was dead to me, nothing else had any attraction. . . . I was therefore often lonely in society, and complete isolation
would have pleased me best" (SE 9:226–27; HA 7:373–74). The erotically
charged scene in which Narcissus fights the captain over the honor of the
captain's wife makes clear that the sexual appeal that Narcissus has for the
Beautiful Soul is also linked to her desire for herself. The Beautiful Soul
tends the wounds of Narcissus "by coaxing and stroking" (SE 9:223; HA
7:368) until the mistress of the house helps her clean up. In the bedroom,
covered with the blood of her lover, the Beautiful Soul sees herself in the
mirror and decides that she is beautiful. During her relationship with Narcissus, she comes not only to admire her naked body but also her naked
soul, as she announces when she decides to let her religious convictions
show: "I removed my mask and began to act always according to the dic-
tates of my heart" (SE 9:230; HA 7:379). Tellingly, given the name of her
lover, this relationship teaches the Beautiful Soul to look inwards, to admire her body and her soul, instead of reaching out.

Her narcissism takes a new turn in her next relationship, with a man
she calls Philo. After Philo drops hints about his sinful past, she perceives
in herself the capacity to sin: "Having occupied myself for a long time with
the state of his soul, I turned my attention to my own. The thought that I
was no better than he came over me and descended like a cloud which
darkened my mind" (SE 9:238; HA 7:392). Whereas other characters frequently use mirror images to prop up positive fantasies about themselves,
the Beautiful Soul becomes aware of her own failings for the first time
when she sees herself reflected in others. Although the coloring of the reflection changes, she still has a relationship with society typical for religious
fanatics in this novel—an inability to see anything but herself in others.

Augustin and the Beautiful Soul are both said to be going ever forward, never backward, but in one sense they move in opposite directions.
While Augustin's love of Sperata replaces his religious feelings, the Beautiful Soul exchanges her mortal lovers for God. The Tower Society, which
claims that Augustin is making progress (SE 9:268; HA:430), is bound to
see his move away from religious fanaticism as healthy; the Beautiful Soul
is the one who praises her own increasing religiosity (SE 9:255; HA 7:420),
about which the Tower Society might have more doubts.

The Beautiful Soul stresses this almost Platonic way in which her physical desire leads her to the divine when she reports that the growth of her
devotion to God and her love for Narcissus are closely interlaced, in that
"Narcissus was the only person whose image hovered before my mind and
claimed all my love," while "the other feeling was not connected with any
image and was inexpressibly pleasant" (SE 9:227; HA 7:374). After her

love for Narcissus fades and after she discovers her sinfulness in Philo, this other imageless and ineffable feeling for God turns into love. Just as the blood of Narcissus makes her aware of her physical beauty, the blood of Jesus cleanses her of the sinfulness she discovers in herself through Philo (SE 9:239; HA 7:393). She compares God's pull on her to the attraction of a lover: "A strong impulse lifted my soul to the cross on which Jesus died. I cannot call it other than an impulse, like that which carries one toward an absent friend, someone one loves dearly . . ." (SE 9:240; HA 7:394). The parallels between Christ and the beloved that the Beautiful Soul draws make clear that Jesus replaces Narcissus and Philo as her lover.

Narcissism also colors this divine love. She loves God in part because he gives her time to indulge in self-contemplation: "[A]t quiet moments I felt that God was granting me time to examine my soul and bring myself ever closer to him" (SE 9:252; HA 7:415). The constitution of her lover as the "Incarnation through which the Word . . . became flesh" (SE 9:239; HA 7:393), instead of as a normal character, makes him a much better mirror for her fantasies. Her repeated insistence on the impossibility of portraying or defining God allows her to model and remodel him according to her changing specifications.[28] The narcissism of these specifications becomes clear upon close analysis of one of her final credos: "[M]y actions are always drawing nearer and nearer to the idea of perfection which I have worked out for myself . . . is this accountable solely to human nature, whose corruption I have become so profoundly aware of? Not for me at least" (SE 9:255-56; HA 7:420). She assumes that God enables her to approach her own ideal, which makes him the perfect lover for a narcissist. Invisible, indescribable, the product of introspective contemplation, he clearly belongs to the Beautiful Soul. Her love of God is therefore nothing but self-love. Like the count, the Harper, and Mignon, the Beautiful Soul indulges in religious fanaticism that takes her out of society.

After such an analysis, it is clear that the Tower Society will medicalize the Beautiful Soul's condition. The medicine of the era would regard her religious feelings as unhealthy because of their asociability. For the Tower Society, the evidence lies in the connections between the Beautiful Soul's religious beliefs and narcissism. Narcissism taints the Beautiful Soul's relationship with all others, including God; the Tower Society views narcissism as sickness; hence, according to the Society, her relationship with God is pathological. The treatment suggested by the physician, that she work in the garden (SE 9:253; HA 7:416), accords perfectly with Zimmermann's notion that gardening helps improve relations with others.[29] Once again, it becomes clear that the Tower Society takes on the Beautiful Soul with an explicitly medical agenda.

HYPOCHONDRIA AND HYSTERIA

The examples of the count, the Harper, Mignon, and the Beautiful Soul have made clear that one form of mental illness, the rapturous ecstasy of religious fanaticism, moves in tandem with introspection and problems of socialization. Another disease, hypochondria, provides further evidence for a connection between mental illness and asociability. Hypochondria, "the fashionable disease of our century,"[30] is far and away the single most frequently found diagnosis in the medical annals of the time.[31] According to one historian, it was the universal danger of the Enlightenment.[32] Another scholar writes that the number of contemporaries who suffered from this malady was uncountable.[33] The subtitle of Johann Ulrich Bilgauer's treatise on the subject reveals the extent of anxieties about hypochondria in the medical literature of the time: . . . *Proof that the Hypochondria of Today is an Almost Universally Prevalent Disease and that It Can Provide a Contribution to Depopulation.*[34] Since the modern understanding of the word scarcely permits such catastrophic views of hypochondria, the eighteenth-century attitude toward the disease needs explanation.

Today, in English and German dictionaries the word "hypochondria" or *Hypochondrie* retains only the restricted sense of "Feeling of a bodily or psychological illness without a pathological basis."[35] Hypochondriacs are those who falsely believe themselves sick. This narrow interpretation of hypochondria was also part of the eighteenth-century definition of the word. Arnold wrote: "In hypochondriac insanity the patient is constantly concerned about his own state of health."[36] For Kant, too, hypochondria was the fanciful disease, "where the patient thinks he finds in himself all diseases about which he reads in books."[37]

In keeping with the holistic tendencies of eighteenth-century medicine, the "diseases" that the hypochondriacs of the Age of Goethe found in themselves, however, did not always have to be somatic. Kant, for instance, included mood changes and imagined misery in his definition of hypochondria.[38] For others, hypochondria had a very general scope, being the cultivation of ungrounded anxieties, not only about physical health but also about business, intellectual riddles, money, and mental problems.

Hypochondria in women could result in hysteria, according to the theories of the time. Hoffmann asserted quite early in the eighteenth century that "the hypochondriacal condition and hysteria represent the same disease and have the same cause and cure."[39] Stahl agreed that "there is no essential difference between these two affections."[40] In 1732, Dr. Thomas Dover's *Treatise on Hypochondriacal and Hysterical Diseases* elaborated the gendered distinction between male hypochondria and female hysteria.[41] Hysteria was said to produce the same symptomatic unfounded worries that hypochondria caused: "That disease in which women invent, exaggerate, and repeat all the various absurdities of which a disordered imagination is capable, has sometimes become epidemic and contagious."[42] By the late eighteenth century there was general unanimity on the subject. Haller, Arnold, Wezel, Gaub, and Weickard all saw the diseases as similar but gender-specific.[43]

In addition, hypochondria led to melancholia, according to some of the era's thinking.[44] Quistorp's play *The Hypochondriac,* for example, takes this link for granted: "It is hypochondria or, to say the same thing another way, melancholia, depression, *passes hysterica;* in short, spleen."[45] Goethe's assumption in *Poetry and Truth* that religion led to hypochondria and from that condition to fixed ideas (usually the cause of melancholia) suggests that he shared his era's understanding of these diseases as being part of a continuum (SE 4:222; HA 9:293).

The era regarded hypochondria and hysteria as the source of a variety of problems, many physical in nature. People who sat extensively were especially prone to hypochondria because it originated in the lower abdomen. Thus academics suffered from the disease, as the encyclopedist Zedler reported: "In general it is called the scholar's sickness because they, by their frequent sitting, again and again put pressure on their stomach, which hinders the movement of the intestines and causes constipation."[46] Businessmen who spent too much time in their offices also frequently fell victim to the disease. One source of the time thundered about the "overwhelming number of people who concern themselves with occupations whose performance requires a lot of sitting or a constricted, forced, and unnatural bodily position. . . ."[47] Hypochondria was a kind of early white-collar, stress-related ailment.

Like hypochondria, hysteria originated in the lower abdomen, but, being a feminine complaint, it was connected with the uterus. Stahl made the link between the two: "It is called a hypochondriacal disease when it attacks men, 'in whom nature makes an effort to be rid of excess blood by vomiting or hemorrhoids'; it is called a hysterical affection when it attacks women 'the course of whose periods is not as it should be.'"[48] Because of this connection with the uterus, scholars like Tissot believed that hysteria had a sexual origin.[49] Whatever the differences between hypochondria and hysteria, however, both were said to result in part from the inability of the bodily fluids in the lower abdomen to move as they should.

At the same time, a luxurious life with too many pleasures, too many books, and not enough discipline was also supposed to cause hypochondria.[50] Foucault interpolates from this thinking the belief that affluence promoted hypochondria because it produced a body that was too soft or porous, and thus vulnerable to the attacks of the "life spirits" *(Lebensgeister)* that caused hypochondria.[51] Another theory posited mental origins of the disease and associated it with a runaway imagination.[52] Thus, physicians of this era had a gamut of explanations for the disease, from purely physical to sociological and psychological.

Regardless of the origins they attributed to the disease, all theoreticians agreed that its sufferers indulged in excessive introspection. Lichtenberg regarded hypochondria as nothing but microscopic self-inspection: "There are serious illnesses, of which one can die . . . there are also some which one scarcely perceives without a microscope, with which however they appear mighty horrible, and this microscope is hypochondria."[53] Whether their complaints were physical, mental, or sociological, all hypochondriacs discovered their problems by examining themselves too closely, which prevented their active participation in the world.[54]

Goethe, too, associated hypochondria particularly strongly with introspection. In *Poetry and Truth*, he asserts that hypochondria drove Count Thoranc to the solitude of his room (SE 4:75; HA 9:87). He describes a local artist as "a very hypochondriac man, withdrawn into himself" (SE 4:92; HA 9:111). He also labels Zimmermann's vanity, which results in the poor treatment of his daughters, "hypochondria" (SE 4:482; HA 10:65). In *Wilhelm Meister's Journeyman Years*, the phrase "self-centered hypochondria" (SE 10:264; HA 8:240) occurs. At another point, he succinctly summed up his philosophy: "Being hypochondriac means nothing but sinking into subjectivity."[55]

Wilhelm Meister's Apprenticeship meticulously replicates this complex of hypochondria and hysteria. Several standard varieties of hypochondriacs appear in it, reflecting the high incidence of this disease in German society of the late eighteenth century. Consonant with its understanding of religious fanaticism as a sickness of sociability, the Tower Society specifically emphasizes the social origins and consequences of hypochondria, particularly its connections with introspection.[56]

Even the modern reader recognizes the countess as a typical hypochondriac. After Wilhelm presses her bosom too heftily, she is convinced that she will develop breast cancer, although her physician, who tells the story to Wilhelm Meister, cannot find any sign of illness:

> [I]ch bin als Arzt gewiß, daß dieser Druck keine üblen Folgen haben werde, aber sie läßt sich nicht ausreden, es sei eine Verhärtung da, und wenn man ihr durch das Gefühl den Wahn benehmen will, so behauptet sie, nur in diesem Augenblick sei nichts zu fühlen; sie hat sich fest eingebildet, es werde diese Übel mit einem Krebsschaden sich endigen. . . . (HA 7:349)

> [{A}s a doctor I am sure that the pressure on her breast will have no bad effects, but she is convinced that there is a lump there and when by feeling

the place I try to dispel this illusion, she says that only then does the pain go away, for she has firmly persuaded herself that this will end in cancer, and with it all her youth and loveliness.] (SE 9:211)

This case accurately reflects both eighteenth-century beliefs about hypochondria as well as modern ones. The countess's hypochondriacal fear of breast cancer despite reassurances from the physician is *eingebildet* (imagined), that is, a product of runaway imagination. It is not surprising that an aristocratic woman should fall prey to this disease, for, as mentioned earlier, it was often attributed to the excessively luxurious lifestyle of the wealthy. Furthermore, the fact that a romantic adventure with Wilhelm Meister initiates the attack suggests that the disease has in part a sexual etiology, which conforms to the gender-based theories of hypochondria and hysteria of the time.

While the novel records many of the eighteenth-century assumptions concerning the origins of hypochondria, it emphasizes above all the linkage between the disease and poor socialization. Although the cancer that the countess claims to feel is imaginary, the physician's use of the word *Wahn* (madness) to describe her state shows that he does not regard her illness as purely fictional. Indeed, the symptoms are quite serious, according to the physician, who regrets that, because of this disease, "she and others" (lost in the translation) can no longer enjoy the "youth" and the "loveliness" of the countess. These "others" are important. The physician uses this disease and the affliction of the count as examples of the one and only "misfortune" *(Unglück)*, the withdrawal from active life that follows the development of an obsessive idea (SE 9:211; HA 7:348). Thus the hypochondria of the countess has highly lamentable societal effects—it draws her inward, preventing her from sharing her beauty and kindness with the rest of society.

Werner is a typical hypochondriac in a specifically eighteenth-century sense. At the beginning of the eighth book, the narrator indicates the severity of Werner's case:

Er war viel magerer als ehemals, sein spitzes Gesicht schien feiner, seine Nase länger su sein, seine Stirn und sein Scheitel waren von Haaren entblößt, seine Stimme hell, heftig und schreiend, und seine eingedrückte Brust, seine vorfallende Schulter, seine farblosen Wangen ließen keinen Zweifel übrig, daß ein arbeitsamer Hypochondrist gegenwärtig sei. (HA 7:498–99)

[He was much thinner, his pointed face seemed sharper and his nose longer, he was bald, his voice was loud and strident and his flat chest, dropping shoulders and pallid cheeks showed quite clearly that this was a sickly creature with a mania for work.] (SE 9:305)

"A sickly creature with a mania for work" is a loose, if informative, translation of *arbeitsamer Hypochondrist*, which could be translated more literally as "an industrious hypochondriac." Werner exemplifies the many businessmen of the eighteenth century who suffered from hypochondria because their work involved too much sitting and worrying. This bourgeois hypochondria does not consist so much of imagined physical illnesses as of stress and anxiety. At the same time, the narrator's exact description of the physical symptoms of Werner's psychological ailment demonstrates once again the extent to which the belief in the unity of mind and body permeates this novel. As in the case of the countess, therefore, the novel records many details of the medical view of hypochondria.

Above all, a poor relationship with society accompanies Werner's hypochondria. His excessive devotion to business and the obsession with money, which destroys his sense of community, leaving him just as isolated as the countess, unite to cause his hypochondria. His addiction to cards (SE 9:306; HA 7:500), a typical product of the ennui of this era, reveals his inability to carry on unstructured relationships with others. Although he gets along well with the Tower Society and is able to function well enough to earn a great deal of money, he does not think about society at large, in the form of the state: "'I can assure you,' said Werner, 'that in all my life I have never thought about the State, and only paid my dues and taxes because that was customary'" (SE 9:311; HA 7:508). Lothario warns him that such an attitude indicates a socialization as severely warped as that of a delinquent father: "A good father is one who at mealtimes serves his children first; and a good citizen is one who pays what he owes the State before dealing with everything else" (SE 9:311; HA 7:508). Lothario's analogy clearly links allegiance to the state with commitment to the family, two ideologies that were rising in importance in the eighteenth century. The structure of his rhetoric, incidentally, uses father and child as an unexpected metaphor for citizen and state, which is a reversal of the usual simile that the state is like a parent to its citizens. In any case, Lothario's revelation to Wilhelm about Mignon's increasingly serious condition immediately follows this discussion, which suggests that, textually, Werner's behavior actually borders on the pathological. Both textually and contextually, Werner's hypochondria is related to an imbalance in his relationship to society.

Aurelie provides the best-documented example of the connection between hypochondria and social isolation. A number of signs indicate that she suffers from a mental affliction. She admits that her love for Lothario pushes her to the verge of insanity: "My mind suffers, my brain is too tense; and so in order to avoid going mad, I return to the feeling that I love him" (SE 9:167; HA 7:279). After she loses control of herself and slashes Wilhelm's palm, she calls herself half-crazy: "'Forgive a woman who is half crazy,' she said" (SE 9:168; HA 7:281). Her brother Serlo uses the word *toll* (crazy) twice with regard to her pathological behavior (SE 9:152-53; HA 7:256–57), which further underscores the medical and psychological nature of Aurelie's problems.

Her insanity has all the symptoms of hypochondria. Aurelie's violent self-criticism is, for instance, typical of the hypochondriac patient, as Zimmermann argues: "A hypochondriac despises no one as much as himself."[57] When she speculates that a German "seriousness" causes her problem (SE 9:166; HA 7:278), she might be referring to *Schwermut*, melancholia, a disease closely linked to hypochondria. Moreover, Aurelie herself diagnoses her sickness as a sort of hypochondria. After explaining to Wilhelm that the purely sexual attentions of her admirers embittered her, she describes her case in medical terms: "You can see how blind and unjust my hypochondria made me, and it grew steadily worse" (SE 9:155; HA 7:260). All signs, including Aurelie's own understanding of her problem, indicate that her illness is a type of hypochondria.

The link between female hypochondria or hysteria and sexuality is also quite clear in Aurelie's case. Raised by a sexually active aunt (SE 9:150; HA 7:252), Aurelie tries to suppress sexuality in her own life on the stage. Since many men are only interested in her body, this suppression proves impossible, which causes her anxiety, nervousness, and anger. Her hypochondria goes into remission when she meets Lothario, but returns with a new vengeance when she loses him. By the time Wilhelm meets her, a few years after the separation, she obsessively keeps a dagger at her side. The repeated references to the *Scheide*, which in German means both "sheath" and "vagina," into which Aurelie puts the dagger (SE 9:152–53; HA 7:256–57) emphasize the weapon's phallic nature, as does Aurelie's erotic behavior when she regains it after squabbling with Serlo over it: "'Forgive me,' she said, kissing the dagger, 'for having been so careless'" (SE 9:152; HA 7:256). Eighteenth-century medicine would certainly agree with Serlo that these sexual references are "crazy" and indicate mental illness.

Significantly, Aurelie identifies strongly with the character she plays in *Hamlet*, Ophelia, who has been for centuries the literary model for female insanity.[58] She reveals her unconscious knowledge of the importance of sexuality by denying its importance in Ophelia. As mentioned earlier, she wants to repress the indecent sexual allusions in *Hamlet:* "But tell me this: Shouldn't the poet have given her in her madness different songs to sing? . . . What is such suggestive and indecent nonsense doing in the mouth of this pure young girl?" (SE 9:152; HA 7:255). By trying to repress the sexual

desire in Ophelia, Aurelie is projecting the innocence that she herself desires but does not possess, thereby revealing the importance of the sexual
element in her own case of hypochondria.

Aurelie is the character most concerned with Germans and Germany.
Her erratic relationship with her audience and German society at large is a
product and symptom of her hypochondria. The severity of her illness increases and decreases according to the changes in her relationship with the
public and with Germany in general. Originally, in her healthy condition,
she has a high opinion of herself and her country; she is as pleased to perform as her audience is to see and hear her, a "public that responded to
everything I offered them" (SE 9:154).[59] As time passes, however, and she
grows, in her own words, increasingly blind, unjust, and splenetic, she also
becomes estranged from her society: "So I began to despise them all intensely, feeling as though the whole nation was purposely prostituting itself by the representatives it sent me" (SE 9:154-55; HA 7:260).

Once she meets Lothario and her health improves, Aurelie regains her
positive attitude toward society (SE 9:157; HA 7:264). Her love of society
is so great that she loses interest in individuals and becomes devoted to the
communality, just as she herself loses her individuality in Lothario: "How
can individuals be so interesting? The question is whether in a mass of
people there is a sufficient distribution of disposition, power and ability
which, when developed by favorable circumstances, can be directed by
outstanding people toward some common goal" (SE 9:157; HA 7:264).
Hypochondria here is associated with the loss of individuality, the rise of
the collective; indeed, one could polemically say it becomes the root of
fascism. Aurelie's positive attitude toward society as a whole does not represent a healthy relationship to society either, because it ignores the individual. After her affair with Lothario ends and her hypochondria returns,
she is once again alienated from the public. Although her audiences adore
her more than ever, they do not realize that emotional anguish is the source
of her energy: "My confused, impetuous, imprecise accents move you
deeply, arouse your admiration, but you don't understand that these are the
anguished cries of an unhappy woman, on whom you have bestowed your
favor" (SE 9:166; HA 7:278). Extreme fluctuations between contempt and
admiration for society characterize Aurelie's attitudes throughout the course
of her hypochondria, suggesting that this illness is related to a problem in
the relationship between society and individual.

In summary, the physician of the Tower Society emphasizes above all
the social ramifications of the hypochondria of the countess, Werner, and
Aurelie. The same obtains for the religious fanaticism of the count, the
Harper, and the Beautiful Soul. While the scientific details of the descriptions of the illnesses reflect many attitudes current in eighteenth-century

thought, they document the connection between mental illness and the relationship between the individual and society particularly well. The assumption that mental illness goes hand in hand with excessive introspection informs the novel's portrayal of sickness. This makes clearer the special interest of the Tower Society, itself admittedly not primarily a medical institution. Its members make use of medicine, because, owing to the implications of monistic philosophy and the increasing importance of medicine, they can interpret societal problems, especially introspection and narcissism, as medical ones. While the Tower Society does not attempt to cure all of those afflicted by a poor relationship to society, it can use them as a foil to foreground their treatment of one character whom they do treat: Wilhelm Meister. If their main goal is the restructuring of society and the readjustment of the relationship of a chosen few like Wilhelm Meister to that society, they can use medicine as part of their project.

6

Dietetics and Homeopathy:
Mastering the Pharmakon

One feature of eighteenth-century medicine's attitude toward illness requires closer examination: a surprising tolerance of disease as part of life. In particular, two medical movements of the time, homeopathy and dietetics, emphasize the importance of incorporating sickness into a program of health. Eighteenth-century medicine's toleration of illness never implies acceptance, however, for it means in the long run to cure patients. The era's medicine thus gambles that it can use the pharmakon for its own purposes, that it can turn poison into medicine. The Tower Society, like the medicine of its time, exhibits a similar tolerance of sickness as part of a plan to achieve health, even when the illnesses are excessive introspection, narcissism, or other poor relationships with society.

SICKNESS AS GENIUS

A general reevaluation of the link between sickness—especially mental illness—and genius, which later culminated in the romantic glorification of altered states of consciousness, began in the second half of the eighteenth century. As an example, the era's changing attitude toward hypochondria demonstrates the new connection between artistry and illness. Originally a somewhat socially objectionable and dangerous disease that afflicted people who had too much time on their hands, or, conversely, worked obsessively, hypochondria took on new dimensions in the eyes of people like Lichtenberg. After describing hypochondria as a "microscope," he remarks: "I believe that, if people really wanted to attach importance to studying the microscopic diseases, they would have the satisfaction of being sick every day."[1] His aphorism leaves open the question of whether there is something actual to see under the microscope. When Lichtenberg refers to the "hermeneutics of hypochondria,"[2] he implies that there is indeed something to interpret. His praise of the character who regards even his good health as a symptom of sickness shows Lichtenberg's acceptance of hypochondria: "A character: seeing above all only the worst, fearing everything, even regarding health as a state in which one did not feel one's sickness."[3] Although he admits in another aphorism that many physical ailments are only imaginary and hence the product of hypochondria, he insists that mental health is usually just as imaginary: "With regard to the body, there are, if not more, then certainly just as many sick in the imagination as really sick; with regard to understanding, just as many, if not many more, healthy in the imagination as really healthy."[4] Lichtenberg implies here that, in order to determine the conditions for their improvement, more people should train the microscope of hypochondria on their psyche.[5] In this respect, he was part of a small group of thinkers of the latter part of the eighteenth and beginning of the nineteenth century who saw merit even in the mental illness most liable to social critique, hypochondria.

Calling for "absolute hypochondria," Novalis radicalized this position at the end of the century. "Hypochondria must become an art—or an education,"[6] because of its beneficial effects: "Hypochondria prepares the way to bodily self-knowledge—self-control—self-vitalization."[7] In another collection of aphorisms, Novalis sees hypochondria as a means toward knowledge of the soul as well as the body: "Concerning hypochondria and jealousy—2 very remarkable phenomena for knowledge of the soul."[8] By 1800, therefore, certain members of the intellectual community were prepared to acknowledge the value of ostensibly "pathological" self-inspection—in particular for the process of education, a project central to *Wilhelm Meister*.

Nor was hypochondria the only disease to develop a range of positive connotations by the end of the eighteenth century. Promies has shown that, even as the bourgeoisie rejected "foolishness" by turning it into an illness, they began to reverse themselves and started to see that newly pathological condition as in part positive. The positive reevaluation of such mental illnesses prepared the way for the subsequent valorization of madness found, for instance, in the *Nightwatches of Bonaventura (Nachtwachen von Bonaventura)* or Hölderlin's *Empedokles*. Theodore Ziolkowski has outlined the celebration of madness in the writings of Novalis and Schelling and the cult of insanity surrounding Hölderlin, recorded in such authors as Bettina von Arnim.[9]

Moving back a few years, though, to the appearance of *Wilhelm Meister's Apprenticeship* in 1795–96, one can say that medicine and literature of the late eighteenth century did not glorify sickness. Nonetheless, the trend toward an appreciation of the values of illness was beginning to make itself felt in eighteenth-century medicine as well. Drawing both on general associations linking illness with inwardness and on the pietist tradition combining self-critiques with self-analysis, medicine turned melancholy into a step toward self-knowledge: "Melancholy is the school of humility, and self-contempt the first step to self-knowledge."[10] Talk of "a sort of sweet melancholy"[11] revealed the attraction that illness was gaining at this time. And, while Aristotle had merely posited a general link between melancholy and genius, eighteenth-century medicine developed its own "scientific" explanation for the relationship between the two: Since melancholics were usually obsessed with fixed ideas, they could usually gain from their lengthy ruminations insights that eluded their healthy, and more distractible, counterparts. Tissot argued the point as follows: "It has been long since noted that this sort of melancholy is sometimes useful for the sciences, because these melancholics stick with a single thought and examine and investigate one single object from all sides without distraction. . . ."[12] No one in the late eighteenth century claimed that the intellectual gains were worth the sufferings produced by illness, but almost everyone acknowledged that sickness could have some beneficial side effects. Like their contemporaries in philosophy, then, physicians of the eighteenth century found both aesthetic and intellectual uses for illness.

Goethe accepted the thinking of his time on the value of illness. Despite his subsequent "distaste for everything pathological"[13] (pronounced in 1821), it is safe to say that, in the 1790s, at least, Goethe viewed "the sickly, the pathological . . . not only as something fully negative, destructive."[14] Goethe's work with Plessing and Krafft indicated his acceptance of the doctrine of humoring certain symptoms of mental illness in order to cure the disease completely. In his poem "The Diary," Goethe writes: "Die Krankheit erst bewähret den Gesunden" (WA 1.5.2:350) [Only sickness protects the healthy].[15] In the *Parliament of West and East*, he portrays Suleika as healing in a way that makes one wish to have a relapse:

> Mit Erstaunen uns umfangend,
> Uns erquickend, heilend, segnend,
> Daß wir uns gesundet fühlen,
> Wieder gern erkranken möchten.
> (*Westöstlicher Divan*, HA 2:66)

> [Embracing us with astonishment,
> refreshing, healing, blessing us,
> so that we, feeling healed,
> would like to sicken again.]

He concludes that the two processes alternate, almost like, to speak in another discourse, yin and yang:

Da erblickst du Suleika
Und gesundetest erkrankend,
Und erkranketest gesundend.

(Westöstlicher Divan, HA 2:66)

[There you see Suleika
and heal while ailing,
and ail while healing.][16]

Typically, Goethe was most interested in a phenomenon like lovesickness, which was on the border of the medical realm. Particularly in the psychological realm of hypochondria, melancholy, and lovesickness, Goethe revealed a willingness to tolerate illness.

Even narcissism, the underlying cause of such psychological illnesses, finds a place in Goethe's worldview. He indulges his narcissism in his exchanges with other people: "I have always paid strict attention to what others might know of me: from them and in them, as in so many mirrors, I can gain a clearer idea of myself . . ." (SE 12:39; HA 13:38). While expressing skepticism in this passage about the phrase, "Know thyself," he nonetheless finds merit in a certain kind of introspection—the kind that involves others.

Given Goethe's acceptance of the limited eighteenth-century philosophical and medical reevaluation of sickness, it is not surprising that sickness in *Wilhelm Meister's Apprenticeship* has a number of positive attributes. The sober Lothario uses Zimmermann's concept of "sweet" illness to express the attraction of disease when he declares that he understands "exactly how some people get to like illnesses that induce pleasant [*süß*, literally, "sweet"] feelings" (SE 9:284; HA 7:464). Characters like the Harper and Mignon make the positive elements of illness most obvious. The Harper's poems command great respect and admiration from virtually all characters in the novel, even though some of his poetic works grow out of his sense of overbearing solitude, while narcissistic and masochistic images that reflect his feelings of guilt and isolation fill others. Similarly, almost everyone in the novel agrees on the beauty of Mignon's poems, although they clearly attest to the severity of her mental disorders. Her poem about Italy reflects the yearnings for Wilhelm and Italy, which are at the root of her health problems. The poem "Heiß mich nicht reden" (HA 7:356) [Bid me not speak] (SE 9:216) expresses an inability to communicate with the ones she loves, suggesting an unhealthy skepticism of language itself. Finally, the poem "So laßt mich scheinen" (HA 7:515) [So let me seem till I become] (SE 9:316) reveals, according to the Tower Society, an "unhealthy" obsession with the soul to the detriment of the body.

In addition to these two characters, whose beneficial sickness has always been apparent, several other characters provide further specific evidence of the linkage between illness, on the one hand, and, on the other hand, genius, poetry, or insight. Despite the serious consequences of her illness, Aurelie is a very positive character. Wilhelm regrets her death immensely: "He had respected her so much and had spent so much time with her that he felt her loss very acutely" (SE 9: 215; HA 7:355). His admiration for her stems, in part, from her penetrating analysis of his character, which produces insights only possible because of her knowledge of her own illness.

Although she admits that Wilhelm understands literature, she justly accuses him of lacking any comprehension of other people: "'For truly,' she went on, 'nothing comes into you from the outside world. I have rarely met anyone who knew so little of the people with whom he lives—indeed fundamentally misjudges them'" (SE 9:153; HA 7:257). Her insights into Wilhelm's character underscore her awareness of the problems of adjusting to society, just as her interest in Ophelia suggests her concern for her sanity. It seems unlikely that she would have such insights if she had developed a healthy relationship with society.

Her sufferings also have a sensational effect on her acting. As noted earlier, the applause for her performances increases as her condition deteriorates (SE 9:166; HA 7:278). She gives her illness free reign in her final performance, which elicits an unheard-of response from the audience: "Tumultuous applause rewarded her anguished efforts. . . ." (SE 9:214; HA 7:354). In addition to granting Aurelie a better understanding of Wilhelm's psychology, then, her mental illness also helps her to act better, which further shows the willingness of this novel to accept certain aspects of sickness as valuable.

In a bizarre way, Sperata's ravings also contain a moment of insight.[17] Her delusion centers on the belief that Mignon will return from the dead and redeem her parents. Sperata is misled in the belief that Mignon's death and resurrection will help her, but she is not entirely mistaken. After all, Sperata's brother-husband is not Mignon's only father, since Wilhelm adopts the child in spirit, if not in law, at the end of book 2: "'My child!' he cried, 'My child! You are mine'" (SE 9:82; HA 7:143). By the time Mignon is terminally ill, Wilhelm has developed a strong sense of guilt with respect to her. At one point he reproaches himself for abandoning her: "You took charge of the poor child, her companionship delighted you, and yet you have cruelly neglected her" (SE 9:308; HA 7:504). The knowledge that his escapade with Philine initiated Mignon's final bout of illness intensifies his guilt feelings, causing him to refer to his "injustice toward the poor creature" (SE 9:321; HA 7:524). Wilhelm is acutely aware that his fiery embrace of Therese is responsible for Mignon's fatal seizure: "'Let me see the child that I have killed,' he cried" (SE 9:334; HA 7:545). By the end of the novel, therefore, Mignon is a standing reproach to Wilhelm. And while this shame apparently cannot be cleansed while Mignon still lives, once she does die Wilhelm can follow the injunction of the ceremonies of the Tower Society and return to life, forgetting his problems with the teenage girl and concentrating on Natalie. Thus, Sperata's obsessive belief that her daughter will die and redeem her parents comes true, in that Mignon's death releases her father figure, Wilhelm, from his guilt. Sperata's sickness, therefore, gives her a certain insight, although admittedly one that she herself fails to understand.

The Beautiful Soul is one more example of the novel's general positive reevaluation of sickness. To begin with, her character shows the prevalence of illness throughout the novel. Since she refers to love as a passion "like any other sickness" (SE 9:220; HA 7:362), many characters must be blissfully ill, given their tendency to fall in love. More importantly, however, she feels that her hemorrhage provides an opportunity to develop her individual way of thinking: "During the nine months of convalescence which I bore patiently, the foundations of my present way of thinking were laid— or so it seems to me now. For during that time my mind received various impulses that helped in the shaping of a specific character" (SE 9:217; HA 7:358). In this citation the Beautiful Soul clearly indicates her belief in sickness as a kind of incubation bed for independent thinking and character.[18] In the case of the Beautiful Soul, even members of the Tower Society admit that there are positive sides to her otherwise unhealthy character. Natalie argues that she is merely "too cultivated" and pleads for understanding for her (SE 9:317; HA 7:518). She even suggests that her aunt is a praiseworthy figure, an example "not to be imitated, but to be striven after" (SE 9:318; HA 7:518). The physician himself reveals his appreciation of her illness by entitling her thoughts the "Confessions of a Beautiful Soul" and mentioning how much he personally values them (SE 9:212; HA 7:350). The Tower Society thereby uses its medicinal representative to indicate the possibility of beauty despite psychic illness.

DIETETICS

In addition to these philosophical and aesthetic speculations on the value of illness, a number of eighteenth-century medical traditions incorporated illness into their health plans. One such tradition was dietetics. According to Boerhaave, who relied in this matter on Galen, dietetics was one of three main branches of medicine, along with surgery and internal medicine.[19] In the eighteenth century, dietetics did not consist merely of dieting, in the modern sense of watching fat and sugar intake, but had to do with the entire way a life was led. For instance, Diaetophilus, an epileptic who compiled a series of recommendations for healthy living, wrote: "I take diet in the broadest sense of the word to be the entire way of life; only with the exclusion of pharmaceutical and surgical interventions."[20] Dietetics was a program of preventative medicine meant to cover every aspect of an entire life.

According to Diaetophilus, each person had to develop the code of behavior that best suited him or her. Psychological dietetics, in particular, varied significantly from one individual to another, amounting to a sort of "private morality." Diaetophilus could not behave "merely according to the morality that applies to all people, but according to the morality peculiar to me, that is codetermined by my physical weaknesses. . . ."[21] Moritz typifies his era's thinking when he insists that each person has to find his or her own equilibrium when searching for this system of psychological dietetics: "Whoever wants to be permanently happy must after a while deduce from careful observations about himself his own psychological dietetics for himself, and strive to become ever more skilled in this healing science."[22] The connections between health and the relationship between the individual and society become apparent in the rhetoric of bourgeois liberalism that inform this discussion, with its emphasis on individual variation and its glorification of personal happiness. The dietetic program was supposed to allow the individual to function happily and healthily in society.

To a certain extent, dietetics accepted the inevitability of illness. The belief, typical for the era, that one only discovered a suitable dietary system after some time implied that the prevention of mental illness was a lifelong process rather than a one-time solution. Insisting that sickness never disappeared entirely and always returned, the dieticians concluded that one need always to be on the lookout for illness, but also be willing to accept illness as an inevitability.

Part of the eighteenth-century willingness to see value in sickness included the belief that at times mental and physical sickness could contribute to a subsequent, more nearly perfect state of health. In his *Medical Hygiene,* Hoffmann rather surprisingly admits that excessively healthful living has its drawbacks: "To live in a medical fashion, that is, according to the strict and academic rules of physicians, is to live miserably and uncomfortably."[23] Because "it is not possible to keep with constant exactitude to the fine borderline beyond which the healthy mental movements become damaging," Diaetophilus, for instance, recommended occasional transgressions of the rules: "[I]t is therefore better sometimes to jump across the line methodically than always to remain underneath it, not attaining one's potential [*Bildung*], stagnating and rotting."[24] The argument that a little sickness tempered with reason could promote one's *Bildung* so that one becomes a happy and healthy individual had its analogies in the theories on pious frauds, which authorized the use of fantasies, untruths, and delusions in order to bring patients back to reason, since both amounted to a partial acceptance of the value of sickness.

Although dietetics emerged from a concern for the individual, it was very much part of the development of the modern state. Captain Cook's discovery that a regular intake of citrus fruit prevented scurvy in sailors was the kind of dietetic thinking that emerged from governmentally sponsored colonial efforts and that European governments impressed upon their own subjects.[25] As individual as each program of dietetics was to be, it was also part of a societal program that connected up with "the regime of hygiene" that Foucault sees arising in the eighteenth century.[26] This new "medical police," a policy that had a policing function, was pioneered in Germany by medical experts like Thomas Rau, who wrote a *Rules of Medical Policy*.[27] Goethe made extensive notes on the educational program of Johann Peter Frank (1745–1821), author of the famous *System of a Medical Policy*.[28] In the *Journeyman Years*, Wilhelm Meister's father worked "with sensible doctors and health policy officers."[29] Thus, Goethe was clearly aware of new medical policies that encouraged the individual to take care of him- or herself for the benefit of the general population.

In *Wilhelm Meister's Apprenticeship*, the Tower Society advocates an Enlightenment program of dietetics. The Beautiful Soul is in agreement with the Tower Society, up to a certain point. She avers that "for seven long years I persisted in this careful diet" (SE 9:237; HA 7:390). Narcissus, one of her lovers, "found this diet rather severe" (SE 9:226; HA 7:373). But despite her adherence to the principles of dietetics, she also, in opposition to the Tower Society, wants certain medical supplements. She insists in the end that medications, rather than dietetic rules, are necessary: "But I was like a sick person without medication who resorts to dieting. It helped somewhat, but not enough" (SE 9:237; HA 7:390).

Once again, the Beautiful Soul is fighting a losing battle, however, for members of the Society expressly prefer a dietary regimen to a momentary cure. Therese uses a metaphor that makes clear that, according to the Tower Society, a permanent dietary rule cures much more certainly than anything else: "Things that are good and moral are like medicine when they [people like Lydia, one of Lothario's girlfriends] feel bad, and any priest or moral teacher is regarded as a physician one dispenses with as soon as possible. I must however confess that morality for me is a kind of diet, but only becomes a diet if practiced as a rule of life . . ." (HA 7:459–60). The similarity posited between clergyman and physician corresponds to the eighteenth-century understanding of the religious and medical disciplines.[30] The insistence on a lifelong dietetic plan to regulate moral and psychological matters is also typical for the era.

As in the medicine of the eighteenth century, dietetics in the novel does not only mean that, for instance, coffee does not become the Beautiful Soul (SE 9:230; HA 7:380) but has to do with an entire way of life. When the Beautiful Soul refers to her "extreme abstemiousness and strict diet," she means "meals, exercise, getting up and going to bed, dressing and going out for rides" (SE 9:234; HA 7:386). Like many of the thinkers of his era, the clergyman views a healthy way of life as an effective program against insanity and does not actually acknowledge a difference between curative and preventative approaches; he says, for instance: "[T]he treatment . . . is the same as one uses to prevent healthy people from going mad" (SE 9:210; HA 7:346). The clergyman's dietetic program resembles the preventative systems of the late eighteenth century in its opposition to emotions and introspection, and in its support for activity.

Many characters in the orbit of the Tower Society have a place for unreason in their daily lives. The characters seem to take the advice of Diaetophilus to heart by tolerating occasional bouts of mental illness in order to prevent them from getting out of hand as they strive to cultivate their development. Serlo's "Children of Joy" *(Kinder der Freude),* the forerunners of the Tower Society, recognize the necessity of madness or foolishness and build this mental illness into their regular life: "These lively people, intelligent and perceptive, well understood that the sum of our existence divided by reason never comes out exactly and that there is always a wondrous remainder" (SE 9:161; HA 7:270). Consonant with Enlightened thinking, though, they do not regard this "wondrous remainder" as entirely positive—indeed they see it as a "troublesome and, if it spreads through the whole mass, dangerous remainder" (SE 9:161; HA 7:270), for which reason they expunge it "by indulging, one day a week, wholeheartedly in foolishness" (SE 9:161; HA 7:270). Rather than celebrating madness, the Children of Joy dose and monitor it as part of their program of mental health: "For without their denying some pet folly, they treated it simply for what it was and nothing more, instead of its becoming through self-delusion a tyrant in the household and secretly enslaving man's reason, which thought it had long ago dispelled it" (SE 9:161; HA 7:270). This thinking clearly emerges from the medical discourse of Goethe's day, which saw the need to undermine madness with madness. Failure to do so could result in an overly confident sanity suddenly discovering it was under the control of "foolishness." Reason would then demonstrate Lichtenberg's situation of inverse hypochondria: believing itself healthy despite actual illness.[31]

The founders and members of the rational Tower Society also believe in a kind of wondrous remainder that accounts for personality—but they regard it as illness. According to Natalie, her uncle refuses to accept the complete rule of reason, admitting the necessity of passionate, unreasonable desires: "Yet he had to admit also that life would lose its savor if he did not sometimes consider himself and passionately indulge in what he could not always approve of or make excuses for" (SE 9:330; HA 7:539). The old man's tolerance for idiosyncratic instincts that stand in opposition to reason amounts to a partial acceptance of individualistic, asocial behavior, which the Tower Society normally considers illness. Similarly, Jarno tells Wilhelm that it is initially good for the young to think highly of themselves and otherwise behave egotistically: "When a man makes his first entry into the world, it is good that he have a high opinion of himself, believe he can acquire many excellent qualities" (SE 9:301; HA 7:493). Only later, according to Jarno, should a person attempt to become one with the larger society. Since Jarno is taking Wilhelm to his initiation at this point, he speaks as a representative of the Tower Society. This statement therefore shows the Tower Society itself joining the Children of Joy and the uncle of Natalie and Lothario not only in using madness to combat illness but also in using the metaphorical meaning of mental illness— asociability, excessive introspection—as a necessary step toward a healthy relationship with society.

In all cases, the eighteenth-century dietetic acceptance of sickness was limited, however, to containing the spread of sickness. For the dieticians, madness, mental illness, and sickness in general were tolerable only as a means to rationality. Thus, while the eighteenth-century physicians had a place for madness in their system, rational behavior still remained firmly in control. It recognized that antitoxins could be toxic and poisons could cure, but still believed it could control the pharmakon.

THE SPECIFICS OF DIETETICS

A look at dietetic regimens actually proposed at the time makes clear the rational side of the eighteenth-century psychological prophylaxis. Despite their emphasis on the necessity for individually tailored dietetic plans, authors like Arnold, Diaetophilus, Zimmermann, and Hufeland advocated a number of general principles for the preservation of mental and spiritual health, adding up to a program of bourgeois living. They tended to overlap with the therapies proposed by philosophical physicians seeking to resocialize their patients. Both set a high premium on regular schedules, adequate physical conditions, and varied activities. Like the philosophical physicians, these dieticians were in fact proposing a system of adjusting to society.

The dietary systems proposed by eighteenth-century German psychologists relied primarily on moderation. Hoffmann asserts that "all excess, even of the best, is harmful to nature."[32] According to Diaetophilus, all of his laws were derived from "the great rule of moderation."[33] A typical first rule for the prevention of insanity was "moderation in eating, drinking, sleeping, and coition."[34] These rules of temperance also applied to the mental faculties, according to Moritz, who wrote that psychological dietetics *(Seelendiätätik)* preserved health and cured disease through principles of "temperance with respect to the inappropriate or irregular use of any faculty of the soul."[35] As can be imagined, this principle of moderation often tended to emphasize abstinence and prohibition of excess, rather than promoting undersatisfied desires.

The physicians of the era were particularly stringent in prohibiting all emotional excesses, which reveals the rational bias of the dietary acceptance of illness. An "appropriate mastery of the passions" showed a proper detachment from the things of the world.[36] Because passions could cause many dangers,[37] a peaceful life, far from crowds, where the individual could properly develop his or her own potential was recommended as the best environment for good health.[38] All of the philosophical physicians agreed that sexual excesses were extremely dangerous for mental health. Hoffmann, for instance, concluded: "Venery is to be neither excessively desired, nor excessively feared. Infrequent, it excites the body; if repeated often, it has a weakening effect."[39] The physicians also insisted on limiting the freedom of the imagination.

The dieticians made positive recommendations as well as prohibitions. Above all, they emphasized work and activity as a means of promoting mental stability. Accordingly, quiet activity was one of the best ways of combating melancholia and ennui.[40]

In his annotation to Kant's essay on the power of the mind to vanquish its own diseases, Hufeland coupled the belief in activity with a condemnation of excessive self-involvement: "I have therefore always found that the more practically active a person's life is, that is, the more he is drawn outwards, the safer he is from hypochondria."[41] The Hufeland citation shows the link between the dieticians' proposals for removing the threat of madness and the dietetic interest in the relationship between individual and society. Activity as a therapy was intended to draw patients out of themselves and into contact with the real world. Kant's essay on the subject also stresses this link. In it, Kant outlined a policy of prevention that emphasized the importance of a stoic regimen for good health. Above all, he counseled that limited sleep ("the bed is a nest for a lot of sicknesses")[42] and plenty of activity, especially for the elderly, were the best guarantors of good health. These suggestions were intended to prevent clients from retreating into nests or beds and encourage them to move out into society. Thus, dietetic discourse on the prevention of madness had ramifications for the issue of sociability.

The Tower Society stands fully behind the dietetic attempt to include madness in a program of general health. They tolerate, but do not glorify, madness; they subordinate illness to health. Lothario, for instance, recovers from his sickness, despite its sweetness. Therese, in the same position of being jilted by Lothario as Aurelie and Lydia, does not torment herself hysterically but throws herself into work. And Natalie's uncle also makes clear that, although passion, desire, and unreason have a place in human experience and are even necessary for life, they cannot be the only side of humanity: "'If I had not resisted myself from youth on,' he would say, 'if I had not striven to extend my mind outward from myself into wider vistas, I would have become a very constricted and thoroughly insufferable person'" (SE 9:330; HA 7:539). Illness for a character like the uncle is only a release with which to prevent more serious problems from arising. After Jarno posits self-interest as an important initial aspect of self-development, he quickly notes that such introspection serves only to prepare the way for entry into society: "but when his development has reached a certain stage, it is advantageous for him to lose himself in a larger whole" (SE 9:301; HA 7:493). The Society of the Tower seems to be arguing that, while mental illness, specifically narcissism, has its uses as an unavoidable and even necessary condition for growth, it must be integrated into an experience of life structured by reason, health, and sociability; they believe they can use the poison to effect a cure.

Working in the dietetic tradition, the physician of the Tower Society forbids excessive emotional outbursts. He warns Aurelie that "intentional revival of passionate feelings" on her part could have serious consequences for her health (SE 9:212; HA 7:349), which turns out to be true (SE 9:214; HA 7:353). Lothario also needs peace and quiet if he is to recover from his wounds, according to Jarno, for which reason Lydia must be spirited away (SE 9:268; HA 7:438). Mignon, too, must preserve, both bodily and spiritually, an equilibrium (SE 9:322; HA 7:525).

Along with emotions, the medicinal authorities in the novel also reject the introspection and asociability associated with madness.[43] The physician of the Tower Society encourages his patients to avoid excessive self-involvement. The clergyman treats the excessive introspection of the Harper with activity and newspaper reading, in order to bring him out of himself. He discourages the Harper's predilection for idiosyncratic behavior and clothing, because they set the self in opposition to the world. His goal is to remind his patients that they are only a small part of a larger organization: "One has to . . . give them the sense of having a common form of life and destiny with many others, and show them that unusual talent, extreme good fortune and excessive misfortune are merely minor deviations from what is normal . . . for nothing brings us closer to madness than distinguishing ourselves from others, and nothing maintains common sense more than living in a normal way with many people" (SE 9:210; HA 7:346–47). The same prescription applies to the Beautiful Soul, who suffers from the same isolation from society that afflicts the Harper. The physician gives the Beautiful Soul the same advice he gives to the Harper when he urges her to spend time observing nature in order to bring her out of herself. In both these cases, as well as in others, the Tower Society equates reason with society and insanity with isolation. And, whatever value it might see in occasional departures from reason and society, it consistently argues that self-involvement detracts from mental health and a felicitous relationship with society.

In keeping with eighteenth-century traditions, the physician regards activity as the standard with which he judges health.[44] The only true misfortunes are fixed ideas that prevent or hinder life (SE 9:211; HA 7:348). For this reason, the physician emphasizes activity in his cure of both the Harper and the Beautiful Soul: "'Man's first task,' he said, 'is to be active, and one should use those intervals when one is obliged to rest, to acquire a clear knowledge of external things, for that will assist us in all our further activity'" (SE 9:253; HA 7:415–16). The rest of the Tower Society is in agreement with the physician. Natalie's and Lothario's uncle, for instance, a guiding light for the Society, believes that activity matters crucially for identity (SE 9:319; HA 7:520). "Purposeful activity" characterizes Therese's life (SE 9:282; HA 7:461); Jarno encourages Wilhelm to "lose himself in a larger whole, learn to live with others, and forget himself in dutiful activity for others" (SE 9:301; HA 7:493). Lothario, too, urges Wilhelm to join the Tower Society and become active (SE 9: 372; HA 7:608). Members of the Tower Society all agree, therefore, in preferring activity to emotions or introspection.

Such a preference typifies the dietetic approach. The Tower Society's adoption of this approach means that frequently its toleration of illness only goes as far as dietetics. The occasional irrational and antisocial act has its place only in a program controlled by reason. For the Tower Society, the fate of characters like the Harper and Mignon show the consequences of uncontrolled illness. In contrast, Serlo and the uncle show the success of allowing small illnesses to take their course.

HOMEOPATHY

In 1796, the same year in which the final installments of *Wilhelm Meister's Apprenticeship* appeared, Samuel Hahnemann (1755–1843) first published the "great law of cure, *similia similibus curantur*,"[45] which was to become a central tenet of homeopathy.[46] Homeopathy takes its name from the practice of using like to cure like. The homeopathic principle of healing began with the notion that the mind-body unity received its life from a "vital principle" that could bring forth its own illnesses: "It is solely the morbidly affected vital principle which brings forth disease."[47] Believing that such self-induced illnesses must have some purpose, Hahnemann devised a medical system, according to which symptoms were cured by administering substances that caused "symptoms that are similar and at the same time, a little stronger" than what the body was itself producing.[48] In another passage he described the homeopathic method as one "which employs against the totality of symptoms of a natural disease a medicine that is capable of exciting in healthy persons symptoms that closely resemble those of the disease itself."[49] He was in essence helping the organism carry out its own program of cure.

Homeopathy emerged from the same progressive tradition that spawned the philosophical physicians. Like the philosophical physicians, Hahnemann believed in the union of mind and body: "[D]iseases of the mind and temper . . . do not form a distinct and wholly separate class from the others."[50] Homeopathy was particularly indebted to Stahl, whose thesis that the anima provided the impetus for all growth, pathological or healthy, in the human organism implied that the soul willed sickness upon itself. This belief inspired the attempts of later philosophical physicians to cure madness by indulging the whims of the mad, which Promies has called the use of "foolishness as medicine."[51] The physicians who humored a patient who believed, say, he was made of glass did so in order to cure the patient of this delusion. In fighting madness with madness, they were arguing—in a way quite similar to homeopathy—that the human organism "knew" what it needed and that the physician had only to strengthen the delusions already present in order to return the patient to sanity.

In the early 1790s Hahnemann worked for the duke of Gotha, not far from Goethe's Weimar. In this time period, Goethe frequently socialized with members of the ducal family, who were related to the family of his own Duke Carl August. In Goethe's autobiographical writings, "Gotha" is as closely interwoven with the completion of *Wilhelm Meister* as the physicians (WA 1.35:35, 278). Indeed, the duke of Gotha and his brother were high on the list of people to receive complimentary copies of the novel when it came out (WA 1.35:46). Some of the medical ideas circulating at the court in Gotha could therefore have easily filtered into the novel.

Admittedly, Goethe does not mention Hahnemann in the 1790s. It is only later that he refers to the physician. In *Faust II*, Goethe parodies homeopathy when Mephistopheles "cures" a woman with a bad foot by stepping on her:

Zu Gleichem Gleiches, was auch einer litt,
Fuß heilet Fuß, so ist's mit allen Gliedern.

(lines 6336–37; HA 3:195)

[*Similia similibus* applies to all disorders;
as foot cures foot, so does each other member.]

(lines 6336–37; SE 2:162)

Despite the mockery, Goethe shows here that the principle of like curing like is the central one that he identifies with homeopathy. Later in life, Goethe makes positive references to homeopathy in his diaries (WA 3.7:213, 221, 3.11:218), suggesting that he is receptive to, if not enthusiastic about, the theory.

In his subsequent discussions of homeopathy, Goethe revealed his understanding of the conceptual connection between homeopathic and dietetic thinking. After a discussion with two young men who were convinced of homeopathy's effectiveness, he wrote: "[I]t seemed to me that whoever lived according to an appropriate diet, paying attention to himself, already unconsciously approached this method" (WA 1.36:183). One could summarize the connection between homeopathy and dietetics as follows: If dietetics was based on the rational control of the pharmakon, homeopathy turned this management of the pharmakon into its central tenet.

Goethe's openness to Hahnemann's medical doctrine makes sense because homeopathy was a logical outgrowth of the tendencies of progressive eighteenth-century medicine. Given Goethe's awareness of the progressive medical tradition and his use of the Tower Society to implement that program, it will not be surprising to find a homeopathic logic in the *Apprenticeship*. But while homeopathy, for all its belief in the unity of mind and body, was most interested in chemical cures for diseases,[52] the Tower Society adopts the homeopathic approach to its own psychological methods by using the irrational beliefs of its patients to cure them. When it offers the Harper a chance to confess so that he can work through his guilt feelings, it shows tolerance for his religious mania. Later it allows him to keep a vial of opium, seemingly according him the right to carry out his death wish. In both cases, the Harper's madness contains the seeds of his attempted cure. Although the physician feels that the religious fervor of the Beautiful Soul is excessive, he uses her religious beliefs to bring her back into the real world by asking her to contemplate God in nature. Natalie's decision to allow Mignon to act out her desire to be an angel is an additional example of the Tower Society's willingness to make use of the irrational, mistaken ideas of patients in order to improve their overall health. Since the Tower Society views those mistaken ideas as illness, it is in effect using sickness to combat sickness. Like homeopathy, it finds a therapeutic function for illness.

The idea of inoculation, imported by Lady Mary Wortley Montagu and others from Constantinople to England in the first half of the eighteenth century, was conceptually parallel to homeopathy, in that it deliberately introduced illness into the body in order to protect the body against illness. In 1796, the year of *similia similibus* and the *Apprenticeship*, Jenner developed the much safer practice of vaccination, the use of milder forms of disease to protect the body against more virulent forms, which also paralleled the homeopathic notion of using small dosages of the cause of an illness in order to stop that illness.[53] Goethe was sympathetic to both inoculation and vaccination.[54] In his autobiography, he refers critically to the reluctance of the Germans to adopt the practice of inoculation and has little nostalgia for the time before vaccination became standard practice (SE 4:38; HA 9:36). In the *Journeyman Years*, in fact, Wilhelm reveals in a letter to Natalie that his father "had worked with sensible doctors and medical policy officials to eliminate the great obstacles that had originally stood in the way of vaccination against the smallpox."[55] Thus, it turns out that the principle of vaccination had played a part in Wilhelm's youth—how important remains yet to be seen.

The year 1796 witnessed the appearance of major developments in vaccination, homeopathy, and the *Apprenticeship*. Inoculation, vaccination, and homeopathy all used sickness against sickness. None of them, however, considered sickness to be a goal in and of itself, any more than dietetics or the rest of eighteenth-century medicine did. Similarly, the Tower Society's homeopathic cures, like its dietetic programs, serve to bring the characters of *Wilhelm Meister's Apprenticeship* to a state of health, not to glorify or celebrate illness. They turn Wilhelm into a master of the pharmakon.

The Uses and Abuses of Bourgeois Society

Since sickness in the eighteenth century and in *Wilhelm Meister's Apprenticeship* is inextricably connected to the patient's behavior in society, its uses and limitations also reflect the advantages and disadvantages of various interpersonal relationships. Just as sickness has some positive sides but must give way to health, a poor relationship with society can have some merit, but a good one is much better. This relativization of the value of sickness and poor relationships with society explains the somewhat contradictory reactions of eighteenth-century medicine and Goethe's novel to the emerging bourgeois civil society of their day. On the one hand, the thinkers of the era attacked that society as the cause of illness; on the other hand, they use it as their model of health. Since they promoted bourgeois society while believing it to cause illness, they had to defend illness as at least necessary, if not positively beneficial.

The relationship between bourgeois society and eighteenth-century medicine, particularly psychiatry, has sparked heated debates on the history of medicine. One tradition of criticism, made famous by French intellectuals such as Foucault, Deleuze, and Guattari, has suggested that eighteenth-century psychiatry aimed to suppress, more or less terroristically, the freedom of the nonbourgeois individual. Another tradition, supported for instance by Lepenies,[56] has argued that the patients of the mental institutions were themselves of the middle class. This meant that the psychology of this era was designed to help the individual and was critical of civilization and society. More recent research has struck a compromise between these two positions, by showing the many facets of both psychiatry and literary depictions of insanity in the late eighteenth century.[57] Works by Schiller, Goethe, Wieland, Spieß, Tieck, and others exhibit, on the one hand, an enlightened attack on asocial behavior and "self-induced" insanity as well as, on the other hand, sympathy with those who have "innocently" lost their sanity because of repression. The bourgeoisie were represented in all categories of mental illness, from physician to patient. Essentially, diseases like hypochondria were the products of, in Sauder's words, a "crisis of the bourgeois human world."[58] *Wilhelm Meister's Apprenticeship* suggests that the philosophical physicians, who favored health, had to accept a limited value for illness because they assumed that bourgeois society was the healthiest way of life, although it caused illness.

Medicine and the philosophy of the eighteenth century were united in laying the blame for the alleged increase of madness upon society. Tissot spoke for many when he attributed the upsurge in insanity to the substantially worse health of people in modern, as opposed to primitive, societies:

> But they [nervous disorders] were certainly much more seldom in those days than nowadays, and for two reasons: The first reason has to do with the fact that in those days human beings were in general much stronger and much more rarely sick and that in those days there were fewer sicknesses of all sorts. The second reason is that the causes that actually produce nervous disorders have for some time now multiplied much more than the more general causes of sicknesses, of which some actually seem to be declining. In this way these sickness have become considerably more frequent than the others.[59]

Christian Garve echoed his Swiss colleague's observation when he pointed out that only the upper classes suffered from an epidemic of insanity and diseases of the imagination: "And insanity, or the predisposition thereto, a fantastic imagination, is just as rare in coarse ages as it is among common and completely uncultured classes."[60] These assumptions had their corollaries in the critique of culture made fashionable in the second half of the eighteenth century by Rousseau. Kant adopted this critique quite early, writing in 1764: "The human being in the state of nature can be subjected only to a few follies and scarcely any foolishness. . . . Which insanity would befall him? . . . Madness . . . is certainly entirely beyond his abilities."[61] Kant went on to make clear that the modern society that he held responsible for the rise in madness was specifically bourgeois: "In the bourgeois constitution can actually be found the means of fermentation for all this corruption which, if they do not actually produce it, certainly serve to maintain and increase it."[62] Reil cited parts of this analysis verbatim in his *Rhapsodies*, a fact that shows how wholeheartedly the medical tradition of the early nineteenth century embraced this critique of middle-class culture.[63]

Such critiques of bourgeois society were actually a sort of self-criticism, however. Despite their belief that bourgeois society was responsible for the inroads of mental illness, Kant and others like him formulated doctrines and philosophies for the emerging middle-class worldview. In the writings of a philosophical physician like Zimmermann, the essentially bourgeois nature of this late-eighteenth-century analysis of insanity becomes clear. Like his contemporaries, Zimmermann was primarily interested in the social origins of mental disorders. In both his books on solitude, he carefully weighed the advantages and disadvantages of solitude. While he acknowledged that humans were social beings, he insisted that society caused many mental disorders. An excessively social existence could hinder individual cultivation. Religious societies were particularly infelicitous environments for the psyche, but the stressful work habits of the bourgeoisie were also dangerous. True freedom was only to be found away from society: "Freedom, true freedom, can nowhere be found so well as in separation from the human throng and all involuntary worldly relationships."[64] Because he believed that "at least a couple of hours a day" all people should be able to say "we are free,"[65] Zimmermann praised this independence as his most important philosophical goal: "Preaching that independence from the world was the intention and the goal of my modest philosophizing in this work on solitude."[66] The contradictory tendencies of Zimmermann's thinking becomes evident in these remarks. On the one hand, Zimmermann insisted that society was often responsible for mental illness; he did not exempt bourgeois society from this analysis. Despite his critique of bourgeois society, however, his remarks also had a liberal bourgeois bent. Although certainly no revolutionary, Zimmermann demanded more room for the individual to develop a strong sense of self that would allow him or her to resist the onslaughts of society, the most potent dangers for the health of the psyche.

Zimmermann's bourgeois individualism typified the philosophical physicians of the era. All of these physicians therefore tried to readjust their mentally ill patients to specifically bourgeois models. They encouraged patients to adopt a bourgeois way of living and admonished the healthy to keep to their middle-class ways. For these people, bourgeois society was a pharmakon, in that it was the cure, as well as one of the causes, of mental illness. Through the physician, bourgeois society perceived the causes of its illnesses and prescribed those very same causes to cure itself. A metaphor for bourgeois society's use of bourgeois lifestyles to cure illnesses that emerged out of those very same lifestyles is the sickly doctor, who must heal himself. Although the trope is old, it shows up again with particular intensity in the eighteenth century. Zimmermann refers to Haller's melancholia and subsequent opium addiction.[67] Numerous works published around the same time as the *Apprenticeship* asserted that Zimmermann himself suffered from "fatal" hypochondria.[68] The bourgeois doctor must heal himself of those illnesses caused by bourgeois life and at the same time must uphold the principles of that bourgeois society.[69]

The Tower Society is cognizant of the contradictions in the life of the sickly bourgeois doctor, promoting his healthful but poisonous society. Its doctor is indeed also sickly: "He was an oldish man who, despite his delicate health, had spent many years in the exercise of such noble duties" (SE 9:210; HA 7:347). And in general, it mirrors these attitudes, alternating between criticism and approval of bourgeois society. Like many in the eighteenth century, the clergyman regards civil, bourgeois society as contributing to mental illness: "Wie vieles ist leider nicht in unserer Erziehung und in unsern bürgerlichen Einrichtungen, wodurch wir uns und unsere Kinder zur Tollheit vorbereiten!" (HA 7:347) [Unfortunately there is much in our educational system and everyday life that preconditions us and our children to madness] (SE 9:210). What the Suhrkamp edition calls "everyday life" is actually "unsere bürgerliche Einrichtungen," literally, "our civilian/ bourgeois arrangements." This thinking clearly emerges from the same tradition as Rousseau, Zimmermann, and Kant. Nor does such thinking remain on the level of bland generalizations. Wilhelm quite specifically blames his father's stiflingly conventional household for his own interest in the theater (SE 9:3; HA 7:11–12), which then leads to his theater mania.[70]

The Society, like the medicine of its time, contradicts itself to a certain extent in that it does not plan to initiate radical changes in "our civil arrangements." Indeed, as an institution, it furthers the goals of this new, civil, bourgeois society. Wilhelm Meister announces that he has acquired the virtues of a bourgeois civilian *(Bürger)* at the end of his apprenticeship

(SE 9:307; HA 7:502); the Tower Society, which has transformed itself into a capital insurance fund (SE 9:345; HA 7:564), insists upon the abolishment of feudal tax privileges (SE 9:310; HA 7:507). Friedrich's reference at the end of the novel to the *Freiredoute* (SE 9:373; HA 7:609), a dance in which all classes and ranks may participate, reminds the reader that the Tower Society also abolishes the exclusivity of the aristocracy by engineering marriages between Lothario, Friedrich, and Natalie, and Therese, Philine, and Wilhelm—an aristocratic family, on the one side, and an illegitimate daughter of a kitchen maid, an actress of uncertain background, and a young merchant's son, on the other side.[71]

Since the Society of the Tower promotes the same culture that is, according to its own physicians, responsible for so much madness, it must therefore be willing to accept the constant return of illness as part of a productive change, indeed, as a pharmakon. Moreover, this illness is not merely an unfortunate by-product of societal changes but also an integral part of those changes. The Tower Society's toleration of illness is an acceptance of the problems that arise for individuals in a society that allegedly causes illness. It is an attempt to manage the pharmakon. The narrator asks: "All transitions are crises, and is not crisis a form of sickness?" (SE 9:309; HA 7:505). No one can maintain that *Wilhelm Meister's Apprenticeship* rejects changes or transitions. Life must of necessity consist of transitions, as both common sense and the novel agree. And if crisis, sickness, and transition are interchangeable words, all three will constantly reappear in life.

When the narrator refers to "crisis," he is referring specifically to a medical problem. It has not been generally noted in criticism of *Wilhelm Meister* that the terminology of "crisis" is also medical. "The change in nature for better or worse," Hoffmann explains, "is called a crisis; the change is a sudden one, either to death or to recovery."[72] These "crises" maintain the same ambiguity that the pharmakon has: "On one occasion, a crisis is salutary and perfect; on another, not salutary and imperfect, indeed, often treacherous."[73] When the narrator of Smollett's *Roderick Random* recovers from a nearly fatal bout of distemper, he writes, for instance, "I had enjoyed a favorable crisis."[74] Thus, in eighteenth-century parlance, in a novel strongly colored by medical discourse, the word "crisis" takes on a specifically medical timbre, relating it to Derrida's understanding of the pharmakon.

The toleration of illness in the novel therefore dovetails neatly with the Tower Society's interpretation of mental illness as a social disorder. Because both the novel and the eighteenth century link mental illness and society, they also link the positive sides of mental illness with societal behavior. Lichtenberg and the early romantics rehabilitated hypochondria because they saw a benefit in introspection, a form of behavior formerly not accepted by society. Likewise, the Tower Society defends the mental illness that it itself helps create by arguing that folly and idiosyncratic, unreasonable, hypochondriac desires must be given space lest they take over. Correspondingly, they believe that a bit of introspection is a normal part of human development. Thus, the network of beliefs in the novel about both the meaning and the uses of sickness reinforces the link between sickness and asociability.

Nonetheless, the Tower Society only endorses sickness and asocial behavior in the context of a program of health and bourgeois society. It believes that it can control the pharmakon, making sure that the poison it provides will heal. As will be seen in the next chapters, these attitudes inform the Tower Society's response to any pathological, antisocial behavior on Wilhelm's part: it tolerates Wilhelm's introspective, narcissistic tendencies, but only as part of a larger strategy to bring him back to bourgeois society and eventually turn him into a pharmaceutical Meister.

7

Wilhelm Meister's Wounds:
Theater Mania and Narcissism

Until now, the obviously sick characters like Mignon and the Harper have been the centers of attention of this study. Yet the novel, the Tower Society, and the reader devote far more attention to Wilhelm Meister and his *Bildung* than to the cures of such characters as Mignon or the Harper. Is medicine just a sideline in the Tower Society's primary business of educating and developing Wilhelm? While Wilhelm Meister may not seem as sick as some of his fellow characters, his case too is a medical one. Because late-eighteenth-century German medicine was increasingly concerned with psychology and the relationship between the individual and society, it was very much interested in the education and development of young representatives of the bourgeoisie like Wilhelm Meister. Just as the medical profession utilized advanced medicine to cure other characters of their "illnesses," the Tower Society uses medicine to cure Wilhelm Meister's wounds and interpret his passion for the theater and his narcissism as "sicknesses."

Unlike Mignon, the Harper, Aurelie, and the Beautiful Soul, Wilhelm seems quite healthy at first. In *The Journeyman Years*, Wilhelm makes clear the importance of medicine and illness in his early life by writing to Natalie that his father had been active in shaping the medical policy of his community (SE 10:291; HA 8:278). Goethe thereby underscores the presence of medicine and medical discourses in Wilhelm's early youth.

Plenty of hints in the *Apprenticeship*, though, point to Wilhelm's illnesses and wounds at the beginning of the novel and show that his apparent healthiness is misleading. The bluntest indication of Wilhelm's poor health is the prevalence of wounds in his early biography.[1] Obsessed by wounds as a child, he writes only the fifth acts of plays, "where everything got confusing and people stabbed each other" (SE 9:17; HA 7:36). Because of this obsession, he identifies with the hero of Torquato Tasso's *Jerusalem Liberated*, Tancred, destined as he is "unwittingly to harm everything he ever loved!" (SE 9:12; HA 7:27).[2] This childhood fascination with wounds signals the significance for Wilhelm of physical injuries.

Although his obsession with wounds has an aggressive streak, in the first part of the novel Wilhelm is actually the recipient of a series of wounds. After his relationship with Mariane ends (for these wounds always occur after pleasurable experiences), he declares that the loss of her, "an early but deep wound" (SE 9:46; HA 7:85), will never heal, although previously he had considered himself "invulnerable" (SE 9:46; HA 7:85). Then, after fencing and preparing for the theater in the idyllic wilds gives Wilhelm an "unusual delight" (SE 9:132; HA 7:223), a marauding band attacks his wandering troupe and shoots him between the left breast and the shoulder, narrowly missing his heart (SE 9:132ff.; HA 7:223ff.). Finally, after an intimate conversation with Aurelie, she leaps up and slashes the palm of his hand. At this point, the narrator tallies up the number of wounds that Wilhelm has sustained: "Along with the two wounds that had not yet fully healed, Wilhelm had now acquired a third . . ." (SE 9:169; HA 7:282). The recurrence of wounds in Wilhelm's early biography means that he is nearly always injured and in need of medical attention.

The narrator prominently positions his résumé of Wilhelm's three wounds at the beginning of the fifth book to indicate the importance of Wilhelm Meister's nearly permanent condition of "having been wounded."[3] The consequences of his loss of Mariane, in accordance with the beliefs of the era concerning the unity of the body and mind, run the gamut of mental and physical symptoms, including "a raging fever, and what followed—medication, overexcitement and lassitude" (SE 9:42; HA 7:77). Similarly, the attack of the robbers keeps Wilhelm confined to his bed for a considerable amount of time. Both of these wounds therefore have important self-evident physical effects on Wilhelm. Moreover, these wounds determine Wilhelm's character significantly: The first awakens a yearning for companionship resolved only by the marriage to Natalie; and the second provides the occasion for meeting Natalie, since Wilhelm might never have met the baroness or received her blessings, had he not fallen victim to the attack of the robbers. These physical wounds, therefore, motivate the plot meaningfully, suggesting the centrality to the novel of Wilhelm's sickness and his need of healing.

In keeping with the belief in the unity of mind and body, Wilhelm's early wounds and injuries have their psychological counterparts. His breakup with Mariane leaves him distraught. He is emotionally "wounded" (SE 9:114; HA 7:194) when Jarno refers to the Harper and Mignon as "an itinerant ballad singer and a silly androgynous creature" (SE 9:113; HA 7:193). On a physical and psychological level, therefore, he needs healing.

Into this medical emergency steps the Tower Society. It heals the physical wounds straightforwardly by hiring surgeons. After the marauding band attacks and wounds Wilhelm, Natalie and her uncle pay for a surgeon, setting the precedent for the Tower Society, which subsequently keeps medical personnel on hand at all times. In paying Wilhelm's medical bills, the Tower Society does more than suture Wilhelm's wounds. It uses its surgeons to accustom him to medicine. At the beginning of his development, Wilhelm Meister, wavering between despair and unrealistic hope about his wounds, has little faith in medical cures. At times, he feels that nothing can change his condition: "I used to think I was indestructible, invulnerable, but now I see that an early but deep wound will never, never heal. I feel that I will take it with me into the grave" (SE 9:46; HA 7:85). At other times he assumes that at least the wounds of geniuses take care of themselves: "'And yet,' said Wilhelm, 'will not a genius be able to save himself, to heal the wounds that he has inflicted on himself?'" (SE 9:67; HA 7:120). Both attitudes indicate a basic disbelief in medicine, which manifests itself in his actions. Out of impatience, for example, with the treatment of his gunshot wound, he breaks it off early: "So he packed his things, . . . without being fully recovered or consulting either the pastor or the surgeon . . ." (SE 9:144; HA 7:242). Such a refusal to submit to the advice of the health-care authorities indicates that Wilhelm does not recognize the need for medical treatment at the beginnings of his sickness.

The Tower Society consistently asserts its right to heal in an effort to persuade Wilhelm of the usefulness of medicine. From the beginning, the stranger, an emissary of the Tower Society, rejects Wilhelm's claim that genius heals its own wounds: "'Not at all,' said the stranger. 'Or if so, then not very effectively'" (SE 9:67; HA 7:120–21). In keeping with this belief, the Tower Society and its allies constantly attempt to intervene in Wilhelm Meister's health. When Aurelie slashes his palm, Wilhelm still acquiesces in her demand that she, rather than a surgeon, treat the wound: "Aurelie would not allow him the services of a surgeon; instead, she bandaged him herself with all sorts of strange speeches, maxims and ceremonies, which made him extremely embarrassed" (SE 9:169; HA 7:282). Aurelie's behavior recalls that of the healing women whom eighteenth-century medicine condescendingly characterized as ineffectual witches. In a medical case of ontogeny repeating phylogeny, Wilhelm recapitulates the history of Western culture by going through a phase of entrusting his health needs to untrained women. The narrative's obvious lack of comprehension for her healing is not surprising, given that the Tower Society apparently wrote it. Wilhelm's embarrassment in this situation suggests that he recognizes the new, professional medical authorities. By the end of the novel, the Tower Society's persistence has paid off: Wilhelm gradually learns an acceptance of medicine and takes the advice of the physician on all issues.

THEATER MANIA

Having accustomed Wilhelm to medicine with its treatment of his wounds, the Tower Society can begin its treatment of his less obvious, but to them more important, illnesses. The emergence of Wilhelm's interest in wounds on the stage (SE 9:17; HA 7:36) suggests that drama is an infectious medium in *Wilhelm Meister's Apprenticeship*. In fact, a good deal of evidence suggests that Wilhelm Meister is "stage-struck," a victim of that eighteenth-century disease, theater mania.[4]

Today, such a mania for the theater would not qualify as an illness; in the eighteenth century, however, it was frequently described as a psychological problem when it afflicted young bourgeois like Wilhelm. At least two accounts of an "unfortunate penchant for theater" appeared in the *Magazine of Experiential Psychology*. Moritz reports that a friend he was treating for a severe case of theater mania, "lived and moved exclusively in the theater world."[5] Serious consequences ensued from the disease: "One of my friends has a son with the best of hearts, whom an unfortunate passion for the theater practically robbed completely of the happiness of his life."[6] A potential complete loss of happiness provided the philosophical physicians of the eighteenth century an excellent excuse to begin their therapies.

At a number of points, the *Apprenticeship* shows its fidelity to the era's belief in the pathological nature of theater mania. Just as Moritz's patient "lebte und webte . . . in der Theaterwelt" [lived and moved . . . in the theater world], Wilhelm "lebte und webte . . . in der shakespearischen Welt" (HA 7:185) [lived and moved in the world of Shakespeare] (SE 9:108). This condition is autistic and narcissistic: Wilhelm doesn't recognize or feel anything outside himself. Wilhelm unwittingly hints at the diseased side of his obsession when he uses the verb *kränken* (variously translated as "to upset," "to hurt," "to grieve" in SE 9:9, 13; HA 7:22, 29) to describe incidents in his early, formative experiences with the theater. Although Wilhelm has in mind the standard meaning of the word—"to vex" or "to irritate"—when he utters it, a meaning which has little to do with sickness, the word itself clearly belongs to the complex *krank* (sick),[7] thereby implying that Wilhelm's obsession has a pathological side. The Tower Society's understanding of Wilhelm's fascination with the theater as an illness in need of curing becomes quite clear when Jarno expressly refers to the abbé's plan of helping Wilhelm's magnificent performance of *Hamlet* as an attempt to heal him (SE 9:337; HA 7:551).

Typically, late-eighteenth-century psychiatric theory counseled humoring the whims of the stagestruck in order to use theater mania against itself.

Moritz, for instance, rejected the treatment of the father of one of his patients, who, like Wilhelm's, strictly prohibited his son's visits to the theater. Such repression generally backfired. Instead, Moritz engaged in a pious fraud by constantly encouraging the young man to cultivate his interest in the theater: "I did anything but discourage him from his decision to dedicate himself to the theater or visiting it daily."[8] When the young man began to moderate his views, claiming he only wanted to test his luck on the stage, Moritz pushed a more radical position: "However, I did not trust this deceptive appearance, but attempted now with all my powers to support his decision for the theater in order to receive a complete victory, or none at all."[9] In the end, the policy forced the young man to think for himself and to face the consequences of his decision: "[W]ith an outbreak of the deepest joy, he embraced me and said: I am not going to the stage, I'm traveling to my parents. —I still did not trust [in this apparent victory] and tried with the strongest counterarguments to bring him back to his first decision. However he departed on the same day to his parents who received their son, who was now completely cured of his fantasy, with open arms."[10] The cure shows typical characteristics of the psychological medicine of the late eighteenth century: deception with good intent and a willingness to accept the fantasies of patients until they themselves reject them.

   In another case, the psychologist Immanuel David Mauchart, who later founded one of the successors to the *Magazine of Experiential Psychology*, the *General Repertory*, described a fanatical theatergoer, who, like Wilhelm, burned all his plays in a desperate attempt to cure himself. This patient had an enlightened father who did not forbid his son's visits to the theater, a tolerant approach that was responsible for the felicitous outcome of the case: "For even the still unnatural vehemence with which he began to implement his decision to recover by burning his collected plays probably did not effect the subsequent complete recovery as much as the continued permission to visit the theater occasionally."[11] Once again, the treatment emphasized indirection, patience, and tolerance.

   The Tower Society uses the same strategy as Moritz and the enlightened father described by Mauchart to cure Wilhelm Meister of his theater mania. As far as the Tower Society is concerned, Werner has the right idea when it comes to Wilhelm's passion for the theater. He encourages Wilhelm to continue his interests as an amateur: "Werner insisted that it was ridiculous to abandon a talent he had exercised with pleasure and some skill, simply because he would never achieve perfection through it. There were always those dull hours that could be filled up in this way, and something would gradually emerge that would give pleasure to us and to others" (SE 9:44; HA 7:82). Carrying on Werner's policy with a more elaborate and elegant theoretical framework, the Tower Society helps and encourages

Wilhelm until he loses interest in the stage. Jarno explains that the abbé hoped to cure Wilhelm's passion for the theater by assisting him in his magnificent performance of Hamlet: "Yes, because he was sure that was the only way to cure you, if you were curable. . . . he hoped that the performance of *Hamlet* would be sufficient to satisfy your desire, and that you would never go on stage again" (SE 9:337–38, HA 7:551). Jarno claims that the cure does not succeed, but this assertion is premature and untenable because Wilhelm quits the theater shortly after this performance. On the very next day, he is completely disillusioned: "The day crept on and none had ever seemed so ordinary to Wilhelm. . . . the interest in *Hamlet* was flagging, and no one found it at all appropriate to repeat it the next day" (SE 9:199; HA 7:329). This cure conforms completely to the tradition of the psychological medicine of the eighteenth century because it accepts and tolerates Wilhelm's fixed, obsessive attachment to the theater until he is ready to give it up of his own accord.[12]

WILHELM'S INWARDNESS

Relying on the tradition of eighteenth-century psychology, which believed that poisons could also be antidotes, the Tower Society uses, along with other art forms, drama, which had exerted such damaging, addictive attractions on Wilhelm, to cure him of that condition which the Tower Society finds underlying most illnesses, narcissism.

Like the sickness of the other characters in the novel, Wilhelm Meister's societal "illness" expresses itself most significantly in introspection and narcissism. From the beginning, this addiction to introspection, self-construction, and self-invention stands out, revealing itself in his constant wish to tell his life story. After he puts Mariane to sleep with his seemingly endless childhood reminiscences, he is tempted to do the same when he meets Jarno: "Wilhelm . . . now felt in the mood to tell his friend and benefactor his whole life story" (SE 9:113; HA 7:193). Similarly, an important part of his proposal to Therese is a "brief" sketch of his personal history (SE 9:309; HA 7:505). This autobiographical urge points to an obsession with himself that is bound to worry the Society, which attempts to cure similar narcissism in characters like the Beautiful Soul, the Harper, Mignon, and the count.

Goethe perhaps anticipated psychoanalytic theories of narcissism by situating the origins of Wilhelm's search for identity in his relationship with his mother.[13] The reader's first extensive introduction to Wilhelm takes place in the form of a discussion between the protagonist and his mother

(SE 9:2ff.; HA 7:11ff.). In this discussion, it becomes clear that his mother now personifies love and support for Wilhelm, although in the earlier, never completed *Theatrical Mission*, she was inattentive to him. In the *Apprenticeship*, she gives him the puppet theater when he is a child and shows understanding for his love of the theater as he grows older, relating his love of the theater to this narcissistic relationship. The change in her character from an inadequate to an exemplary mother allows Wilhelm to grow up in an ideal bourgeois family, which sets the stage for Wilhelm's early narcissism.[14] In this novel, the mother's main activity consists of reminiscing with Wilhelm about his childhood, that is, providing him with an image of himself. These details suggest that, by fulfilling all his desires, the ideal bourgeois mother gives her child its first taste of mirroring, a taste so good that it keeps looking for additional narcissistic relationships. The novel thereby implicates the bourgeois family as a toxin as well as promoting it subsequently as a cure.

The pathology of Wilhelm's initial relationships with others becomes clearest in his affair with Mariane. She and his mother play the same role in their conversations with Wilhelm. Just as his mother had, Mariane seems willing to spend hours listening to him relate his childhood experiences. Most interestingly, in book 1, chapter 2, Wilhelm discusses a puppet performance of the biblical story of David with his mother; in the following chapter, the same conversation, without interruption or repetition, continues—the only difference being the presence of Mariane instead of Wilhelm's mother. She has replaced his mother as interlocutor.

Although Kittler, and in his wake a number of other critics, claim that Mariane does not fully supplant Wilhelm's mother because she does not come from the same bourgeois background,[15] in fact she does have a bourgeois heritage. Her maid, Barbara, reports: "In her early youth she had been provided with everything, but her family lost its fortune through a series of complicated circumstances" (SE 9:292; HA 7:477). Nonetheless, she has clearly fallen from her bourgeois standing and is now too bohemian to please Wilhelm's parents. Her relationship with Wilhelm turns into a specular one, which, in the world this novel represents, might work between mothers and sons, but not between husbands and wives.

Wilhelm projects his desires onto Mariane in order to transform her into the mirroring figure he wants. According to the narrator, he uses all his faculties to convert her into an object worthy of his affection: "His heart strove to ennoble the object of his affections, and his mind to lift them both on to a higher plane" (SE 9:16; HA 7:33). Mariane knows, however, that Wilhelm's projections fail to portray her psyche accurately: "[S]he found nothing in herself . . . for her mind was empty and her heart had no resistance"

(SE 9:16; HA 7:34). Wilhelm's construction of her identity in his own image means that, when he considers his beloved "half—more than half—of himself" (SE 9:16; HA 7:33), he is more accurate than he realizes.

Because his heart and mind color his perception of her so extensively, his relationship with her is essentially an echoing one:

> Happy youth, happy those first gropings for love, when we converse readily with ourselves, delighting in echoes of our own conversation and satisfied when our invisible partner merely repeats the last syllables of what we have just uttered!
> Wilhelm was in this state during the first days of his love for Mariane—and even more so later, when he began to shower her with all the wealth of his feelings and to regard himself as a beggar living from what she gave him in return. (SE 9:30; HA 7:57)

The narrator uses Wilhelm's love affair as an example for the general principle that first loves are specular. The love between Augustin and Sperata would be confirming evidence of this principle, as is Mignon's infatuation with Wilhelm. Not surprisingly, Wilhelm's relationship with Mariane induces him to talk "to himself, no matter where he was" (SE 9:16; HA 7:34). In Mariane, then, Wilhelm creates and finds the same sort of unquestioning, mirroring support that he had found or wanted to find in his mother.

Because the Tower Society is interested in readjusting its patients to society, it would already have ample reason to intervene in such solipsistic thinking. Wilhelm's introspection, however, has psychological consequences that make even clearer its connections with illness. Typically for characters who believe they are united with their mirror images, the achievement of unity with his mirror image ushers in for Wilhelm a euphoric phase that contrasts sharply with Mariane's depression: "But Wilhelm soared happily in loftier regions. For him, too, a new world had opened up, a world with vistas of endless delight" (SE 9:16; HA 7:34). Conversely, the melancholy that results from Wilhelm's loss of Mariane (SE 9:41–42; HA 7:77) is also typical, reminiscent of the depressions that befall Augustin and Mignon when they lose, respectively, Sperata and Wilhelm. The text thus not only describes the relationship between Mariane and Wilhelm as narcissistic, it also shows the health consequences of such relationships.

Wilhelm's subsequent love affairs follow the pattern set while courting Mariane. In the countess, for instance, he finds a new mirror image. Originally, Wilhelm goes to her castle in order to "derive insights" about, among other things, himself (SE 9:88; HA 7:154). Admittedly, the narrator claims that Wilhelm desires general knowledge of humanity, life, and art as well as specific knowledge about himself, but other indicators suggest that Wilhelm is primarily interested in himself at this point. Öhrgaard demonstrates convincingly that the castle bears many similarities to the home of Wilhelm's parents, which leads him to conclude that the noble couple acts as a set of substitute parents.[16] Given the narcissism inherent in the relationship with the mother in this novel, this would indicate Wilhelm's attempt to find some image of himself in the countess. The presence of Wilhelm Meister's initials on the clasp of the countess's bracelet—a detail noted by the narrator before he describes the first and last embrace of the lovers (SE 9:118; HA 7:201)—further suggests that Wilhelm's love of the countess is actually self-love.

DRAMA AS DRUG

The Tower Society, which works so hard to help characters like the Harper, Mignon, and the Beautiful Soul adjust to society despite their excessive introspection, must try to "cure" Wilhelm's narcissism, too. To heal Wilhelm's excessively introspective psyche and bring him back in touch with society, the Tower Society's members prefer the indirect methods of the medicine of their era, in particular, theater and painting. With both theater and painting, the Tower Society pits Wilhelm's narcissistic imagination against itself by using media in which Wilhelm initially sees himself, thereby using his sickness to cure itself.

One of the therapies that the Tower Society uses to heal Wilhelm of his introspection and encourage him to develop extroverted relationships with others involves Wilhelm's childhood love and "illness," the theater. The stranger reveals the Tower Society's belief in the efficacy of drama as a tool for improving the relationship between the individual and society when he proposes impromptu skits as good exercise: "It is the very best way to take people out of themselves and, by way of a detour, return them to themselves" (SE 9:67; HA 7:119). Here literature, in the form of drama, is quite literally a pharmakon, a detrimental, addictive influence on Wilhelm's life that must not only be cured but is also part of a cure. These spontaneous performances represent the beginnings of the Society's comprehensive theatrical therapy, which starts by drawing Wilhelm out of himself and concludes with a theatrical representation of his healing.

The pharmaceutical nature of theater in Wilhelm's life is specifically linked with narcissism. The Society's therapy reveals its connections to the medicine of the philosophical physicians not only in its reliance on creative outlets like drama but also in its attempt to pit Wilhelm's introspection against itself. Originally, Wilhelm derives a strong narcissistic pleasure from the theater. As a child, Wilhelm most admires those dramas in which he has a chance to star (SE 9:14; HA 7:30). Later, the stranger picks up on

Wilhelm's desire to see himself in dramas he reads, and he makes the extemporaneous acting exercises more appealing to the young man by promising that they bring the actor back into himself.

The novel details most exactly the introspection in Wilhelm's relationship with Shakespeare.[17] When Jarno introduces Wilhelm to Shakespeare's writings, they fulfill the protagonist's narcissistic fantasies anew. Wilhelm tells Jarno that Shakespeare's dramas reflect all the intuitions, thoughts, and feelings of his childhood: "Presentiments that I have had from youth on, without being aware of them, about human beings and their destinies, all these I have found confirmed and enlarged in Shakespeare's plays" (SE 9:112; HA 7:192). Later on, Jarno agrees with Wilhelm, asserting that, because Wilhelm only plays himself when he takes on Hamlet's role, he never really learns to act: "You, for example, played Hamlet quite well and a few other roles, where your character, your physical appearance and your mood of the moment assisted you" (SE 9:337; HA 7:550–51).

Predictably, this solipsism has psychological consequences. Wilhelm's feeling of unity with Shakespeare's literary works provokes a euphoric state, in which he feels rejuvenated and ready to take on the whole world: "The few glances that I have cast into Shakespeare's world have impelled me more than anything else to take more resolute steps into the real world, to plunge into the flood of destinies that hangs over the world and someday, if fortune favors me, to cull several drafts from the great ocean of living nature and distribute these from the stage to the thirsting public of my native land" (SE 9:113; HA 7:192). Although Jarno welcomes his client's resolution to take a more active role in the world as a sign that the dramatic cure is working, Wilhelm's enthusiasm is too reminiscent of his exaltation in the heyday of his narcissistic relationship with Mariane to qualify as a true turn away from introspection. Indeed, another passage makes clear that his love of the theater shares with his love of Mariane an excessive reliance on projection: "Wilhelm was still at that happy stage in life when it seems inconceivable that there could be any blemish on a girl one loves or an author that one admires. Our feelings are so absolute and so all of a piece that we assert a similar perfection and harmony in the objects" (SE 9:176; HA 7:293).[18] Just as Wilhelm falsely attributes qualities to Mariane that she does not possess, he attributes a unity he desires for himself to these plays.

Eventually, Wilhelm refines his sense of identity with Shakespeare by assuming, first, the identity of Henry IV and, second, that of Hamlet. In the case of Henry IV, Wilhelm contents himself with dressing up and acting like the prince (SE 9:123–24; HA 7:210–11). In order to study Hamlet's character more thoroughly, however, Wilhelm memorizes his speeches, especially, significantly enough, the monologues (SE 9:128; HA 7:217). When he can imitate Hamlet's emotions as well as his words, he achieves a feeling of identity with his hero: "I also believed that I was really getting into the spirit of the part by somehow myself assuming the weight of his profound melancholy and, beneath this burden, following my model through the strange labyrinth of so many different moods and peculiar experiences. I learnt the part and tried it out, feeling that I was becoming more and more identified with my hero" (SE 9:128; HA 7:217). Wilhelm's decision to take upon himself the burden of Hamlet's melancholy is a crucial step, for it reveals the basic tendency of the therapy of this era to use illness against itself. The Tower Society plans to wean Wilhelm of his introspection and depression by initially indulging his self-destructive desires in letting him play the notoriously introverted melancholy prince.[19]

Wilhelm's rapid loss of interest in the theater after the performance of *Hamlet* signifies not only the cure of his theater mania but also the progress in the treatment of his introspection. The contradictions and incongruities within the characters of the drama quickly take the wind out of his narcissistic fantasies (SE 9:128; HA 7:217). At first, Wilhelm attempts to provide Hamlet with a unified character, a task that requires an immense amount of extratextual information, especially about Hamlet's childhood. Eventually he concludes that Hamlet is overweight, blond, and blue-eyed, because the text says that the prince is Danish and tires easily when fencing:

> The fencing is hard for him, sweat runs off his face, and the queen says: "He's fat and scant of breath." How can you imagine him, except as blond and portly? For people who are dark-haired are rarely like that when they are young. And do not his fits of melancholy, the tenderness of his grief, his acts of indecisiveness, better suit someone like that than a slim youth with curly brown hair from whom one would expect more alacrity and determination? (SE 9:185; HA 7:306)

With good reason, Aurelie rejects Wilhelm's approach to literary characters as fatal to the imagination: "You are spoiling my whole image of him. . . . Get rid of that fat Hamlet!" (SE 9:185; HA 7:307). Wilhelm himself indicates his dissatisfaction with the results of his analysis, which alienate him from his former mirror image: "The more I worked myself into the part, the more I have become aware that my physical appearance has absolutely none of the characteristics Shakespeare gave to Hamlet" (SE 9:184; HA 7:306). In a significant step, Wilhelm finally comes to know the alterity of one of the objects of his affection. Whereas he loses Mariane long before he realizes that she has a life full of feelings beyond his comprehension, he is able to determine that Hamlet represents something different from himself before losing track of the play.

A close reading of Wilhelm's initiation into the Tower Society at the end of the seventh book shows its significance as a recapitulation of the dramatic therapy that the Tower Society applies to Wilhelm's problems with society. Kittler and Haas have pointed out the connections between this initiation scene and the theater: One of the episodes of the initiation specifically refers to Wilhelm's performance of *Hamlet*, the opening and closing of curtains recalls the curtains that come up frequently in Wilhelm's memories of his childhood theatrical experiences, and both the initiation and the performance contain inexplicable appearances and disappearances.[20]

In addition to its drama, however, the initiation scene also has medical aspects. The use of the former chapel as a stage (SE 9:301; HA 7:493) parallels the refurbishing of religious tenets with psychological beliefs and hints at a project involving the treatment of the soul in a modern way. Having established a medical stage, the initiation emphasizes the need for healing. The first man who appears in the scene brings up the topic of illness by reminding Wilhelm of the lovelorn prince: "Where do you think the sick prince is languishing at the moment?" (SE 9:302; HA 7:494). Wilhelm then reinforces the suggestions of the presence of illness by assigning the blame for his past errors on mistaken imagination: "'What error can the man be referring to,' he asked himself, 'except that which has dogged me all my life: . . . imagining I could acquire a talent to which I had no propensity?'" (SE 9:302; HA 7:495).[21] Admittedly, Wilhelm presumably uses the verb "to imagine" *(einbilden)* in a casual and nonmedical way. Nonetheless, the Tower Society, with its medical approach to the imagination, feels entitled to treat Wilhelm's false ideas about his teleology.

After illness makes its presence felt, the Tower Society uses the initiation to demonstrate Wilhelm's newfound health. In a typically tolerant way, these physicians view his past illnesses, not as regrettable, but as stepping-stones toward healing: "You are saved, and on the way to your goal. You will not regret any of your follies . . ." (SE 9:303; HA 7:495). Not just an imprecise term, "follies" *(Torheiten)* can refer to a treatable mental illness. The ghost who sounds like Wilhelm's father metaphorically rephrases this medical sentiment when he declares: "Steep slopes can only be scaled by bypaths . . ." (SE 9:303; HA 7:495). Both of these statements mirror the medical belief in the value, albeit limited, of sickness.

At the end of the scene, the language of healing predominates, as hints concerning Wilhelm's new health come more quickly. Words like *Heil* (hail) and *heilig* (holy)—etymologically related to *Heilung* (healing), of course[22]— occur repeatedly on the last page of the chapter. The Tower Society chooses a direct translation of one of the aphorisms of Hippocrates, one of the most highly respected medical authorities in the eighteenth-century tradition,[23] for the very first sentence of the Certificate of Apprenticeship—"art is long, life is short, judgment difficult, opportunities fleeting" (SE 9:303; HA 7:496) comes from "Vita brevis, ars longa, occasio praeceps, experientia fallax, iudicium difficile."[24] The preponderance of signals concerning health at the end of the initiation contrasts sharply with the emphasis on illness at the beginning of the scene, suggesting that Wilhelm enacts the story of his recovery as part of a general medicinal therapy.

THE VISUAL ARTS AGAINST NARCISSISM

In addition to drama, another of Wilhelm's childhood loves plays an important role in the Tower Society's treatment of Wilhelm's excessive introspection: the visual arts. Once again, the Tower Society chooses medicine from the creative world to treat Wilhelm's sickness. Once again, it uses something that originally panders to Wilhelm's narcissistic desires in order to combat that narcissism. And once again, it divides its therapy into two major parts, with the second part retelling the story of Wilhelm's development from introvert to extrovert.

The Tower Society knows both of Wilhelm's love of art and of the solipsism inherent in this love. The loss of his grandfather's art collection left Wilhelm as disconsolate as the loss of a lover: "Those were the first sad days of my life" (SE 9:37; HA 7:69). Later in the novel, this sense of emptiness overtakes Wilhelm and other characters after the shattering of a narcissistic love relationship, a fact that suggests that narcissism also informs this love of painting. The stranger, an emissary of the Tower Society, accuses him of only seeing himself in his favorite painting, that of the lovelorn prince (SE 9:38; HA 7:70). The stranger's sentiments clearly indicate that the Tower Society intends to fight Wilhelm's introversion, but this does not prevent the Society from using his narcissism against itself.

The painting of the lovelorn prince (reprinted on the cover of this book) depicts the court physician's discovery that the prince Antiochus Soter suffers from lovesickness on account of his father's bride. After the physician diagnoses Antiochus's love, he convinces the father, King Seleukos I of Syria, to give up his bride for the sake of his son.[25] In the eighteenth century, this story had recognizable medical value, because it showed the dependency of the body on the soul and the importance of psychic desires for physical well-being. Gaub, for instance, mentions it in his treatise of 1763, *De regimine mentis*,[26] a book that Goethe knew and recommended to the young psychiatrist Karl Wiegand Maximilian Jacobi, who frequently visited him in the 1790s.[27] It is therefore not surprising that the medical authorities of the Tower Society make such enthusiastic use of this painting in their program of philosophical medicine.

Although the Tower Society intends to use the painting to quash

Wilhelm's narcissism, they begin by encouraging him to find similarities between himself and the artwork. In fact, the stranger's accusation that Wilhelm's interest in the painting actually derives from the young man's self-interest perhaps motivates him to associate his life with it. The comparison does not, after all, make much sense at first glance: When the painting still belonged to the Meister family, Wilhelm was neither a prince, nor consciously interested in the wife of his father, nor lovesick. When the stranger admonishes Wilhelm not to look for himself in this painting, he perhaps subtly suggests precisely that course of action. In so doing, he takes the first step in his therapy of using Wilhelm's introspective love of theater to resocialize the young man properly. Such a therapy conforms with the eighteenth-century medical belief in the usefulness of illness in the struggle for health.

In the next passage to mention the painting, Wilhelm Meister himself finds a connection between it and his own experience. While under medical treatment, his youthful dreams reappear as he thinks of the beautiful Amazon: "[H]e also remembered the sick prince with the beautiful loving princess approaching his bed" (SE 9:139; HA 7:235). Once again, the comparison is daring. Wilhelm does not know that Natalie nurtures love for him just as Stratonike in the Plutarchian story harbors sympathies for the lovesick prince. Wilhelm's automatic identification of an unknown woman as the bride of the father of his alter ego and his incipient hope that she will one day be his are also thoroughly unjustified. The peculiar lack of justification for the connection between Wilhelm's life and this painting suggests that the Tower Society has a specific agenda in mind when the stranger proposes to Wilhelm that his interest in the picture is narcissistic.

Shortly after Wilhelm's visit to the Hall of the Past, Jarno shows uncharacteristic understanding, if not actual sympathy, for those who identify with artworks: "It is true that many of them are reminded of their own wretched deficiencies when they are in the presence of great works of art and of nature, that they take their conscience and morality with them to the opera . . ." (SE 9:352; HA 7:574). Jarno curtly describes such naive viewers and readers as "those poor devils, those human beings you speak of" (SE 9:352; HA 7:574), indicating that he cannot seriously be proposing projection and narcissism as a general form of art appreciation. Everything that he and the Tower Society say against introspection would contradict this. Instead, it seems more likely that Jarno defends, in Wilhelm's presence, people who find themselves in paintings when they are "poor devils," that is, when they are laden down with needs, cares, desires, and hatreds and need solace—or even medicine—in art.[28] He supports treating art as medicine when patients require it.

Finally, with a series of questions, Friedrich prods Wilhelm into seeing the meaning of the painting: "What's the name of that old goatee with the crown, pining away at the foot of the bed of his sick son? What's the name of the beauty who enters with poison and antidote simultaneously in her demure, roguish eyes? Who is that botcher of a doctor who suddenly sees the light and for the first time in his life can prescribe a sensible remedy, give medication which is a complete cure and is as tasty as it is effective?" (SE 9:371; HA 7:606). Friedrich's insistent emphasis on the physicians, prescriptions, medicine, and cures underscores the therapeutic nature of the painting. Moreover, like the stranger and Jarno, Friedrich encourages Wilhelm to find himself in this portrayal of the medical world, thereby seemingly encouraging his narcissism, but only as part of a long-range effort to cure him of his illness permanently.

Like the initiation scene, the Hall of the Past offers an explanation of Wilhelm's cure. In the hall, Wilhelm discovers, enshrined in art, a positive account of his own development. This story of his healing begins with a pictorial biography that specifically takes the importance of self-reflection into account when it begins with "that first delicate awakening of self with which the maiden delays drawing water while she gazes admiringly at her own reflection" (SE 9:331; HA 7:541). Although this cycle of paintings includes the narcissistic gaze at oneself in the water, it also clearly places this activity (1) in the realm of the feminine and (2) at the beginning of a career, which implies, since Wilhelm must "become a man," his need to overcome this introspection. Looking for himself in the art of the Hall of the Past, Wilhelm discovers that self-analysis must remain at the beginning of one's life.

Once again, the signs of success come rapidly. Immediately after Friedrich's forward question, the final barriers to Wilhelm's marriage with Natalie fall, and he can enter matrimony a "healthy" man. As will be seen in the next chapters, Wilhelm's marriage with Natalie shows that the Tower's creative therapies have in fact brought Wilhelm into society. The Tower Society has been able to use Wilhelm's initially narcissistic desires to see himself in drama, and the visual arts to cure him of that introspection.

8

Wilhelm's Lovesickness: Cross-Dressing and Homosexuality

Wilhelm's wounds, his obsession with the theater, and his narcissism can all be seen as symptoms of lovesickness, the disease that the philosophical physicians took so seriously.[1] Mignon's case and the Beautiful Soul's off-hand remark that love is a passion, "like all other sickness" (SE 9:220; HA 7:362), show that the novel agrees with its era's medicine in interpreting lovesickness as a disease, one naturally in need of a cure. The Tower Society operates on the assumption that Wilhelm is particularly in need of medical guidance in his affectional and romantic life.

THE ONE-SEX SYSTEM

Wilhelm's need for medical guidance in his love life has to do with the epistemic and social changes of the 1790s in Germany that *Wilhelm Meister's Apprenticeship* records so sensitively. According to Thomas Laqueur, one of the changes that took place in the eighteenth century was the decline of the "one-sex system." Concerning gender, Laqueur postulates that a "radical eighteenth-century reinterpretation of the female body in relation to the male" took place, largely emerging from a medical tradition.[2] Previously, from antiquity through the Renaissance and beyond, there was a "one-sex model," in which men and women were on a continuum, with women simply less developed than men and thus quite similar to boys.[3] Subsequently, however, in the "two-sex model," men and women became two "opposite and incommensurable biological sexes."[4] Under the one-sex model, it was considered possible, if not likely or desirable, for women to become men, which allowed for a gray area of indeterminacy that permitted a certain limited space for sexually odd, androgynous, cross-dressed, or transsexual

144

people. Under the two-sex model no such uncertainty or ambiguity between the sexes existed, for which reason clothing codes also became more and more strict with regard to gender. The Tower Society helps Wilhelm negotiate this difficult transition in gender relations.

The development of the two-sex system aligns with the transition Foucault sees from the ancient male love of boys to the modern love of women, a transition he suggests is recorded in an exemplary way in Goethe's *Faust*.[5] Since, as Kittler has noted, *Wilhelm Meister* picked up the developments in the bourgeois family with remarkably sensitivity,[6] it would not be surprising to find traces of the changes with regard to gender in Goethe's novel. Indeed, alongside an emergent two-sex model (to be discussed in the next chapter) appear remnants of the one-sex model, comprising the transvestite and hermaphroditic aspects of the story.

To summarize Laqueur's notion of the one-sex system: Previously, thinking on gender had been based on Galen, the pre-Christian Roman physician, who had in essence argued that women were simply "men turned inside out,"[7] inviting his readers to "turn outward the woman's, turn inward, so to speak, and fold double the man's, and you will find the same in both in every respect."[8] Testicles became ovaries, menstruation became hemorrhoids, and penises became either clitorises or vaginas, depending on the physician.[9] According to Galen, the main difference between men and women was that men had more body heat. The basic similarity of male and female bodies allowed women to become men by simply warming up. Women were therefore merely cooler than men on the heat continuum, or, in Laqueur's paraphrase, "[W]omen, whatever their special adaptations, are but variations on the male form, the same but lower on the scale of being and perfection."[10] In this tradition, women have the potential to develop toward masculinity, but are restricted from going all the way, while men can move up and down along the gender continuum. The Tower Society takes it upon itself to show Wilhelm how to move up and down this gender continuum in a salutary way.

THE SIGNS OF WILHELM'S LOVESICKNESS

Of the three wounds tallied up at the beginning of book 5 (SE 9:168; HA 7:282), all stem in one way or another from Wilhelm's more or less romantic relationships with women. Mariane's apparent betrayal produces the first bout of lovesickness, which eventually results in such symptoms as fever, tension, and fatigue (SE 9:41–42; HA 7:76–77).[11] Natalie voluntarily accepts responsibility for the attack of the robbers, because she and her family were the intended victims (SE 9:134; HA 7:227). In any case,

Wilhelm's love of her subsequently leaves him in a state of emotional and physical unrest: "In these circumstances neither his mind nor his body could be at rest, by night or by day" (SE 9:349; HA 7:570). The wounds caused by Aurelie's knife slashing are also the product of unhealthy emotional relationships between the sexes.

Wilhelm's lovesickness is also connected to the medical issues discussed in the previous chapter: his mania for the theater and his narcissism. The loss of Mariane induces significant psychic pain by causing Wilhelm to forsake the theater, a connection to which Wilhelm himself alludes when he wonders: "Was it simply my love for Mariane that made me so enthralled by the theater? Or was it love of art that made me so captivated by her?" (SE 9:165; HA 7:377). A similar linkage of lover and theater occurs when the narrator reports that Wilhelm finds Shakespeare as perfect as a young man finds his new girlfriend (SE 9:176; HA 7:293). The gunshot wound follows the hilarious and carefree performance of the duel between Hamlet and Laertes. Aurelie's knife slash also occurs in a dramatic milieu. The mania for the theater therefore belongs inextricably to the complex of physical wounds and lovesickness.

The story of Wilhelm's narcissism is also the story of his failed love affairs. His relationship with Mariane is compared to an echo (SE 9:30; HA 7:57); he quite literally echoes Mignon when he reconstructs her poetry (SE 9:83; HA 7:145-46). He goes to the count's castle, where he falls in love with the countess, in order to find out about himself (SE 9:88; HA 7:154). Similarly, his desire to marry Therese is also a product of his search for a mirror image.

Thus all of the problems discussed in the previous chapter can be seen in the specific "disease" of lovesickness and the Tower Society's treatment of that disease. Wilhelm's lovesickness manifests itself in a number of attitudes toward gender that the Society believes it must cure. The Society combats his attraction to androgynous transvestites and his incipient homosexuality, using the scientific and medical discourses that the eighteenth century was fashioning to establish and master new gender relationships.

THE BOTCHED CURE

One attempted treatment of Wilhelm's lovesickness comes early in the novel to give the reader an example of a botched cure. Werner, not a member but an affiliate of the Tower Society, performs the unsuccessful operation, which resembles the work of an incompetent dentist: "Wilhelm . . . left his friend in a disturbed and vexed state of mind, like someone having a defective but firmly rooted tooth grasped by a clumsy dentist, who vainly tries to dislodge it" (SE 9:33; HA 7:62). The dental metaphor reminds the reader of the medical nature of Wilhelm's problem and sets up Werner's activities as a foil for the Tower Society's successful cure.

Werner's discussions with Wilhelm make clear that the reader should not expect much of his work. After Werner declares, "I think there is nothing in life more sensible than making profit out of the follies of others" (SE 9:18; HA 7:36), Wilhelm replies, "I would think it a nobler pleasure to cure people of their follies" (SE 9:18; HA 7:37). Werner's mundane concern with profit prevents him from entering the ranks of the healers in the novel.

Against his era's medical advice, Werner uses direct argumentation, proof, and witnesses to cure one symptom of Wilhelm's lovesickness, his refusal to believe in Mariane's infidelity. Even after Wilhelm accepts the veracity of Werner's suspicions about Mariane, the young businessman continues his bad medicine, directly attacking the malignant passion with proof and stories: "Werner, of necessity the only person that Wilhelm could confide in, did all he could to pour fire and flame onto this hateful passion, the dragon in his entrails. The occasion was so apposite, the evidence so everpresent, that he made use of everything he heard in the way of rumors and stories" (SE 9:42; HA 7:77). Just as the priest's therapy causes Sperata to lose her sanity, Werner's treatment finally makes Wilhelm sick: "He did this so systematically and with such vehemence and savagery that he did not leave his friend one consoling moment of illusion, one escape hatch from his despair" (SE 9:42; HA 7:77). While Werner's rationalistic approach does not allow for "one consoling moment of illusion," Goethe and the Tower Society follow the new psychological medicine of the late eighteenth century, with its pious frauds that agreed with the fictions of the patient until he or she was ready to relinquish them.

The philosophical physicians, who liked to believe that nature was on their side, would be particularly interested in nature's use of sickness to combat itself. Thus the Tower Society records in the novel that nature used illness to grant Wilhelm a respite from Werner's medicine: "And so nature, determined not to lose a favorite son, afflicted him with sickness, so that he had, in his own way, time to breathe" (SE 9:42; HA 7:77). In *Poetry and Truth*, Goethe describes another situation in which a physical illness provided relief from psychological problems: "So I spent my days and nights in great unrest, in delirium and exhaustion, and it was actually a relief when this finally resulted in a rather violent bodily illness, so that a physician had to be called and every means taken to calm me" (SE 4:166; HA 9:216). Thus Goethe and the novel both seem to be granting illness a pharmaceutical power to heal, despite its fundamentally injurious nature.

CROSS-DRESSING AND ANDROGYNY

While Werner tries to repress Wilhelm's irrational behavior regarding Mariane, the Tower Society uses Wilhelm's disordered love to cure him of his lovesickness. The Tower Society's treatment of Wilhelm makes clear that it believes that, at the root, Wilhelm's lovesickness stems from his insufficient manliness. An important part of its program of socializing is its effort to develop his gender identity.

The most obvious symptom of Wilhelm's inadequate masculinity, in the mind of the Tower Society, is his fascination with transvestites of androgynous appeal. In the novel, androgynous, cross-dressed women exert a powerful attraction on the hero. Mariane's mannish attire lends her boyish good looks. Wilhelm tells Mariane that one of his first literary loves, Chlorinde in Torquato Tasso's *Jerusalem Liberated*, charmed him because of her androgynous nature (SE 9:11; HA 7:26). Wilhelm's acquaintance, the baroness, loves to disguise herself as a page boy or a hunter (SE 9:110; HA 7:188). One of the women to whom Wilhelm proposes, Therese, dresses frequently as a man, partly in order to impress the man whom she loves (SE 9:278; HA 7:454–55). And the woman whom Wilhelm finally does marry, Natalie, has haunted him as "the lovely Amazon" (SE 9:139, 314; HA 7:235, 513) long before he knows her personally. Goethe's own era found even more of the female characters androgynous: Aurelie, according to Schiller, is destroyed by her own androgyny,[12] and even Philine, of all characters, is, according to Jenisch, a "moral hermaphrodite."[13]

Fitting into this pattern as well, of course, is Wilhelm's attraction to Mignon, one of the most famous and influential androgynous and transvestite characters in German literature.[14] Although characters like Aurelie urge her to wear feminine clothing suitable for her sex, she insists on wearing boyish clothing. Neither Wilhelm (SE 9:50; HA 7:91) nor the surgeon (SE 9:149; HA 7:236–37) can determine her gender at first, while the narrator refers to her with pronouns of three different genders.[15] Her Italian heritage fits well with her cross-dressing, for, in his essay "Women's Roles on the Roman Stage Played by Men" (written in 1788, before the completion of the *Apprenticeship*), Goethe asserts that "the modern Romans have in general a special tendency to exchange clothes of both sexes in masquerades" (WA 1.47:270).

The many sumptuary laws proclaimed from the Middle Ages through the Enlightenment show that the classical era was not naive about representation. It knew that signs of clothing could be manipulated to disguise class or—increasingly more important—gender, but this possibility did not result in complete skepticism with regard to the system of representation;

rather, it resulted in watchful vigilance. Jarno mirrors this mentality in *Wilhelm Meister*, when he distinguishes between "dainty hermaphrodites," like the baroness, who merely appear to be men but do not possess manly virtues, and "real amazons," like Therese, who both appear and act masculine (SE 9:269; HA 7:439). While he warns of the possibility of subverting and misusing the semantic system of clothing as signifier for character, he does not fundamentally attack the validity of the union between clothes, body, and characters.[16]

Jarno's assertion that he can distinguish, not just between a cross-dressed woman and a biological man but between artificial hermaphrodites and real amazons, is comparable to the Tower Society's belief that it can ensure that its pharmakon, its *Bildung*, will cure and not poison. Just as the pharmakon disrupts the binarism between toxin and antitoxin, the transvestite pharmaceutically confuses male and female. In her analysis of the frequent occurrence of drag shows in socially conservative institutions, Garber suggests these institutions are using transvestism as "a version of the poison as its own remedy."[17] By showing the distance between the signifier (a woman in drag, say) and the signified (a man), the transvestite foregrounds representation in a way that challenges the notion of a perfectly transparent language. The Tower Society is playing with poison when it plays with cross-dressers: transvestism is a symbol for the breakdown of an entire semiotic system, yet the Tower Society hopes to manage it successfully in order to cure the system.

The Tower Society's use of medicine in its work with transvestites is additional evidence pointing to the pharmaceutical nature of the cross-dresser in *Wilhelm Meister*. Garber points out that frequently in transvestism the doctor is "the ultimate agent of discovery."[18] In *Wilhelm Meister*, Mignon is afraid to see the surgeon about her arm because "he had thought she was a boy" (HA 7:236-37). Actually, everyone knows about Mignon's gender status at this point except for the Tower Society: Jarno scornfully calls her a hermaphrodite, and the surgeon thinks she is a boy. But once the Tower Society fixes her gender as a girl passing for a boy, it uses her for its own gender constructions. Indeed, although it pathologizes her condition, regarding her as a kind of poison, it also medicalizes her in the sense that it turns her into a kind of medicine, a pharmakon. Despite her noxious androgyny, she becomes, like all the mannish women in the *Apprenticeship*, part of Wilhelm's cure.

Most of the transvestites in *Wilhelm Meister* are like Mignon in that they go from female to male. Goethe would almost certainly have known of some of the many examples of such behavior in the eighteenth century, behavior that was fairly common and becoming threatening to society. Whereas medieval and Renaissance sumptuary laws had been directed primarily at members of the bourgeoisie who attempted to dress in a way that was above their station, eighteenth-century laws tended to target women who dressed as men. While there was some admiration for women who were forced to take on a man's role in order to survive,[19] female-to-male cross-dressers were increasingly seen as dangerous or at least unsettling to the gender constructions developing in the era.[20] In England there were fifteen cases of women prosecuted for impersonating men between 1761 and 1815.[21] In Paris, an ordinance of 1800 strictly forbade female-to-male cross-dressing.[22] And in Germany, Catharina Margarethe Linck had been executed in 1721 for impersonating a man and marrying a woman.[23] Goethe's interest in the "gynocracy" of the "Bohemian Amazons" and the attendant male revolution against that assertion of power by women (WA 1.42:93–94) suggests his awareness of the anxieties that female insubordination could cause.

When the women in the novel cross-dress, they generally seem to take on male characteristics that go beyond clothing. Thus, at the beginning of the *Apprenticeship*, when Mariane enters her room dressed as an officer and confronts her servantwoman about the choice of her lover, she is at her most obstreperous and least ladylike. As Mariane puts aside her phallic "sword and plumed hat" (SE 9:1; HA 7:9), Barbara, the servantwoman, seizes the initiative, and attempts to change her charge into a woman by changing her wardrobe: "I have to see to it that you are soon in a long dress again . . . I hope that you will apologize, as a girl, for the harm you did me as a flighty officer: off with that coat and with everything underneath it. It's an uncomfortable costume, and dangerous for you, I see" (SE 9:2; HA 7:10). Barbara clearly believes that Mariane is developing manly qualities by wearing men's clothes. When Mariane subsequently contemplates her own heroic behavior in the face of rejection by a world that does not understand her illegitimate child, she agrees with Barbara that male character traits deserve masculine attire: "Don't I deserve to appear in men's clothing today? Haven't I been bold?" (SE 9:294; HA 7:480). Mariane's question implies that men's clothes are a reward for particularly courageous behavior. Similarly, the Beautiful Soul is pleased that her father considers her almost a son (SE 9:218; HA 7:360), and she is proud of her "manly defiance" (SE 9:230; HA 7:379). Later in the novel, Therese apologizes to Wilhelm that her men's clothing is "unfortunately . . . only a costume" (SE 9:273; HA 7:446). The novel presents the aspirations of these women to manliness as something to be proud of. This positive assessment of masculinity in women is generally what explains the affirmative treatment that women who cross-dressed as men received in the eighteenth century. Many eighteenth-century thinkers, such as, for instance, Kant, found it understandable that a woman would try to live as a man, because they assumed that everyone agreed that men were naturally better.[24]

The novel puts clear limits on these aspirations, however. Natalie, a wealthy and powerful "Amazon," could seriously destabilize the gender structures that, as shall be seen, the Tower Society is constructing. Therese's more overt cross-dressing, which first appeals to Wilhelm but which he then rejects, stands as an implicit warning—perhaps to Natalie, and certainly to readers—that women must not take their desires to become men too seriously, lest they be relegated to also-rans in the marriage contest.[25]

Male-to-female cross-dressing was also an important phenomenon in the eighteenth century. Edward Hyde, Lord Cornbury, the colonial governor of New York and New Jersey from 1702 to 1708, dressed as a woman, apparently in order to represent his relative and sovereign, Queen Anne.[26] His behavior attributes great power to the ability of clothes to represent concepts like the monarchy, even across the barrier of gender. More sensational still was the Chevalier d'Eon, born in 1728, who was, according to Garber, "the most famous transvestite in Western history." Born a man, trained as a spy, d'Eon cross-dressed until the English judicial courts and French royal court required that his gender identity be fixed. It was decided he was a woman. At the time, the world was astonished that a woman had passed as a man so long; when, however, d'Eon died in 1810 and the surgeon determined that he had anatomically normal male genitals, the world—including the surgeon and d'Eon's female companion, Mrs. Cole—was just as surprised to discover that a man had passed as a woman for so long.[27] So spectacular was d'Eon's story that Havelock Ellis wanted to name the phenomenon of cross-dressing "eonism."

Goethe mentioned the chevalier in a letter to his wife (23 September 1814; WA 4.25:41), but there were other cross-dressers even closer to home. August, the duke of Sachsen-Gotha and Altenburg (1772–1822), with whom Goethe had some contact and with whose older relatives Goethe had been quite close in the 1790s, dressed in women's clothes at his court.[28] In a coded way, Goethe refers somewhat negatively to the duke's proclivities when he complains about him as "problematic," "effeminate," and "pleasant yet disgusting."[29]

Goethe's contempt for the young Duke August suggests that he may have associated cross-dressing with a certain fear of emasculation. In any case, male-to-female cross-dressing in his works is often portrayed negatively. While many of the female characters in *Wilhelm Meister* aspire to male virtues by wearing masculine clothes, the male characters do not explicitly reciprocate so often. The closest thing to overt male transvestism takes place in Wilhelm's mind, when he sees Philine with a young person in an officer's uniform, who he somewhat irrationally assumes is his long-lost mistress, Mariane. Although he sees a man, he cries out: "[L]et us see the disguised girl!" (HA 7:337). In fact, the "girl" is Friedrich, dressed up as a girl dressed up as an officer. The Shakespearean quality of the multiple disguises points, incidentally, to the archaism in Friedrich's character that manifests itself in his baroque "foolishness" as well.

Otherwise, to find male characters in Goethe's oeuvre who explicitly don female attributes, one must leave the *Apprenticeship* and turn to, for instance, *Faust*, where the move is associated with shame. When Mephistopheles adopts the appearance of the Phorkyas he cries out: "Then I, o shame!, will now be called hermaphroditic!" (*Faust* 8029; SE 2:204; HA 3:243). Similarly, in the classical Walpurgisnacht, Thales expresses concern about the ambivalent gender of Homunculus:

> Auch scheint es mir von andrer Seite kritisch:
> Er ist, mich dünkt, hermaphroditisch.
>
> (HA 3:250)

> [Unless I err, there is another problem:
> He seems to be hermaphroditic.]
>
> (*Faust* 8255–56; SE 2:210)

This negative portrayal of male-to-female sex changes shows that Goethe's gender continuum—like that of many writers—often seems slanted against women. While it may be advantageous for women to don male clothing, it is shameful for men to lose their gender identity.

In his essay on the theatrical cross-dressing for the Roman stage, however, Goethe expresses himself positively about male-to-female transvestism. The cross-dressed actors inspire in him "a previously unknown pleasure" (WA 1.47:272), in fact, because they represent artifice, rather than crude reality: "In such a performance the concept of imitation, the thought of art, always remained lively and, through the clever play, only a sort of self-conscious illusion was produced" (WA 1.47:272). Goethe's analysis thus closely aligns with Garber's in that it is neither "fooled" by the cross-dresser, nor does it look "through" the cross-dresser to determine the real sex, but it appreciates the artifice of the performance of gender: "[O]ne experienced here the pleasure of seeing, not the thing itself, but its imitation, of being entertained, not by nature, but by art, looking at, not an individual, but a result" (WA 1.47:274).

The pleasure of seeing artifice, rather than nature, emerges partly because the consciousness associated with artifice can tell the audience more specifically about the nature of that which is depicted. For this reason, one learns more about femininity from the cross-dressed male actor than from a real woman, according to Goethe: "The youth has studied the characteristics of the female sex in its essence and behavior; he knows them and produces them as an artist; he does not play himself, but a third and actually foreign nature. We get to know this nature all the better because someone has observed and thought about it, and not the thing, but rather the result of the thing, is performed for us" (WA 1.47:272). In his essay on Roman cross-dressing, Goethe does not say whether he would find female-to-male cross-dressing so informative about masculinity as male-to-female cross-dressing is for him about femininity, but one of his favorite actresses in Weimar, Christiane Becker, née Neumann (also known as "Euphryosyne"), frequently played men's roles in the 1790s.[30] In 1791, she played a certain "Arthur" quite to Goethe's satisfaction (WA 1.35:19). In 1794, she not only played the role of Jacob in Iffland's "Old and New Time" ("Alte und neue Zeit"), but she actually delivered a prologue to the play, written by Goethe, in which she drew attention to her cross-dressing: "I'm supposed to be called Jacob? A boy?" (WA 1.13.1:164). In *Wilhelm Meister*, Goethe carries on the experiment of determining whether cross-dressed female characters can show Wilhelm Meister how masculinity functions, allowing him to learn to perform his gender.

Wilhelm benefits from the cross-dressing of the female characters, because he can specularly identify with their androgyny and learn masculinity from them. Thus he loves Mariane, dressed as an officer, because she mirrors—or, to use Goethe's word, echoes—him (SE 9:30; HA 7:57). Similarly, his mirror relationship with Mignon allows him to explore a whole range of emotions, variously identifiable as female, childish, or poetic. Further indication that Wilhelm mirrors these cross-dressed women is his attempt, identical to their own, to achieve masculinity by dressing up as a "real" man, the count. The baroness, who enjoys dressing up as "a page boy, or a huntsman" (SE 9:110; HA 7:188), encourages Wilhelm to follow her example, and dress up as the count. At this point in his development, he is therefore in a situation similar to the women, who are aspiring to manly power by wearing male clothing. The difference, of course, is that Wilhelm will be able to become a man.

The use of the semiotics and didactics of drag to allow Wilhelm to become a man is clearest in his relationship with Natalie, whom he first sees dressed in her (obviously male) uncle's coat, for which reason he calls her "the lovely amazon" through most of the novel. When he first sees her, he is lying wounded, tended by his similarly wounded mirror image, Mignon, and Philine, who serves as a caring, nurturing, maternal figure (SE 9:132–33; HA 7:224–25). He is thus in a childlike state of undifferentiated gender, mirroring androgynous characters and happy to view the woman with a man's coat as an androgynous amazon, or to speak psychoanalytically, a mother with a phallus.[31] Natalie, however, attempts to show him the importance of shedding his androgynous nature and becoming a man by handing him her phallus or avuncular coat (SE 9:135; HA 7:228). With this move, she reveals herself as a woman and dresses him up as a man.

The Tower Society uses Wilhelm's interest in androgynous characters to attract him to women like Natalie and allow him to develop the masculinity they desire for him, which demonstrates the basic homeopathic structure of the Tower Society's cures. For the Tower Society's male "patients," whose telos is manhood, this strategy offers great possibilities: they can move, via the symbolism of drag, from self-identification with androgynous women to self-identification as men. Cross-dressing becomes the mechanism through which Wilhelm can use a series of women for his own individuation and development. This makes his story of becoming a man a rich one, full of psychological complexity, while at the same time it clearly relegates the position of the female to that of a stage that one goes through.

The Tower Society thus uses the transvestite "as a figure for development, progress, or a 'stage of life,'" a strategy that Garber considers "to a large extent a refusal to confront the extraordinary power of transvestism to disrupt, expose, and challenge."[32] Garber repeatedly calls this looking through rather than at the transvestite;[33] the attitude corresponds to the notion of a transparent signifying system. Goethe, in his essay on women's roles in the Roman theater, shows his awareness of looking at the transvestite as an artistic phenomenon; the Tower Society is not so astute, however. Just as the Tower Society believes it can manage the pharmakons of art and language to get the cures it wants, so it attempts to use androgyny and cross-dressing to develop a strong man.

HOMEOPATHY AGAINST HOMOSEXUALITY

To most readers today, transvestism always has a touch of homosexuality, despite the repeated declarations of sexologists that the two phenomena are distinct. Particularly titillating is the possibility that relationships will turn out to be homosexual if the travesty continues too long or too successfully and makes its way into the bedroom. The eighteenth century seems to have shared this understanding of homosexuality, too. Alan Bray notes that, while Renaissance male-to-female transvestite prostitutes apparently wanted in fact to pass as females for mercenary reasons, "the transvestism of the eighteenth-century . . . was about homosexuality."[34] Terry Castle adds, "[T]o don the garments of the opposite sex was to enter a world of sexual deviance"; she suggests that the connection between sodomy and transvestism became quite common in the eighteenth century.[35] Randolph Trumbach's work has also shown that cross-dressing definitely distinguished the "mollies," or male homosexuals, and that some observers, like John Cleland, author of *Fanny Hill*, suspected that cross-dressed women probably had sex with other women.[36]

A great deal of evidence suggests that the eighteenth century was increasingly concerned with same-sex attractions, for a number of reasons.[37] Foucault argues that "homosexuality became a problem—that is sex between men became a problem—in the 18th century" because of the decline of the cult of friendship.[38] David Halperin specifically cites "the eighteenth-century discovery and definition of sexuality" as one of the temporal milestones allowing homosexuality to come on line.[39] Some of the elements that scholars have identified as contributing to the development of a new understanding of sexuality include the rise of medical, vs. religious, conceptions of sexuality[40] and the interiorization of societal constraints against homosexuality.[41] "[I]n the cities of northern Europe, especially in those like London, Paris, and Amsterdam, which had populations of half a million," these and other changes, such as urbanization, industrialization, and the rise of market economies[42] and bourgeois families, led to the appearance around 1700 of "a minority of markedly effeminate men whose most outstanding characteristic was that they desired to have sex only with other males."[43]

Germany was not far behind in its development of something like a gay male subculture. Joan de Jean has shown how classics, one of the first fields to discuss homosexuality in detail, was particularly important in the development of discussions of sexuality in Germany.[44] In the field of classics, one professor, Christoph Meiners (1747–1810) of Göttingen, whom Goethe refers to frequently in the course of his life (see, for instance, "Tag- und Jahreshefte 1801"; WA 1.35:107), felt it important to publish his "Observations on the Male Love of the Greeks."[45] Sometimes it was hard to distinguish between homosexuality as the object of these classicist discussions and a homosexual desire among the interlocutors of the discussion. Winckelmann's work, which Goethe of course greatly admired, was a prominent example of the homosexually colored discussion of antiquity that helped structure modern understandings of homosexuality.

Male homosexuality was said to permeate Berlin in particular. In 1782, an "Austrian officer"—generally said to be Johann Friedel[46]—wrote that the city was filled with homosexual men: "Almost no good-looking boy is safe from these gentlemen. As soon as they spot one, they chase after him like a stag in rut."[47] There were even bordellos catering to male homosexuals at the time: "You will find here houses that exist under the honorable title of boy establishment [*Knabentabagie*]," wherein one finds "a gathering of ten to twelve boys of various ages, men of various character at their sides; on each face womanly lust."[48] From this evidence, Steakley concludes that in Berlin "a fairly continuous homosexual subculture was in place by the late eighteenth century."[49]

An aura of homosexuality surrounded Frederick the Great.[50] The eighteenth-century traveler Honoré Gabriel Riquetti (1749–91), writing under the pseudonym of the Comte de Mirabeau, alleged that there were all-male orgies at Frederick's court, particularly among the "mignons" of Frederick's brother, Prince Heinrich (1726–1802).[51] In a chapter entitled "On Frederick's Alleged Greek Taste in Love," Zimmermann, who attended the king in his last days, defended him against the rumors about his sexuality, rumors that he nonetheless passed on: "Frederick lost much sensual pleasure through his distaste for women. But he obtained it again in his dealings with men and had retained from the history of philosophy that it was said of Socrates he had loved contact with Alcibiades."[52] Although certain modern readers might try to explain away such a passage merely as evidence of the cult of friendship, eighteenth-century readers like Zimmermann understood that the references to misogyny, excessive male bonding, and Socrates[53] amounted to libel. Later in the chapter, Zimmermann concedes the frequency of the rumors about Frederick: "It was rumored: 'He had really loved many of his pages, many an Antinous, many a beautiful youth, not as Socrates had actually loved the beautiful Alcibiades—but as the Jesuits, according to his own account, so often loved their beautiful pupils.'"[54] Just as he tries to save Socrates from his reputation as a pederast (while getting in a jibe at the Jesuits), Zimmermann tries to explain away Frederick's behavior. He develops a rather elaborate tale involving a venereal disease that required an operation on the king's private parts. The operation, referred to as "a ghastly cut,"[55] led to a deformation of the genitals that supposedly made the king too self-conscious to court women.

It is no surprise that a physician should analyze and solve the problem of the king's alleged homosexuality, because medicine was increasingly interested in the subject in the eighteenth century. Its concern with the mind and morals of its patients helped foster its interest in sexuality. Significantly, there is a rise of psychiatric commentary on sexuality. In a survey conducted between 1791 and 1794, H. B. Wagnitz reports that insane asylums are among the institutions incarcerating sodomites.[56] Wagnitz's numbers are small (0.5 percent of the inmates in Bayreuth were incarcerated because of *Sodomiterey*), but they indicate a slowly rising interest on the part of medicine in the formerly religious category of sexual deviance. Similarly, Karl Philipp Moritz's *Magazine of Experiential Psychology* records a number of instances of homoerotic love in a medical/psychological context. Some, such as the translation of H. Cardus's Renaissance memoirs, refer disparagingly to the "disgusting suspicion of pederasty,"[57] while others refer somewhat more tolerantly to a reciprocal love that differs from the sort that shows up in almost every eighteenth-century novel only in that both partners are of the same sex and that it is more consistently medicalized.[58]

Despite the tolerance evinced in some of the articles in Moritz's *Magazine*, the medical discussion of sexuality usually found homosexuality to be a pathological condition. In his *Essay on those Sicknesses that Arise from Self-Abuse*, Simon-André Tissot rages against female masturbation and particularly "the feminine disgrace which happens with the clitoris [*Küzler*]"[59]:

> Nature tends to play sometimes, and creates female personages of a sort who, because of the size of their clitoris and out of ignorance about its proper usage, fall into an abuse and want to play the man. Stimulated, they stimulate others and attempt to create hereby for themselves the pleasure of true intercourse. This sort of female personage hates men and is their enemy; they were not unknown to the ancients, who called them "tribates" (lewd women who perform shameful acts with their own sort) and divided them into various categories; writers also did not silently ignore these appellations and they attributed the establishment of this order to the young Sappho.[60]

As the passage from Tissot suggests, attacks on homosexuality often came within the framework of the massive eighteenth-century assault on masturbation. When they concerned male homosexuality, such attacks emerged from an obsession with semen that reflected both bourgeois interest in an economy of saving and a more generally phallocentric world. Already Boerhaave worried that "rash expenditure of semen brings on a lassitude, a feebleness, a weakening of motions, fits, wasting, dryness, fevers, aching of the cerebral membranes, obscuring of the senses, and above all the eye, a decay of the spinal chord, a fatuity, and other like ends."[61] Tissot cited the Roman authority Galen to show that the loss of one half an ounce of semen did more damage than the loss of forty ounces of blood.[62] Condemnations of male homosexuality came particularly in discussions of the misuse of semen. In 1729, for instance, the nineteen-year-old "victim" of two separate "fellatio attacks" subsequently died, apparently because of "exhaustion caused by the unnatural loss of semen."[63]

Moderation was of course the watchword for eighteenth-century medicine—nowhere more so than in the realm of sexuality. While excessive expenditures of semen were a health problem for eighteenth-century physicians, ascetic retention of semen was also dangerous. Some of the most virulent and open descriptions of homosexuality as a disease come in analyses performed by Zimmermann of the medical consequences of celibacy. When defending Frederick the Great, he suggested that Jesuits actually committed sodomitical sins that Socrates was merely alleged to have committed. In a passage of *About Solitude* that amounts to a polemic against Catholicism, he argued that the repression of the passions in the cloisters resulted in an explosion of irrational acts, including suicides, unnatural emissions during religious services,[64] castration, love madness, and pederasty. He cited a church father who lived in an age of great monasteries as noting that "pederasty was in his time so common that a youth could scarcely escape it."[65]

Once medicine began treating homosexuality as a disease in need of a cure, the pharmakon entered the picture, and with it literature. The emergence of a medical interest in homosexuality went hand in hand with a rising literary interest in the subject. A physician, Smollett, produced in *Roderick Random* one of the first "medico-moral" depictions in English literature of a homosexual subculture.[66] German literature also quickly recorded the phenomenon of homosexuality, particularly male homosexuality. In Christoph Martin Wieland's novel *Agathon* (first edition 1766), important as a prototype for the bildungsroman, several characters desire younger boys to serve as "Ganymedes."[67] Wieland's poem "Juno and Ganymede" is filled with humorous and lascivious passages of a rococo sort, which intimate a thorough knowledge of homosexual practices. Indeed, according to Gleim, the reproach went around in literary circles that it was from Wieland that German youth first heard about "Greek love," that is, homosexuality.[68]

Goethe was no exception to the eighteenth-century German literary trend of appropriating homosexuality as a theme. Although Gilman is generally correct when he observes that "Goethe's clearly autobiographical mode would have made the poetic representation of homoeroticism too immediate for his audience as well as himself,"[69] there are some places where Goethe becomes more audacious. In one couplet, Goethe coquettishly suggests that he is familiar with pederasty:

> Knaben liebt ich wohl auch,
> doch lieber sind mir die Mädchen,
> Hab ich als Mädchen sie satt
> dient sie als Knabe mir noch.

> (WA 1.53:16)

> [Boys I have loved as well,
> but I prefer the girls,
> if I tire of her as a girl,
> she can still serve me as a boy.]

Whether or not the couplet is autobiographical, it reveals that Goethe was familiar with same-sex sexual practices, as do a number of his literary works. For instance, in the "Book of the Cupbearer" in the *Parliament of East and West* (HA 2:89–99), Goethe works with some of the poems of the Persian poet Hafez that extol the beauty of boys. In addition, Goethe's translation of the passage in Benvenuto Cellini in which the Italian artist responds to Baccio Bandinelli's insult, "Oh, be quiet, you sodomite!," provides further evidence of the translator's knowledge of homosexual practices: "Oh, you fool, I said, you go beyond the limit! But would God that I understood such a noble art, for we read that Jupiter practiced it with Ganymede and here on earth the great emperors and kings are in the habit of doing the same; I however, a low and humble little person, wouldn't know how to reconcile myself to such a strange custom" (WA 1.44:196). Throughout Goethe's works, then, in all genres, Goethe expresses a willingness to handle, however gingerly, the theme of homosexuality.[70]

Goethe is famous for having declared late in life that "Greek love" was both in and against nature,[71] thereby granting homosexuality the pharmaceutical role of being both one thing and its opposite, a role that accorded well with homosexuality's new medical status. In general, Goethe uses homosexuality as a pharmakon, an antitoxic toxin. *Faust* provides a good example: Hints of Mephisto's homosexuality are sprinkled throughout *Faust*, culminating in Mephisto's besotted admiration for the bodies of the male angels in the final scenes. Nonetheless, Mephisto is necessary for Faust's development and salvation—his venomous sodomy is a cure for the play's hero.

In 1796, the same year in which he completed *Wilhelm Meister's Apprenticeship*, Goethe published the *Letters from Switzerland (Briefe aus der Schweiz)*, a collection of letters putatively from the youth of the protagonist of one of his other novels, Werther. It turns out that Werther, who of course kills himself because of a heterosexual infatuation with Charlotte, begins his erotic development with a homoerotic infatuation: "I arranged for Ferdinand to bathe in the lake; how splendidly my young friend is built! how proportionate are all of his parts! what a fullness of form, what a splendor of youth, what a profit for me to have enriched my imagination with this perfect example of human nature. . . . I see him as Adonis felling the boar, as Narcissus mirroring himself in the Spring" (WA 1.19:213). The allusions to Adonis and Narcissus—two beautiful mythological male youths fated to tragic deaths—obliquely confirms the homoeroticism of this passage. It is significant that at the same time that Goethe is completing his narrative of Wilhelm Meister's development into a heterosexual hero, he returns to one of his other heterosexual protagonists and places a homoerotic event at the beginning of his development.

In *Wilhelm Meister* homosexuality similarly appears as a kind of inoculation, causing a sickness that subsequently ensures a greater health. While there is a subtle hint of possible lesbianism or tribadism in Philine's affair with the "girl" (who turns out to be Friedrich), these allusions to homosexuality otherwise hover around the men in the novel, particularly Wilhelm. At least one male character besides Wilhelm can be construed as touched by a whiff of homosexuality—Philo, the beloved of the Beautiful Soul. The Beautiful Soul had fallen in love with him, but when he confessed certain things that he had withheld from her, she could "assume the worst" (SE 9:238; HA 7:392): "With infinite sadness of heart I saw in Philo some sort of counterpart to the hero of Wieland's novel *Agathon*, who had to repay the cost of his education in the sacred grove of Delphi with heavy overdue interest" (SE 9:238; HA 7:392). Subsequently in describing this catastrophe, the Beautiful Soul alludes to David and Bathsheba (SE 9:239; HA 7:393). In his commentary, Trunz implies that these confessions are sexual, and assumes that they are heterosexual (HA 7:776–77). David, however, is linked not only to Bathsheba but also to Jonathan. And Agathon is quite definitely linked not only to Danae, as Trunz emphasizes, but also to homosexual love, specifically in the Delphic groves that the Beautiful Soul mentions. As mentioned earlier, in *Agathon*, as in his other works, Wieland treats the subject of homosexuality. In one case, the protagonist, Agathon, who as a youth dreams of being loved by the gods like Ganymede, is homosexually abused by a priest disguised as Apollo in the groves of Delphi.[72] Homosexual abuse, rather than heterosexual activity, could therefore easily explain why Philo's confession prompts "experiences which were quite new" to the Beautiful Soul (SE 9:238; HA 7:392). Importantly, this touch of homosexuality causes the Beautiful Soul to realize that she is no better than he is and to recognize the evil within her. This process of self-recognition then contributes to her development. The poison of homosexuality is therefore part of her cure.

Wilhelm's attraction to officers, boyish Italian waifs, figures on horseback in greatcoats, and "comely young huntsmen" (SE 9:273; HA 7:446) seems to have a homoerotic component even if these androgynous characters turn out to be women—respectively, Mariane, Mignon, Natalie, and Therese. Such passages suggest that Wilhelm's interest in women dressed as men is actually an interest in women who are becoming men.

Mariane offers the earliest allusion in the novel to Wilhelm's homosexual component when she compares him to Jonathan, King David's intimate male friend. Mariane can easily transfer her love from Wilhelm's puppet of Jonathan to its owner: "It was Jonathan she loved. Him she treated with particular delicacy, and in the end transferred her cherishing embraces from the puppet to Wilhelm" (SE 9:5; HA 7:16). In comparing Wilhelm to Jonathan, Mariane links her beloved to a man whose love for another man, King David, was "passing the love of women" (2 Sam. 1:26). For eighteenth-century Christendom, Jonathan was a symbol of male-male love. To be sure, this love was not always perceived sexually, but it did indicate feelings strong enough that it certainly could cover and protect any man who wished to describe his homoerotic desire.[73] Thus, by playing Jonathan to Wilhelm's David, Mariane intuits the existence of the homoerotic energies in her beloved and attempts to mobilize them.

Mignon adds significantly to the air of homosexuality around Wilhelm. To begin with, for many eighteenth-century Northern Europeans, Mignon's Italian origins would be sexually somewhat suspect. G. S. Rousseau has shown how Italy was quickly becoming a Mecca for homosexuals in the eighteenth century.[74] Winckelmann's move to Rome points to the currency of this belief among German homosexuals, too.[75] Goethe also considered Italy a homoerotic environment, as his letter of 29 December 1787, to the duke of Weimar, Carl August, suggests. In this letter, he refers to "a remarkable phenomenon that I have seen nowhere as strong as here, that is the love of men amongst themselves" (WA 4.8:315). Goethe even invokes the trope of the "love that dare not speak its name" when he concludes, "It is a material about which can scarcely be spoken, let alone written" (WA 4.8:315). As Gilman notes, it is no accident that the *Italian Journey* is sprinkled with references to Winckelmann and Ganymede.[76] Much of Goethe's remaining oeuvre suggests strongly that Italy is associated with sexuality in his writing: the Roman Elegies and the Venetian Epigrams are examples. Particularly his translations suggest that this Italian sexuality is slightly queer. In addition to the Cellini translation that refers to sodomy, Goethe also translated one of Richard Payne Knight's travel journals to Sicily for inclusion in his study of Phillip Hackett, the Prussian artist who spent much time in Italy. While this journal does not mention sexuality in any particular way, Knight, who was infamous in the eighteenth century because of his *Discourse on the Worship of Priapus and its Connection with the Mystic Theology of the Ancients* (1786–87), was part of a homocentric and phallus-obsessed world of Northern European connoisseurs that vibrated with homosocial and homosexual tensions.[77] All of this suggests that in Goethe's world Mignon's Italian nature contributes to the queerness of her sexuality.

In addition, although editors of Goethe editions anxiously insist that "Mignon," like *Liebling*, could apply innocently to both men and women,[78] the name was, like Ganymede, a byword for a male homosexual prostitute in the late eighteenth century.[79] Gloria Flaherty's discovery of certain shamanic qualities in Mignon have homosexual as well as hermaphroditic connotations, too.[80]

Mignon's boyishness is particularly important because Wilhelm thinks he might have had sex with her and thereby caused her trauma. It has rarely been remarked that Mignon's androgyny brings Wilhelm perilously close to pederasty. While ambiguous sex with the epicene Mignon seems possible to Wilhelm, his heterosexual activities with Philine, the woman with whom he in fact did have intercourse that night, prove much more difficult for him to accept. Her kisses on the street embarrass him (SE 9:75; HA 7:133). When the supermanly stable master and Friedrich fight over her, he finds the men fascinating but refuses to honor her with a glance (SE 9:80; HA 7:141). Thus, rather than accept a sexual relationship with Philine, Wilhelm's consciousness shifts to less feminine substitutes like Mignon or his masculine rivals for her attention.

The most obvious instance of homoeroticism in the Wilhelm Meister story is the tale of the fisherman's son, which Goethe splices as a flashback into *Wilhelm Meister's Journeyman Years*, decades after the *Apprenticeship*, almost as if he intended to drive home the homosexuality of Wilhelm's youth for those who had ignored the subtler signs. Just as, in 1796, Goethe had added a retrospective homoerotic incident to the beginning of Werther's life, so, in the *Journeyman Years*, he adds a homoerotic flashback to the story of *Wilhelm Meister* that he first published in 1796. The story of the fisherman's son, with whom Wilhelm falls in love, is the only new incident that readers learn about Wilhelm's early life. Wilhelm tells the story himself, in a letter in which he excuses himself from his heterosexual duties of being with his wife, Natalie. As Eissler notes, the story is told haltingly; it is divided into several sections by dashes or asterisks in the text, suggesting its emotional weight.[81] Wilhelm is supposed to return from a visit to family friends by nightfall, "for it seemed utterly impossible to sleep anywhere but in one's own accustomed bed" (SE 10:285; HA 8:270). The parental concern about sleeping arrangements proves justified, because Wilhelm spends the afternoon with a new friend, "a boy to whom I had been especially drawn as soon as he had appeared" (SE 10:286; HA 8:271), in a sultry, sensual environment—learning to fish, which in this case turns out be a metaphorical activity. He is surrounded by dragonflies, for which his friend uses an unusual name, *Sonnenjungfern* (HA 8:272), literally meaning "sun virgins," suggesting that virginity is at stake. Eventually, he and his friend are both naked together in the water, overwhelmed by each other's beauty, and, after dressing again, exchange fiery kisses: "So beautiful was the human form, of which I had never had any notion. He seemed to look at me with the same attention. Quickly dressed, we still faced each other without veils. Our hearts were drawn to one another, and with fiery kisses we swore eternal friendship" (SE 10:287; HA 8:272). The scene has the same erotic implications as the one in the *Letters from Switzerland* in which Werther watches Ferdinand bathe. Even Trunz has to remark on the "soft erotic tones" of the "first friendship" (HA 8:636).[82] Within the narrative, the pastor's wife also suspects that something is wrong when she refuses to let Wilhelm take his new friend home, "quietly remarking that it was not proper" (SE 10:287; HA 8:272).

Eissler believes the situation is inappropriate because of the class differences between the two boys, but mythological allusions suggest that sexuality probably plays a role as well. When the fisherman's son dies, trying to rescue some wayward swimmers, Goethe links him to Hyacinth— a male lover of Apollo who is killed by Zephyr, who is also in love with the youth[83]—just as he had linked Ferdinand to other doomed, erotically charged male figures from Greek mythology. As his friend is dying, Wilhelm blithely falls in love with a girl with whom he walks in a garden where the beautiful hyacinths are past their prime. Goethe provides his readers with one flashback on Wilhelm Meister's youth to emphasize the importance of Wilhelm's male-male attraction at the beginning of his development. Like the hyacinth, this development is natural, but blooms early in the spring of the young man's life and passes away before the peak of the human cycle.

Although the flowers in the garden point to the fleeting nature of Wilhelm's homosexual desire, Wilhelm himself is of course still overwhelmed by the death of his friend when he sees "naked, gleaming white bodies, brilliant even in the dim lamplight" (SE 10:289; HA 8:275). Seeing his friend's body among the dead, Wilhelm floods "his broad chest with countless tears" (SE 10:289; HA 8:276). That these unending tears might be a euphemism for another, less easily mentioned bodily fluid, is intimated when Wilhelm admits: "I had heard something about rubbing being helpful in such a case, so I rubbed my tears in, and deceived myself with the warmth that I generated" (SE 10:289; HA 8:276). Like Rousseau's supplement, this rubbing arouses only deceptive warmth. The final indication of the erotics of this mortuary encounter comes when Wilhelm tries to resuscitate the dead boy, an effort that glides smoothly into memories of their kiss in the lake: "In my confusion I thought of blowing breath into him, but the rows of pearly teeth were firmly clamped shut, and the lips, on which our parting kiss still seemed to linger, refused the slightest sign of response" (SE 10:289; HA 8:276). The deathbed scene further emphasizes the erotic nature of the friendship between the boys.

This homoerotically charged episode is also closely related to medicine, as Wilhelm claims that it motivates his desire to become a surgeon. Even more importantly, the inoculative nature of this experience is made quite clear when, in the very same letter, Wilhelm reports that his father was an early proponent of inoculations against smallpox (SE 10:391; HA 8:278). This early homoerotic episode becomes a controlled exposure that makes him immune to the "disease" of homosexuality. Thus the pharmaceutical nature of homosexuality is linked to medicine, which is both the supplier of metaphors for Wilhelm's development and the product of that development.

Homosexuality is thus like transvestism and androgyny in the world of *Wilhelm Meister*. All are tolerated, like disease, at the beginning of development, as a phase that leads, by a pharmaceutical, or inoculative, logic to gender division. Rather than being directly repressed, such tendencies are confronted homeopathically. In the *Apprenticeship* the Tower Society not only tolerates Wilhelm's relationship with Mignon but also introduces Wilhelm to Therese and Natalie when these women are in men's clothing. It uses androgynous cross-dressers who appeal to incipient homosexual desires in Wilhelm to bring him to the heterosexuality that it considers healthy.

9

Building a Family Out of
the Two Sexes

While the Tower Society uses homeopathic methods to combat aspects of Wilhelm Meister's gender identity and sexuality of which it disapproves, it also offers positive models for the goals that it would like to instill into its ward. The Society attempts to direct Wilhelm away from his homosexual love of transvestites toward a love of characters who complement, rather than mirror, him in familial structures. Specifically, they want him to develop relationships with other characters based on the model of the husband and the father. Whereas they had used the homoerotic attractions against themselves in order to correct any wayward tendencies in Wilhelm Meister, they use art to direct Wilhelm toward their final, heterosexual goals.

THE TWO SEXES

In promoting a view of the two sexes as complementary and utterly different, the Tower Society participates in the "radical eighteenth-century reinterpretation of the female body in relation to that of the male" that Thomas Laqueur has documented.[1] Just as a physician had articulated the one-sex model of humanity, medicine played an important role in changing the gender paradigms. The eighteenth-century vitalist belief in the unity of mind and body paved the way for an anthropology that allowed genitals and other biological facts to have an important role in determining psychology, socialization, and appropriate behavior for members of both sexes. Much of Stahl's work had specifically to do with feminine maladies, for the function of menstruation and its connections to psychological illnesses had been a major question in medicine since Harvey's discovery of the circulatory system in 1628.[2] From 1748 to 1752, Stahl's student Johann Storch published a study of women's diseases consisting of eight books in nine volumes.[3]

Anatomy played an important role in the further medical solidification of the two-sex system. In 1788, the German anatomist Jakob Ackermann called for a thorough study of the gender-determined aspects of every facet of the body. Soon medical anatomists like Goethe's friend Samuel Thomas von Soemmerring were searching for sexual difference in skeletons. After analyzing this anatomical research, Londa Schiebinger concludes, "[B]y the 1790s, European anatomists presented the male and female body as each having a distinct telos—physical and intellectual strength for the man, motherhood for the woman."[4]

The two-sex system also had repercussions in medical thinking on mental health, as well. Rather than men and women being on a continuum of susceptibility to madness, they were prone to incommensurable, completely different, diseases. As early as 1732, Thomas Dover had divided hypochondria and hysteria on the basis of gender distinctions.[5] Both Thomas Arnold and Samuel Tissot emphasized the connections between menstruation and madness, particularly hysteria.[6] Carl Friedrich Pockels, the coeditor of Moritz's *Magazine of Experiential Psychology*, went on to produce a five-volume study of the female sex and a four-volume one of the male sex.[7] In general, women were considered especially likely to go mad, partly because of biological facts such as menstruation and partly because of social constraints that prevented them from getting enough movement.[8] This thinking became increasingly important in the nineteenth century, when, as Elaine Showalter writes, psychiatrists saw their "task with respect to women as the preservation of brain stability in the face of almost overwhelming physical odds."[9]

While women were especially prone to poor mental health, the sexual act was particularly dangerous for men,[10] because of the incredible rarity and value to the body of semen, for which reason many physicians argued that men should determine when intercourse takes place. Concerning when the sexual act should happen, one man writes: "I also believe that it is easy to perceive nature's distinct signal that absolutely no deliberative vote [on the incidence of the sexual act] should be accorded woman—on account of her overpowering charms, her readiness, which is less damaging to her, and her most beautiful virtue, her modesty."[11] As Laqueur has argued, it was the physicians of the late eighteenth and early nineteenth centuries who determined that women did not need to or were not even able to have orgasms. One corollary of this thinking was that women, being less sexual, should find it easier to be more faithful.[12] Thus, the medical rethinking of the unity of mind and body allowed for physicians to distinguish "scientifically" between the psychology of men and women and thus to dictate the "healthiest" behavior for the two genders.

Of course, these new eighteenth-century gender distinctions appear not only in medicine. As Schiebinger writes, "[B]y the 1790s the theory of sexual complementarity had swept Europe and passed, in some cases, into national legislation."[13] Such thinking about the complementary nature of gender is evident in Rousseau's writing, particularly in *Emile*, in which gender-specific systems of education are proscribed for boys and girls.[14] In Germany these beliefs resurface in Kant's alignment of men with science and reason and women with feeling and sense,[15] in Schiller's essays on feminine grace *(Anmut)* and masculine dignity *(Würde)*,[16] and in Fichte's speculations on the necessity for a masculine, rational, active component and a feminine, loving, passive component in a complete family.[17] The family itself helped strengthen the new set of gender distinctions, because this "polarization of sexual stereotypes" resulted from the rise of the bourgeois family—between 1780 and 1810, according to one estimate—consisting of a relatively small, self-contained unit, in which the father worked away from home while the mother, in the absence of large numbers of relatives or servants, took care of the children.[18]

All of these broader developments in the gender divisions of the eighteenth century worked to create a sense of fragmentation and lack in individuals. Industrialization and capitalism resulted in the alienation of workers from their products. At home, as documented by, for instance, the *Apprenticeship*, the rise of the bourgeois family created a strong bond to the mother for many children born into the new society. The inevitable oedipal breakage of this mother-child bond produced a sense of loss. The gender divisions themselves, based on the notion of complementarity, make sure that every man feels he needs a woman and every woman a man. This sense of fragmentation and its heterosexual cure should turn up in the *Apprenticeship*.[19]

In this context, androgyny becomes a yearning for a mythic, lost wholeness. Plato's *Symposium*, with its story of prehistoric, androgynous wholes that split up into men and women and Carl Gustav Jung's argument that the hermaphrodite represents the perfect human[20] both show the long tradition behind this interpretation of androgyny as wholeness. Many of Rousseau's early works, which use androgynous figures as symbols for strong wholeness, indicate that androgyny was increasingly used to combat the sense of fragmentation and loss in the eighteenth century.[21] This mythic sense of a lost wholeness shows up in the *Apprenticeship*'s nostalgia for the doomed characters like Mignon.

LEARNING TO BE A HUSBAND

Although, as the previous chapter showed, traces of an older one-sex system remain in the transvestism and androgyny of *Wilhelm Meister*, overall the Tower Society endorses the emerging two-sex system.[22] Because the Tower Society ardently subscribes to this new view of the complementarity of the sexes, Wilhelm must learn to accept and love the alterity of women.[23] It is particularly consistent in attributing lack and inadequacy to its male characters who feel most strongly the loss of the mythic wholeness of androgyny. It cures these characters of their sense of fragmentation by offering the promise of heterosexual complementarity.

Philine offers Wilhelm his first real chance to appreciate alterity. Whereas Mignon attempts to mirror every aspect of Wilhelm, even denying her own gender, Philine, a happy "non-narcissist,"[24] makes no attempt to imitate him. The only female character who never copies his attire by wearing male clothes, she bears little resemblance to Wilhelm.

Wilhelm, however, does not take advantage of the chance to appreciate her otherness. He learns to love her only by mimicking other men, showing that narcissism structures his psyche at the beginning of the novel. His mirror image comes not from Philine, but from Wilhelm's rivals, as the scene in which Friedrich and the stablemaster fight for Philine shows: "What he saw was an exaggerated display of his own self, for he too had been consumed by fierce jealousy, and if his sense of propriety had not prevented him, he too would have indulged his wildest fancies, gleefully and maliciously harmed his beloved, and challenged his rival. He would gladly have obliterated everybody who seemed to be there just to exasperate him" (SE 9:80; HA 7:140). Wilhelm finds, in the masculine stablemaster and the passionate Friedrich, images of male desire that appeal to him far more than the object of that desire, which he too would like to wound.[25] He therefore diligently avoids looking at Philine and concentrates exclusively on the two men fighting for her: "The duel was for Wilhelm an additional externalization of his own feelings. He couldn't deny that he himself would have liked to direct a rapier, or still better, a sword, at the stablemaster, although he soon observed that the man was a far better fencer than he was. But he did not deign to cast on Philine a single glance . . ." (SE 9:80–81; HA 7:141). Although Wilhelm is still narcissistically infatuated with images—not of Philine, who eludes his memory as quickly as she leaves his bed, but of his male competitors for her—he moves in a direction approved by the Tower Society by imitating men who love women as wives.[26] His narcissism here functions as a means of his cure.

The countess, whose adoption of Philine at the castle suggests that she is a higher class version of the same principle, also inspires a similar sort of triangulated desire, in that Wilhelm looks to her husband for a sense of masculine identity. Wilhelm imitates the count by dressing up in his clothes, literally stepping into the shoes of the father. The count discovers Wilhelm by glimpsing him in a mirror (SE 9:111; HA 7:190), reinforcing the whole narcissistic tone of this episode. This kind of mirroring helps him learn to imitate men who love women for their alterity rather than for their specularity.

The Tower Society builds upon these developments by using its artistic therapy to instill the hoped-for desire in Wilhelm's mind. As shown earlier, the paintings of the Hall of the Past have a salutary effect on Wilhelm's narcissism, which the Tower Society is treating (SE 9:332; HA 7:541). He likes them because they tickle his narcissistic fantasy by relating his own story, but also because they offer an escape from solipsism. Rather than merely finding a static depiction of himself in the Hall of the Past, he sees a possible present and future (SE 9:331; HA 7:541). The present and the future consist not in Wilhelm as narcissist, gazing at himself in the well, but as a father with a wife: "This is how everything was, and this is how everything will be. . . . The picture of this mother clasping her child will survive many generations of happy mothers. Some father in a future century will delight in this bearded man casting aside all seriousness and joking with his son. Bashful brides will sit like that one for all time, silently asking to be consoled and persuaded; impatient like this one, all bridegrooms will stand, listening to find out when they may enter" (SE 9:331; HA 7:541). These models set Wilhelm's thoughts moving toward the Tower Society's ideal of the family, an ideal that, despite Wilhelm's exclamations about its timelessness, in fact corresponds to a newly arising bourgeois familial conception, based on the two-sex model.

After the visit to the Hall of the Past, the Tower Society uses Therese as a teacher to provide Wilhelm with more direct help in developing the attitude toward the two sexes that they consider appropriate. She had herself undergone a transition from a narcissistic love of a parent to an understanding of the complementary love of spouses,[27] so Wilhelm could find her especially approachable. Once again, the principle of the pharmakon emerges, as her sickness turns out to be useful in his cure.

Therese's first love is as introspective as Wilhelm's. In a precise analogy to his case, she finds her first mirror image in her father. Just as Wilhelm has a somewhat strained relationship with his father, Therese dislikes her mother, whose dissolute life allows for loose morals and inconstancy: "She was impulsive, erratic, with no concern for her household nor love for me, her only child . . . the delight of the circle she gathered around herself. Her circle was certainly never large, or did not remain so for long, and consisted mainly of men . . ." (SE 9:273–74; HA 7:447).[28] While Wilhelm makes up for his tense paternal relationship by having a close relationship with his mother, Therese believes her father differs significantly and positively from her mother (SE 9:273; HA 7:447). Typically for the narcissist, Therese misapprehends the situation, because her father is the one, according to the abbé, who commits adultery right under the nose of his spouse (SE 9:343; HA 7:560). Nonetheless, she identifies with her ideal version of her father, in essence denying her own gender, as Mignon had done with Wilhelm (SE 9:274; HA 7:447). A gaze into his eyes fuels a mirror fantasy: "When I looked into his eyes, it was as though I was peering into my own self. For it was in the eyes that I resembled him most" (SE 9:274; HA 7:447).[29] Eventually, she gets to live entirely alone with her father, but this happy situation does not last long, because he suffers a stroke (accurately described),[30] loses his ability to speak, and dies, leaving behind a testament that bequeaths everything to his wife, seemingly repudiating his love for his daughter (SE 9:276; HA 7:450).

The ruins of Therese's specular relationship with her father leave her prepared for the lesson that she learns from Lothario: Men and women must be fundamentally different, and love each other because of those differences. In a long passage, Lothario insists that, while disharmony epitomizes the masculine world of politics and business, the housewife has a true internal autonomy: "[M]an . . . for the sake of some goal he never attains, . . . must every moment abandon that highest of all goals: harmony within himself. But the sensible housewife really governs, rules over all that is in the home" (SE 9:277; HA 7:452). This new sense of identity does not emerge from a sense of unity and oneness with the beloved, but from a strong sense of difference between the genders.

By the time Wilhelm meets Therese, he, too, wants to base his love on difference. Whereas he perceives his own life story as a constant state of confusion, a string of "one mistake after another, one false step after the other" (SE 9:273; HA 7:446), he views her life as a unified whole: "Your appearance, your whole nature, and everything around you, show that you have reason to be satisfied with the life you have led, its clear and steady progress, with no time wasted, and no regrets to labor over" (SE 9:273; HA 7:446). Therese smilingly protests that he should listen to her tale before he makes such conclusions. After he hears her out, however, he repeats his praises of her steadfastness: "He admired Therese for not feeling any need to change her way of life despite the unexpected sad change in her expectations. 'How happy those are,' he said to himself, 'who do not have to reject the whole of their past life in order to accommodate themselves to fate!'" (HA 7:449). Wilhelm's opinion about Therese's life story unconsciously echoes the opinions that Lothario had expressed to Therese about women in general—that they possess an autonomy that Wilhelm lacks, as do, according to Lothario, all men.

Much like Lothario, then, Wilhelm chooses to ask for Therese's hand in marriage precisely because of her differences. She has qualities that he lacks, but that his son needs. Thus, he attempts to construct a family based on the models that Therese reported Lothario as giving and similar to the ones portrayed in the Hall of the Past: "[He felt that] he must now find a mother for the boy, and he could not find a better one than Therese . . . a wife and companion like her seemed the only possible person to whom he could safely entrust himself and his loved ones" (SE 9:309; HA 7:504). Wilhelm is still searching for a mother at this point, but now he needs a mother for his son, rather than for himself. Having learned the Tower Society's vision of the family from Lothario, Therese, and the Hall of the Past, he accepts it as his own desire.

Both Lothario and Wilhelm ascribe to femininity a kind of wholeness that this era also attributes to androgyny, for which reason it is not surprising that the women in this novel are able to cross-dress, as mentioned in the previous chapter, and achieve a limited sort of masculinity, while the reverse is more difficult for the men in the novel.[31] Perhaps because this androgynous wholeness must be illusory, according to the newer anthropology of complementarity, both Therese and Wilhelm plunge into the same sort of desperate melancholy that afflicts such characters as the Harper and Mignon when their relationships fail. Therese utters words of uncharacteristic pessimism and despair as she watches her marriage plans disintegrate: "I am very upset . . . I fear we are all being deceived, and in such a manner that we shall never straighten things out" (SE 9:329; HA 7:537). Wilhelm also has a severe relapse at the close of the relationship with Therese. Desperate for maternal affection again, he seeks a mother in his own son: "'Come, dear boy,' he said to his son . . . , 'may you be and remain everything for me. You were given to me in place of your dear mother, you shall replace that second mother I had intended for you; now you have a larger gap to fill. . . . Come, son! Come, brother-man [*Bruder*], let's saunter about [*hinspielen*] in the world, without any particular goals, as well as we can!'" (SE 9:349; HA 7:564). The translation "brother-man" diminishes the ambiguity of *Bruder;* additionally, the translation of "saunter" for *hinspielen,* related to *spielen* (to play), makes Wilhelm's sentiments seem less childish and regressive than they are. The change in his address from "son" to "brother" shows his regression into childhood behavioral patterns, paralleling Mignon's confusion of "beloved" and "father" in "Know you the land." At this point, plagued by mental and physical restlessness, Wilhelm has an acute sense of the meaninglessness of life: "[H]e could see the whole chain of his life, but at the moment it lay in pieces which would not join together again" (SE 9:349–50; HA 7:570). Near the end of the *Apprenticeship* the situation becomes so bad that Wilhelm, like the Harper and the count before him, puts his own existence into question: "He became so lost in these lugubrious reflections that he sometimes seemed to himself like a ghost, and even when he was feeling and touching objects outside himself, he could hardly resist the sense of not knowing whether he was alive or not" (SE 9:350; HA 7:571). This principle of dissociation from the real world is characteristic for narcissism as well as for many of the mental illnesses of the late eighteenth century.[32] Wilhelm's restlessness, despair, and disbelief all make clear that his condition is a serious illness.

Wilhelm's final relationship with Natalie is the Tower Society's idea of a cure. Although many critics regard Wilhelm's marriage as beneficial, Helmut Ammerlahn is probably the first to refer to it specifically as a "cure."[33] In her first incarnation as an amazon, Natalie, like Therese, functions as a medicine against Wilhelm's excessive introspection, because Natalie's initial attraction for Wilhelm stems from her amazonian nature.[34] Like the princess in the painting of the lovelorn prince, whose eyes, according to Friedrich's innuendo-ridden speech at the end of the novel, contain both *"Gift und Gegengift"* (HA 7:606) [poison and antidote] (SE 9:371), Natalie first appeals to Wilhelm's narcissistic side before curing him of introspection. Wearing male clothes when he first sees her (SE 9:134; HA 7:226), she belongs to the category of women with whom he has mirroring relationships. As noted earlier, she quickly signals her intention to cure him of this desire for the same by giving her masculine garb to him (SE 9:135; HA 7:228).

Later, he confuses Natalie's handwriting with that of her sister, the countess (SE 9:311, 313; HA 7:508, 510), putting Natalie into the category of women who inspire the triangulated desire that causes Wilhelm to imitate their beloveds. And, indeed, at this point Wilhelm feels that only Lothario deserves Natalie (SE 9:273; HA 7:445), while Natalie herself expresses her unique and overwhelming love for her brother (SE 9:330; HA 7:538). Natalie comes closest to desiring a mirror image in the passage where she tells Wilhelm that her brother alone can provide her with a sense of wholeness and completion: "[M]y life is so intensely bound up with that of my brother, that when he suffers pain, so do I, and the joys he experiences are what gives me happiness. I can truly say that only through him have I learnt that the heart can be moved and uplifted, that there is joy and love in the world, and feeling which brings contentment beyond all need . . ." (SE 9:330; HA 7:538). These signs suggest that Wilhelm at this point loves her as a way of identifying with Lothario, just as he had loved Philine in order to be more like the masculine stablemaster.

As Wilhelm learns masculinity from the stablemaster, he learns to love women from Lothario. Jane K. Brown has noted that a "Lothario" was a womanizer throughout the eighteenth century, at least since a character by that name had appeared in *The Fair Penitent* (1703) by Nicholas Rowe (1674–1718).[35] Daniel Jenisch's scornful reference to Lothario's "chasing after, crawling around women" shows that Goethe's contemporaries believed that this particular "Lothario" definitely lived up to his name.[36] Some comment on Lothario's behavior is certainly warranted, given that, within fifty pages, the reader learns of romances with seven women conducted by the baron: Aurelie (SE 9:258; HA 7:422), Lydie (SE 9:261; HA 7:427), another unidentified "lady" (SE 9:263; HA 7:429), Therese (SE 9:269; HA 7:441), Therese's mother (under the guise of Frau von St. Alban; SE 9:280; HA 7:458), his tenant (SE 9:284; HA 7:464), and her daughter (SE 9:288; HA 7:466). If the Tower Society wants to teach Wilhelm to love women, it has certainly found an experienced teacher in Lothario. By the end of the novel, Wilhelm transcends his teacher and loves Natalie as the missing element in his family—his wife and his child's mother.

In order to understand the cure that Natalie offers, it is necessary to examine her way of loving. Rather than relying on identification with others, she complements them. Natalie's relationships with others rely on the assumption that a fundamental flaw characterizes human nature. She tells Wilhelm: "I would almost be inclined to say that it is better to err because of principles than to do so from arbitrariness of nature, and my observation of human beings tells me that there is always some gap in their natures which can only be filled by a principle expressly communicated to them" (SE 9:323; HA 7:527). This absence in human nature, requiring rules and laws, determines her view of humanity. The expressly communicated principle does not always fill the gap in human nature correctly, she admits, because some principles can mislead: "'I have always thought,' said Natalie, 'that our principles are merely supplements to our existence. We are all too ready to give our faults the semblance of valid principles'" (SE 9:346; HA 7:565). Nonetheless, according to Natalie, laws, principles, and concepts—regardless of their good or bad effects—are the supplements, or pharmakons, that give people identity and plenitude.

This assumption implies that other people cannot provide one with a full image of oneself. Natalie therefore uses the empty space, the absence, that she sees in human nature as the mold in which she casts her own identity. She thrives on the chance to fill gaps and correct human error. Her uncle equates her nature with that which the outside world lacks: "Natalie can truly be said to be in a state of bliss on this earth, for her nature never demands anything but what the world desires and needs" (SE 9:330; HA 7:539). The text provides numerous examples of Natalie's desire to alleviate society's needs with clothes for the poor (SE 9:254; HA 7:418), medical care for the wounded Wilhelm (SE 9:133–39; HA 7:226–36), or appropriate ideals for children: Therese quotes her as saying, "[I]f we just take people as they are . . . we make them worse; but if we treat them not as they are but as they should be, we help them become what they can become" (SE 9:326; HA 7:531). Natalie tries to be the presence for the absence in

human nature, the fulfillment of every wish, the good supplement to existence. More specifically, this aspiration to be what her society lacks means
that she tries to differ from that which she loves.

Natalie's desire to fulfill Wilhelm's needs prompts her decision to marry
him. Friedrich's prediction that she will not marry until someone lacks a
bride proves true: "I don't believe you will marry until some bride or other
is missing, and you, with your customary generosity, will provide yourself
as a supplement to someone's existence" (SE 9:346; HA 7:565). The need
that Natalie can fill is Wilhelm's need for a mother for his child. From the
first episode in which he meets Natalie formally for the first time, when
Felix slumbers softly between them (SE 9:314; HA 7:513), to her final
decision to marry Wilhelm, which is precipitated by Felix's illness (SE
9:372; HA 7:609), the text repeatedly emphasizes her excellent qualities as
a mother for Wilhelm's son. Natalie therefore provides Wilhelm with a
new model for love. Rather than mirroring him, she strives to be what he is
not. She embodies the new spirit of complementarity in gender relations.

Friedrich's comparison between Wilhelm and Saul, the son of Kis, who
goes out in search of his father's she-asses and ends up a king, neatly sums
up the Tower Society's account of Wilhelm's development.[37] Saul had been
an important element in Wilhelm's personal mythology ever since he staged
a puppet show of the David story. As a child and as a young man, Wilhelm
identifies with David (SE 9:3; HA 7:13), while Mariane favors Jonathan
(SE 9:5; HA 7:15–16). Of course, this bodes poorly for the fate of their
relationship. It also indicates that Wilhelm still associates himself with the
generation of the children. By the time Wilhelm reaches the Hall of the
Past and sees paintings that quite possibly refer to Saul's progress,[38] he
finds Saul's life to be one of general applicability. At the end of the novel,
it becomes clear just how applicable Saul's story is to Wilhelm. Just as
Saul went out looking for his father's she-asses, Wilhelm unwittingly begins his search for himself by looking for the female who, in the Tower
Society's vision of the family, belongs to his father—his mother. Through
this search he outgrows his adolescence and serendipitously discovers a
real sense of identity as the head of his own family.

LEARNING TO BE A FATHER

Just as the Tower Society had used the art in the Hall of the Past to
teach Wilhelm about the alterity of women and the role of the husband, it
uses art, specifically *Hamlet*, to mold Wilhelm into a father.[39] The news of
the death of Wilhelm's father at the beginning of the fifth book (SE 9:170;
HA 7:284) sets the stage for Wilhelm's performance of Shakespeare's play,

in which Wilhelm begins to understand the dynamics of father-son relationships and familiarize himself with the role of the father.

In its rendition of the play, the novel emphasizes Hamlet's relationship
with his father, especially the scenes in which Hamlet and the ghost of his
father converse. The ghost reminds Wilhelm of his father: "Wilhelm thought
it [the voice] sounded like that of his own father" (SE 9:195; H 7:322).
This encounter with the ghost provokes "these mysterious feelings and
memories" (SE 9:195; HA 7:323) that cause Wilhelm to lose control of
himself on the stage and thereby to act even better than usual. Like Aurelie,
Wilhelm responds with theatrical creativity to his emotional crises.

The initiation ceremony continues this dramatic therapy, also with the
effect of helping Wilhelm make contact with the world of fathers. When
the ghost reappears during this scene in the tower, he makes clear that the
experience on the stage has an effect on Wilhelm Meister's actual life: "'I
am your father's ghost,' said the figure in the frame, 'and I depart in peace,
for all I wished for you has been fulfilled more than I myself could imagine'" (SE 9:303; HA 7:495). The ghost's "I" could possibly refer to several
characters: Wilhelm's father, the ghost of Hamlet's father, or the actor who
portrays the ghost—according to Jarno, the abbé or his twin brother (SE
9:338; HA 7:551). If the abbé or his twin brother is speaking for himself
when he states that his wishes for Wilhelm Meister are better fulfilled than
he could have hoped for, then the Tower Society implies that, when it helps
Wilhelm put on a spectacular performance of *Hamlet*, it has cured him of
more than his obsession for the theater. It turns out that, in accordance with
the rules of eighteenth-century dramatic therapy, precisely this play and
this encounter with the ghost help Wilhelm Meister by allowing him to act
out his relationship with his father.

The indication of the success of this therapy comes quickly. As soon as
Wilhelm has read through enough of the Hippocratic "Certificate of Apprenticeship," he requests permission to ask a question concerning the identity of Felix's father. The abbé responds enthusiastically: "Praise be to you
for asking that question! . . . Hail to you, young man. Your apprenticeship
is completed" (SE 9:304; HA 7:497). Immediately, the abbé presents
Wilhelm with Felix, who emerges from behind the scenes: "Take unto yourself this lovely child from our hands, turn around, and dare to be happy"
(SE 9:304; HA 7:497). The usage of the word *Heil* (hail) connotes healing.[40] The abbé's enthusiastic response indicates that Wilhelm's acceptance
of his paternity was ardently desired, as does the presumably preplanned
presence of Felix behind the curtains. The call for Wilhelm to dare to be
happy, a call that suggests the definite, positive effects on Wilhelm's mental health of his acknowledgment of his fatherhood further implies that the
Tower Society views this scene as a successful cure.

Both Meister and the Tower Society agree that the Society deserves the credit for bringing Wilhelm's paternity to light. Although he and Mariane have a child very early in the novel, Wilhelm admits this only at the end of his development. Even though Barbara shows him letters from Mariane that assert his paternity in no uncertain terms (SE 9:295; HA 7:483), he does not believe that he fathered Felix until he receives confirmation from the Tower Society. Only then does Wilhelm "feel" his fatherhood, a gift for which he thanks the Society: "'Ja, ich fühl's,' rief er aus, 'du bist mein! Welche Gabe des Himmels habe ich meinen Freunden zu verdanken!'" (HA 7:497) ["Yes, oh yes," said Wilhelm, "you are indeed mine! What a gift this is from Heaven that I have to thank my friends for!"] (SE 9:304).[41] Of course, until recently, even twentieth-century physicians have not been able to determine paternity with any degree of certainty. Several characters in the *Apprenticeship* make clear that it was also difficult in the eighteenth century. Therese's mother mentions the uncertainty of fatherhood—indeed, her own example makes the uncertainty of motherhood clear—while Friedrich makes untranslatable German puns (based on the words *zeugen* [to beget] and *überzeugen* [to convince]) on the theme: "Die Vaterschaft beruht überhaupt nur auf der Überzeugung; ich bin überzeugt, und also bin ich Vater" (HA 7:559) [Fatherhood rests only on conviction; I am convinced, therefore I am the father] (SE 9:342).[42] These lines remind the reader that the paternity that Wilhelm "feels" has little to do with any biological relationship to Felix, especially as the Tower Society makes no effort to prove its contention. The contrast between Wilhelm's rejection of Barbara's assurances of fatherhood and his acceptance of the Society's designation of him as a father reflects the transfer of legitimacy in matters of childbirth from midwives, who probably looked much like Barbara, to the new "man-midwives" or obstetricians. It also shows the authority that Wilhelm has invested in the Tower Society as a healing institution.

With his marriage to Natalie and his acceptance of Felix as son, Wilhelm becomes head of a family and thereby resolves his societal problems, as far as the Tower Society is concerned. As a result of this progress, he feels obliged to make long-term plans and commitments, a sentiment that demonstrates his status as a virtuous citizen: "Everything he planned was now to mature for the boy, and everything he built was to last for several generations. His apprenticeship was therefore completed in one sense, for along with the feeling of a father he had acquired the virtues of a solid citizen. His joy knew no bounds" (SE 9:307; HA 7:502).[43] The connections between Wilhelm's paternity and his membership in civil, bourgeois society, or patriarchy, underscore the meaning of Wilhelm's accession to the roles of father and husband in the family. For the Tower Society, the successful achievement of such familial positions implies a proper entry into society.

Wilhelm's happiness is therefore not only personal, but also of societal import. He has, in becoming a member of the family, lost his narcissistic introversion and become involved with the rest of society.

The Tower Society brings Wilhelm into its new bourgeois society by teaching him its era's new medical anthropology, an anthropology that emphasizes the complementarity of the sexes. With Lothario ventriloquizing through Therese and Natalie, the Society teaches Wilhelm to love women as others, not as mirroring mothers. He himself becomes comfortable with his roles as bourgeois father and husband, achieving a position in society that the Tower Society regards as healthy.

Conclusion:
The Meaning of Health

Doctor's orders: Wilhelm's *Bildung* consists of taking his poisonous medication in the proper dose in order to ensure a salutary outcome, an outcome that will allow Wilhelm himself to become a master of the pharmakon. Wilhelm Meister's development most certainly qualifies as a cure—but a cure that is as noxious as it is beneficent. The pharmaceutical nature of Wilhelm's drugs—the ambivalence of *Bildung*—is a by-product of the medical discourse that informs *Wilhelm Meister's Apprenticeship.*

The difficulties with a simple affirmation of the beneficial nature of Wilhelm Meister's cure stem primarily from the eighteenth-century approach to the mind-body problem. Throughout the eighteenth century, physicians from Stahl and Haller to Weickard and Zimmermann insisted that, contrary to Cartesian tenets separating the *res extensa* from the *res cogitans*, mind and body were one. This renewed belief in the unity of mind and body produced both a reaction against mechanistic medicine, as practiced by Boerhaave and Hoffmann, and an interest in the soul. Goethe not only reduplicates this interest in medical aspects of the soul in his novel, but actively theorizes his era's discussion of the mind-body problem. The Tower Society, the institution most linked in the novel to the medical profession, adopts a belief in the unity of mind and body and diagnoses the separation of mind and body of such ailing characters as the Beautiful Soul and Mignon as unhealthy.

While surgeons and traditional physicians suffer some neglect in the novel, and must even tolerate unflattering portrayals of their work, the eighteenth-century "philosophical physicians," who dealt with mental, spiritual, and psychological complaints, bask in the center of attention. In particular, the case of Augustin, the Harper, shows how accurately Goethe noted his era's most advanced psychological medicine. The origins of the Harper's disease in a poor relationship with society and an obsession on a

178

fixed idea conform to eighteenth-century thoughts on the etiology of madness. The symptoms, including melancholia, disbelief in the existence of himself or the world, and occasional fits of rage, fit into the era's clinical pictures of religiously inspired insanity. The attempts at curing Augustin with a combination of wholesome living at the clergyman's estate and a few so-called pious frauds, designed to trick the patient out of his madness, accurately mirror the thinking of progressive German physicians like Zimmermann.[1] Even the failure of the therapy, as exemplified by Augustin's suicide with a razor blade, underscores Goethe's attempt to reproduce the medical language of his time faithfully, for the prospect of suicides in the new institutions, where the mentally ill had a relatively great deal of freedom of movement, was frequently discussed.[2]

The eighteenth-century medical belief in the unity of mind and body helped the physicians assume a more imposing position in their era's intellectual landscape. With their new competence in matters concerning the mind, the spirit, and the psyche, they began to take an active role in philosophy, theology, and even the arts. In the *Apprenticeship*, too, the physician assumes a newly significant position as an important collaborator in the Tower Society's schemes to improve Wilhelm Meister and the world. Like the eighteenth-century physicians, who railed against the dangers of the imagination, the physician in Goethe's novel finds a "destructive imagination" in the cases of the countess, Aurelie, the count, Sperata, the Harper, and Mignon.[3] Just as the eighteenth century witnessed the banishment of the fool from court and stage and the entrance of foolishness, characterized by an excess of wit, into the ranks of psychological diseases,[4] the society of the *Apprenticeship* regards the antics of Friedrich and Philine as slightly deranged. Moreover, just as early psychologists like Moritz and Mauchart began analyzing literary works for hints about psychological character, Aurelie and Wilhelm Meister probe Ophelia's speeches for clues to her psychic constitution, while Natalie and the physician study Mignon's slips of the tongue and poetry for insight into her past. Finally, like the physicians of Goethe's age who increasingly contested the competence of religion in matters of spiritual health, the physicians in the *Apprenticeship* feel obliged, in the cases of Sperata, the Harper, and the Beautiful Soul, to intervene in order to heal the damage done by their priestly counterparts. Significantly, the physicians, Natalie, Lothario, and the abbé—in short, the characters in the orbit of the Tower Society—stand on the side of this new medicine, which has extraordinary powers to treat "illnesses" that had in earlier centuries not been matters of health at all.

One of the new "sicknesses" that this new medicine intends to treat is asociability caused by narcissism or excessive introspection. For the physicians of the eighteenth century, many forms of mental illness, including religious fanaticism and hypochondria, originated in an inadequately formed sense of belonging to society. In accordance with this tradition, the psychologically ill in Goethe's novel are also not sociable and extroverted enough.

On the one hand, the disease of those whom the Tower Society finds excessively religious[5] stems from introspection, narcissism, or an otherwise poor relationship with society: the count who has joined the Moravian religious community is obsessed with the image of himself he sees when Wilhelm wears his clothes. The Harper, a former monk, fixates on the loss of his sister and his fear of death at the hands of a young boy, and sings of solitude. Mignon, a daily churchgoer with psychosomatic heart problems, also demonstrates the linkage between a poor relationship with society and religious extremism. A poor relationship with society causes her religious hallucination when a group of bandits, who mistreat her and separate her from her original community, drives her to such madness that she has a vision of Mary; this hallucination, a symptom of insanity, then causes a further disruption of her relationship with society when it causes her to take a vow of silence. Finally, the Beautiful Soul, committed to pursuing her form of religion, can see only herself in those she loves, including God, which shows once again the connections between religious extremism and solipsism.[6]

Besides religious fanaticism, the diseases of hypochondriacs are also linked to asociability.[7] The countess, with a common form of hypochondria, believes that she has breast cancer, which means that she can no longer contribute her "youth" and "loveliness" to "others" (SE 9:211; HA 7:349).[8] Werner, a typical eighteenth-century hypochondriac, worries not so much about his health but about his financial well-being. His disease, however, has the same effect as that of the countess: his refusal to pay taxes and the uncomfortable home he prepares for his family demonstrate his lack of full participation in society. Finally, Aurelie, who identifies herself and her worries as "hypochondriac" (SE 9:155; HA 7:260), has extreme difficulty relating to her audience, the German public. In this novel, both religious fanatics and hypochondriacs have poor relations with society. By assuming competence for these "diseases" of the spirit and the imagination, the Tower Society also takes on responsibility for "curing" these relationships with society.

The Tower's attitude toward these ailments is not as cut-and-dried as might be expected, for, like the physicians of the eighteenth century, it grants sickness a certain amount of worth. The physician and other members of the Tower Society are aware of the links between sickness and insight and creative genius in such characters as Aurelie, Sperata, and the Beautiful Soul, as well as the Harper and Mignon. More importantly, because they understand the use of the pharmakon—the strategy of fighting fire with fire—they are willing to use illness homeopathically or inoculatively in their struggles against illness. The physician directs the Harper's suicidal drive against itself when he allows Augustin to carry a vial of opium. Similarly, he uses the Beautiful Soul's "pathological" religious fanaticism against itself when he urges her to look for God in nature as part of his attempt at bringing her out of herself. Moreover, when members of the Tower Society, including Lothario and his uncle, give into their whims occasionally, and when members of the Society's precursor, the "Children of Joy," spend one full day of the week acting as fools, they in effect permit some irrational behavior as a sort of safety valve that prevents the onset of insanity.

This toleration of sickness, however, never exceeds the bounds of a larger dietetic plan favoring health. Behind the plan to allow Mignon to wear angel's clothes, for instance, is the hope of bringing her back down to earth. And behind the occasional toleration of irrational behavior is a highly rational program, which rejects emotions and introspection in favor of activity. The Tower Society believes it can administer exactly the right dosage of its poisonous medicine, its pharmakon, in order to bring about health.

Like the religious fanatics and hypochondriacs of the novel, Wilhelm Meister also suffers from poor health, a fact that is underscored by his many wounds at the beginning of the novel.[9] His mania for the theater is another indication of his sickness,[10] which, as in the case of the other sick characters of the novel, has above all an important impact on his relationship with society, making him too introspective. The Society asserts its medical authority over Wilhelm when it treats his wounds. It then allows Wilhelm to act in a magnificent performance of *Hamlet* as part of its plan to cure him of his theater mania, just as it sometimes tolerates illnesses in other characters as part of its dietetic plan. Similarly, it cures Wilhelm's narcissism by encouraging him to find himself in a series of creative works, including, besides *Hamlet*, the painting of the lovelorn prince, the dramatic initiation at the end of book 7, and the paintings in the Hall of the Past.[11] The Tower Society first uses Wilhelm's narcissistic desires to lure him into finding himself solipsistically in all of these artworks; from these paintings and plays, however, Wilhelm learns to avoid excessive introversion and thus becomes a "healthy" member of society.

Put more concretely, Wilhelm's diseased narcissism amounts to a kind of lovesickness, an inability to choose and maintain a love that the Tower considers appropriate. Homeopathically, the Tower Society allows Wilhelm to exercise his homosexually tinged love of characters in masculine garb, because it can direct this love toward the heterosexuality that it favors. Inoculating Wilhelm with male-male affection, it encourages Wilhelm to admire and imitate men who love women. It camouflages its feminine ideals

(Therese and Natalie) as male impersonators when it first presents them to Wilhelm, thus using Wilhelm's attraction to mirroring cross-dressers to catch him for their plan.

For the Tower, the family is the locus of healthy non-narcissistic relationships based on an appreciation of otherness. In the family, the young Wilhelm learns to replace his desire for maternal, mirroring, androgynous figures with a desire for wives and children. The Society watches with approval as Wilhelm moves away from specular relationships with characters including his mother, Mariane, and Mignon. The Tower shows Wilhelm pictures of ostensibly eternally valid familial models in the Hall of the Past, which leads Wilhelm to understand the role of the husband as differing from that of the wife and children. Therese lectures him further on the subject. In Natalie, who makes a policy of molding herself into the opposite of her social counterparts, he finds the incarnation of this alterity.[12] By introducing the protagonist to Shakespeare and above all *Hamlet*, the Tower Society encourages Wilhelm to reconcile himself with the role of the father as well as that of husband. By the end of the dramatic initiation scene, Wilhelm accepts his role as father of Felix. The Tower Society thus inculcates Wilhelm with a two-sex view of humanity, according to which men and women have very different natures and roles to play, roles that are complementary and, in the family, add up to a whole.

To summarize coarsely and negatively, *Bildung* in *Wilhelm Meister* consists of heterosexual male socialization concluding with the acquisition of wife, children, and property. Without such a clear statement of the nature of *Bildung*, discussions of *Wilhelm Meister* can get lost in the fog of generalities about the humanistic values of the Age of Goethe. This dry-eyed assessment of the nature of *Bildung* is not meant as a critique of the novel, however, but rather as a critique of the Tower Society and those readers who promote its ideals blindly. The conclusion that the Tower Society endorses the late-eighteenth-century German bourgeois family as the drug that cures excessive introspection could lead readers to believe that the late-nineteenth-century critics who saw the book as a manual for correct bourgeois living were actually right.[13] For a number of reasons, however, this interpretation must be rejected.

First of all, the Tower Society is not identical with the novel. Admittedly, some overlap between the Tower Society and the novel exists, because the Tower Society apparently structures the plot, by secretly pulling the strings that control Wilhelm's life. Moreover the novel seems to be the file, called "Wilhelm Meister's Apprenticeship," stored in the archives of the Tower (SE 9:309; HA 7:505). Thus the Tower Society not only manages Wilhelm's life but also in a very specific sense apparently writes the account of his life.

But even if the Tower is the author of the "Apprenticeship," its text could know and say more than it does, as is often the case with literary works. Literature often reveals the weaknesses in the intent of its authors because of its ability to assert at the same time one thing and its opposite, to be both poison and antidote—in a word, because of its pharmaceutical quality. The fundamental distinction between the Tower Society and the novel is that the Tower believes it can control the pharmakon, while the novel reveals what Benjamin Bennett calls "radical irony."[14] The Tower Society operates on the assumption that it can manage the dosage of its poisonous medicine to Wilhelm and ensure a healthy outcome. In contrast, the novel itself takes more seriously the eighteenth-century medical notion that every medicine can also be a poison. It does not back up the Tower's claim to complete control of the healing process. In undermining the Tower's claim to completely beneficent healing, the novel simultaneously shows the ambiguity and ambivalence of literature.

There are suggestions that the novel's "real" author, Goethe, knew more than its putative author, the Tower Society. As much as he was aware of and supported the progressive medicine of his era, he understood the limitations of its practitioners. For all his familiarity with the physicians of Weimar, Goethe treated his own doctor, Hufeland, with a certain amount of disrespect, apparently passing on the book that Hufeland had given him to his mother unopened and quickly losing contact with the man after he moved to Berlin, despite his growing fame.[15] Zimmerman came in for a certain amount of criticism in *Poetry and Truth;* many physicians, along with other eighteenth-century figures, were lampooned in such writings as the "Xenien." This is not to deny Goethe's interest in the progressive medical research of his day, but simply to point out that this interest was always tempered.

Many of Goethe's works bear witness to his conscious effort to relativize the medical program. The Hippocratic sentiments expressed at the beginning of the "Certificate of Apprenticeship," "Art is long, life is short" (SE 9:303; HA 7:496), also occur in *Faust*, significantly enough in the mouth of Wagner: "Ach Gott! Die Kunst ist lang, Und kurz ist unser Leben" ("Nacht," line 558; HA 3:25) [Alas, that art is long and human life so short!] (SE 2:19). The fact that Wagner, who, as a bumbling pedant, plays a kind of fool in *Faust*, utters the same words that open the Tower Society's chief document of initiation suggests that Goethe referred to this medical doctrine with a certain irony. Even within the *Apprenticeship*, the ambiguous position of Friedrich, both fool and casual associate of the Tower Society, ironizes medicine. On the one hand, Friedrich's wit is instrumental in applying the medicinal message of the painting of the lovelorn prince to Wilhelm's case; on the other hand, he is himself not completely sane and,

even more telling, he delivers, at the end of the novel, "a ridiculous encomium on medicine" (SE 9:371; HA 7:606). He is a kind of pharmakon for
the pharmaceutical field itself—while he actually implements the cure, he
also casts doubt on the notion of cures.

The Tower Society's inability to provide a final cure for many of the
characters in the novel ironizes its medicine even more seriously. The Tower
cannot even rid Augustin, the Harper, of his fixed obsession, which means
that it cannot actually cure his melancholy. Often, medicine seems only
able to ease the pain of those suffering from illnesses. The physician who
treats Sperata relieves her from the anguish that her priest had caused but
does not prevent her death (SE 9:362; HA 7:591). When the physician of
the Tower Society suggests that Aurelie read the "Confessions of the Beautiful Soul," he does indeed ease her pain: "Das heftige und trotzige Wesen
unsrer armen Freundin war auf einmal gelindert" (HA 7:355) [The poor
woman's violence and pity suddenly all calmed down] (SE 9:215). Like
the Italian physician, however, he is not able to prevent his patient's death.
The Beautiful Soul's "calming," expressed in the German with precisely
the same verb, *lindern*, recurs when the physician discusses Mignon's case:
"[W]o wir nicht helfen können, sind wir doch schuldig zu lindern" (HA
7:525) [{E}ven if we cannot help, we have an obligation to appease] (SE
9:321). Needless to say, the physician is also unable to cure her, an inadequacy that results in her death. The Society's inability to give permanent
assistance to most of the sick characters in the novel points to a further
ironization of its use of its era's advanced medicine.

In particular, objections to the connection between the Tower Society's
model of the family and health have every justification. Goethe might have
been the first to agree with such objections, since he left a family that, with
its hardworking, somewhat authoritarian father, supportive and loving
mother, and two surviving children, was precisely what the Tower Society
endorses. Instead, Goethe spent many years of life as a bachelor and subsequently lived with Christiane Vulpius, in a relationship that, as it was not
initially sanctioned by the church and never fully accepted by Weimar society, was not at all similar to the ideal envisioned by the Tower Society.

Linking Wilhelm's final health to his ascent to the role of father in the
family seems to condemn to illness characters unable to conform to this
heterosexual model. The Harper and the Beautiful Soul, permanently isolated from their families, presumably cannot hope to attain health. Laertes,
who lost his bride on the day of the wedding (SE 9:129–30; HA 7:219–20),
also probably has no hope of recovering from his asocial misogyny (SE
9:55; HA 7:100), venereal disease, inability to stand solitude, melancholy
thoughts about the past, and sense of the "fragmentation of life" (SE 9:159;
HA 7:267).[16] Similarly, characters who chose to live in other family struc-

tures, such as, for instance, the one in which Serlo grew up, which did not differentiate between child and parent, setting even the infant to work on the stage (SE 9:160; HA 7:268),[17] would, given the medical discourse of this novel, have no reason to hope for health.

The Tower's family model is particularly open to criticism for its neglect of women's health. If, for Wilhelm Meister, health means overcoming his narcissistic relationship with his mother and learning to move into the role of the father, what does health mean for women? Because the novel cannot answer the question, many of its female characters die or are infirm: the Beautiful Soul spends her whole life suffering from disorders of the blood that cause hemorrhages; Aurelie never overcomes her love of Lothario and dies a death that is gentle only after a violent struggle (SE 9:215; HA 7:355); Mariane, already suffering from depression during her relationship with Wilhelm (SE 9:16; HA 7:34), dies a wretched and lonely death (SE 9:298; HA 7:481); Mignon, subject to heart seizures, falls victim to a massive attack when she sees Therese embrace Wilhelm (SE 9:333; HA 7:544).[18] Mariane Hirsch argues that the women in this novel must die precisely because of the linkage between paternity and health. Since women obviously are not encouraged to leave the narcissistic maternal sphere and replace the father in an extroverted paternal world, they have no way out of the excessive introspection that this novel labels both motherly and pathological.[19]

Even Wilhelm's cure is ambivalent. Although he achieves the status of propertied family man that the Tower Society regards as healthy, this view of healthiness contains the seeds of unhealthiness. The family that Wilhelm, Natalie, and Felix form at the end of the *Apprenticeship* is suspiciously similar to the family in which Wilhelm grew up. It has the professional father with an estate to take care of, the loving mother, and even the ancestral artworks that Wilhelm loved as a child. Thus, like bourgeois society at large, this family structure, while in the final analysis allegedly "healthy," produces the same pathologies that it cures.

The continuation of Wilhelm's story in the *Journeyman Years* hints that this solution does not work for him. After a single night with his wife, he leaves her to go "journeying" and study medicine—Natalie returns the favor by leaving him behind in Europe while she emigrates to America. By the time Goethe published the *Journeyman Years*, his faith in both the curative powers of the family and the ability of readers to understand his ironization of the cure had dimmed to the point that he had to spell out more clearly the deleterious side effects of Wilhelm Meister's cure.

Wilhelm thus undergoes a "cure," but the value of this cure remains profoundly ambivalent. The deep irony surrounding the Tower Society's cure of Wilhelm might seem to leave readers in the same interpretative impasse that characterizes the analysis of the *Apprenticeship* as a bildungs-roman. If one cannot ascertain whether Wilhelm's cure is beneficial or pernicious, one cannot determine if the novel is (as Schiller asserted) edifying or (as Novalis argued) corrupt. Nonetheless, those critics who first proposed an analysis of the medical discourse in the novel have rendered the discipline a service, because this approach contributes significantly to an understanding of *Wilhelm Meister's Apprenticeship*.

To begin with, the study of eighteenth-century medical writings clarifies the nature of the illness of minor characters like the count and countess, Werner, and Laertes, and more important characters such as Mignon, the Harper, the Beautiful Soul, and Aurelie, as well as, most importantly of all, Wilhelm Meister. This would be in any case of interest philologically and historically. In addition, it makes clear the consistent efforts of the Tower Society to employ the most advanced medicine of its time to heal all of these characters, particularly Wilhelm Meister. Whatever one thinks of Wilhelm at the end of the novel, he does undergo a rigorous and comprehensive program of treatment designed to combat his narcissism and bring him into the world of the fathers. Paying close attention to the medical discourses of the novel puts this plot movement into sharp relief.

While an analysis of the novel's medical discourse cannot give a final evaluation of the merit of this cure, it can explain why the assessment of the cure's value would be so difficult to determine. Specifically, pointing out the eighteenth-century medical context of Wilhelm's *Bildung* can help explain the seeming contradictions of the bildungsroman. These contradictions spring from a medical thinking imbued with homeopathic notions, ideas like inoculation and vaccination, a medical thinking very aware of the close relationship between the poison and the cure. At the very foundation of the medical discourse that informs this novel is the concept of the pharmakon, with its built-in indeterminacy. Thus a medical analysis of the drug goes hand in hand with a literary analysis of irony. Close attention to medical discourses in the *Apprenticeship* therefore inevitably leads to, brings out, and illuminates the basic structures of the novel that assure interpretive deadlock.

If any cure can also be a poison for one and the same individual, it stands to reason that what helps one person might harm another. This structure clarifies why Wilhelm's *Bildung* might not have a beneficial effect for the Beautiful Soul and could be disastrous for Mignon and Mariane. The variously positive and negative effects of *Bildung* mirror developments in eighteenth-century medicine, which, while beneficial for certain individuals, contributed to the development of medical institutions that had developed new kinds of oppression. The Tower Society that cures the young bourgeois Wilhelm, but is complicitous in the death of Mignon and the

Harper, is analogous to the medical institutions, like the clinic and the insane asylum, whose rise Foucault has eloquently chronicled. The novel documents the rise of those Enlightenment institutions whose dialectic of liberating the bourgeoisie but restructuring society in more subtly oppressive ways Horkheimer and Adorno explore. The medical discourses informing the novel help explain the presence of these structures in *Wilhelm Meister*.

The presence of markers from the history of medicine and its institutions in *Wilhelm Meister* shows that the notion of the cure is historically bound. Especially once "health" leaves the more objective physical realm of broken bones, foul bodily fluids, and chemicals, it becomes more and more subjective, requiring increasingly complicated ethical decisions. While earlier mechanistic physicians had the relatively straightforward task of maintaining the corporeal machine in good working order,[20] the new philosophical physicians had the more difficult job of defining and preserving the mental faculties. Even the physician Hufeland recognized it would be particularly difficult to establish the definition of mental health: "Normally one answers the question [what is insanity] thus: One says madness is unreason, the opposite of healthy reasonable thought, . . . but from this it would follow . . . that one would have to have certain concepts and characteristics of that which we call reason, which I however search for in vain."[21] The uncertainty about the meaning of sanity in the Age of Goethe suggests that readers nowadays are under no obligation to accept any definition of mental health from that era as binding or worthy of emulation. One era's definition of health might not correspond to another's.[22]

In its own day, the *Apprenticeship* probably did have certain limited goals concerning the advancement of medicine and the clarification of medicine's limits. Its most important contribution now to medicine is the eighteenth-century awareness that health and sickness are part of a humanly constructed system of signification. This is not to deny that sickness exists and that modern medicine can take practical steps against that sickness. But the modern assumption that medical matters are based on extralinguistic realia needs occasional tempering, lest it be forgotten that not all the categories established and used by medicine are "real."[23] The self-evidently constructed nature of a bygone medical system, such as one finds in a sensitive novel of an earlier era, like the *Apprenticeship*, allows one to see more clearly the issues of signification in the medicine of today—particularly when an eighteenth-century novel like the *Apprenticeship* lays bare the production of the "healthiness" of the bourgeois lifestyle, including heterosexual marriage and property management. Many modern medical presuppositions are remnants of the changes that took place in medicine and society at large in the eighteenth century. Since *Wilhelm*

Meister acutely recorded many of those changes, it can prove useful in critiquing those still-current presuppositions.

Once it becomes clear that medicine is a system of signification, its presence in the novel allows not only for a critique of medicine but also for a study of it as a metaphor for other systems of signification. Goethe can write about signification in general while he writes about medicine. In the grand scheme of signification, according to Foucault, one of the biggest changes to take place around the publication of *Wilhelm Meister's Apprenticeship* was the epistemic transformation between the classical and the modern. Goethe's novel carefully registers this change. The Tower Society holds onto a classical notion of sickness structured like a sign, with a (generally verbalized) signifying symptom pointing clearly to a signified illness. Analogously, it regards literature and works of art as endowed with certain transparent meanings. For the Tower Society, for instance, Mignon's poems reveal her inner psychic traumas, the Beautiful Soul's "Confessions" educate their reader about the need for moderate religious feelings, and the written account of Wilhelm's *Apprenticeship* contributes to Wilhelm's healthy development.

The novel, however, suggests that something like Foucault's modern episteme structures it at the highest level. It indicates that a certain residue remains when the medical discourse attempts to transform the signifiers of the characters into illnesses. Mignon's poem, "Heiß mich nicht reden, heiß mich schweigen" (HA 7:356) [Bid me not speak, let me be silent] (SE 9:216), appears, seemingly by chance and without motivation, at the end of book 5, immediately before the Beautiful Soul's "Confessions"—perhaps in order to discourage readers from moving too quickly from the signifier of texts to the signified. Mignon and the Harper stand mutely, difficult to interpret, because they point to what Foucault calls the "radical intransitivity" of language in modern poetry.[24] The narrator, when describing Wilhelm's reaction to reading the file in the Tower Society's archive on his apprenticeship, carefully avoids calling that text a mirror image and instead compares it to a portrait (SE 9:309; HA 7:505). This is a tactful maneuver, not an open break with the Tower Society, for the Tower Society regards the portrait as absolutely interpretable but the novel, through its inclusion of characters like Mignon and the Harper, allows for textual levels that are not so interpretable.

In the *Journeyman Years*, which thematize the historical rupture between the older world of Wilhelm's youth and the new world of the nineteenth century, Goethe continues to discuss medicine and meaning in ways that foreshadow Foucault. The modern medical distrust of the ability to represent reality causes what Foucault calls the "turn inward" to find factual, nonlinguistic realities. The *Journeyman Years* records this turn with its increasing emphasis on dissection as a medical tool (SE 10:321–29; HA 8:322–34). Wilhelm and the physicians still need to convey their insights to one another, so they attempt to subordinate art to the goal of completely clear communication. Wilhelm thinks his theater is useful because it teaches him how the body functions, while his teacher uses Greek sculptures to teach anatomy and is creating artificial body parts to avoid the problems of acquiring human corpses.

In the chapter preceding the discussion of dissection, Hersilie depicts the key to the casket that remains a mystery for the rest of the novel (SE 10:321; HA 8:321). This mysterious casket is the flip side of the modern distrust of language as a communicating device. The casket represents the increasingly opaque work of art or literature, which does not lend itself to use by the Tower Society or anyone else. It is the legacy of Mignon, who cries:

> Ich möchte dir mein ganzes Innre zeigen,
> Allein das Schicksal will es nicht.
>
> (HA 7:356)

> [My inmost heart to thee I'd open,
> But fate decrees I may not so.]
>
> (SE 9:216)

Mignon herself has become in the *Journeyman Years* a completely free-floating signifier, almost entirely dissociated from the "real" character that Wilhelm knew in the *Apprenticeship*. Halfway through the novel, Wilhelm meets a painter who has made a profession out of selling portraits of Mignon and who can also sing the songs from the *Apprenticeship* composed by her and the Harper (SE 10:254–59; HA 8:226–32). As humorous and parodic as this Cervantean scene is, it also points to the increasing disconnection between works of art and their source. It suggests that the signifier (in this case, the image of Mignon) no longer limpidly refers to the signified (the living person, Mignon).

One result of the increasing disconnection between the conceptions of art and life was the gradual loss of medical interest in literary contributions to medicine. Ziolkowski has demonstrated that after the 1790s psychiatry increasingly became a specialized medical field, interested in scientifically proven facts, unintelligible to the uninitiated, and not open to suggestions from literature. Concomitantly, literature began depicting the insane with mounting disregard for medicine's portrayal of the facts.[25] Despite the breach between medical and literary discourses, literature remains interested in the mentally and physically ill—not primarily because literature wants to offer an alternate therapy, but because medicine allows literature to discuss systems of signification. *Wilhelm Meister's Apprenticeship*, written on the cusp of the changing relationship between literature and psychiatry that Ziolkowski describes, is already intensely and primarily interested in medicine as a system of signification.

As Ziolkowski notes, the linkage between medicine and literature as systems of signification becomes clear when madness and psychology are introduced via discussions that Wilhelm Meister and Aurelie have concerning Hamlet and Ophelia (SE 9:145–48; HA 7:244–49).[26] The novel thereby shows the importance of the literary structuring of psychological states. Other illnesses, too, are narratively constructed: The pathologies of the Beautiful Soul and the long case histories of Augustin, the Harper, and his sister-wife, Sperata, come to mind. The use of the poetry of the Harper and Mignon as evidence for their sickness further intensifies the connection between literature and medicine, as does the use of the Beautiful Soul's writings to ameliorate Aurelie's condition.

The constructed nature of medical thinking becomes even more apparent in the case of Wilhelm Meister. His illnesses emerge in his childhood reading of Tasso's *Jerusalem Liberated* and his performances on the stage. Exemplified by theater mania, excessive introspection, and inadequate masculinity, they are not "naturally" identifiable as diseases. The Tower Society, which controls the medicine and the writing in the novel, turns Wilhelm's life into a case study of illness, archiving it as the "Apprenticeship." In their signification of him, they construct and cure his illness.

If medicine orders Wilhelm's life, its power has only grown since *Wilhelm Meister* was published. In the last two centuries, it has constructed not only many illnesses but also some of the larger categories that are at the foundation of modern society. As the Tower Society constructs the illnesses of Wilhelm and other characters in the novel, it demonstrates the construction of some of these larger fictions that still rule life today, like race, class, sexuality, and gender. The novel shows both how medicine is actually involved with these constructions and how medical constructions can stand as metaphors for the development of these categories.

An undercurrent of medicalized racial thinking eddies through the novel. In the *Apprenticeship*, when the Harper first appears, there is some concern about whether he is a Jew (SE 9:72; HA 7:128). The Harper's beard revitalizes fears that he is a "Jewish spy" after the robber band attacks (SE 9:142; HA 7:239). The Harper's subsequent sickness and his possible Jewishness coincide well in this era, for, from the eighteenth century on, the sickly Jew was a staple of medical discussions.[27] A top priority of the clergyman helping the Tower Society treat the Harper is the removal of his Jewish beard (SE 9:210; HA 7:347). For the longest time, his refusal to give up his beard remains a telling sign of his insanity (SE 9:364–65; HA

7:596). When the Tower Society believes it has cured the Harper, it specifically alludes to the Jewish subtext, when it declares "the beard was gone, his hair was cared for" (SE 9:364; HA 7:595). At times the "disease" of unkempt Jewish hair threatens to spread to Wilhelm: Werner, who is at this point working with the Tower Society, is concerned that Wilhelm will look like a Jew unless he puts his hair into a pigtail (SE 9:307; HA 7:501). Thus, the Tower Society and its friends help cement the cliché of the sickly Jew and work to cure Wilhelm of his possible case of "Jewishness."

In the *Journeyman Years*, the issue of the Jew becomes more pronounced and the Tower Society's anxiety about Jews reaches the point that they exclude Jews from the utopian community they want to construct in the States. Benjamin Bennett, intriguingly arguing that the Jews symbolize readers in the Wilhelm Meister novels, suggests that the Tower Society's anti-Semitism is the final twist of irony distancing the novel from the content of the Tower Society's message.[28] This idea would accord well with the theory that Goethe's novel is commenting on the medical discourses that help construct society rather than merely transmitting them.

While the Jews become very important in the *Journeyman Years*, in the *Apprenticeship* they are not as much an issue as the Italians. Italians, by dint of the association with the Harper, Sperata, and Mignon, are also pathologized, in accordance with the medical thinking of the time. Zimmermann found the Italians particularly prone to melancholia because of their mystical religion, Catholicism, and their hot, dry climate.[29] But the Northerners are allowed their illnesses as well. The count's Anglophilia alludes to the madness of the English. The discussion of the character Hamlet centers around his Nordic melancholia. Wilhelm, who first flirts with the Italian sickness brought by Mignon and the Harper, must be inoculated against the Nordic sickness by playing Hamlet. The medical thinking in the novel, which the Tower Society controls, thus is part of a trend creating racial distinctions based on medicine.

As the previous two chapters have shown, the novel's medical discourse also devotes considerable attention to the construction of categories of sexuality and gender. It pathologizes androgyny and the homosexual possibilities associated with blurred gender lines. Mignon's case of androgyny is so serious that she dies, while the Beautiful Soul's manliness embitters her life. Therese's embrace of Lothario's clear distinctions between the two genders saves her from her cross-dressing tendencies. Natalie's amazonian quality is just a small dose of toxin that cures Wilhelm's androgynous tendencies homeopathically. Her health and his become assured when she transfers her uncle's coat to him.

As part of the construction of gender, the Tower's medical discourse classifies heterosexual relationships as healthy. Augustin and Sperata's incestuous relationship, which is based on identity and thus analogous to a homosexual relationship, has deleterious health consequences, both for their child and for them. Conversely, the triple marriage orchestrated by the Tower Society at the end of the novel, between Friedrich and Philine, Lothario and Therese, and Wilhelm and Natalie, is a veritable orgy of sexual difference. Philine is woman personified; while observing her courtship with the hypermasculine stable master and Friedrich, Wilhelm got his first lesson in heterosexual difference. Lothario and Therese promote a concept of a healthy relationship based on absolute gender difference; Therese's account of this philosophy to Wilhelm reinforces the lesson he learned from observing Philine and Friedrich. As for his own marriage, Wilhelm is only judged worthy of it when he has taken on the masculine mantle Natalie offers him.

Friedrich calls this triple marriage at the end of the book a *Freiredoute*, a dance in which both nobility and bourgeoisie take part (SE 9:373; HA 7:609, 811). For three mésalliances to take place at one time was by no means common in the eighteenth century. Goethe is clearly playing with issues of class here, too, issues that consciously determined identity in the eighteenth century more than they do now. Indeed, then they were as constitutive of identity, and as questionable, as sexuality is today. In *Wilhelm Meister's Apprenticeship*, medicine also seems to play a role in class identity as well. Purely aristocratic couples, like the count and countess or Augustin and Sperata, tend to be sick, contributing to the notion that the aristocracy had spent itself and was losing vitality and health. At the same time, bourgeois society, with its stress, leads to the hypochondria of characters like Werner. When the pastor points out that much "in our educational system and everyday life" (SE 9:210; HA 7:347) causes madness, the German word translated as "everyday" is *bürgerlich*, literally, "bourgeois." On the other hand, those progressive elements of the upper and middle classes that leave behind the worst characteristics of their origins and are not hidebound in their observance of class structure—upwardly mobile bourgeoisie and reform-minded aristocracy open to marriage with the newcomers—are healthy.

The novel therefore clearly suggests that medicine is an apt metaphor for the forces of signification that create such signifiers as race, gender, sexuality, and class. There are of course other orders besides that of the doctors. While medicine has a hand in the construction of many categories in modern society, including ones that go far beyond the generally recognized bounds of sickness, it is not the only such institutional force in modern society. Law, for instance, has similarly worked on the configuration of modern identity—so have the new disciplines in academe, particularly the human sciences, like economics, politics, and anthropology. Medicine plays an especially important role in the construction of such categories in *Wilhelm*

Meister, but it can stand as an example of many of the new forces structuring modern life and society.

Perhaps because its account of the power of the medical discourse over society was so believable, *Wilhelm Meister's Apprenticeship* became vastly important in the nineteenth century, grounding a new genre of novels that tested the mettle of authors from Jean Paul to at least Thomas Mann and promoted serious thought by philosophers from Hegel to Dilthey and beyond. In 1863, a French commentator called it a guide for the young bourgeoisie in this century;[30] in 1886, a German book used it as the basis for a primer for proper living.[31] Much of its success probably emerged from the relevancy of the medical ideas about the two-sex system and gender complementarity promulgated in it by the Tower Society. These ideas struck a sympathetic chord with readers, who often overlooked Goethe's ironization of them; arguably, the *Journeyman Years* was neglected in the nineteenth century largely because its irony was too strong for readers. The ideas about gender, sexuality, race, and class that captured the attention of the reading public were transmitted by both high and low culture throughout the nineteenth and even into the twentieth centuries.

This account of *Wilhelm Meister's* sensitivity to the development of modern social constructs of race, gender, sexuality, and class does not necessarily imply, however, that the novel offers a system of medicine to be emulated. What it offers is a credible account of the systems that structure the world in those terms. If the novel is truly a pharmakon, then it can also critique precisely those structures that it described and arguably helped build. Perhaps it even shows why they should be changed. The traditional reading of the *Apprenticeship* overlooked its irony, while readings reacting to the traditional ones have disregarded the skill with which the novel portrays the systems it ironizes. Admittedly, Wilhelm Meister's *Bildung* is a kind of healing. But having established that, the critic must turn to the story of the doctor and the doctor's orders. Such an analysis shows how medicine is a discourse that can be manipulated in order to structure society and the lives of individuals in that society. Further reflection on the role of medicine in the novel reveals how medicine produces even larger discursive structures of race, gender, sexuality, and class. In short, readers can learn from *Wilhelm Meister* more about discourses like medicine that structure their society.

Notes

PREFACE

1. Avital Ronell, *Crack Wars: Literature, Addiction, Mania* (Lincoln: University of Nebraska, 1992).

2. An interpretation to which Nietzsche alludes in an aphorism in *Human, All-Too-Human*: "Already and Still. A: 'German prose is still quite young: Goethe says that Wieland is its father.' B: 'So young and already so ugly!' C: 'But—as far as I know, Bishop Ulfila already wrote German prose; it is therefore almost fifteen hundred years old.' B: 'So old, and still so ugly!'" *Menschliches Allzumenschliches II*, aphorism 90. Friedrich Nietzsche, *Sämtliche Werke: Kritische Studienausgabe in 15 Bänden*, ed. Giorgio Colli and Mazzino Montinari (Munich: DTV, 1980), 2:593–94.

CHAPTER 1: MEDICINE IN GOETHE'S TIME, LIFE, AND WORKS

1. Michel Foucault, *The Order of Things: An Archaeology of the Human Sciences* (New York: Vintage, 1973), 308.

2. Barbara Duden, *The Woman Beneath the Skin: A Doctor's Patients in Eighteenth-Century Germany* (Cambridge: Harvard University Press, 1991). Thomas Laqueur, *Making Sex: Body and Gender from the Greeks to Freud* (Cambridge: Harvard University Press, 1990), 145.

3. Foucault, *Order of Things,* 221.

4. Londa Schiebinger, *The Mind Has No Sex? Women in the Origins of Modern Science* (Cambridge: Harvard University Press, 1989), 190–91, 226.

5. Michel Foucault, "The Politics of Health in the Eighteenth Century," in *The Foucault Reader*, ed. Paul Rabinow (New York: Pantheon, 1984), 279–82.

6. Laurence Rickels, *The Case of California* (Baltimore: Johns Hopkins University Press, 1991), 158–59. For a review of the literature on the history of adolescence, see John Neubauer, *The Fin-de-Siècle Culture of Adolescence* (New Haven: Yale University Press, 1992), 3–6.

7. Henry Louis Gates Jr., "Editor's Introduction: Writing 'Race' and the Difference It Makes," *Critical Inquiry* 12, no. 1 (Autumn 1985): 7. Critically, Gates notes that "our conversations are replete with usages of race which have their sources in the dubious pseudosciences of the eighteenth and nineteenth centuries" (4).

8. A good start for information on the homosexual subcultures of the eighteenth century would be the essays in *Sexual Underworlds of the Enlightenment*, ed. G. S. Rousseau

and Roy Porter (Manchester: Manchester University Press, 1987). See also Kent Gerard and Gert Hekma, eds., *The Pursuit of Sodomy: Male Homosexuality in Renaissance and Enlightenment Europe*. For information specifically about Germany, see Robert Tobin, *Warm Brothers: Queer Theory and the Age of Goethe* (Philadelphia: University of Pennsylvania Press, 2000).

   9.   Donna Haraway, "The Biopolitics of Postmodern Bodies: Determinations of Self in Immune System Discourse," *Differences* 1, no. 1 (Winter 1989): 13.

   10.   Richard Harrison Shryock, *The Development of Modern Medicine: An Interpretation of the Social and Scientific Factors Involved* (London: Gollancz, 1948), 87.

   11.   Gloria Flaherty, *Shamanism and the Eighteenth Century* (Princeton: Princeton University Press, 1992), 100.

   12.   Count Buffon (1707–88) attempted to show environmental causes for race. The English surgeon John Atkins concluded from his research that Blacks and Whites were fundamentally different in *The Navy-Surgeon; or, A Practical System of Surgery* (London, 1734). Richard H. Popkin, "Medicine, Racism, Anti-Semitism: A Dimension of Enlightenment Culture," in *The Languages of Psyche: Mind and Body in Enlightenment Thought. Clark Library Lectures, 1985–1986*, ed. G. S. Rousseau (Berkeley: University of California Press, 1990), 414.

   13.   *Über die körperliche Verschiedenheit des Negers vom Europäer* (Frankfurt and Mainz, 1785). Discussed by Schiebinger, *Mind Has No Sex?*, 211.

   14.   Sander Gilman, *The Case of Sigmund Freud: Medicine and Identity at the Fin de Siècle* (Baltimore: Johns Hopkins University Press, 1993), 10–55. Popkin also provides an account of European thinkers from Voltaire to Goebbels who regarded Judaism, more or less metaphorically, as a disease that had infected Europe ("Medicine, Racism, Anti-Semitism," 413).

   15.   Foucault, *Order of Things*, 299–300.

   16.   Ian Watt, *The Rise of the Novel: Studies in Defoe, Richardson, and Fielding* (Berkeley: University of California Press, 1964).

   17.   Diaetophilus (Karl W. F. L. Drais), *Physische und Psychologische Geschichte seiner siebenjaehrigen Epilepsie*, 2 vols. (Zürich, 1798). Sander Gilman refers to him in connection with the rise of narratives of sickness in *Freud, Race, and Gender* (Princeton: Princeton University Press, 1993), 132.

   18.   Julia Epstein, "Historiography, Diagnosis, and Poetics," *Literature and Medicine* 11, no. 1 (Spring 1992): 24; emphasis Epstein's. This entire issue of *Literature and Medicine* is entitled "The Art of the Case History," ed. Joanne Trautmann Becks and Anne Hunsaker Hawkins, and contains a number of good articles on the subject.

   19.   Duden, *Woman Beneath the Skin*, 63.

   20.   *Gnothi Sauton oder Magazin zur Erfahrungsseelenkunde* (1782–92). See note at beginning of book for information on citations of Moritz. For more on Moritz's psychological thought, see Rainard Bezold, *Popularphilosophie und Erfahrungsseelenkunde im Werk von Karl Philipp Moritz* (Würzburg: Königshaus und Neumann, 1984). See also Lothar Müller, *Die kranke Seele und das Licht der Erkenntnis. Karl Philipp Moritz' Anton Reiser* (Frankfurt a/M: Athenäum, 1987).

   21.   For an informative article on Moritz's friendship with Goethe and the traces that that friendship left in *Wilhelm Meister's Apprenticeship*, especially in the figure of Laertes, see Hans-Jürgen Schings, "Wilhelm Meisters Geselle Laertes," *Euphorion* 77, no. 4 (1983): 419–37. In addition, Schings's commentary in the Münchner Ausgabe gives a good account of Goethe's borrowings from Moritz (MA 5).

   22.   Marie Mulvey Roberts and Roy Porter, introduction to *Literature and Medicine in the Eighteenth Century*, ed. Marie Mulvey Roberts and Roy Porter (New York: Routledge, 1993), 1.

23. Simon Richter, *Laocoon's Body and the Aesthetics of Pain: Winckelmann, Lessing, Herder, Moritz, Goethe* (Detroit: Wayne State University Press, 1992), 90–130.

24. These works have been translated in Kenneth Dewhurst and Nigel Reeves, *Friedrich Schiller: Medicine, Psychology, and Literature, with the First English Edition of His Complete Medical and Psychological Writings* (Berkeley: University of California Press, 1978). There is a large body of literature on Schiller's psychological theories, including, for instance: Walter Hinderer, "Die Philosophie der Ärzte und die Rhetorik der Dichter: Zu Schillers und Büchners ideologisch-ästhetischen Positionen," *Zeitschrift für deutsche Philologie* 109, no. 4 (1990): 502–20; Heinrich Schipperges, "Der Medicus Schiller und das Konzept seiner Heilkunde," in *Schiller und die höfische Welt*, ed. Achim Aurnhammer (Tübingen: Niemeyer, 1990), 134–47; Jean-Jacques Alcandre, "Médecine et écriture dramatique, A propos du jeune Schiller," in *Conscient, inconscient dans le texte littéraire: Cahiers d'études germaniques* 10 (1986): 211–27; Wolfgang Riedel, *Die Anthropologie des jungen Schiller. Zur Ideengeschichte der medizinischen Schriften und der "Philosophischen Briefe"* (Würzburg: Königshaus und Neumann, 1985).

25. For a collection of sources in Goethe's writings on his interest in medicine, see Manfred Wenzel, *Goethe und die Medizin: Selbstzeugnisse und Dokumenta* (Frankfurt a/ M: Insel, 1992).

26. *Goethe's Collected Works*, ed. Victor Lange, Eric A. Blackall, and Cyrus Hamlin, 12 vols. (Boston: Suhrkamp, 1982), 4:196. Future references to this edition will be indicated parenthetically in the text, by the abbreviation SE. *Goethes Werke: Hamburger Ausgabe in 14 Bänden*, ed. Erich Trunz, 8th ed. (Munich: Beck, 1981), 9:259. Future references to this edition will be indicated with the abbreviation HA.

27. Conversations with Lavater, 16–18 July 1774. *Johann Wolfgang von Goethe: Gedenkausgabe der Werke, Briefe und Gespräche*, ed. Ernst Beutler, 25 vols. (Zürich: Artemis, 1949), 22:54. Future references to this edition will be indicated by the abbreviation AA.

28. Theodore Ziolkowski, *German Romanticism and Its Institutions* (Princeton: Princeton University Press, 1990), 178.

29. In 1796 alone, see: 10 January, "Pause in the novel . . . Hufeland"; 26 February, "Novel. Evenings Hufeland"; 2 March, "Novel . . . at Hufeland's"; 1 June, "Early novel . . . Hufeland." *Goethes Werke: Herausgegeben im Auftrage der Großherzogin Sophie von Sachsen*, 143 vols. (1887–1919; reprint, Munich: DTV, 1987), 3.2:38, 40, 44. Future references to this edition will be indicated, parenthetically in the text or in endnotes, by the abbreviation WA.

30. WA 3.2:57, 59, 70, 225, 240, 306, 309, plus many more references in subsequent volumes.

31. "Tag- und Jahreshefte 1794"; HA 10:441.

32. "Jahres- und Tageshefte 1795"; WA 1.35:60.

33. *Goethe in vertraulichen Briefen seiner Zeitgenossen*, ed. Wilhelm Bode, 3 vols., (Berlin and Weimar: Aufbau, 1979), 2:32.

34. WA 3.1:122.

35. In 1796: "Pause in novel . . . Loder" (10 January); "Early novel . . . Loder" (12 January); "Novel. Evening Loder" (5 March); WA 3.2:38, 40, 41. For more on Goethe's relationships with the physicians of Weimar, see Albrecht Gittinger, "Krankheit und heilender Eingriff: Goethes *Wilhelm Meister*" (diss., Heidelberg, 1980), 18ff.

36. Soemmering to Goethe, 27 January 1795. *Goethe und Soemmerring: Briefwechsel 1784–1828*, ed. Manfred Wenzel, Soemmerring-Forschungen 5 (Stuttgart: Fischer, 1988), 91.

37. "It was said that a Chinese mandarin addressed a letter from China to 'the illustrious Boerhaave, physician in Europe,' and it reached him." Lester King, *The Medical World of the Eighteenth Century* (Chicago: University of Chicago Press, 1958), 62.

38. SE 4:257, 5:711; HA 9:344, 10:314.

39. HA 9:277. In his notes, Goethe adds Hufeland to this list and connects medicine more specifically to literature, as opposed to "the general development of culture": "Physicians affect literature. Unzer. Zimmermann. *Tissot.* later Hufeland." WA 1.27:388–89.

40. 1 July 1795; WA 3.2:34.

41. Goethe to the Großherzog Carl August, 4 November 1781; WA 4.5:209. In a letter to Carl Ludwig Knebel (1744–1834), 3 February 1782, Goethe asserts that he and Knebel are both "personal and court physicians": "I entertain you with nothing but pleasure. Inwardly it looks a lot different, which no one can know better than we personal and court physicians." WA 4.5:257.

42. "Eine alte Kranckheit zerrüttet die Einsiedlische Famielie, der Häusliche, politische, moralische Zustand hat auf den Vater so gewürckt, daß er nahe an der Tollheit, wahnsinnige, wenigstens schwer erklärliche Handlungen vorgenommen hat." Goethe to the Großherzog Carl August, 4 November 1781; WA 4.5:209.

"Moralisch" is translated here as "morals," but one should bear in mind that psychologists of the era were drawing heavily upon religious vocabulary in order to discuss psychological matters. Thus, while a term like "moralisch" maintain some of its religious sense of "moral," it increasingly referred to the state of the psyche and also had a sense related more closely to the term "morale." A similar caveat applies to translations of the word "soul," which can also be used in both a religious context and a psychological one, where it will tend to mean something more like "psyche."

Goethe's treatment of Ernst Hildebrand von Einsiedel is discussed by Vivian Yvonne Greene, "The Artistic Value of Emotional Disorder for Goethe," diss., U of Illinois at Urbana, 1976.

43. Goethe to Charlotte von Stein, 5 September 1785; WA 4.7:87. Sigmund Freud discusses this incident in "Goethe-Preis 1930: Ansprache im Frankfurter Goethe-Haus," in *Gesammelte Werke: Chronologisch Geordnet,* ed. Anna Freud, 18 vols. (London: Imago, 1948), 14:548–49, as does Kurt Robert Eissler, *Goethe: A Psychoanalytic Study, 1775–1786,* 2 vols. (Detroit: Wayne State University Press 1963), 2:990.

44. *Campagne in Frankreich*; HA 10:331. For more on the Plessing episode, see Eissler, *Goethe,* 1:3–17. See also Gottfried Diener, *Goethe's "Lila": Heilung eines "Wahnsinns" durch "psychische Kur"* (Frankfurt a/M: Athenäum, 1971), 58ff.

45. Goethe to Krafft, 13 July, 1779; WA 4.4:46.

46. Goethe to Krafft, 2 November 1778; WA 4.3:252.

47. Goethe to Krafft, 14 December 1778; WA 4.3:263.

48. For more information on Krafft, see Diener, *Goethe's "Lila,"* 103ff., and Greene, "Artistic Value of Emotional Disorder for Goethe," 108ff.

49. Paul Henry Gerber, *Goethe's Beziehung zur Medizin* (Berlin: Karger, 1900), 70.

50. Letter of 1 July 1771.

51. 30 November 1772 and 1 December 1772.

52. Frank Nager, *Der heilkundige Dichter: Goethe und die Medizin,* 3d. ed. (Zürich: Artemis, 1992), 141.

53. Ibid., 206–20.

54. Paul Diepgen, "Goethe und die Medizin," *Klinische Wochenschrift* 11, no. 39 (24 September 1932): 1615.

55. Ziolkowski, *German Romanticism and Its Institutions,* 170–76.

56. Conversation reported by Chancellor Friedrich v. Müller, 21 April 1824. AA 23:338.

57. *Wilhelm Meisters theatralische Sendung.* Referred to in a letter to Knebel, 21 November 1782; WA 4.6:96.

58. Nicholas Boyle, *Goethe: The Poet and The Age,* 2 vols. (Oxford: Oxford University Press, 1992) 1:342.

59. The last chapters were apparently finished on 16 June 1796. WA 4.3:44.

60. W. Daniel Wilson, "Weimar Politics in the Age of the French Revolution: Goethe and the Spectre of Illuminati Conspiracy," *Goethe Yearbook* 5 (1990): 174. Rosemarie Haas, *Die Turmgesellschaft in "Wilhelm Meisters Lehrjahren": Zur Geschichte des Geheimbundromans und der Romantheorie im 18. Jahrhundert* (Frankfurt a/M: Lang, 1975).

61. Ziolkowski, *German Romanticism and Its Institutions,* 178.

62. As fascinating as the *Journeyman Years* are, this study will regard them primarily as an outgrowth of and comment on the *Apprenticeship*. A thorough study of the *Journeyman Years* would exceed the space limitations of this book and is, in a sense, less urgent, because the *Journeyman Years* did not reenter the general discourse in the way that the *Apprenticeship* did. While the *Apprenticeship* sparked immediate strong response and quickly became a classic of nineteenth-century bourgeois society, the *Journeyman Years* was largely neglected.

63. The pattern follows that of Goethe's Faust story, which appeared as the "Urfaust" in the early 1770's, followed by *Faust. A Fragment (Faust. Ein Fragment)* in 1790, *Faust. Part I (Faust, I. Teil)* in 1808, and *Faust II* in 1832.

64. See especially Schiller's letters to Goethe on 5 and 8 July 1796, in *Briefe an Goethe. Hamburger Ausgabe in 2 Bänden*, ed. Karl Robert Mandelkow, 2d ed. (Munich: Beck, 1982), 1:242, 246–47.

65. "Le guide moral du jeune bourgeois au 19ème siécle." Emile Montegut, *La Revue des deux mondes,* 1863, 194–95. For the use of the novel as a "besondere Hodegetik," see Georg Stanitzek, "Bildung und Roman als Momente bürgerlicher Kultur: Zur Frühgeschichte des deutschen 'Bildungsromans,'" *Deutsche Vierteljahresschrift* 62.3 (September 1988): 439.

66. Wilhelm Dilthey, *Das Erlebnis und die Dichtung*, 6th ed. (Berlin and Leipzig: Teubner, 1919), 393–94. For additional comments by Dilthey on the "Bildungsroman," see also *Das Leben Schleiermachers* (Berlin and Leipzig: Teubner, 1922), 1:317.

67. Max Wundt, *Goethes Wilhelm Meister und die Entwicklung des modernen Lebensideals* (Berlin and Leipzig: Göschen, 1918). Melitta Gerhard, *Der deutsche Entwicklungsroman bis zu Goethes "Wilhelm Meister* (Halle: Niemeyer, 1926; reprint, Bern: Franke, 1968). A good German collection is *Zur Geschichte des deutschen Bildungsromans,* ed. Rolf Selbmann, Wege der Forschung 640 (Darmstadt: Wissenschaftliche Buchgesellschaft, 1988). A representative sampling of essays in English on the history of the bildungsroman and interpretations of *Wilhelm Meister* as a bildungsroman can be found in *Reflection and Action: Essays on the Bildungsroman,* ed. James Hardin (Columbia: University of South Carolina Press, 1991). An excellent interpretation of the history of the bildungsroman is offered by Todd Kontje, *The German Bildungsroman: A History of a National Genre* (Columbia: Camden, 1993).

68. Letter to Goethe, 8 July 1796; *Briefe an Goethe,* 1:247.

69. Although his title makes explicit that *Wilhelm Meister* contributed to the development of "the modern ideal of life," Wundt admits that the novel's conclusion does not live up to its own standards (*Goethes Wilhelm Meister und die Entwicklung des modernen Lebensideals,* 208ff.). Critics who follow this line of reasoning include Kurt May, "*Wilhelm Meisters Lehrjahre,* ein Bildungsroman?" *Deutsche Vierteljahresschrift* 31 (1957): 33; and Hans Eichner, "Zur Deutung von Wilhelm Meisters Lehrjahren," *Jahrbuch des Freien Deutschen Hochstifts* (1966).

70. Friedrich Schlegel, "Über Goethes Meister," in *Schriften zur Literatur,* ed. Wolfdietrich Rasch, 2nd. ed (Munich: DTV, 1985).

71. Hans-Egon Hass, "Goethe's *Wilhelm Meisters Lehrjahre,*" *Der Deutsche Roman,* 2 vols., ed. Benno v. Wiese (Düsseldorf: Bagel, 1963), 1:132–210.

72. Benjamin Bennett, *Beyond Theory: Eighteenth-Century German Literature and the Poetics of Irony* (Ithaca: Cornell University Press, 1993), 3, 41–42.

73. Novalis, "Fragmenten und Studien 1799–1800," *Novalis: Schriften. Die Werke Friedrich von Hardenbergs*, ed. Paul Kluckhohn and Richard Samuel, 2d ed., 5 vols. (Stuttgart: Kohlhammer, 1977–88), 3:638–39.

74. Karl Schlechta, *Goethes Wilhelm Meister* (Frankfurt a/M: Klostermann, 1953) 112. See also Heinz Schlaffer, "Exoterik und Esoterik in Goethes Romanen," *Goethe-Jahrbuch* 95 (1978): 225.

75. Friedrich Kittler, "Über die Sozialisation Wilhelm Meisters," in *Dichtung als Sozialisationsspiel*, ed. Gerhard Kaiser and Friedrich Kittler (Göttingen: Vanderhoeck & Ruprecht, 1978), 82, 87–88.

76. See Gerhard Kaiser and Friedrich Kittler, introduction to *Dichtung als Sozialisationsspiel*, 14.

77. Hannelore Schlaffer, *Wilhelm Meister. Das Ende der Kunst und die Wiederkehr des Mythos* (Stuttgart: Metzler, 1980).

78. Todd Kontje, *Private Lives in the Public Sphere: The German "Bildungsroman" as Metafiction* (University Park: Pennsylvania State University Press, 1992).

79. Kittler, "Über die Sozialisation Wilhelm Meisters," 99–109.

80. Jochen Hörisch, *Gott, Geld und Glück: Zur Logik der Liebe in den Bildungsromanen Goethes, Kellers und Thomas Manns* (Frankfurt a/M: Suhrkamp, 1983), 35.

81. Dennis Mahoney, "The Apprenticeship of the Reader: The Bildungsroman of the 'Age of Goethe,'" in Hardin, *Reflection and Action*, 97–117.

82. An indication of the link betweem medicine and linguistics can be found in the word, "semiotics," which today primarily signifies the doctrine of signs, but which has, since its earliest attestations down to the present day, always had, both in English and in German, the specific technical meaning in medicine of the study of symptoms. Indeed, Locke, who studied and practiced medicine, drew upon medical vocabulary when he introduced the word "semiotics" to philosophy in his *Essay Concerning Human Understanding* (Patrick Romanell, *John Locke and Medicine* [New York: Prometheus, 1987], 15, 34, 143). Early citations in dictionaries of both languages tend to come from the medical world. Looking up "Zeichenlehre" (the doctrine of signs) in Adelung's eighteenth-century dictionary, one finds the following definition: "In a narrower sense, in medicine, the science of properly judging the state of a sickness from its signs; semiotics" (Johann Christoph Adelung, *Grammatisch-kritisches Wörterbuch der Hochdeutschen Sprache*, 2d ed. [Leipzig, 1801], 4:1670). The authoritative early nineteenth-century *German Dictionary of Jacob Grimm and Wilhelm Grimm* gives a similar definition: "in medicine, the diagnosis, earlier called semiotics" (*Deutsches Wörterbuch von Jacob und Wilhelm Grimm*, ed. Ludwig Sütterlin [Leipzig: Hirzol, 1960],15:483). Another early dictionary concurs: "in the medical sciences, the science of properly evaluating the reason and the state of a sickness based on its signs [. . .] (semiotics)" (Joachim Heinrich Campe, *Wörterbuch der deutschen Sprache*, 5 vols. [Braunschweig: Schulbuchhandlung, 1811], 5:828). Since these early German dictionaries abhor the loanword, they don't have an entry for "Semiotik," but in their entries for German translations of the word they acknowledge the common currency of the Greek term, specifically in the medical arena.

The early physicians Lazer Riverius, Hermann Boerhaave, and Friedrich Hoffmann all devoted sections of their medical handbooks to "semiotics," which was one of the five traditional "institutes" of seventeenth-century medicine (Friedrich Hoffmann, *Fundamenta Medicinae*, trans. Lester S. King [Halle, 1695; New York: American Elsevier, 1971], xi). "Semiotics" take up about one fifth of Hoffmann's *Fundamenta Medicinae* (83–102). Lavater refers to "medicinal semeiotics, or the signs of health and sickness," in his *Essays on Physiognomy* (Johann Caspar Lavater, *Essays on Physiognomy for the Promotion of Knowledge and the Love of Mankind*, trans. Thomas Holcroft, 3 vols. [London, 1789], 3:79). Although Lavater's physiognomical doctrines might seem to make him the master semiotician of the body, he freely cedes "medicinal semeiotics" to the physicians: "Not I, but an experienced physician ought to write on the physiognomonical and pathognomonical semeiotica of health and sickness . . ." (79). In 1785, one such physician, Johann Daniel Metzger described "semiotics" as "the theory of signs," divided "into the physiological and pathological" (*Grundsätze der allgemeinen Semiotik und Therapie* [Königsberg, 1785], 3). The title of his book, *Principles of General Semiotics and Therapy*, indicates the strength at that time of the understanding of semiotics as medical interpretation. As late as 1813, Landré-Beauvais published a work entitled *Semiotics or Treatise on the Signs of Maladies* (King, *Medical World of the Eighteenth Century,* 1063–65). See my essay, "Prescriptions: The Semiotics of Medicine and Literature," *Mosaic.* 33, no. 4 (December 2000): 174–92.

83. Hellmut Ammerlahn, "Goethe und Wilhelm Meister, Shakespeare und Natalie: Die klassische Heilung des kranken Königssohns," *Jahrbuch des Freien Deutschen Hochstifts,* 1978, 47–84.

84. Hannelore Schlaffer, *Wilhelm Meister,* 155.

85. Hans-Jürgen Schings, *Melancholie und Aufklärung: Melancholiker und ihre Kritiker in Erfahrungsseelenkunde und Literatur des 18. Jahrhunderts* (Stuttgart: Metzler, 1977) is an extremely influential study of eighteenth-century medicine. Since the publication of that work, Schings has produced a number of essays on eighteenth-century medicine and *Wilhelm Meister,* some of which are cited here: "Agathon-Anton Reiser-Wilhelm Meister: Zur Pathogenese des modernen Subjekts im Bildungsroman," in *Goethe im Kontext,* ed. Wolfgang Wittkowski (Tübingen: Niemeyer, 1984), 42–68. "Der anthropologische Roman: Seine Entstehung und Krise im Zeitalter der Spätaufklärung," in *Deutschlands kulturelle Entfaltung: Die Neubestimmung des Menschen,* ed. Bernhard Fabian, Wilhelm Schmidt-Biggermann, and Rudolf Vierhaus, Studien zum achtzehnten Jahrhundert 2/3 (Munich: Kraus, 1980), 247–75. "Symbolik des Glücks: Zu Wilhelm Meisters Bildergeschichte," in *Johann Wolfgang von Goethe: One Hundred and Fifty Years of Continuing Vitality,* ed. Ulrich Goebel and Wolodymyr Zyla (Lubbock, Tex.: Texas Tech Press, 1984), 155–77. "Wilhelm Meisters schöne Amazone," *Jahrbuch der deutschen Schillergesellschaft* 29 (1985): 141–206.

86. Gloria Flaherty, "The Stage-Struck Wilhelm Meister and Eighteenth-Century Psychiatric Medicine," *Modern Language Notes* 110 (1986), 493–515.

87. David Roberts, *The Indirections of Desire: Hamlet in Goethes "Wilhelm Meister"* (Heidelberg: Carl Winter Universitätsverlag, 1980).

88. Hörisch, *Gott, Geld und Glück,* 20–80. Another interpretation with a Lacanian subtext emphasizing mirroring is Clark Muenzer's *Figures of Identity: Goethe's Novels and the Enigmatic Self* (University Park: Pennsylvania State University Press, 1984).

89. Kontje, *German Bildungsroman,* 52.

CHAPTER 2. THE MIND-BODY PROBLEM

1. Liliane Weissberg, *Geistersprache: Philosophischer und literarischer Diskurs im späten achtzehnten Jahrhundert* (Würzburg: Königshaus & Neumann, 1990), xi, 161–62.

2. For an introduction to ancient (and, for that matter, modern) philosophical thought on the subject, see the article on "Leib-Seele-Verhältnis" in *Historisches Wörterbuch der Philosophie,* ed. Joachim Ritter and Karlfried Grüner (Darmstadt: Wissenschaftliche Buchgesellschaft, 1980), 5:186–205. See also "Mind-Body Problem," in *The Encyclopedia of Philosophy,* ed. Paul Edwards (New York: Macmillan, 1967), 5:336–46. For medieval responses to the mind-body problem, see Jean Starobinski, *Geschichte der Melancholiebehandlung von den Anfängen bis 1900* (Basel: n.p., 1960).

3. See, for instance, Johann Georg Zimmermann, who writes that Georg Ernst Stahl developed, while reading Descartes on the mind-body problem, "at every page an irresist-

ible disgust at this worldly wisdom born of the imagination" [bei jeder Seite einen unwiderstehbaren Eckel gegen diese in der Einbildung erzeugte Weltweisheit]; Zimmermann, *Das Leben des Herrn von Haller* (Zürich, 1755), 15. Cited by Reinhard Mocek, "Zum Mechanismus-Vitalismus-Paradigma der Stahl Ära," in *Georg Ernst Stahl (1659–1734): Hallesches Symposium 1984*, ed. Wolfgang Kaiser and Arina Völker (Halle: Martin-Luther-Universität Halle-Wittenberg, 1985), 34.

4. René Descartes, "Treatise on Man" and "Description of the Human Body," in *The Philosophical Writings of Descartes*, trans. John Cottingham, Robert Stoothoff, and Dugald Murdoch, 3 vols. (Cambridge: Cambridge University Press, 1985–91), 1:99–108, 314–24.

5. In his "Sixth Meditation. The Existence of Material Things, and the Real Distinction between Mind and Body," Descartes observes that only "one small part of the brain, namely the part which is said to contain the 'common' sense, affects the mind." The translator John Cottingham notes that in a letter dated 21 April, 1641, Descartes declared that the "conarion" was the seat of the common sense. Descartes, *Philosophical Writings of Descartes*, 2:59.

6. See Anselm Model, *Metaphysik und reflektierende Urteilskraft bei Kant: Untersuchungen zur Transformierung des leibnizschen Monadenbegriffes in der "Kritik der Urteilskraft"* (Frankfurt a/M: Athenäum, 1987), 291. See also L. J. Rather, *Mind and Body in Eighteenth-Century Medicine. A Study Based on Jerome Gaub's "De regimine mentis"* (London: Wellcome Historical Medical Library, 1965).

7. "Leibniz applies the separation of the dimension of the *res cogitans* (simple monads) and the *res extensa* (composite physical world) more consistently than Descartes." Model, *Metaphysik und reflektierende Urteilskraft bei Kant,* 291.

8. Gottfried Wilhelm Leibniz, "Considerations on the Principles of Life, and on Plastic Natures; By the Author of the System of Pre-Ordained Harmony" (1705), in *Philosophical Papers and Letters*, ed. Leroy E. Loemker, 2 vols. (Chicago: University of Chicago Press, 1956), 2:955. See also the Correspondence with Arnauld, 14 July 1686 and 9 October 1687, 1:507–37. For these passages in their original languages, see *Die philosophischen Schriften von Gottfried Wilhelm Leibniz*, ed. C. J. Gerhardt, 7 vols. (Berlin, 1885; reprint, Hildesheim: Olms, 1961), 6:541, 2:111–29.

9. Gerd Fabian, "Beitrag zur Geschichte des Leib-Seele-Problems (Lehre von der prästabilisierten Harmonie und vom psychophysischen Parallelismus in der Leibniz-Wolffschen Schule)," in *Friedrich Mann's Pädagogisches Magazin* 1012 (Langensalza: Hermann Beyer & Söhne, 1925), 29ff.

10. Christian Wolff, *Vernünftige Gedancken von Gott, der Welt, und der Seele des Menschen, auch allen Dingen überhaupt*, 3d ed. (Halle, 1725) 1:478.

11. Ibid.

12. Ibid.

13. Ibid., 479.

14. For more on the mind-body problem in early-eighteenth-century Germany, see Schings, "Der anthropologische Roman," 250. See also Fabian, "Beitrag zur Geschichte des Leib-Seele-Problems."

15. Shryock, *Development of Modern Medicine,* 23.

16. Johann Georg Sulzer, *Kurzer Begriff aller Wißenschaften und andere Theile der Gelehrsamkeit, worin jeder nach seinem Inhalt, Nuzen und Vollkommenheit kürzlich beschrieben wird*, 2d ed. (Leipzig, 1759), 130, 137.

17. Johannes Steudel, *Leibniz und die Medizin: Rede bei Übernahme des Rektoramtes der Rheinischen Friedrich-Wilhelms-Universität zu Bonn, 15 November 1958* (Bonn: Hanstein, 1960).

18. Werner Leibbrand and Annemarie Wettley, *Der Wahnsinn: Geschichte der abendländischen Psychopathologie* (Freiburg: Alber, 1961), 252–53.

19. Ibid., 251–55, 329–34.

20. For an introduction to Boerhaave's thinking, see King, *Medical World of the Eighteenth Century*, 59–121.

21. Andrew Cunningham, "Medicine to Calm the Mind: Boerhaave's Medical System, and Why It Was Adopted in Edinburgh," in *The Medical Enlightenment of the Eighteenth Century*, ed. Andrew Cunningham and Roger French (Cambridge: Cambridge University Press, 1990), 54.

22. Christian Probst, "Das Menschenbild der praktischen Medizin im 18. Jahrhundert, gezeigt an den Beispielen der Iatromechanik und des Epidemismus," in *Deutschlands kulturelle Entfaltung: Die Neubestimmung des Menschen*, ed. Bernhard Fabian, Wilhelm Schmidt-Biggemann, Rudolf Vierhaus, Studien zum achtzehnten Jahrhundert 2/3 (Munich: Kraus, 1980), 157.

23. Christian Probst, *Der Weg des ärztlichen Erkennens am Krankenbett: Herman Boerhaave und die ältere Wiener medizinische Schule* (Wiesbaden: Franz Steiner, 1972), 26.

24. Hoffmann, *Fundamenta Medicinae*, 11.

25. Johanna Geyer-Kordesch, "German Medical Education in the Eighteenth Century: The Prussian Influence," in *William Hunter and the Eighteenth-Century Medical World*, ed. W. F. Bynum and Roy Porter (Cambridge: Cambridge University Press, 1985), 194. See also Shryock, *Development of Modern Medicine,* 28.

26. Roger French, "Sickness and the Soul: Stahl, Hoffmann, and Sauvages on Pathology," in Cunningham and French, *Medical Enlightenment of the Eighteenth Century*, 98.

27. Ibid., 97.

28. Hoffmann, *Fundamenta Medicinae*, 12–13.

29. Ibid., 51–52.

30. Ibid., 55.

31. *L'homme machine* (1748). For more information on La Mettrie, see Bernd A. Laska's excellent introduction to Julian Offray de La Mettrie, *Der Mensch als Maschine*, trans. Bernd A. Laska (Nürnberg: LSR, 1985).

32. La Mettrie, *Der Mensch als Maschine,* 67.

33. Ibid.

34. Wolfgang Promies, *Die Bürger und der Narr oder das Risiko der Phantasie. Sechs Kapitel über das Irrationale in der Literatur des Rationalismus* (München: Hanser, 1966), 230.

35. Karl Eduard Rothschuh, "Leibniz, die prästabilisierte Harmonie und die Ärzte seiner Zeit," in *Akten des internationalen Leibniz-Kongresses, Hannover, 14–19 November 1966,* 6 vols. (Wiesbaden: Steiner, 1969), 2:240.

36. Johanna Geyer-Kordesch, "Georg Ernst Stahl's Radical Pietist Medicine and Its Influence on the German Enlightenment," in Cunningham and French, *Medical Enlightenment of the Eighteenth Century*.

37. Lester S. King, *The Philosophy of Medicine: The Early Eighteenth Century* (Cambridge: Harvard University Press, 1978), 143–51.

38. Ernst Platner, *Ernst Platners vermischte Aufsätze über medicinische Gegenstände* (Leipzig, 1796), 144.

39. Immanuel Kant, "Träume eines Geistersehers, erläutert durch Träume der Metaphysik," in *Werke in Sechs Bänden*, ed. Wilhelm Weischedel, 6 vols. (Wiesbaden: Insel, 1960–64), 1:939.

40. Shryock, *Development of Modern Medicine,* 28.

41. A collection of articles on Stahl's chemical thinking is available in *Chemie im achtzehnten Jahrhundert: Auf dem Weg zu einer internationalen Wissenschaft: Georg Ernst Stahl (1659–1734) zu 250. Todestag*, Staatsbibliothek Preußischer Kulturbesitz, 23 (Wiesbaden: Reichert, 1984).

42. "The unity of the body and soul, for which Stahl argues, directly challenged a somatically oriented medicine as well as post-Cartesian philosophy." Geyer-Kordesch, "Georg Ernst Stahl's Radical Pietist Medicine," 68.

43. Rothschuh, "Leibniz, die prästabilisierte Harmonie und die Ärzte seiner Zeit," 238.

44. Leibbrand and Wettley, *Der Wahnsinn*, 314.

45. George Ernst Stahl, *Über den mannigfaltigen Einfluß von Gemütsbewegungen auf den menschlichen Körper (Halle, 1695) . . .*, ed. Bernward Josef Gottlieb (Leipzig: Barth, 1961), 25.

46. Ibid., 37.

47. Ibid.

48. Johann Geyer-Kordesch, "Die 'Theoria medica vera' und Georg Ernst Stahls Verhältnis zur Aufklärung," in Kaiser and Völker, *Georg Ernst Stahl*, 84.

49. Simon-Andre Tissot, *Abhandlung über die Nerven und deren Krankheiten*, trans. J. C. G. Ackermann, 2 vols. (Frankfurt, 1782), 1:218.

50. Andreas Rüdiger, *Herrn Christian Wolffens Meinung von dem Wesen der Seele und eines Geistes überhaupt; und D. Andreas Rüdigers Gegen-Meinung* (Leipzig, 1727), § 12 (no page numbers).

51. Ibid., § 12, no page numbers.

52. Ibid., § 12, no page numbers.

53. For more on Krüger, plus a good summary of developments in eighteenth-century medicine, see Wolfram Mauser, "Johann Gottlieb Krügers 'Träume': Zu einer wenig beachteten literarischen Gattung des 18. Jahrhunderts," in *Goethe aus interkulturellen Perspektive*, ed. Adrian Fink and Gertrud Gréciano (Strasbourg: Institut d'études allemandes, Université de Sciences Humaines de Strasbourg, 1988).

54. Johann Gottlob Krüger, *Diät oder Lebensordnung*, 2d ed. (Halle, 1763), 346.

55. Ibid.

56. Ibid., 492.

57. Hence Promies's argument that Haller's experiments were attempts at compromise between Stahl and Boerhaave (*Die Bürger und der Narr*, 230–34).

58. Platner, *Ernst Platners vermischte Aufsätze*, 144–48.

59. Haller used painful stimulants like fire, acid, and sharp instruments to determine if the soul reacted to physical changes in the body. Pain indicated that the body part in question was linked to the conscious and sensible soul. Haller regretted that sometimes the pain produced by exposing the bodily part was so great that he could not determine if stimulation of the parts caused any additional pain. According to Shryock, there were six hundred experiments in all, of which Haller performed two hundred himself (*Development of Modern Medicine*, 65). Simon Richter provides illuminating insights into the relationship of Hallerian pain and eighteenth-century aesthetics in general in *Laocoon's Body and the Aesthetics of Pain*, 32, 93–108.

60. Shryock, *Development of Modern Medicine*, 61.

61. Albrecht von Haller, *Von den empfindlichen und reizbaren Teilen des menschlichen Körpers*, trans. and ed. Karl Sudhoff (Leipzig: Barth, 1922). Haller determined, incidentally, that parts of the tendons, bones, brain membranes, corneas, and organs like the intestines and the heart were merely irritable and had no connection with the soul, whereas other parts—muscles, skin, and certain organs—were sensible, which indicated the presence of the soul.

62. John Neubauer, *Bifocal Vision: Novalis' Philosophy of Nature and Disease* (Chapel Hill: University of North Carolina Press, 1971), 21.

63. Melchior Adam Weickard, *Entwurf einer einfachern Arzeneykunst oder Erläuterung und Bestätigung der Brownischen Arzneylehre* (Frankfurt a/M, 1795).

64. Rather, *Mind and Body in Eighteenth-Century Medicine*, 34. Metzger, incidentally,

called Gaub "without doubt still the greatest pathologist of our times." *Vermischte medicinische Schriften*, 2d ed., 2 vols. (Königsberg, 1784), 2:282.

65. Ernst Anton Nicolai, *Gedancken von den Würckungen der Einbildungskraft in den menschlichen Körper*, 2d ed. (Halle, 1751), 49.

66. Johann Georg Zimmermann, *Von der Erfahrung in der Arzneykunst*, "Neue Auflage" (Zürich, 1777), 315.

67. Johann Georg Zimmermann, *Ueber die Einsamkeit*, 4 vols. (Frankfurt, 1785), 1:117.

68. See Schings, *Melancholie und Aufklärung*, 63–64.

69. Zimmermann, *Von der Erfahrung in der Arzneykunst*, 635ff., for the effects of the passions on the body, and 682ff., for the effects of intellectual activity.

70. Thomas Arnold, *Beobachtungen über die Natur, Arten, Ursachen und Verhütung des Wahnsinns oder der Tollheit*, 2 vols. (Leipzig, 1784–88), 2:64.

71. Lavater, *Essays on Physiognomy*, 1:24. See Sander L. Gilman, "The Struggle of Psychiatry with Psychoanalysis: Who Won?" *Critical Inquiry* 13, no. 2 (Winter 1987): 293–313; and idem, *Wahnsinn, Text und Kontext: Die historischen Wechselbeziehungen der Literatur, Kunst, und Psychiatrie* (Frankfurt a/M and Bern: Peter Lang, 1981).

72. For an entertaining introduction to Mesmer and the whole world of eighteenth-century psychologists, see: Peter Sloterdijk, *Der Zauberbaum: Die Entstehung der Psychoanalyse im Jahr 1785: Ein epischer Versuch zur Philosophie der Psychologie* (Frankfurt a/M: Suhrkamp, 1985). For a more scholarly approach, see Maria Tatar, *Spellbound: Studies on Mesmerism and Literature* (Princeton: Princeton University Press, 1978).

73. Weickard referred skeptically to "the beautiful cures that are related to us about electric shocks." Melchior Adam Weickard, *Der philosophische Arzt*, 2d ed., 4 vols. (Frankfurt, 1782–85), 2:32.

74. Eberhard Gmelin, "Geschichte eines periodischen Wahnsinns," *Allgemeines Repertorium* 4 (1798): 154.

75. Hermann Boerhaave, *Kurze Lehr-Sätze von Erkennung und Heilung der Krankheiten* (Berlin, 1763), 371, aphorism 1089.

76. Starobinski, *Geschichte der Melancholiebehandlung*, 51.

77. Shryock, *Development of Modern Medicine*, 159. See also Erna Lesky, *The Vienna Medical School of the Nineteenth Century* (Baltimore: Johns Hopkins University Press, 1976), 8–12, 111.

78. Weickard, *Der philosophische Arzt*, 1:115.

79. Adolph Freiherr von Knigge, *Über den Umgang mit Menschen*, 5th ed., 3 vols. (Frankfurt, 1796), 1:98.

80. La Mettrie, *Der Mensch als Maschine*, 21–27. Johann Karl Wezel, *Versuch über die Kenntniß des Menschen*, 2 vols. (Leipzig, 1784; reprint, Frankfurt a/M: Athenäum, 1971), 1:82, 187

81. Rather, *Mind and Body in Eighteenth-Century Medicine*, 89.

82. Gert Mattenklott, *Melancholie in der Dramatik des Sturm und Drang*, Studien zur Allgemeinen und Vergleichenden Literaturwissenschaft 1 (Stuttgart: Metzler, 1968; reprint, Königstein/Ts: Athenäum, 1985), 22. The page number is that of the reprint.

83. Starobinski, *Geschichte der Melancholiebehandlung*, 56.

84. Hoffmann, *Fundamenta Medicinae*, 43.

85. Duden, *Woman Beneath the Skin*, 151–53.

86. Moritz, "Grundlinien zu einem ohngefähren Entwurf in Rücksicht auf die Seelenkrankheitskunde," *MzE* 1, no. 1 (1783): 31.

87. Arnold, *Beobachtungen*, 2:202.

88. Ziolkowski, *German Romanticism and Its Institutions*, 152.

89. Ernst Platner, *Anthropologie für Aerzte und Weltweise* (Leipzig, 1772), xvff. Cited in Schings, *Melancholie und Aufklärung*, 24.

90. Wezel, *Versuch über die Kenntniß des Menschen*, 1:7.

91. Ibid., 1:7–8.

92. Weissberg, *Geistersprache*, 21.

93. Wolfram Mauser, "Anakreon als Therapie? Zur medizinisch-diätetischen Begründung der Rokokodichtung," *Lessing Yearbook* 20 (1988): 87–120.

94. Schings, "Der anthropologische Roman." See also Horst Thomé, *Roman und Naturwissenschaft: Eine Studie zur Vorgeschichte der deutschen Klassik* (Frankfurt: Peter Lang, 1978).

95. Friedrich Schiller, "Versuch über den Zusammenhang der thierischen Natur des Menschen mit seiner geistigen," in *Schillers Werke. Nationalausgabe. Philosophische Schriften*, ed. Benno von Wiese, Erster Teil (Weimar: Böhlhaus, 1962), 20:64–65. For translations, see Dewhurst and Reeves, *Friedrich Schiller*. For further secondary literature, see note 24 in chapter 1.

96. Ziolkowski, *German Romanticism and Its Institutions*, 170.

97. Richter, *Laocoon's Body and the Aesthetics of Pain*, 32.

98. Model, *Metaphysik und reflektierende Urteilskraft bei Kant*, 12–13. According to Model, the first still preserved letter by Kant was written to Haller, a fact that further demonstrates the importance of medicine to the philosopher (316).

99. Ziolkowski, *German Romanticism and Its Institutions*, 150. See also Bennett, *Beyond Theory*, 240.

100. The medical section of the *Streit der Fakultäten* was written as an answer to what Kant called Hufeland's "edifying and delightful work." Hufeland republished it separately then under the title. *Von der Macht des Gemüths durch den bloßen Vorsatz seiner krankhaften Gefühle Meister zu sein* (On the power of mood to be Master of its pathological feelings purely through resolution), ed. Christoph Wilhelm Hufeland (Leipzig, 1824).

101. Immanuel Kant, "Gedanken von der wahren Schätzung der lebendigen Kräfte und Beurtheilung der Beweise, deren sich Herr von Leibniz und andere Mechaniker in der Streitsache bedient haben . . . ," *Werke* 1:1–218. Discussed by Model, *Metaphysik und reflektierende Urteilskraft bei Kant*, 334.

102. Kant, "Träume eines Geistersehers," 1:939. For a much more thorough analysis of the mind-body problem in Kant's "Träume," see Weissberg, *Geistersprache*, 34–61. See also Steudel, *Leibniz und die Medizin*, 20.

103. Kant, *Kritik der Urteilskraft*, § 65, *Werke* 5:486.

104. Gerhard Sauder, *Empfindsamkeit*, Band 1: *Voraussetzungen und Elemente* (Stuttgart: Metzler, 1974), 109.

105. 21 March 1830; AA 24:405.

106. *Xenien*, 83; HA 1:220.

107. Goethe's "Anmerkungen" to *Rameau's Neffe* (WA 1.45:197). See also Goethe's review of the *Bekehrungsgeschichte des vormaligen Grafen J. F. Struensee; nebst desselben eigenhändiger Nachricht, von der Art, wie er zu Änderung seiner Gesinnung über die Religion gekommen ist* (Conversion story of the former Count J. F. Struensee), by Dr. B. Münter, in the *Frankfurter gelehrte Anzeigen*. WA 1.37:254.

108. HA 9:273.

109. *Über Laokoon* (1798); HA 12:61–62.

110. Letter of 1 July; HA 6:33; SE 11:23.

111. Duden, *Woman Beneath the Skin*, 142–70.

112. Robert A. Erickson, "William Harvey's *De Motu Cordis* and 'The Republick of Literature,'" in Roberts and Porter, *Literature and Medicine in the Eighteenth Century*, 58–83.

113. Richter argues that, in his essay on Laocoon, Goethe has the Hallerian, medical sense of "Reiz" in mind (*Laocoon's Body and the Aesthetics of Pain*, 174).

114. W. Daniel Wilson, "Science, Natural Law, and Unwitting Sibling Incest in Eighteenth-Century Literature," *Studies in Eighteenth-Century Culture* 13 (1984): 249–70.

115. Hannelore Schlaffer, *Wilhelm Meister,* 74. Hellmut Ammerlahn, "Wilhelm Meister's Mignon: Ein offenbares Rätsel; Name, Gestalt, Symbol, Wesen und Werden," *Deutsche Vierteljahresschrift* 42, no. 1 (1968): 91–94.

116. Kurt Robert Eissler provocatively claims that this scene "admits of only one interpretation": "a masterly description, realistic down to the smallest detail, of a girl having an orgasm." Eissler, *Goethe,* 2:870. Discussed by Roberts, *Indirections of Desire,* 81. See also Robert Tobin, "The Medicinalization of Mignon," in *Goethes Mignon und ihre Schwestern: Interpretationen und Rezeption* (New York: Peter Lang, 1993), 48–49. This volume contains a number of important studies of Mignon.

117. Schiebinger, *Mind Has No Sex?,* 168–69. Laqueur, *Making Sex,* 155.

118. Stephan Koranyi, *Autobiographik und Wissenschaft im Denken Goethes* (Bonn: Bouvier, 1984), 197–98.

119. For more on the Beautiful Soul's sexuality, see Frederick J Beharriell, "The Hidden Meaning of Goethe's 'Bekenntnisse einer schönen Seele,'" in *Lebendige Form,* ed. by Jeffrey L. Sammons and Ernst Schürer (München: Fink, 1970), 37–62. See also Jill Anne Kowalik, "Feminine Identity Formation in *Wilhelm Meisters Lehrjahre,*" *MLQ* 53, no. 2 (June 1992): 149–72.

120. For similar argumentation, see also Schings, "Agathon-Anton Reiser-Wilhelm Meister," 50–51.

Chapter 3. Surgical, Internal, and Psychological Medicine

1. Duden, *Woman Beneath the Skin,* 64.

2. Johann Christian Reil, *Rhapsodieen über die Anwendung der psychischen Curmethode auf Geisteszerrüttungen* (Halle, 1803; Amsterdam: Bonset, 1968), 26.

3. Johann Friedrich Heynatz, *Versuch eines möglichst vollständigen synonymischen Wörterbuches der Deutschen Sprache* (Berlin, 1795), s.v. "Bader, Barbier, Bartscherer, Feldscher oder Feldscherer, Wundarzt, Chirurgus," 381.

4. *Deutsches Wörterbuch von Jacob und Wilhelm Grimm,* ed. Sütterlin, s.v. "Wundarzt," vol. 14, no. 2, column 1770.

5. Schiebinger, *Mind Has No Sex?,* 105.

6. Heynatz, *Versuch,* 381–82.

7. Ferdinand Gregorovius, *Göthe's Wilhelm Meister in seinen socialistischen Elementen entwickelt,* 2d ed. (Schwäbisch Hall, 1855), 181.

8. Johann Zachariä Platner, *Gründliche Einleitung in die Chirurgie oder kurze Anweisung aller Kranckheiten, so denen Chirurgis vorkommen,* 2 vols. (Leipzig, 1757), 1:14.

9. Shryock, *Development of Modern Medicine,* 90, 146–49.

10. HA 7:585. The passage is on p. 359 of SE 9, but the translation substitutes the more general "medical" for "surgical."

11. Shryock, *Development of Modern Medicine,* 52.

12. *Deutsches Wörterbuch von Jacob und Wilhelm Grimm,* ed. Sütterlin, s.v. "Wundarzt," vol. 14, no. 2, column 1770. For Heynatz, *Medicus* was merely an unnecessary foreign word for "physician" [*Arzt*]. Heynatz, *Versuch,* s.v. "Arzt, Doktor, Medicus," 254.

13. Thomas Broman, "Transformation of Academic Medicine in Germany, 1780–1820" (diss., Princeton University, 1987).

14. Dorothea Erxleben (1715–62), "Germany's first woman MD," practiced medicine

and received her medical degree from Halle in 1754, by royal dispensation from Frederick the Great. Erxleben was however an exception—no more women graduated from the medical school at Halle until 1901! Schiebinger, *Mind Has No Sex?*, 250–57.

15. *Faust I*, "Outside the City Gate," 1035ff; SE 2:29; HA 3:39. Trunz explains the meaning of the alchemical terminology in his commentary, HA 3:528–29. For more on alchemy and Goethe, see Ronald Gray, *Goethe the Alchemist* (Cambridge: Cambridge University Press, 1952).

16. Johann August Unzer, *Medicinisches Handbuch* (Lüneberg, 1770), 268.

17. Christian Wilhelm Hufeland, "Ueber den Mißbrauch des Opiums bei Kindern, nebst der Geschichte einer Opiatvergiftung in den ersten Tagen des Lebens" (1801), in *Christoph Wilhelm Hufeland: Kleine Medizinische Schriften*, 4 vols. (Berlin, 1822–28), 3:398.

18. Hufeland, *Die Kunst, das menschliche Leben zu verlängern* (Jena, 1797), 485. Apparently, Hufeland presented a copy of this book to Goethe, who however immediately passed it on to his mother unopened. Gittinger, "Krankheit und heilender Eingriff," 20.

19. The "Brunonian" system was founded by John Brown (1735–88). His *Elementa medicinae* (1780) set up a new school of thought in medicine which classified all illness into the two large categories of "sthenie" (overstimulation) and "asthenie" (understimulation). Although Goethe was skeptical of Brown's speculative medicine (Shryock, *Development of Modern Medicine*, 67), he apparently found the revolutionary medical system fascinating, for he turned his attention to it repeatedly in his writings (HA 9:450; WA 3.3:53).

20. Weickard, *Der philosophische Arzt*, 1:6.

21. Nicolai, *Gedancken von den Würckungen der Einbildungskraft in den menschlichen Körper*, 47.

22. Krüger, *Diät oder Lebensordnung*, 396.

23. Ibid.

24. On druggists and apothecaries, see King, *Medical World of the Eighteenth Century*, 1–29. On the (largely female) medicinal cooks, see Schiebinger, *Mind Has No Sex?*, 112–16.

25. *Deutsches Wörterbuch von Jacob und Wilhelm Grimm*, ed. Sütterlin, s.v. "Leibarzt," vol. 6, column 590.

26. Championing the 1770s is Gerhard Sauder, *Empfindsamkeit*, 1:106. Preferring the 1780s is Schings, *Melancholie und Aufklärung*, 145.

27. Hufeland, "Geschichte der Gesundheit, nebst einer physischen Charakteristik des jetzigen Zeitalters" (Berlin, 1812), in *Christoph Wilhelm Hufeland: Kleine Medizinische Schriften*, 4:379.

28. Johann Daniel Metzger, "Beytrag zu einer medicinischen Topographie der Stadt Königsberg," in *Vermischte medicinische Schriften*, 2:141.

29. See H. B. Wagnitz, *Historische Nachrichten und Bemerkungen über die merkwürdigsten Zuchthäuser in Deutschland. Nebst einem Anhang über die zweckmäßigste Einrichtung der Gefängnisse und Irrenanstalten* (Halle, 1791–94).

30. He also treated Goethe in 1801 (Nager, *Der heilkundige Dichter,* 31). From Goethe's diaries and letters, it is clear that he socialized with Reil as the occasion arose and thanked him for his influential book, *Rhapsodies on the Use of the Psychic Cure Method (Rhapsodieen über die Anwendung der psychischen Curmethode)*, as soon as it was published, in August 1803. (Reil is referred to in the following passages: WA 3.3:59, 73, 77, 4.16: 269, 328, 461)

31. Ziolkowski, *German Romanticism and Its Institutions*, 202, 152.

32. Reil, *Rhapsodieen*, 11–12.

33. For more on visits to the insane asylum, as well as Goethe's reaction to this practice, see Anke Bennholdt-Thomsen and Alfredo Guzzoni, "Der Irrenhausbesuch," *Aurora* 42 (1982): 82–110. See also F. Fischer, "Goethe über Irrenanstalten und Geisteskrankheiten," *Psychiatrisch-Neurologische Wochenschrift* 43 (23 January 1903): 474.

34. See Starobinski, *Geschichte der Melancholiebehandlung,* 54–81, for a summary.

35. Gesa Wunderlich, *Krankheits- und Therapiekonzepte am Anfang der deutschen Psychiatrie: Haindorf, Heinroth, Ideler* (Husum: Matthieson, 1981), 86.

36. Diener, *Goethes "Lila,"* 160. For more on the English tradition, see also Werner Obermeit, *"Das unsichtbare Ding, das Seele heißt": Die Entdeckung der Psyche im bürgerlichen Zeitalter* (Frankfurt a/M: Syndikat, 1980).

37. Ziolkowski, *German Romanticism and Its Institutions,* 143.

38. Klaus Dörner, *Bürger und Irre* (Frankfurt a/M: Europäische Verlagsanstalt, 1969), 105–16.

39. "Aus dem Mercure de France dieses Jahres, Nro 2," *MzE* 7, no. 2 (1789): 112–14.

40. Michel Foucault, *Madness and Civilization: A History of Insanity in the Age of Reason,* trans. Richard Howard (New York: Vintage, 1988), 245.

41. Knigge, *Ueber den Umgang mit Menschen,* 1:152. Reil also advocated violence only at the beginning of the treatment and absolutely forbade it in the case of mentally retarded patients (*Rhapsodieen,* 188–89, 220–32).

42. Zur Hellen, "Ueber Seelenkrankheit und einen Seelenkranken Menschen," *MzE* 7, no. 2 (1789): 124.

43. Reil, *Rhapsodieen,* 241.

44. Ibid., 244.

45. Foucault, *Madness and Civilization,* 249.

46. Franz Loquai, *Künstler und Melancholie in der Romantik* (Frankfurt a/M: Peter Lang, 1984).

47. Boerhaave, *Kurze Lehr-Sätze von Erkennung und Heilung der Krankheiten,* 371.

48. Hoffmann, *Fundamenta Medicinae,* 94.

49. Knigge, *Über den Umgang mit Menschen,* 1:152.

50. Immanuel Mauchart, "Über den eigentlichen Sitz des Wahnsinns," *Allgemeines Repertorium für empirische Psychologie und verwandte Wissenschaften* 2 (1792): 46–47.

51. Ibid., 48.

52. On the usage of the theater and the fine arts for therapy, see, for instance, Martin Schrenk, *Über den Umgang mit Geisteskranken: Die Entwicklung der psychiatrischen Therapie vom "moralischen Regime" in England und Frankreich zu den "psychischen Curmethoden" in Deutschland* (Berlin: Springer, 1973), 70ff.

53. J.H.K., "Ein Brief die Seelenheilkunde betreffend," *MzE* 3, no. 1 (1785): 89–90.

54. In his prefatory remarks to the letter, Moritz praises it despite its bad style and religious undertones: "The following letter contains, despite the effusive and simplistic style, very reasonable thoughts, and is all the more noteworthy, as it seems to come from someone who has not studied, who judges simply according to his right feeling, without preformed opinions." *MzE* 3, no. 1 (1785): 89.

55. Mauchart, "Über den eigentlichen Sitz des Wahnsinns," 50–51.

56. First published by Moritz in the *Magazine,* it was later mentioned by Mauchart in "Über den eigentlichen Sitz des Wahnsinns," 21, 50.

57. Ernestine Christiane Reiske, "Heilung des Wahnwitzes durch Erweckung neuer Ideen, in zwei Beispielen," *MzE* 3, no. 3 (1785): 214.

58. Moritz, "Revision der drei ersten Bände dieses Magazins," *MzE* 4, no. 1 (1786): 34.

59. J.H.K., "Ein Brief," 90.

60. At least, the physician thought it was a lie. Moritz actually did die of tuberculosis at an early age.

61. Eighteenth-century medicine considered this cure a minor sensation. Reil mentions it (*Rhapsodieen,* 285). Müller discusses this case at length (*Die kranke Seele und das Licht der Erkenntnis,* 72ff.).

62. Albrecht Schöne, "Interpretationen zur dichterischen Gestaltung des Wahnsinns in der deutschen Literatur," diss., Münster, 1951. Anke Bennholdt-Thomsen and Alfredo Guzzoni, *Der "Asoziale" in der Literatur um 1800* (Königstein: Athenäum, 1979). Jutta Osinski, *Über Vernunft und Wahnsinn: Studien zur literarischen Aufklärung in der Gegenwart und im 18. Jahrhundert* (Bonn: Bouvier, 198). Georg Reuchlein, *Bürgerliche Gesellschaft, Psychiatrie, und Literatur: Zur Entwicklung der Wahnsinnsthematik in der deutschen Literatur des späten 18. und frühen 19. Jahrhunderts* (München: Fink, 1986).

63. Ziolkowski, *German Romanticism and Its Institutions,* 155.

64. Georg Reuchlein, *Die Heilung des Wahnsinns bei Goethe: Orest, Lila, der Harfner und Sperate. Zum Verhältnis von Literatur, Seelenkunde und Moral im späten 18. Jahrhundert* (Frankfurt a/M: Peter Lang, 1983).

65. *Allgemeines Repertorium* 2 (1792): 30–31.

66. Georg Christoph Lichtenberg, *Südelbücher,* ed. Franz H. Mautner (Frankfurt a/M: Insel, 1983), B72, 41. See also Arnold, *Beobachtung,* 1:214; Zimmermann, *Von der Erfahrung in der Arzneykunst,* 642–85; and Reil, *Rhapsodieen,* 292.

67. Arnold, *Beobachtungen,* 1:194.

68. Zimmermann, *Von der Erfahrung in der Arzneikunst,* 642–85. See also Reil, *Rhapsodieen,* 346; and Weickard, *Der philosophische Arzt,* 3:157.

69. Gittinger, "Krankheit und heilender Eingriff," 49ff. Eugen Wolff, *Mignon: Ein Beitrag zur Geschichte des Wilhelm Meister* (Munich: Beck, 1909), 149–50. Both refer to Zimmermann, *Von der Erfahrung in der Arzneykunst.*

70. Reil, *Rhapsodieen,* 292.

71. Goethe to K.F.M. Graf Brühl, 1 October 1818; WA 4.29:299.

72. For contrary theses, see: Schöne, "Interpretationen zur dichterischen Gestaltung des Wahnsinns in der deutschen Literatur," 62–64; Gittinger, "Krankheit und heilender Eingriff," 90–105; and Paul J. Möbius, *Über das Pathologische bei Goethe,* 2d ed (Leipzig, 1898; Munich: Matthes, 1982), 149.

73. "Nachteilige Wirkung der Einsamkeit auf die Leidenschaften, zumal bey Einsiedlern und Mönchen," in Zimmermann, *Ueber die Einsamkeit,* 2:204–452.

74. Zimmermann, *Ueber die Einsamkeit,* 2:292.

75. "Aus einem Brief," *MzE* 5, no. 1 (1787): 78–79; "Merkwürdige Beispiele von Lebensüberdruß," *MzE* 6, no. 3 (1788): 194–95.

76. "Ein Kindermörder aus Lebensüberdruß," *MzE* 2, no. 1 (1784): 15–17.

77. Boerhaave, *Kurze Lehr-Sätze von Erkennung und Heilung der Krahnkheiten,* aphorisms 1118–19.

78. Hoffmann, *Fundamenta Medicinae,* 72.

79. Christian Wilhelm Hufeland, "Medizinische Praxis der Landesgeistlichen" (1811), in *Christian Wilhelm Hufeland: Kleine Medizinische Schriften,* 3:233–39.

80. Gittinger, "Krankheit und heilender Eingriff," 90ff.

81. Ulrich Nassen, "Trübsinn und Indigestion—Zum medizinischen und literarischen Diskurs über Hypochondrie im 18. Jahrhundert," in *Fugen. Deutsch-Französisches Jahrbuch für Textanalytik* (Freiburg: Walter, 1980), 170–86.

82. Reil, *Rhapsodieen,* 314ff.

83. Ibid., 210. See also Moritz, "Revision der ersten Bände des Magazins," 31.

84. Reuchlein, *Die Heilung des Wahnsinns,* 84ff.

85. Gittinger, "Krankheit und heilender Eingriff," 90–105. Reuchlein, *Die Heilung des Wahnsinns,* 86.

86. Schrenk, *Über den Umgang mit Geisteskranken,* 47. Gittinger, "Krankheit und heilender Eingriff," 90–105.

CHAPTER 4. THE PHYSICIAN'S POWER

1. Sulzer, *Kurzer Begriff aller Wißenschaften*, 157–60.

2. Cited in Müller, *Die kranke Seele und das Licht der Erkenntnis*, 66. Müller devotes an entire chapter, "Porträt eines philosophischen Arztes," to Herz.

3. Cited in ibid.

4. Cited in ibid.

5. Karl Philipp Moritz, "Über den Endzweck des Magazins zur Erfahrungsseelenkunde," *MzE* 8, no. 1 (1791): 9.

6. Rather, *Mind and Body in Eighteenth-Century Medicine*, 50.

7. La Mettrie, *Der Mensch als Maschine*, 20–21. Perhaps this attack on the philosophers is one of the ideas that La Mettrie stole from Gaub, if Gaub's complaints to Haller are based on the truth (Rather, *Mind and Body in Eighteenth-Century Medicine*, 13).

8. Zimmermann, *Von der Erfahrung in der Arzneykunst*, book 1.

9. Moritz, footnote to "Grundlinien," 28.

10. Immanuel D. Mauchart, "Vorrede," *Allgemeines Repertorium* 1 (1792): iii–iv.

11. Johann Gottfried Herder, "Vom Erkennen und Empfinden der menschlichen Seele," in *Herders Werke in fünf Bänden*, 4th ed. (Berlin: Aufbau, 1969), 3:18.

12. For an explanation of the eighteenth-century understanding of the poet as body-oriented (in contrast to the the mind-oriented philosopher), see Weissberg, *Geistersprache*, 20–21.

13. Herder, "Vom Erkennen und Empfinden der menschlichen Seele," 3:18.

14. Kant, "Träume eines Geistersehers," 1:939. For more on the subject, see Weissberg, *Geistersprache*, 34–61.

15. Model, *Metaphysik und reflektierende Urteilskraft bei Kant*, 325.

16. George Berkeley, "Letter to Thomas Prior," in *Works*, ed. Alexander Campbell Fraser, 4 vols. (Oxford: Oxford University Press, 1901), 3:306. Cited in King, *Medical World of the Eighteenth Century*, 31–53.

17. Simon-André Tissot, *Von der Gesundheit der Gelehrten* (Leipzig, 1775), 1.

18. Zur Hellen, "Ueber Seelenkrankheit und einen Seelenkranken Menschen," 116.

19. Cited by Wunderlich, *Krankheits- und Therapiekonzepte am Anfang der deutschen Psychiatrie*, 85.

20. Ibid., 55.

21. Moritz, "Revision der ersten Bände des Magazins," 31.

22. For more examples on this subject, see Schings, *Melancholie und Aufklärung*. See also Weissberg, *Geistersprache*, 62–91.

23. Carl Friedrich Pockels, in his addendum to Daniel Jenisch's "Über die Schwärmerey und ihre Quellen in unseren Zeiten," *MzE* 5, no. 3 (1787): 226.

24. Arnold, *Beobachtung*, 2:351–52.

25. Weickard, *Der philosophische Arzt*, 4:188.

26. Zimmermann, *Von der Erfahrung in der Arzneykunst*, 702.

27. Mauchart, "Verstand in der Raserey," *Allgemeines Repertorium* 4 (1798): 83.

28. Tissot, *Von der Gesundheit der Gelehrten*, 98.

29. Cited by Goethe in "Windischmann, Über etwas das der Heilkunst Noth thut." *WA* 1.41.2:160.

30. Moritz called Socrates one of the best "moral physicians" *(moralische Ärzte)*. Moritz, "Grundlinien," 31.

31. Novalis, "Das Allgemeine Brouillon," in *Novalis: Schriften: Die Werke Friedrich von Hardenbergs*, ed. Paul Kluckhohn and Richard Samuel, 2d ed., 5 vols. (Stuttgart: Kohlhammer, 1977–88), 3:315.

32. "Der Arzt ist ein Künstler . . ." Kant, "Der Streit der Fakultäten," in *Werke in Sechs Bänden*, 6:288.

33. Johann Daniel Metzger, "Ueber die Wirkung der Arzneymittel im M.K.," in *Vermischte medicinische Schriften*, 1:230.

34. Diaetophilus, *Physische und Psychologische Geschichte seiner siebenjaehrigen Epilepsie*, 2:302. See also Reil, *Rhapsodieen*, 23.

35. Adelung, *Grammatisch-kritisches Wörterbuch der Hochdeutschen Sprache*, col. 1648.

36. See Broman, "Transformation of Academic Medicine in Germany." For a discussion of Boerhaave's belief that theory was science, practice art, see also Richard Toellner, "Medicina Theoretica—Medicina Practica: Das Problem des Verhältnisses von Theorie und Praxis in der Medizin des 17. und 18. Jahrhunderts," in *Theoria cum Praxi: Zur Verhältnis von Theorie und Praxis im 17. und 18. Jahrhundert: Akten des IV. Internationalen Leibniz-kongresses*, 4 vols. (Wiesbaden: Franz Steiner, 1982), 2:69–73.

37. Zimmermann, *Von der Erfahrung in der Arzneykunst*, 338–52.

38. Sauder, *Empfindsamkeit*, 1:154–76.

39. Hoffmann, *Fundamenta Medicinae*, 55–60.

40. Nicolai, *Gedancken von den Würkungen der Einbildungskraft in den menschlichen Körper*, 46. For more on Nicolai's "Therapie imaginaria," see Mauser, "Anakreon als Therapie?," 87–100.

41. Mauchart, "Ueber den eigentlichen Sitz des Wahnsinns," 3.

42. Arnold, *Beobachtungen*, 2:351.

43. Ibid., 361.

44. Zimmermann, *Von der Erfahrung in der Arzneykunst*, 102.

45. For more on the increasingly problematic status of the imagination, see Promies, *Die Bürger und der Narr*, 202ff.

46. "Tag- und Jahreshefte 1805"; HA 10:490. Discussed by Promies, *Die Bürger und der Narr*, 170.

47. "sie hat sich fest *eingebildet*, es werde dieses Übel mit einem Krebsschaden endigen." HA 7:349, emphasis mine. The Suhrkamp edition translates *sich einbilden* as "to persuade oneself" (SE 9:211), which misses the nuance present in its relationship to the word *Einbildungskraft* (imagination).

48. Nicolai, *Gedancken von den Würckungen der Einbildungskraft in den menschlichen Körper*, 46.

49. For more on the imagination, but without reference to the medical tradition, see Monika Fick, "Destruktive Imagination: Die Tragödie der Dichterexistenz in *Wilhelm Meisters Lehrjahren*," *Jahrbuch der deutschen Schillergesellschaft* 29 (1985): 207–47.

50. Lichtenberg, *Südelbücher*, KA5, 32.

51. Ibid., J510, 389.

52. Reil, *Rhapsodieen*, 401.

53. Karl Friedrich Flögel, cited by Promies, *Die Bürger und der Narr*, 40. See also Wolf Lepenies, *Melancholie und Gesellschaft* (Frankfurt a/M: Suhrkamp, 1969), 92.

54. Moritz, "Vorwort," *MzE* I, no. 1 (1783): n.p. See also Mauchart, who declared "it belongs to the plan of this repertory to analyze dramatic works" (*Allgemeines Repertorium* 1 [1792]: 266), and included reviews of fictional works, by, for instance, Kotzebue, in the volumes of his journal.

55. Weissberg, *Geistersprache*, 20–21.

56. A view to which Goethe expressly ascribed, incidentally, in his essay, "Hör-, Schreib- und Druckfehler" (ca. 1820). WA 1.41:183–88.

57. "fast gehört der Fall in Ihr Fach, lieber Pastor." HA 7:348. The Suhrkamp translation elides the "fast" too much for my purposes here: "I believe this case belongs in your territory. . . ." SE 9: 211.

58. See Schings's commentary in the Münchner Ausgabe of the *Lehrjahre.* MA 5:794.

59. Letter to Augustin Trapp, 28 July 1770; WA 4.1:242.

60. "die Behandlung des Geistlichen hatte ihre Vorstellungsart so verwirrt, daß sie, ohne wahnsinnig zu sein, sich in den schlimmsten Zuständen befand." HA 7:587. The Suhrkamp translation changes the grammar and glosses over the use of the word *Behandlung* (treatment): "[T]he priest having so confused her that, without being mad, she found herself in the strangest state of mind." SE 9:359.

CHAPTER 5. RAPTURE AND MELANCHOLY, HYPOCHONDRIA AND HYSTERIA

1. For more on the interrelationship of the two aspects of the Tower Society—trainer of young men like Wilhelm Meister and reorganizer of society—see Haas, *Die Turmgesellschaft in "Wilhelm Meisters Lehrjahren.*

2. Bernd Nitzschke, "Goethe ist tot, es lebe die Kultur," introduction to Möbius, *Über das Pathologische bei Goethe*, 20–21.

3. For more on the links between religious fanaticism, *Schwärmerei*, acedia, and melancholia, see Schings, *Melancholie und Aufklärung.*

4. Goethe to Lavater, 22 June 1781; WA 4.5:147.

5. For instance, Zur Hellen, "Beispiel und Folgen einer schwärmerischen Sehnsucht nach dem Tode," *MzE* 2, no. 1 (1784): 53–56. See also Schings, *Melancholie und Aufklärung,* 165–200.

6. Carl Friedrich Pockels, addendum to Jenisch, *MzE* 5, no. 3 (1787): 226.

7. HA 7:191, 196. Translated as "quietly brooding," SE 9:112, and "wrapped up in himself," SE 9:115.

8. Sauder, *Empfindsamkeit,* 1:152.

9. For more on the close connections between the count's melancholy, disturbances of the "Ich," and narcissism, see Hörisch, *Gott, Geld und Glück,* 69.

10. F. A. Stroth, "Zweifel an eigener Existenz," *MzE* 2, no. 1 (1784): 59–60. Z.L.A. Schl., "Einige Bemerkungen über etliche im ersten Stück des zweiten Bandes des Magazins befindliche Aufsätze," *MzE* 4, no. 3 (1786): 281.

11. Zimmermann, *Ueber die Einsamkeit,* 2:192.

12. As early as 1911, Ernst Berendt pointed out the connections between this poem and Obereit's medicinal writings in *Goethes Wilhelm Meister: Ein Beitrag zur Entstehungsgeschichte* (Dortmund: Ruhfus, 1911), 67ff. See also Schings's commentary on this poem in the Münchner Ausgabe, MA 5:742.

13. Zimmermann, *Ueber die Einsamkeit,* 2:151.

14. One thinks of Wilhelm's reaction to Mariane (SE 9:30; HA 7:57), and Mignon's to Wilhelm (SE 9:83; HA 7:145–46).

15. For more on eighteenth-century scientific attitudes toward incest and nature and their application to this scene, see Wilson, "Science, Natural Law, and Unwitting Sibling Incest," 249–70.

16. §69. For more on this subject, see Ilse Graham, *Goethe: Portrait of the Artist* (Berlin and New York: de Gruyter, 1977), 205. See also Achim Aurnhammer, *Androgynie: Studien zu einem Motiv in der Europäischen Literatur* (Köln, Wien: Böhlen, 1986), 166ff.

17. Interestingly, "anastomosis" is also a medical term, showing up, for instance, in Benjamin Rush's treatises on medical taxonomies. It has origins in anatomy, where it refers to the connections between veins and nerves, as well as in botany, where it refers to the connections between plant veins. That the word could float between medical taxonomies

and Goethe's writings on plants is not surprising, for a number of reasons. To begin with, in an older tradition botany was intimately connected with medicine, as many medications were made from herbs. This notion began to die out as the physicians discredited druggists and associated medical cooking with superstitious old women (Schiebinger, *Mind Has No Sex?*, 112–16, 241–44). More importantly for Goethe and his era, the later eighteenth century attempted to apply the Linnean botanical model throughout nature and society, and particularly to medicine. The use of this medical term to describe the lily, with which the Harper identifies, is a subtle example of the influence that medical discourses have on the description of the Harper and a suggestion that a medical eye is overseeing the Harper's development.

18.　Schöne argues that Augustin's fear of Felix is also a fear of a projection of himself, which would further support the thesis that Augustin's relationships with others suffer from his inability to escape himself or his projections. Schöne, "Interpretationen zur dichterischen Gestaltung des Wahnsinns in der deutschen Literatur," 65.

19.　See Zimmermann's tirades against monks and celibacy in both *Von der Erfahrung in der Arzneykunst* and *Ueber die Einsamkeit*.

20.　*Allgemeines Repertorium* 3 (1793): 313.

21.　Weissberg, *Geistersprache*, 93, 103.

22.　Monika Fick, "Mignon—Psychologie und Morphologie der Geniusallegorie in *Wilhelm Meisters Lehrjahren*," *Sprachkunst* 13 (1982): 19. Aurnhammer, *Androgynie*, 166. William Gilby, "The Structural Significance of Mignon in *Wilhelm Meisters Lehrjahre*," *Seminar* 16 (1980): 139–40. Per Øhrgaard, *Die Genesung des Narcissus: Eine Studie zu Goethe: "Wilhelm Meisters Lehrjahre,"* trans. Monika Wesemann (Copenhagen: Københavns Universität, 1978), 78.

23.　Gilby is one of the few critics to note Wilhelm's partial authorship of this poem ("Structural Significance of Mignon," 141).

24.　Goethe to Schiller, 18 March 1795; WA 4.10:244.

25.　May, "*Wilhelm Meisters Lehrjahre*, ein Bildungsroman?," 24–25. Wundt, *Goethes Wilhelm Meister und die Entwicklung des modernen Lebensideals,* 211ff. Erich Trunz, HA 7:767. For a gallant defence of the Beautiful Soul, see Daniel J. Farrely, *Goethe and Inner Harmony: A Study of the "schöne Seele" in the "Apprenticeship of Wilhelm Meister"* (Shannon, Ireland: Irish University Press, 1973).

26.　Bernhard Greiner, "Dialogisches Wort als Medium des Über-Sich-Redens: Goethes 'Bekenntnisse einer schönen Seele' im *Wilhelm Meister* und die Friederiken-Episode in *Dichtung und Wahrheit*," in *Freiburger literaturpsychologische Gespräche*, Bd. 11, *Über sich selber reden: Zur Psychoanalyse autobiographischen Schreibens*, ed. Johannes Cremerius, Wolfram Mauser, Carl Pietzcker, and Frederick Wyatt (Würzburg: Königshausen & Neumann, 1992), 95–120.

27.　Beharriel, "Hidden Meaning of Goethe's 'Bekenntnisse einer schönen Seele,'" 37–62. Kowalik, "Feminine Identity Formation in *Wilhelm Meisters Lehrjahre*," 149–72.

28.　Øhrgaard, *Die Genesung des Narcissus,* 149ff.

29.　Wolfgang Kehl, "'Die Schönheiten der Natur gemeinschaftlich betrachten': Zum Zusammenhang von Freundschaft, ästhetischer Naturerfahrung und 'Gartenrevolution' in der Spätaufklärung," in *Frauenfreundschaft—Männerfreundschaft: Literarische Diskurse im 18. Jahrhundert*, ed. Wolfram Mauser and Barbara Becker-Cantarino (Tübingen: Niemeyer, 1991), 174–75, 182.

30.　An anonymous writer cited by Franz Loquai, *Künstler und Melancholie in der Romantik,* 31.

31.　Müller, *Die kranke Seele und das Licht der Erkenntnis,* 93.

32.　Ibid., 93.

33. Promies, *Die Bürger und der Narr,* 238–39.

34. . . . *Beweis, daß die Hypochondrie heutigen Tages eine fast allgemein verbreitete Krankheit ist, und daß sie eine Ursache der Entvölkerung abgeben kann.* Gert Mattenklott has the full citation in the bibliography of *Melancholie in der Dramatik des Sturm und Drang.*

35. *Der grosse Duden,* vol. 5, *Fremdwörterbuch,* 3d ed. (Mannheim: Dudenverlag, 1974), 307.

36. Arnold, *Beobachtung,* 1:179.

37. Kant, "Streit der Fakultäten," 6:378. Discussed at length in Nassen, "Trübsinn und Indigestion."

38. Ziolkowski, *German Romanticism and Its Institutions,* 150.

39. Hoffmann, *Fundamenta Medicinae,* 80.

40. Cited in Foucault, *Madness and Civilization,* 145. He discusses the relationships between the two diseases at length and in detail (136–58).

41. George S. Rousseau, "Cultural History in a New Key: Towards a Semiotics of the Nerve," in *Interpretation and Cultural History,* ed. Joan H. Pittock and Andrew Wear (London: Macmillan, 1991), 45–46.

42. Joseph Raulin, *Traité des affections* (Paris, 1758), xx. Cited by Foucault, *Madness and Civilization,* 138–39.

43. Linking the two ailments, Arnold cited Syndenham (*Beobachtungen,* 1:184). Wezel referred to Haller when connecting the two diseases (Wezel, *Versuch über die Kenntniß des Menschen,* 1:188). Weickard classified both as asthenic diseases (*Entwurf einer einfachern Arzeneykust,* 272). See also Sauder, *Empfindsamkeit,* 1:152; and Rather, *Mind and Body in Eighteenth-Century Medicine,* 189.

44. Sauder, *Empfindsamkeit,* 1:147–54.

45. Quistorp, "Der Hypochondrist." Cited by Promies, *Die Bürger und der Narr,* 238.

46. Johann Heinrich Zedler, *Großes Universal-Lexikon aller Wissenschaften und Künste,* 64 vols. (Leipzig, 1735), 13:1479.

47. Cited by Nassen, "Trübsinn und Indigestion," 175.

48. Foucault, *Madness and Civilization,* 145. He cites Stahl, *Theorie medica vera,* 453.

49. See Tissot, *Abhandlung über die Nerven und deren Krankheiten,* 2:72–99.

50. Ibid., 351.

51. Foucault, *Madness and Civilization,* 149–50.

52. See Loquai's summary of the theories in Zedler and other encyclopedias of the era.

53. Lichtenberg, *Südelbücher,* J673, 399.

54. See Kay Flavell, "Goethe, Rousseau, and the 'Hyp,'" in *Oxford German Studies* 7, ed. D. F. Glanz (Oxford: Clarendon Press, 1973), 5–23.

55. Conversation with Riemer, 3 May 1814. AA 22:722.

56. Schings, "Symbolik des Glücks," 170.

57. Zimmermann, *Ueber die Einsamkeit,* 1:59. Much later, while discussing Byron's poetry, Goethe himself associates "hypochondriac passion" and violent "self-hatred." "Tag- und Jahreshefte 1816"; HA 10:520.

58. Elaine Showalter, *The Female Malady: Women, Madness, and English Culture, 1830–1980* (New York: Penguin, 1985), 10.

59. The original maintains more clearly the specularity of this relationship: "wie ich wirkte, wirkte die Menge wieder auf mich zurück; ich war mit meinem Publikum in dem besten Vernehmen," literally, "as I affected the crowd, so it affected me. . . ." HA 7:258.

CHAPTER 6. DIETETICS AND HOMEOPATHY

1. Lichtenberg, *Südelbücher*, J673, 399.
2. Ibid., J748, 404.
3. Ibid., J595, 394.
4. Ibid., J178, 367.
5. For more on the increasingly popular image of hypochondria, see Müller, *Die kranke Seele und das Licht der Erkenntnis,* 172ff. See also Nassen, "Trübsinn und Indigestion," 175ff.
6. Novalis, "Terplitzer Fragmente," 101, in Kluckhohn and Samuel, *Novalis: Schriften,* 2:614.
7. Novalis, "Terplitzer Fragmente," 68, in Kluckhohn and Samuel, *Novalis: Schriften,* 2:607.
8. Novalis, "Logologische Fragmente," 128, in Kluckhohn and Samuel, *Novalis: Schriften,* 2:555. All Novalis citations are also discussed by Neubauer, *Bifocal Vision,* 36–37.
9. Ziolkowski, *German Romanticism and Its Institutions,* 204–5.
10. Zimmermann, *Ueber die Einsamkeit,* 3:182.
11. Ibid., 4:34, 181–82. For more on the subject, see Schings, *Melancholie und Aufklärung.* See also Sauder, *Empfindsamkeit,* 1:151.
12. Tissot, *Von der Gesundheit der Gelehrten,* 54–55.
13. Goethe to Carl August, 25 February 1821; WA 4.34:142.
14. Henry von Witzleben, "Goethe und Freud," *Studium Generale* 19 (1966): 614.
15. See Hans Rudolf Vaget, *Goethe—Der Mann von 60 Jahren: Mit einem Anhang über Thomas Mann* (Königstein: Athenäum, 1982).
16. For literally thousands more Goethe citations on the subject of health, see Gertrud Hager, *Gesund bei Goethe: Eine Wortmonographie* (Berlin: Akademie, 1955).
17. For more on Sperata's illness, see Thomsen and Guzzoni, *Der "Asoziale" in der Literatur um 1800,* 186ff. See also Reuchlein, *Die Heilung des Wahnsinns,* 86–88; and idem, *Bürgerliche Gesellschaft, Psychiatrie, und Literatur,* 158–61.
18. Robert R. Heitner, who argues that the Beautiful Soul is "purified by sickness" and who refers to her therapeutic hemorrhages, picks up this line of reasoning in "Goethe's Ailing Women," *MLN* 95, no. 3 (1980): 505.
19. Hermann Boerhaave, *Wie studiert man Medizin,* trans. and ed. Franz-Josef Schmidt (Hamm, Westf.: printed as manuscript, n.p., 1975).
20. Diaetophilus, *Physische und Psychologische Geschichte seiner siebenjaehrigen Epilepsie,* 2:170.
21. Ibid., 313.
22. Moritz, "Zur Seelendiätätik," *MzE* 1, no. 1 (1783): 83–84.
23. Hoffmann, *Fundamenta Medicinae,* 104.
24. Diaetophilus, *Physische und Psychologische Geschichte seiner siebenjaehrigen Epilepsie,* 2:405.
25. Shryock, *Development of Modern Medicine,* 70.
26. Foucault, "Politics of Health in the Eighteenth Century," 282–84.
27. *Medizinische Polizeiordnung* (1764). Foucault, "Politics of Health in the Eighteenth Century," 278.
28. The German title is *System einer medizinischen Polizei.* Goethe's notes are in the "Vorbereitung zur zweiten Reise nach Italien," WA 1.34.2:190.
29. "mit verständigen Ärzten und Polizeiverwandten bemüht." HA 8:278. The

"Polizeiverwandten" are translated as "police officials" (SE 10: 291), but in the context of the discussion, which centers on vaccination, it makes more sense that they are actually "health policy officials," in the sense of the "medizinische Polizei" (medical policy) of physician-authors like Rau and Frank.

30. See Hufeland, "Medizinische Praxis der Landesgeistlichen," 4:233–39.

31. Interestingly, in his study of Balzac's *Sarrazine,* Roland Barthes uses the same mathematical metaphor of the remainder to describe the incomprehensible unique essence of a character that transcends rationality. The character Sarrazine is said to be, "from a classical viewpoint," the intersection of a number of psychological characteristics:

> What gives the illusion that the sum is supplemented by a precious remainder (something like *individuality*, in that, qualitative and ineffable, it may escape the vulgar bookkeeping of compositional characters) is the Proper Name. (Roland Barthes, *S/Z,* trans. Richard Miller [New York: Hill and Wang, 1974], 190–91; emphasis by Barthes)

Whereas, however, by Balzac's day this individuality is "precious," Serlo, a member of a generation that predates not only the society of "Sarrazine," but also the Tower Society, regards such a remainder as surprising and dangerous. While Balzac is clearly in what Foucault calls the modern age, with its belief in something beyond language (like, for instance, a self), Serlo is still very much in the classical era, which believed in representation and would regard Sarrazine as representing those character traits Barthes mentions. Serlo's concern about the "wondrous remainder" is a symptom of the increasing skepticism about representation that was to bring in the modern era.

32. Hoffmann, *Fundamenta Medicinae,* 103.

33. Diaetophilus, *Physische und Psychologische Geschichte seiner siebenjaehrigen Epilepsie,* 2:165.

34. Arnold, *Beobachtung,* 2:351.

35. Moritz, "Zur Seelendiätätik," 83.

36. Arnold, *Beobachtungen,* 2:351, 356.

37. Hoffmann, *Fundamenta Medicinae,* 51–52. Zimmermann, *Von der Erfahrung in der Arzneykunst,* 642–85.

38. Zimmermann, *Ueber die Einsamkeit,* 4:87ff.

39. Hoffmann, *Fundamenta Medicinae,* 109.

40. Zimmermann, *Ueber die Einsamkeit,* 3:154.

41. Hufeland's annotations to his edition of the medical part of Kant's "Streit der Fakultäten," published separately as *Von der Macht des Gemüths durch den bloßen Vorsatz seiner kranken Gefühle Meister zu sein,* ed. Christian Wilhelm Hufeland (Leipzig, 1824), 27–28.

42. Kant, "Streit der Fakultäten," 6:376.

43. In his personal life as well, Goethe became extremely suspicious of excessive introspection. See Eissler, *Goethe,* 2:1155–65.

44. Philippe Buschinger, *Die Arbeit in Goethes Wilhelm Meister* (Stuttgart: Heinz, 1986).

45. Constantine Herring, introduction to Samuel Hahnemann, *Organon of Homeopathic Medicine,* 4th American ed. (New York, 1860), 3.

46. Hahnemann first employed this concept in his "Essay on a New Principle for Ascertaining the Curative Powers of Drugs." King, *Medical World of the Eighteenth Century,* 167.

47. Hahnemann, *Organon of Homeopathic Medicine,* § 12. For more on Hahnemann, see Hans Joachim Schwanitz, *Homöopathie und Brownianismus, 1795–1844: Zwei wissenschaftstheoretische Fallstudien aus der praktischen Medizin* (Stuttgart: Fischer, 1983).

48. Hahnemann, *Organon of Homeopathic Medicine,* § 48, 119.

49. Ibid., § 70, 133.

50. Ibid., § 210, 186.

51. Promies, *Die Bürger und der Narr,* 158.

52. Hahnemann, *Organon of Homeopathic Medicine,* 187.

53. Shryock, *Development of Modern Medicine,* 70.

54. Diepgen, "Goethe und die Medizin," 1615.

55. "Die großen Hindernisse, welche der Einimpfung der Blattern anfangs entgegenstanden, zu beseitigen, war er mit verständigen Ärzten und Polizeiverwandten bemüht." HA 8:278. See also n. 29.

56. In addition to Lepenies, *Melancholie und Gesellschaft,* see also Dörner, *Bürger und Irre,* who pointed out (esp. 80ff.) that eccentricity was a completely acceptable bourgeois tradition in eighteenth-century England.

57. Osinski, *Über Vernunft und Wahnsinn,* 38–58. Reuchlein, *Bürgerliche Gesellschaft, Psychiatrie, und Literatur,* 60–67.

58. Sauder, *Empfindsamkeit,* 1:153.

59. Tissot, *Abhandlung über die Nerven und deren Krankheiten,* 1–2.

60. Christian Garve, "Ueber die Rollen der Wahnwitzigen in Shakespears Schauspielen, und über den Charakter Hamlets insbesondere," in *Popularphilosophische Schriften im Faksimiledruck,* ed. Kurt Wölfel, 2 vols.(Stuttgart: Metzler, 1974), 2:434.

61. Immanuel Kant, "Versuch über die Krankheiten des Kopfes," in *Werke in Sechs Bänden,* 1:898–99.

62. Ibid., 1:899.

63. Reil, *Rhapsodieen,* 12.

64. Zimmermann, *Ueber die Einsamkeit,* 4:87–88.

65. Ibid., 197.

66. Ibid.

67. Ibid., 2:185

68. Johann Ernst Wichmann, *Zimmermanns Krankheitsgeschichte* (Hannover, 1796). Heinrich Matthias Marcard, *Beitrag zur Biograhie des seligen . . . Zimmermanns* (Hamburg, 1796). Simon-André Tissot, *Zimmermanns Lebensgeschichte* (Zürich, 1797). Goethe alludes to the published accounts of Zimmermann's illness in *Poetry and Truth* (SE 4:481; HA 10:65; see commentary, 10:601).

69. Compare to the situation of the Jewish doctor in Gilman, *Case of Sigmund Freud.*

70. Wundt argued that the theater was the only way out for German youth who felt oppressed by eighteenth-century German bourgeois culture, *Goethes Wilhelm Meister und die Entwicklung des modernen Lebensideals,* 193. See also Gonthier-Louis Fink, "Die Bildung des Bürgers zum 'Bürger': Individuum und Gesellschaft in 'Wilhelm Meisters Lehrjahren,'" *Recherches Germaniques* 2 (1972): 7.

71. Fink, "Die Bildung des Bürgers zum 'Bürger,'" 3–37. See also Rolf-Peter Janz, "Zum sozialen Gehalt der 'Lehrjahre,'" in *Literaturwissenschaft und Geschichtsphilosophie. Festschrift für Wilhelm Emrich,* ed. H. Arntzen (Berlin: Walter de Gruyter, 1975), 320–40.

72. Hoffmann, *Fundamenta Medicinae,* 101.

73. Ibid., 102.

74. Tobias Smollett, *The Adventures of Roderick Random* (1748), ed. Paul-Gabriel Boucé (New York: Oxford University Press, 1979), 193.

CHAPTER 7. WILHELM MEISTER'S WOUNDS

1. For more on wounds, see A. G. Steer, "The Wound and the Physician in Goethe's *Wilhelm Meister,*" in *Studies in German Literature of the Nineteenth and Twentieth Centu-*

ries: Festschrift for Frederic E. Coenen, ed. Siegfried Mews (Chapel Hill: University of North Carolina Press, 1970), 11–23.

2. For more on the importance of Tasso's *Jerusalem Delivered* for Wilhelm Meister see Monika Fick, *Das Scheitern des Genius* (Würzburg: Königshausen & Neumann, 1987), 70–72. See also Schings, "Symbolik des Glücks," 155–77; and idem, "Wilhelm Meisters Schöne Amazone," 141–206.

3. Nanine Charbonnel, *L'impossible pensée de l'éducation* (Cousset-Fribourg, Switzerland: Editions Delval, 1987), 19.

4. See Flaherty, "Stage-Struck Wilhelm Meister and Eighteenth-Century Psychiatric Medicine," 493–515.

5. "lebte und webte bloß in der Theaterwelt." Karl Philipp Moritz, "Ein Unglücklicher Hang zum Theater," *MzE* 3, no. 1 (1785): 91.

6. Ibid., 90.

7. *Der grosse Duden,* vol. 7, *Etymologie: Herkunftswörterbuch der deutschen Sprache,* 3d ed. (Mannheim: Dudenverlag, 1974), 366.

8. Moritz, "Ein Unglücklicher Hang zum Theater," 93.

9. Ibid., 95–96.

10. Ibid., 96.

11. I. D. Mauchart, "Eine Geschichte eines unglücklichen Hangs zum Theater," *MzE* 7, no. 3 (1789): 275.

12. For more on the cure of Wilhelm's passion for the theater, see Kittler, "Uber die Sozialisation Wilhelm Meisters," 88.

13. Jacques Lacan, "The Mirror Stage," in *Ecrits,* trans. Alan Sheridan (New York: Norton, 1977), 4.

14. Hörisch, *Gott, Geld und Glück,* 38ff. See also Kittler, "Über die Sozialisation Wilhelm Meisters," 15–25.

15. For more on the bourgeois nature of Wilhelm's family and the nonbourgeois nature of his early relationships with characters besides his mother, see Kittler, "Uber die Sozialisation Wilhelm Meisters," 30–40; and Hörisch, *Gott, Geld, und Glück,* 38ff. See also Beate Hansel, *Die Liebesbeziehung des Helden im deutschen Bildungsroman* (Frankfurt a/ M: Lang, 1986), 32–36.

16. Öhrgaard, *Die Genesung des Narcissus,* 80.

17. For more on the connections between Shakespeare and both Goethe's and Wilhelm Meister's "pathological interiority," see Fick, *Das Scheitern des Genius,* 114–19.

18. Like the Beautiful Soul, who transferred her physical love of Narcissus to a divine love of God, Wilhelm platonically shifts from loving a (female) human to loving abstract art.

19. Goethe refers to the perception of Hamlet as melancholy in *Poetry and Truth:* "Hamlet and his monologues were spectres that continued to haunt all youthful minds. Everyone knew the main passages by heart and gladly recited them, and everyone thought he had a right to be as melancholy as the prince of Denmark, though he had seen no ghost and had no royal father to avenge" (SE 4:42; HA 9:582). For more on Hamlet as melancholy *(schwermüthig),* see Garve, "Ueber die Rollen der Wahnwitzigen in Shakespears Schauspielen." See also Weickard, *Der philosophische Arzt,* 1:215–19.

20. Haas, *Die Turmgesellschaft in "Wilhelm Meisters Lehrjahren,"* 28–38. Kittler, "Uber die Sozialisation Wilhelm Meisters," 88.

21. "'Von welchem Irrtum kann der Mann sprechen', sagte er zu sich selbst, 'als von dem, der mich mein ganzes Leben verfolgt hat, . . . daß ich mir einbildete, ein Talent erwerben zu können, zu dem ich nicht die geringste Anlage hatte!'" HA 7:495.

22. *Der grosse Duden,* 7:256–57.

23. Müller, *Die kranke Seele und das Licht der Erkenntnis,* 48–63. See also Stephan

Koranyi, *Autobiographik und Wissenschaft im Denken Goethes* (Bonn: Bouvier, 1984), 224–26.

24. See Trunz's commentary, HA 7:793. See also Flaherty, "Stage-Struck Wilhelm Meister and Eighteenth-Century Psychiatric Medicine," 510. The Tower cites many other Hippocratic sentences in the *Lehrbrief* as well. See Karl Deichgraber, "Goethe und Hippokrates," *Archiv für die Geschichte der Medizin* 29 (1937): 27–56.

25. The best essay on this painting is Ammerlahn, "Goethe und Wilhelm Meister, Shakespeare und Natalie," 47–84, which contains a more extensive bibliography for readers interested in further study of the painting's role in the novel.

26. Rather, *Mind and Body in Eighteenth-Century Medicine,* 150.

27. Flaherty, "Stage-Struck Wilhelm Meister and Eighteenth-Century Psychiatric Medicine," 510ff.

28. For more on Jarno's toleration of narcissistic approaches to art, see Schlaffer, *Wilhelm Meister,* 80–81.

CHAPTER 8. WILHELM'S LOVESICKNESS

A much more extensive treatment of homosexuality and Goethe and his Age can be found in my book *Warm Brothers: Queer Theory and the Age of Goethe* (Philadelphia: University of Pennsylvania Press, 2000).

1. Arnold, *Beobachtungen,* 1:194. Zimmermann, *Von der Erfahrung in der Arzney-kunst,* 642. Reil, *Rhapsodieen,* 346. Weickard, *Der philosophische Arzt,* 3:157.

2. Laqueur, *Making Sex,* 4.

3. Ibid., 63–107.

4. Ibid., 154.

5. Michel Foucault, *The History of Sexuality,* vol. 2: *The Uses of Pleasure,* trans. Robert Hurley (New York: Vintage, 1990), 229–30.

6. Kittler, "Über die Sozialisation Wilhelm Meisters."

7. Vern L. Bullough, "Medieval Medical and Scientific Views of Women," *Viator* 4 (1973): 492.

8. Galen, *On the Usefulness of the Parts of the Body,* ed. and trans. Margaret May, 2 vols. (Ithaca: Cornell University Press, 1968), 2:628–29.

9. Laqueur, *Making Sex,* 8ff.

10. Ibid., 5.

11. Kurt Robert Eissler, the noted psychoanalyst, claims that Goethe's narration of this sickness "could almost be included in a textbook of so-called psychosomatic medicine.'" Eissler, *Goethe,* 2:722.

12. Schiller to Goethe, 2 July 1796; *Briefe an Goethe,* ed. Mandelkow, 2:233.

13. Daniel Jenisch, *Ueber die hervorstechendsten Eigenthümlichkeiten von Meisters Lehrjahren* (Berlin, 1797), 79–80.

14. Paul Derks discusses the cross-dressed characters who appeared in Mignon's wake in the early nineteenth century. *Die Schande der heiligen Päderastie: Homosexualität und Öffentlichkeit in der deutschen Literatur, 1750–1850* (Berlin: Verlag Rosa Winkel, 1990), 413.

15. Catriona MacLeod, "Pedagogy and Androgyny in *Wilhelm Meisters Lehrjahre,*" *MLN* 108 (1993): 389–426. Aurnhammer, *Androgynie,* 166ff.

16. On the union of body and clothes, see Gerhard Neumann, "'Ich bin gebildet genug, um zu lieben und zu trauern': Die Erziehung zur Liebe in Goethes *Wilhelm Meister,*" in *Liebesroman—Liebe im Roman,* ed. Titus Heydenreich and Egert Pöhlmann (Erlangen: Universitätsbibliothek Erlangen-Nürnberg, 1987), 51–52.

17. Margerie Garber, *Vested Interests: Cross-Dressing and Cultural Anxiety* (New York: Routledge, 1992), 66.

18. Ibid., 203.

19. Martha Vicinus, "'They Wonder to Which Sex I Belong': The Historical Roots of Modern Lesbian Identity," in *The Lesbian and Gay Studies Reader*, ed. Henry Abelove, Michèle Aina Barale, and David Halperin (New York: Routledge, 1993), 436–37.

20. Kristina Straub, "The Guilty Pleasures of Female Theatrical Cross-Dressing and the Autobiography of Charlotte Clarke," in *Body Guards: The Cultural Politics of Gender Ambiguity*, ed. Julia Epstein and Kristina Straub (New York: Routledge, 1991), 142–66.

21. Lillian Faderman, *Surpassing the Love of Men: Romantic Friedship and Love between Women from the Renaissance to the Present* (New York: Morrow, 1981), 58.

22. Garber, *Vested Interests,* 153.

23. Faderman, *Surpassing the Love of Men,* 51. Vicinus, "'They Wonder to Which Sex I Belong,'" 439.

24. Schiebinger, *Mind Has No Sex?,* 230.

25. The relationship between Natalie and Therese stands in a hallowed tradition going back at least to Shakespeare, an author who was of course immensely important for Goethe and whose works play an important role in *Wilhelm Meister*. Writing about similar structures in *Twelfth Night*, in which Olivia is, like Natalie, a strong, independent woman, and Viola, like Therese, is a parody of a woman trying to be a man, Jean Howard notes that "the figure of the male-attired woman [is] used to enforce a gender system that is challenged in other contexts by that figure" (Jean Howard, "Cross-Dressing, the Theatre, and Gender Struggle in Early Modern England," *Shakespeare Quarterly* 39, no. 4 [1988]: 432). Therese's presence suggests that mobility is possible on the gender continuum, but that too much of a good thing is not desirable. Her own manliness points to the Tower Society's belief that it can manage its poisons, using such potentially dangerous behavior salubriously.

26. Garber, *Vested Interests,* 53.

27. Gary Kates, "D'Eon Returns to France: Gender and Power in 1777," in Epstein and Straub, *Body Guards,* 167–94. Garber, *Vested Interests,* 265. Vern Bullough, *Sexual Variance in Society and History* (New York: Wiley, 1976), 488–90.

28. Derks, *Die Schande der heiligen Päderastie,* 413.

29. "Tag- und Jahreshefte 1808"; WA 1.36:34.

30. Goethe in fact listed "disguised pants roles" as one of her specialities (WA 1.36:245).

31. For a discussion of Natalie's imaginary maternal phallus and the uncle's coat, see Eissler, *Goethe,* 2:905. Kittler, "Über die Sozialisation Wilhelm Meisters," 51. Neumann, "'Ich bin gebildet genug,'" 51.

32. Garber, *Vested Interests,* 16.

33. Ibid., 150.

34. Alan Bray, *Homosexuality in Renaissance England* (London: Gay Men's Press, 1982), 88.

35. Terry Castle, *Masquerade and Civilization: The Carnivalesque in Eighteenth-Century English Culture and Fiction* (Stanford, Calif.: Stanford University Press 1986), 47.

36. Randolph Trumbach, "London's Sapphists: From Three Sexes to Four Genders in the Making of Modern Culture," in Epstein and Straub, *Body Guards,* 121.

37. Readers versed in gay and lesbian studies may be somewhat surprised to hear of a discussion of "homosexuality" in the eighteenth century. After all, the word "homosexuality" is a product of nineteenth-century sexological discourses, just as the word "transvestite" is the invention of the twentieth-century sexologist Magnus Hirschfeld. And just as Bray suggests that transvestites fulfilled very different societal functions in the eighteenth century than they had in the sixteenth, many modern historians of sexuality posit the creation of the "homosexual," a person whose identity is based upon his or her sexuality, in the

nineteenth century. They argue that individual sodomitical acts performed before the invention of the "homosexual" did not constitute an identity. Such arguments for a true history of sexuality are powerful indeed, but they can be overstated. Since most of them emerge from a Foucauldian perspective, it is helpful to remember that Foucault argues that the concept of "man" itself emerged somewhere around 1800. Thus rather than pinning the appearance of homosexuality on the coining of the word "homosexual," it is more appropriate to relate the development of a homosexual personality to the appearance of personality, individual uniqueness, "humanity" in general. Such a move corresponds more accurately to the development of sexuality and allows the reader to talk about homosexuality in relationship to a group of texts from the emergence of the modern era, including Goethe's *Wilhelm Meister.* Michel Foucault, *The History of Sexuality,* vol. 1: *An Introduction,* trans. Robert Hurley (New York: Random House, 1980), esp. 43. David Halperin, *One Hundred Years of Homosexuality and Other Essays on Greek Love* (New York: Routledge, 1990). David Greenberg, *The Construction of Sexuality* (Chicago: University of Chicago Press, 1988).

38. Bob Gallagher and Alexander Wilson, "Sex and the Politics of Identity: An Interview with Michel Foucault," in *Gay Spirit: Myth and Meaning,* ed. Mark Thompson (New York: St. Martin's Press, 1987), 33.

39. Halperin, *One Hundred Years of Homosexuality,* 26. See also Michael S. Kimmel, "'Greedy Kisses' and 'Melting Extasy,'" in *Love Letters Between a Certain Late Nobleman and the Famous Mr. Wilson,* ed. Michael S. Kimmel (New York: Harrington Park, 1990), 6.

40. Michel Rey, "Police and Sodomy in Eighteenth-Century Paris: From Sin to Disorder," in Gerard and Hekma, *Pursuit of Sodomy,* 129–46.

41. James Steakley, "Sodomy in Enlightenment Prussia: From Execution to Suicide," in Gerard and Hekma, *Pursuit of Sodomy,* 163–76.

42. John D'Emilio, "Capitalism and Gay Identity," in *Making Trouble: Essays on Gay History, Politics, and the University* (New York: Routledge, 1992), 3–17.

43. Randolph Trumbach, "The Birth of the Queen: Sodomy and the Emergence of Gender Equality in Modern Culture, 1660–1750," in *Hidden from History: Reclaiming the Gay and Lesbian Past*, ed. Martin Duberman, Martha Vicinus, and George Chauncey Jr (New York: Meridian, 1990), 130.

44. Joan de Jean, "Sex and Philology: Sappho and the Rise of German Nationalism," *Representations* 27 (Summer 1989): 148–71.

45. Christoph Meiners, *Vermischte philosophische Schriften*, 3 vols. (Leipzig, 1775), 1:61–121.

46. Manfred Herzer, "Bibliographie zur Homosexualität: Die nicht-belletristische deutschsprachige Literatur bis 1899," in *Der unterdruckte Sexus: Historische Texte zur Homosexualität,* ed. Joachim J. Hohmann (Lollar: n.p., 1977), 179. See also Steakley, "Sodomy in Enlightenment Prussia," 169.

47. [Johann Friedel], *Briefe über die Gallanterien von Berlin, auf einer Reise gesammelt von einem österreichischen Offizier* (Gotha, 1782), 152. Cited in Steakley, "Sodomy in Enlightenment Prussia," 169.

48. *Briefe* 153, 171. Cited in Steakley, "Sodomy in Enlightenment Prussia," 169–70.

49. Steakley, "Sodomy in Enlightenment Prussia," 170.

50. Ibid., 167. Derks, *Die Schande der heiligen Päderastie,* 91, 268.

51. G. S. Riquetti, *Secret History of the Court of Berlin,* ed. Oliver H. G. Leigh (Washington, D.C.: n.p., 1901). Cited in G. S. Rousseau, *Perilous Enlightenment: Pre- and Postmodern Discourses: Sexual, Historical* (Manchester: Manchester University Press, 1991), 25. Bullough, *Sexual Variance in Society and History,* 484.

52. Johann Georg Zimmermann, *Fragmente über Friedrich den Großen: Zur Geschichte seines Lebens, seiner Regierung, und seines Charakters,* 3 vols. (Leipzig, 1790), 1:13.

53. For more on Socrates as an eighteenth-century code word for homosexuality, see Derks, *Die Schande der heiligen Päderastie,* 60.

54. Zimmermann, *Fragmente über Friedrich den Großen,* 85–86.

55. Ibid., 70.

56. Wagnitz, *Historische Nachrichten und Bemerkungen,* 2.2:14. For a reference to similar developments in Paris, see Rey, "Police and Sodomy in Eighteenth-Century Paris," 146.

57. "Auszug aus dem Leben H. Cardus," *MzE* 6, no. 1 (1788): 93. The correspondent who reports being abused by a preacher as a child is perhaps male and would therefore also be referring to a homosexual act. "Aus einem Brief," *MzE* 5, no. 1 (1787): 78–79

58. "Aus einem Brief," *MzE* 8, no. 1 (1791): 11–14. The author points to the breakdown of the friendship cult when he concludes his letter: "[T]a paidixa liegen gewis nicht zum Grunde, dafür stehe ich; aber Freundschaftsgefühle äussern sich doch auch nicht so" (14) [{P}ederasty is certainly not the reason, of that I am sure; but the feelings of friendship don't express themselves this way either]. See also "Auszug aus einem Brief," *MzE* 8, no. 2 (1791): 160–65.

59. Simon-André Tissot, *Versuch von denen Krankheiten, welche aus der Selbstbefleckung entstehen* (Frankfurt a/M, 1771), 39.

60. Ibid., 39–40. Tissot refers interested readers to a 1730 dissertation on the subject by T. Tronchin. For more on tribades, see Laqueur, *Making Sex,* 53.

61. *Institutiones medicinae.* Cited in Bullough, *Sexual Variance in Society and History,* 496.

62. Tissot, *Versuch von denen Krankheiten, welche aus der Selbstbefleckung entstehen,* 398.

63. Steakley, "Sodomy in Enlightenment Prussia," 164.

64. Here the notorious passage from Goethe's "The Diary" ["Das Tagebuch"] comes to mind:

> "That even in the church (I blush) with heaven's King
> Racked on his cross, before the priest and all,
> My impudent hero made his curtain call!"

> ["Und als ich endlich sie zur Kirche führte,
> Gesteh ich's nur, vor Priester und Altare,
> Vor deinem Jammerkreuz, blutrünstger Christe,
> Verzeih mir's Gott, es regte sich der Iste."]

Both English and German are available in SE 1:186–87.

65. Zimmermann, *Ueber die Einsamkeit,* 2:233.

66. Rousseau, *Perilous Enlightenment,* 15, 19, 22.

67. For Psyche's adventures with the sodomitical sea pirate, see Christoph Martin Wieland, *Werke,* ed. Fritz Martini and H. W. Seiffert, 5 vols. (Munich: Hanser, 1964–68), 1:395–96. For the shadowy seductions at Delphi, see 1:559–60.

68. Gleim to Wieland, 2 January 1774. Heinrich Pröhle, *Lessing, Wieland, Heinse: Nach den handschriftlichen Quellen in Gleims Nachlasse dargestellt,* 2d ed. (Berlin, 1879), 267.

69. Sander Gilman, *Inscribing the Other* (Lincoln: University of Nebraska Press, 1991), 49.

70. For more on Goethe and sexuality, see Derks, *Die Schande der heiligen Päderastie,* 247–95. See also Sander L. Gilman, *Goethe's Touch: Touching, Seeing, and Sexuality* (New Orleans, La.: The Graduate School of Tulane University, 1988); and idem, *Sexuality: An*

Illustrated History: Representing the Sexual in Medicine and Culture from the Middle Ages to the Age of AIDS (New York: Wiley, 1989), 221–28.

71. 7 April 1830; AA 23:686. The trope also appears in Voltaire's essay on Socratic love, in which he writes: "How can it be that a vice, one which would destroy the human race if it became general, an infamous assault upon nature, can nevertheless be so natural?" He answers his question by suggesting that boys are girl-like and thus able to confuse male desire, a line of argument that relies upon the one-sex theory of gender. Bullough, *Sexual Variance in Society and History,* 490.

72. Wieland, *Werke,* 1:555–60.

73. For some examples of how the story of David and Jonathan was also appropriated by women, see Faderman, *Surpassing the Love of Men,* 107, 121.

74. Rousseau, *Perilous Enlightenment,* 172–99. See also Robert Aldrich, *The Seduction of the Mediterranean: Writing, Art, and Homosexual Fantasy* (London: Routledge, 1993).

75. Derks, *Die Schande der heiligen Päderastie,* 174–215.

76. Gilman, *Sexuality,* 223.

77. Rousseau, *Perilous Enlightenment,* 68–137.

78. Trunz in HA 7:726. See also Schings's commentary in MA 5:736.

79. Wolff, *Mignon,* 110.

80. Flaherty, *Shamanism and the Eighteenth Century;* on Mignon: 179–82; on Shamans and hermaphroditism and homosexuality: 35, 93, 118.

81. Eissler, *Goethe,* 2:1449.

82. The story even makes it into Bullough's history of sexual variance as evidence for the strong tradition of male-male eroticism in nineteenth-century Germany (*Sexual Variance in Society and History*, 535).

83. Lord Byron and his circle used "hyacinth" as a code word for homosexual amours. See Louis Crompton, *Byron and Greek Love: Homophobia in Nineteenth-Century England* (Berkeley: University of California Press, 1985), 127–29, 141–42, 179.

CHAPTER 9. BUILDING A FAMILY OUT OF THE TWO SEXES

1. Laqueur, *Making Sex,* 4.

2. Georg Ernst Stahl, *Ausführliche Abhandlung von den Zufällen und Kranckheiten Des Frauenzimmers . . .* (Extensive treatment of the incidents and sicknesses of women . . .) (Leipzig, 1724).

3. Duden, *Woman Beneath the Skin,* 187–88.

4. Schiebinger, *Mind Has No Sex?,* 188–91.

5. *Treatise on Hypochondriacal and Hysterical Diseases.* Discussed in Rousseau, "Cultural History in a New Key," 45–46.

6. Arnold, *Beobachtung,* 2:180–200. Tissot, *Abhandlung über die Nerven und deren Krankheiten*, 72–99.

7. Carl Friedrich Pockels, *Der Mann, ein anthropologisches Charaktergemälde seines Geschlechtes: Ein Gegenstück zu der Charakteristik des weiblichen Geschlechts*, 4 vols. (Hanover, 1805–8); and idem, *Versuch einer Charakteristik des weiblichen Geschlechts*, 5 vols. (Hanover, 1799–1802). Discussed in Schiebinger, *Mind Has No Sex?,* 265.

8. Zimmermann, *Von der Erfahrung in der Arzneykunst,* 600, 733.

9. Showalter, *Female Malady,* 74.

10. Zimmermann, *Von der Erfahrung in der Arzneykunst,* 600. Tissot does point out, however, that too much sex is also dangerous for women, in *Abhandlung über die Nerven und deren Krankheiten*, 1:69.

11. Diaetophilus, *Physische und Psychologische Geschichte seiner siebenjaehrigen Epilepsie*, 2:345.

12. Laqueur, *Making Sex*, 24ff.

13. Schiebinger, *Mind Has No Sex?*, 226.

14. Ibid., 221–22.

15. Ibid., 271.

16. See, for instance, H. A. Korff, *Geist der Goethezeit*, 4th ed., 4 vols. (Leipzig: Koehler and Amerlang, 1958), 2.2:334. For the gender distinctions Schiller made in "Ueber die nothwendigen Grenzen beim Gebrauch der schönen Form" [On the necessary boundaries in the use of the beautiful form], see also Weissberg, *Geistersprache*, 238–39.

17. Karen Kenkel, "The Personal and the Philosophical in Fichte's Theory of Sexual Difference," in *Impure Reason: Dialectic of Enlightenment in Germany*, ed. W. Daniel Wilson and Robert C. Holub (Detroit: Wayne State University Press, 1993), 278–300.

18. Karen Hausen, "Family and Role-Division: The Polarisation of Sexual Stereotypes in the Nineteenth Century—An Aspect of the Dissociation of Work and Family Life," in *The German Family: Essays on the Social History of the Family in Nineteenth- and Twentieth-Century Germany*, ed. Richard Evans and W.R. Lee (Totowa, N.J.: Barnes and Noble, 1981), 51–83. See also Dieter Schwab, "Familie," in *Geschichtliche Grundbegriffe: Historisches Lexikon zur politisch-sozialen Sprache in Deutschland*, ed. O. Brunner, W. Conze, and R. Kosselek, 3 vols. (Stuttgart: Klett, 1975), 2:253–301. For a dissenting view, see Werner Conze, "Neue Literatur zur Sozialgeschichte der Familie," *Vierteljahrschrift für Sozial- und Wirtschaftsgeschichte* 71, no. 1 (1984): 59–72.

19. Hörisch, *Gott, Geld, und Glück*.

20. Gray, *Goethe the Alchemist*, 224.

21. Robert Ellrich, "Rousseau's Androgynous Dream: The Minor Works of 1752–62," *French Forum* 13 (1988): 319–38.

22. MacLeod, "Pedagogy and Androgyny in *Wilhelm Meisters Lehrjahre*," 389.

23. Gerhart Neumann, "Wissen und Liebe: Der auratische Augenblick im Werk Goethes," in *Augenblick und Zeitpunkt: Studien zur Zeitstruktur und Zeitmetaphorik in Kunst und Wissenschaften*, ed. Christian W. Thomsen and Hans Holländer (Darmstadt: Wissenschaftliche Buchgesellschaft, 1984), 290.

24. Öhrgaard, *Die Genesung des Narcissus*, 61.

25. See Roberts, *Indirections of Desire*, 78.

26. See Eve Kosofsky Sedgwick, *Between Men: English Literature and Male Homosocial Desire* (New York: Columbia University Press, 1985), for a Girardian explanation of this kind of triangulated desire.

27. For an interesting psychoanalytic discussion of Therese's development, see Kowalik, "Feminine Identity Formation in *Wilhelm Meisters Lehrjahre*," 149–72.

28. In her low morality, Therese's mother resembles Aurelie's aunt (SE 9:150; HA 7:252).

29. Therese's eyes catch Wilhelm's attention immediately (SE 9:270; HA 7:441–42).

30. Diepgen, "Goethe und die Medizin," 1615.

31. In some ways, then, androgyny tends to fall into the female category. Randolph Trumbach notes that, although eighteenth-century scholars theoretically regarded hermaphrodites as between the sexes, in practice they often referred to them as female ("London's Sapphists," 117).

32. Zimmermann, *Ueber die Einsamkeit*, 2:192.

33. Ammerlahn "Goethe und Wilhelm Meister, Shakespeare und Natalie," 48.

34. Roberts, *Indirections of Desire*, 117–29. Schings, "Wilhelm Meisters schöne Amazone," 186ff.

35. Jane K. Brown, "The Theatrical Mission of the *Lehrjahre*," in *Goethe's Narrative*

Fiction: The Irvine Goethe Symposium, ed. William J. Lillyman (Berlin: Walter de Gruyter, 1983), 70–71.

36. Jenisch, *Ueber die hervorstechendsten Eigenthümlichkeiten von Meisters Lehrjahren*, 200.

37. As Schings has pointed out in the annotations to the Münchner Ausgabe of the *Lehrjahre*, the paradigmatic usage of the lucky conclusion of Saul's search for his father's she-asses first appears in Wieland's *Don Sylvio von Rosalva*, book 1, chapter 8. MA 5:856.

38. The series in the hall that begins with the young maid at the well and concludes with coronation ceremonies at the altar (SE 9:331–32; HA 7:541) at least mirrors, if not refers to, Saul's story.

39. For more on Wilhelm's use of *Hamlet* to overcome his complexes about his father, see Hans Mayer, *Goethe: Ein Versuch über den Erfolg* (Frankfurt a/M: Suhrkamp, 1973), 25–31; Muenzer, *Figures of Identity*, 58; Ammerlahn, "Goethe und Wilhelm Meister, Shakespeare und Natalie," 58ff.; Fick, *Das Scheitern des Genius*, 139–48; and Eissler, *Goethe*, 2:920–30.

40. *Der grosse Duden*, 7:256–57.

41. Note that the translation glosses over the phrase "ich fühl's."

42. For more on determining paternity and the Name-of-the-Father in modern society, see Kittler, "Uber die Sozialisation Wilhelm Meisters," 91–92.

43. The translation glosses over the phrase "Er fühlte es" [he felt it].

Conclusion: The Meaning of Health

1. The most thorough treatments of the Harper's cure are by Reuchlein, *Die Heilung des Wahnsinns* and *Bürgerliche Gesellschaft, Psychiatrie, und Literatur zur Entwicklung der Wahnsinnsthematik*.

2. Martin Schrenk, *Über den Umgang mit Geisteskranken: Die Entwicklung der psychiatrischen Therapie vom "moralischen Regime" in England und Frankreich zu den "psychischen Curmethoden" in Deutschland* (Berlin: Springer Verlag, 1973), 47.

3. For a nonmedical view of the imagination in the *Lehrjahre*, see Fick, "Destruktive Imagination," 207–47.

4. Promies, *Die Bürger und der Narr*.

5. Schings, *Melancholie und Aufklärung*, 73–164.

6. Müller, *Die kranke Seele und das Licht der Erkenntnis*, 304–20.

7. Nassen, "Trübsinn und Indigestion," 171–86.

8. The Suhrkamp translation drops the phrase "für sie und andere" [for herself and others].

9. Steer, "The Wound and the Physician in Goethe's Wilhelm Meister," 11–23.

10. Flaherty, "Stage-Struck Wilhelm Meister and Eighteenth-Century Psychiatric Medicine," 493–515.

11. Öhrgaard, *Die Genesung des Narcissus*.

12. The reading of the *Lehrjahre* most similar to this one is by Hörisch, *Gott, Geld und Glück*, 30–99.

13. Klaus F. Gille, *Goethes Wilhelm Meister: Zur Rezeptionsgeschichte der Lehr- und Wanderjahre* (Königstein: Athenäum, 1979).

14. Bennett, *Beyond Theory*. Friedrich Schlegel was of course the first critic to emphasize the novel's irony, in "Über Goethes Meister," reprinted in *Schriften zur Literatur*, ed. Wolfdietrich Rasch, 2d ed (Munich: DTV, 1985).

15. Gittinger, "Krankheit und heilender Eingriff," 18–32.

16. Schings, "Wilhelm Meisters Geselle Laertes," 419–37.

17. For a good interpretation of Serlo's childhood, see Kittler, "Über die Sozialisation Wilhelm Meisters," 62–68.

18. Heitner, "Goethe's Ailing Women," 497–515.

19. Marianne Hirsch, "Spiritual 'Bildung': The Beautiful Soul as Paradigm," in *The Voyage In: Fictions of Female Development*, ed. Elizabeth Abel, Marianne Hirsch, and Elizabeth Langland (Hanover, N.H.: University Press of New England, 1983), 23–48.

20. Probst, "Das Menschenbild der praktischen Medizin," 155–70.

21. Christian Wilhelm Hufeland, "Ueber den Wahnsinn, seine Erkenntniß, Ursachen, und Heilung," in *Christian Wilhelm Hufeland: Kleine Medizinische Schriften*, 4:15.

22. See Susan Sontag, *Illness as Metaphor* (New York: Vintage, 1979); and idem, *AIDS and its Metaphors* (New York: Farrar, Straus, and Giroux, 1989), for more on the quandaries resulting from the blurring of the boundaries between strictly mechanical medicine and psychological, philosophical, and religious thinking.

23. Sander Gilman, *Difference and Pathology: Stereotypes of Sexuality, Race, and Madness* (Ithaca: Cornell University Press, 1985), 25.

24. Foucault, *Order of Things*, 43–44.

25. Ziolkowski, *German Romanticism and Its Institutions*, 139.

26. Ibid., 171.

27. Gilman, *Difference and Pathology*, 150–62; idem, *Case of Sigmund Freud*, 11–68; and idem, *Freud, Race, and Gender*, 20.

28. Bennett, *Beyond Theory*, 62.

29. Johann Georg Zimmermann, *Von der Einsamkeit* (Frankfurt, 1777), 70–71, 90, 94, 102; and idem, *Ueber die Einsamkeit*, 1:300, 2:214–95.

30. Emile Montegut, *La Revue des deux mondes*, 1863, 194–95.

31. Stanitzek, "Bildung und Roman als Momente bürgerlicher Kultur," 439.

Bibliography

GOETHE EDITIONS

Briefe an Goethe: Hamburger Ausgabe in 2 Bänden. Edited by Karl Robert Mandelkow. 2d ed. Munich: Beck, 1982.

Goethes Briefe: Hamburger Ausgabe in 4 Bänden. Edited by Karl Robert Mandelkow. Hamburg: Wegner, 1965.

Goethe's Collected Works. Edited by Victor Lange, Eric A. Blackall, and Cyrus Hamlin. 12 vols. Boston: Suhrkamp, 1982.

Goethes Gespräche in 4 Bänden. Edited by Wolfgang Herwig. Zürich: Artemis, 1971.

Goethes Werke. Hamburger Ausgabe in 14 Bänden. Edited by Erich Trunz. 11th ed. Munich: Beck, 1981.

Goethes Werke: Herausgegeben im Auftrage der Großherzogin Sophie von Sachsen. Weimar: Böhlau, 1888; reprint, Tokyo: Sansyusya, 1975.

Sämtliche Werke nach Epochen seines Schaffens: Münchner Ausgabe. Munich: Hanser, 1986.

OTHER SOURCES

Adelung, Johann Christoph. *Grammatisch-kritisches Wörterbuch der Hochdeutschen Sprache.* 2d ed. Leipzig: Breitkopf und Härtel, 1801.

Alcandre, Jean-Jacques. "Médecine et écriture dramatique, Apropos du jeune Schiller." *Conscient, inconscient dans le tête littéraire: Cahiers d'études germaniques* 10 (1986): 211–27.

Aldrich, Robert. *The Seduction of the Mediterranean: Writing, Art, and Homosexual Fantasy.* London: Routledge, 1993.

Allgemeines Repertorium für empirische Psychologie und verwandte Wissenschaften. Edited by I. D. Mauchart. Nürnberg: Felsecker, 1792–98.

Ammerlahn, Hellmut. "Goethe und Wilhelm Meister, Shakespeare und Natalie: Die klassische Heilung des kranken Königsohns." *Jahrbuch des Freien Deutschen Hochstifts,* 1978, 47–84.

———. "Wilhelm Meisters Mignon—ein offenbares Rätsel: Name, Gestalt, Symbol, Wesen, und Werden." *Deutsche Vierteljahresschrift* 42, no. 1 (1968): 89–116.

227

Arnold, Thomas. *Beobachtungen über die Natur, Arten, Ursachen und Verhütung des Wahnsinns oder der Tollheit.* Translated by Johann Christian Gottlieb Ackermann. 2 vols. Leipzig: Friedrich Gotthold Jacobäer und Sohn, 1784–88.

Aurnhammer, Achim. *Androgynie: Studien zu einem Motiv in der Europäischen Literatur.* Köln: Böhlen, 1986.

Baeumer, Max L., and Edith Potter. "Reader-Response and 'Inward-Form' in Goethe's Early Criticism." In *Goethe as a Critic of Literature,* edited by K. J. Kink and M. L. Baeumer, 57–85. Lanham, Md.: University Press of America, 1984.

Barner, Wilfried. "Geheime Lenkung: Zur Turmgesellschaft in Goethes *Wilhelm Meister.*" In *Goethe's Narrative Fiction: The Irvine Goethe Symposium,* edited by William J. Lillyman, 85–109. New York: Walter de Gruyter, 1983.

Barthes, Roland. *S/Z.* Trans. Richard Miller. New York: Hill and Wang, 1974.

Beharriell, Frederick J. "The Hidden Meaning of Goethe's 'Bekenntnisse einer schönen Seele.'" In *Lebendige Form: Interpretationen zur deutschen Literatur. Festschrift für Heinrich E. K. Henel,* edited by Jeffrey L. Sammons and Ernst Schürer, 37–62. Munich: Fink, 1970.

Behler, Ernst. "What It Means to Understand an Author Better Than He Understands Himself: Idealistic Philosophy and Romantic Hermeneutics." In *Literary Theory and Criticism: Festschrift Presented to Réné Wellek,* edited by Joseph P. Strelka, 1:69–92. 2 vols. New York: Peter Lang, 1984.

Bennett, Benjamin. *Beyond Theory: Eighteenth-Century German Literature and the Poetics of Irony.* Ithaca: Cornell University Press, 1993.

Bennholdt-Thomsen, Anke, and Alfredo Guzzoni. *Der "Asoziale" in der Literatur um 1800.* Königstein: Athenäum, 1979.

———. "Der Irrenhausbesuch." *Aurora* 42 (1982): 82–110

———. "Nachwort." In vol. 10 of *Magazin zur Erfahrungsseelenkunde.* Lindau: Antiqua Verlag, 1979.

Berendt, Ernst. *Goethes Wilhelm Meister: Ein Beitrag zur Entstehungsgeschichte.* Dortmund: Ruhfus, 1911.

Berghahn, Klaus L., and Beate Pinkernel. *Am Beispiel "Wilhelm Meister": Einführung in die Wissenschaftsgeschichte der Germanistik.* 2 vols. Königstein: Athenäum, 1980.

Bezold, Rainard. *Popularphilosophie und Erfahrungsseelenkunde im Werk von Karl Philipp Moritz.* Würzburg: Königshaus und Neumann, 1984.

Blackall, Eric A. *Goethe and the Novel.* Ithaca: Cornell University Press, 1976.

Blessin, Stefan. *Die Romane Goethes.* Königstein: Athenäum, 1979.

Boerhaave, Hermann. *Kurze Lehr-Sätze von Erkennung und Heilung der Krankheiten.* Berlin: Haude und Spener, 1763.

———. *Wie studiert man Medizin.* 1727. Translated and edited by Franz-Josef Schmidt. Reprint, Hamm, Westfalen: n.p., 1975.

Bonnet, Charles. *Analytischer Versuch über die Seelenkräfte.* Translated by Christian Gottfried Schütz. 2 vols. Bremen: Cramer, 1770–71.

———. *Betrachtungen über die Natur.* 1764. Trans. Johann Daniel Titius. 4th ed. 2 vols. Leipzig: Junius, 1783.

Borchardt, Hans Heinrich. "Bildungsroman." In *Reallexikon der deutschen Literaturgeschichte.* 2d ed. Berlin: Walter de Gruyter, 1955.

———. *Der Roman der Goethezeit.* Stuttgart: Urach, 1949.

Boyle, Nicholas. *Goethe: The Poet and the Age*. 2 vols. Oxford: Oxford University Press, 1992.

Bray, Alan. *Homosexuality in Renaissance England*. London: Gay Men's Press, 1982.

Broman, Thomas. "Transformations of Academic Medicine in Germany, 1780-1820." Diss., Princeton University, 1987.

Brown, Jane K. *Goethe's Cyclical Narratives: "Die Unterhaltungen deutscher Ausgewanderten" and "Wilhelm Meisters Wanderjahre"*. Chapel Hill: University of North Carolina Press, 1975.

――――. "The Theatrical Mission of the 'Lehrjahre.'" In *Goethe's Narrative Fiction: The Irvine Goethe Symposium,* edited by William J. Lillyman, 69–84. New York: Walter de Gruyter, 1983.

Bullough, Vern L. "Medieval Medical and Scientific Views of Women." *Viator* 4 (1973).

――――. *Sexual Variance in Society and History*. New York: Wiley, 1976.

Buschinger, Philippe. *Die Arbeit in Goethes Wilhelm Meister*. Stuttgart: Heinz Akademischer Verlag, 1986.

Campe, Joachim Heinrich. *Wörterbuch der deutschen Sprache*. 5 vols. Braunschweig: Schulbuchhandlung, 1811.

Castle, Terry. *Masquerade and Civilization: The Carnivalesque in Eighteenth-Century English Culture and Fiction*. Stanford, Calif.: Stanford University Press 1986.

Charbonnel, Nanine. *L'impossible pensée de l'éducation. Sur le Wilhelm Meister de Goethe*. Cousset-Fribourg, Switzerland: Editions Delval, 1987.

Chemie im achtzehnten Jahrhundert: Auf dem Weg zu einer internationalen Wissenschaft: Georg Ernst Stahl (1659–1734) zu 250. Todestag. Edited by Michael Engel. Wiesbaden: Reichert, 1984.

Conze, Werner. "Neue Literatur zur Sozialgeschichte der Familie." *Vierteljahrschrift für Sozial- und Wissenschaftsgeschichte* 71, no. 1 (1984): 59–72.

Corngold, Stanley. *The Fate of the Self: German Writers and French Theory*. New York: Columbia University Press, 1986.

Crompton, Louis. *Byron and Greek Love: Homophobia in Nineteenth-Century England*. Berkeley: University of California Press, 1985.

Cunningham, Andrew. "Medicine to Calm the Mind: Boerhaave's Medical System, and Why It Was Adopted in Edinburgh." In *The Medical Enlightenment of the Eighteenth Century*, edited by Andrew Cunningham and Roger French. Cambridge: Cambridge University Press, 1990.

Darnton, Robert. *Mesmerism and the End of the Enlightenment in France*. Cambridge: Harvard University Press, 1968.

Degering, Thomas. *Das Elend der Entsagung: Goethes "Wilhelm Meisters Wanderjahre."* Bonn: Bouvier, 1982.

Deichgraber, Karl. "Goethe und Hippokrates." *Archiv für die Geschichte der Medizin* 29 (1937): 27–56.

De Jean, Joan. "Sex and Philology: Sappho and the Rise of German Nationalism." *Representations* 27 (Summer 1989): 148–71.

D'Emilio, John. *Making Trouble: Essays on Gay History, Politics, and the University.* New York: Routledge, 1992.

Derks, Paul. *Die Schande der heiligen Päderastie: Homosexualität und Öffentlichkeit in der deutschen Literatur, 1750–1850*. Berlin: Verlag Rosa Winkel, 1990.

Descartes, René. *The Philosophical Writings of Descartes.* Translated by John Cottingham, Robert Stoothof, and Dugald Murdoch. 2 vols. Cambridge: Cambridge University Press, 1984.

———. *"Über den Menschen" (1632) sowie "Beschreibung des menschlichen Körpers" (1648).* Translated and edited by Karl E. Rothschuh. Heidelberg: Lambert Schneider, 1969.

Dessoir, Max. *Geschichte der neueren deutschen Psychologie.* 2d ed. Vol. 1. Berlin: Dunker, 1902.

Deutsches Wörterbuch von Jacob und Wilhelm Grimm. Edited Ludwig Sütterlin. Leipzig: Hirzol, 1960.

Dewhurst, Kenneth, and Nigel Reeves. *Friedrich Schiller: Medicine, Psychology, and Literature, with the First English Edition of His Complete Medical and Psychological Writings.* Berkeley: University of California Press, 1978.

Diaetophilus (Karl W. F. L. Freyherr von Drais]. *Physische und Psychologische Geschichte seiner siebenjaehrigen Epilepsie, Nebst angehaengten Beitraegen zur körperlichen und Seelendiaetetik für Nervenschwache.* 2 vols. Zürich: Orell, Füßli, und Co., 1798.

Diener, Gottfried. *Goethes "Lila" Heilung eines "Wahnsinns" durch "psychische Kur."* Frankfurt a/M: Athenäum, 1971.

Diepgen, Paul. "Goethe und die Medizin." *Klinische Wochenschrift* 11, no. 39 (24 September 1932): 1611–16.

Dilthey, Wilhelm. *Das Erlebnis und die Dichtung.* 6th ed. Berlin: Teubner, 1919.

———. *Das Leben Schleiermachers.* Berlin and Leipzig: Teubner, 1922.

Dörner, Klaus. *Bürger und Irre. Zur Sozialgeschichte und Wissenschaftssoziologie der Psychiatrie.* Frankfurt a/M: Europäische Verlagsanstalt, 1969.

Duden, Barbara. *The Woman Beneath the Skin: A Doctor's Patients in Eighteenth-Century Germany.* Translated by Thomas Dunlap. Cambridge: Harvard University Press, 1991.

Der Duden in zehn Bänden. Vol. 7, *Etymologie. Herkunftswörterbuch der deutschen Sprache.* Mannheim: Bibliographisches Institut, 1963.

Duncan, Bruce. Review of *Figures of Identity,* by Clark S. Muenzer. *Eighteenth-Century Studies* 20, no. 2 (Winter 1986–87): 255–57.

Eichner, Hans. "Greatness, Saintliness, Usefulness: Character Configurations in Goethe's Oeuvre." *Goethe's Narrative Fiction. The Irvine Goethe Symposium,* edited by William J. Lillyman, 38–54. New York: Walter de Gruyter, 1983.

Ellrich, Robert. "Rousseau's Androgynous Dream: The Minor Works of 1752–62." *French Forum* 13 (1988): 319–38.

Epstein, Julia. "Historiography, Diagnosis, and Poetics." *Literature and Medicine* 11, no. 1 (Spring 1992): 23–44.

Erickson, Robert A. "William Harvey's *De Motu Cordis* and 'The Republick of Literature.'" In *Literature and Medicine in the Eighteenth Century,* edited by Marie Mulvey Roberts and Roy Porter, 58–83. New York: Routledge, 1993.

Eissler, Kurt Robert. *Goethe: A Psychoanalytic Study, 1775–1786.* 2 vols. Detroit: Wayne State University Press, 1963.

Faderman, Lillian. *Surpassing the Love of Men: Romantic Friedship and Love between Women from the Renaissance to the Present.* New York: Morrow, 1981.

Farrelly, Daniel J. *Goethe and Inner Harmony: A Study of the "schöne Seele" in the "Apprenticeship of Wilhelm Meister".* Shannon, Ireland: Irish University Press, 1973.

Fichte, Johann Gottfried. *Grundlage des Naturrechts nach Prinzipien der Wissenschaftslehre.* Hamburg: Felix Meiner, 1960.

Fick, Monika. "Destruktive Imagination: Die Tragödie der Dichterexistenz in *Wilhelm Meisters Lehrjahren.*" *Jahrbuch der deutschen Schillergesellschaft* 29 (1985): 207–47.

———. "Mignon—Psychologie und Morphologie der Geniusallegorese in *Wilhelm Meisters Lehrjahren.*" *Sprachkunst* 13 (1982): 3–49.

———. *Das Scheitern des Genius. Mignon und die Symbolik der Liebesgeschichten in "Wilhelm Meisters Lehrjahre."* Epistemata: Reihe Literaturwissenschaft, 20. Würzburg: Königshausen und Neumann, 1987.

Fink, Gonthier-Louis. "Die Bildung des Bürgers zum 'Bürger': Individuum und Gesellschaft in *Wilhelm Meisters Lehrjahre.*" *Recherches germaniques* 2 (1972): 3–37.

Fischer, F. "Goethe über Irrenanstalten und Geisteskrankheiten." *Psychiatrisch-Neurologische Wochenschrift* 43 (23 January 1903): 474.

Flaherty, Gloria. *Shamanism and the Eighteenth Century.* Princeton: Princeton University Press, 1992.

———. "The Stage-Struck Wilhelm Meister and Eighteenth-Century Psychiatric Medicine." *Modern Language Notes* 110 (1986): 493–515.

Flavell, Kay. "Goethe, Rousseau, and the 'Hyp.'" In *Oxford German Studies 7,* edited by D. F. Glanz, 5–23. Oxford: Clarendon Press, 1973.

Foucault, Michel. *The History of Sexuality.* Vol. 1, *An Introduction.* Translated by Robert Hurley. New York: Random, 1980.

———. *The History of Sexuality.* Vol. 2, *The Uses of Pleasure.* Translated by Robert Hurley. New York: Vintage, 1990.

———. *Madness and Civilization: A History of Insanity in the Age of Reason.* Translated by Richard Howard. New York: Vintage, 1988.

———. *The Order of Things: An Archaeology of the Human Sciences.* New York: Pantheon, 1970.

———. "The Politics of Health in the Eighteenth Century." In *The Foucault Reader,* edited Paul Rabinow. New York: Pantheon, 1984.

French, Roger. "Sickness and the Soul: Stahl, Hoffmann, and Sauvages on Pathology." In *The Medical Enlightenment of the Eighteenth Century,* edited Andrew Cunningham and Roger French. Cambridge: Cambridge University Press, 1990.

Freud, Sigmund. *Gesammelte Werke, Chronologisch Geordnet.* Edited by Anna Freud. 18 vols. London: Imago, 1948.

Friedel, Johann. *Briefe über die Gallanterien von Berlin, auf einer Reise gesammelt von einem österreichischen Offizier.* Gotha, 1782.

Gadamer, Hans-Georg. *Wahrheit und Methode: Grundzüge einer philosophischen Hermeneutik.* Tübingen: Mohr, 1960.

Galen. *On the Usefulness of the Parts of the Body.* Edited and translated by Margaret May. 2 vols. Ithaca: Cornell University Press, 1968.

Gallagher, Bob, and Alexander Wilson. "Sex and the Politics of Identity: An Interview with Michel Foucault." In *Gay Spirit: Myth and Meaning,* edited by Mark Thompson, 25–35. New York: St. Martin's Press, 1987.

Gallas, Helga. *Das Textbegehren des Michael Kohalhaas: Die Sprache des Unbewußten und der Sinn der Literatur.* Reinbek bei Hamburg: Rowohlt, 1981.

Garve, Christian. "Ueber die Rollen der Wahnwitzigen in Shakespears Schauspielen, und über den Charakter Hamlets ins besondere" (1796). In vol. 2 of *Christian Garve: Popularphilosophische Schriften über literarische, ästhetische und gesellschaftliche Gegenstände im Faksimiledruck,* edited by Kurt Wölfel. Stuttgart: Metzler, 1974.

Gates, Henry Louis, Jr. "Editor's Introduction: Writing 'Race' and the Difference It Makes." *Critical Inquiry* 12, no. 1 (Autumn 1985): 1–20.

Garber, Margerie. *Vested Interests: Cross-Dressing and Cultural Anxiety.* New York: Routledge, 1992.

Gerard, Kent, and Gert Hekma. *The Pursuit of Sodomy: Male Homosexuality in Renaissance and Enlightenment Europe.* New York: Harrington Park, 1989.

Gerber, Paul Henry. *Goethe's Beziehung zur Medicin.* Berlin: Karger, 1900.

Gerhard, Melitta. *Der deutsche Entwicklungsroman bis zu Goethes "Wilhelm Meister."* Halle: Niemeyer, 1926; reprint, Bern and Munich: Franke, 1968.

Gervinius, G. G. *Geschichte der Deutschen Dichtung.* Edited by Karl Bartsch. 5th ed. Leipzig: Engelmann, 1874.

Geyer-Kordesch, Johanna. "Georg Ernst Stahl's Radical Pietist Medicine and Its Influence on the German Enlightenment." In *The Medical Enlightenment of the Eighteenth Century,* edited by Andrew Cunningham and Roger French. Cambridge: Cambridge University Press, 1990.

———. "Die 'Theoria medica vera' und Georg Ernst Stahls Verhältnis zur Aufklärung." In *Georg Ernst Stahl (1659–1734): Hallesches Symposium 1984,* edited by Wolfgang Kaiser and Andreas Völker, 89–98. Halle: Wissenschaftspublizistik der Martin-Luther-Universität Halle-Wittenberg, 1985.

Gilby, William. "The Structural Significance of Mignon in *Wilhelm Meisters Lehrjahre.*" *Seminar* 16 (1980): 136–50.

Gille, Klaus F., ed. *Goethes Wilhelm Meister: Zur Rezeptionsgeschichte der Lehr- und Wanderjahre.* Texte der deutschen Literatur in wirkungsgeschichtlichen Zeugnissen, 3. Königstein/Ts: Athenäum, 1979.

———. *"Wilhelm Meister" im Urteil der Zeitgenossen: Ein Beitrag zur Wirkungsgeschichte Goethes.* Van Gorcum's Literaire Bibliotheek, 19. Assen: Van Gorcum, 1971.

Gilman, Sander L. *The Case of Sigmund Freud: Medicine and Identity at the Fin -de-siècle.* Baltimore: Johns Hopkins University Press, 1993.

———. *Difference and Pathology: Stereotypes of Sexuality, Race, and Madness.* Ithaca: Cornell University Press, 1985.

———. *Freud, Race, and Gender.* Princeton: Princeton University Press, 1993.

———. *Goethe's Touch: Touching, Seeing, and Sexuality.* New Orleans, La.: The Graduate School of Tulane University, 1988.

———. *Sexuality: An Illustrated History: Representing the Sexual in Medicine and Culture from the Middle Ages to the Age of AIDS.* New York: Wiley, 1989.

———. "The Struggle of Psychiatry with Psychoanalysis: Who Won?" *Critical Inquiry* 13, no. 2 (Winter 1987): 293–313.

———. *Wahnsinn, Text und Kontext. Die historischen Wechselbeziehungen der Literatur, Kunst und Psychiatrie.* Europäische Hochschulschriften, ser. 1, Dt. Sprache u. Literatur, 417. Literatur und Psychologie, 8. Frankfurt a/M and Bern: Peter Lang, 1981.

Gittinger, Albrecht. "Krankheit und heilender Eingriff: Goethes 'Wilhelm Meister.'" Medical diss., University of Heidelberg, 1980.

Gnothi Sauton oder das Magazin für Erfahrungsseelenkunde als ein Lesebuch für Gelehrte und Ungelehrte. Edited by Carl Phillip Moritz, with help from Karl Friedrich Pockels and Salomon Maimon. 1783–92. Facsimile reprint, edited by Anke Bennholdt-Thomsen and Alfredo Guzzoni, Lindau: Antiqua, 1979.

Goethe in vertraulichen Briefen seiner Zeitgenossen. Edited by Wilhelm Bode. 3 vols. Berlin and Weimar: Aufbau-Verlag, 1979.

Goethe und Soemmerring: Briefwechsel, 1784–1828. Edited by Manfred Wenzel. Soemmerring-Forschungen 5. Stuttgart: Fischer, 1988.

Graham, Ilse. *Goethe: Portrait of the Artist.* Berlin and New York: Walter de Gruyter, 1977.

Gray, Ronald D. *Goethe the Alchemist.* Cambridge: Cambridge University Press, 1952.

Green, Vivian Yvonne. "The Artistic Value of Emotional Disorder for Goethe." Diss., University. of Illinois, Urbana-Champaign, 1976.

Greenberg, David. *The Construction of Sexuality.* Chicago: University of Chicago Press, 1988.

Gregorovius, Ferdinand. *Göthe's Wilhelm Meister in seinen socialistischen Elementen entwickelt.* 2d ed. Schwäbisch Hall: n.p., 1855.

Greiner, Bernhard. "Dialogisches Wort als Medium des Über-Sich-Redens: Goethes 'Bekenntnisse einer schönen Seele' im *Wilhelm Meister* und die Friederiken-Episode in *Dichtung und Wahrheit.*" In *Freiburger literaturpsychologische Gespräche*, Bd. 11: *Über sich selber reden. Zur Psychoanalyse autobiographischen Schreibens*, edited by Johannes Cremerius, Wolfram Mauser, Carl Pietzcker, and Frederick Wyatt, 95–120. Würzburg: Königshausen & Neumann, 1992.

Haas, Rosemarie. *Die Turmgesellschaft in "Wilhelm Meisters Lehrjahren": Zur Geschichte des Geheimbundromans und der Romantheorie im 18. Jahrhundert.* Frankfurt a/M: Peter Lang, 1975.

Hager, Gertrud. *Gesund bei Goethe: Eine Wortmonographie.* Deutsche Akademie der Wissenschaften zu Berlin, Veröffentlichung des Instituts für Deutsche Sprache und Literatur, 5. Berlin: Akademie, 1955.

Hahnemann, Samuel. *Organon of Homeopathic Medicine.* 4th American ed. New York, 1860.

Haller, Albrecht. *Von den empfindlichen und reizbaren Teilen des menschlichen Körpers.* Translated and edited by Karl Sudhoff. Klassiker der Medizin, 27. Leipzig: Johann Abrosious Barth, 1922.

Halperin, David. *One Hundred Years of Homosexuality and Other Essays on Greek Love.* New York: Routledge, 1990.

Hampton, Wilborn. "Comic Actor Tries His Hand as the Melancholy Prince." *New York Times,* 2 June 1989, C3.

Hansel, Beate. *Die Liebesbeziehungen des Helden im deutschen Bildungsroman und ihr Zusammenhang mit der bürgerlichen Konzeption von Individualität.* Europäische Hochschulschriften, Reihe I, Deutsche Sprache und Literatur, 901. Frankfurt a/M, Bern, and New York: Peter Lang, 1986.

Haraway, Donna. "The Biopolitics of Postmodern Bodies: Determinations of Self in Immune System Discourse." *Differences* 1, no. 1 (Winter 1989): 3–43.

Hardin, James, ed. *Reflection and Action: Essays on the Bildungsroman.* Columbia: University of South Carolina Press, 1991.

Hass, Hans-Egon. "Goethes *Wilhelm Meisters Lehrjahre.*" In *Der Deutsche Roman*, vol. 1: *Vom Barock bis zur Gegenwart: Struktur und Geschichte*, edited by Benno von Wiese, 132–210. Düsseldorf: A. Bagel, 1963.

Hausen, Karin. "Family and Role Division: The Polarisation of Sexual Stereotypes in the Nineteenth Century—An aspect of the Dissociation of Work and Family Life." In *The German Family: Essays on the Social History of the Family in Nineteenth- and Twentieth-Century Germany,* edited by Richard J. Evans and W. Robert Lee, 51–83. Totowa, N.J.: Barnes and Noble, 1981.

Heitner, Robert R. "Goethe's Ailing Women." *Modern Language Notes* 95, no. 3 (1980): 497–515.

Herder, Johann Gottfried. *Herders Werke in fünf Bänden*, 4th ed. Berlin and Weimar: Aufbau-Verlag, 1969.

Hermann, Helene. "Die psychologischen Anschauungen des jungen Goethe und seiner Zeit (Erster Teil)." Diss., Friedrich-Wilhelm-Universität zu Berlin, 1904.

Hertwig, Hugo. *Der Arzt, der das Leben verlängerte: Das Leben und Wirken des großen Hufeland, 1762–1800*. Berlin: Otto Schaffer, 1941.

Herzer, Manfred. "Bibliographie zur Homosexualität: Die nicht-belletristische deutschsprachige Literatur bis 1899." In *Der unterdruckte Sexus: Historische Texte zur Homosexualität*, edited Joachim J. Hohmann. Lollar: n.p., 1977.

Hinderer, Walter. "Die Philosophie der Ärzte und die Rhetorik der Dichter: Zu Schillers und Büchners ideologisch-ästhetischen Positionen." *Zeitschrift für deutsche Philologie* 109, no. 4 (1990): 502–20.

Hirsch, Marianne. "Spiritual 'Bildung': the Beautiful Soul as Paradigm." In *The Voyage In: Fictions of Female Development*, edited by Elizabeth Abel, Marianne Hirsch, and Elizabeth Langland, 23–48. Hanover, N.H.: University Press of New England, 1983.

Hißmann, Michael. *Anleitung zur Kenntniß der auserlesenen Literatur in allen Theilen der Philosophie*. Göttingen and Lemgo: Meyer, 1778.

Historisches Wörterbuch der Philosophie. Edited by Joachim Ritter and Karlfried Grüner. Darmstadt: Wissenschaftliche Buchgesellschaft, 1980.

Hörisch, Jochen. *Gott, Geld, und Glück: Zur Logik der Liebe in den Bildungsromanen Goethes, Kellers, und Thomas Manns*. Edition Suhrkamp 1180, Neue Folge, 180. Frankfurt a/M: Suhrkamp, 1983.

Howard, Jean. "Cross-Dressing, the Theatre, and Gender Struggle in Early Modern England." *Shakespeare Quarterly* 39, no. 4 (1988): 418–40.

Hufeland, Christian Wilhelm. *Kleine Medizinische Schriften*. 4 vols. Berlin: Reimer, 1822-28.

———. *Die Kunst, das menschliche Leben zu verlängern*. Jena, 1797.

Husemann, Friedrich. *Goethe und die Heilkunst: Betrachtungen zur Krise in der Medizin*. Dresden: Emil Weise, 1936.

Ideler, Karl Wilhelm. *Grundriß der Seelenheilkunde*. 2 vols. Berlin: Enslin, 1835–38.

Janz, Rolf-Peter. "Zum sozialen Gehalt der Lehrjahre." In *Literaturwissenschaft und Geschichtsphilosophie: Festschrift für Wilhelm Erich*, edited by Helmut Arntzen et al., 320–40. Berlin and New York: Walter de Gruyter, 1975.

Jenisch, Daniel. *Ueber die hervorstechendsten Eigenthümlichkeiten von Meisters Lehrjahren; oder über das, wodurch dieser Roman ein Werk von Göthen's Hand ist. Ein ästhetisch-moralischer Versuch*. Berlin: Johann Georg Langhilf, 1797.

Kaltenbrunner, Gerd-Klaus. "Von einem, der auszog, das Leben zu verlängern. Erinnerungen an Christoph Wilhelm Hufeland und seine Makrobiotik." *Neue Deutsche Hefte* 34, no. 2 (1987): 254–65.

Kant, Immanuel. *Von der macht des Gemüths durch den bloßen Vorsatz seiner kranfhaften Gefühle Meister zu sein*. Edited by C. W. Hufeland. Leipzig: Reclam, 1824.

———. *Werke in Sechs Bänden*. Edited by Wilhelm Weischedel. 6 vols. Wiesbaden: Insel, 1960–64.

Kates, Gary. "D'Eon Returns to France: Gender and Power in 1777." In *Body Guards: The Cultural Politics of Gender Ambiguity*, edited by Julia Epstein and Kristina Straub, 167–94. New York: Routledge, 1991.

Kehl, Wolfgang. "'Die Schönheiten der Natur gemeinschaftlich betrachten': Zum Zusammenhang von Freundschaft, ästhetischer Naturerfahrung, und 'Gartenrevolution' in der Spätaufklärung." In *Frauenfreundschaft-Männerfreundschaft: Literarische Diskurse im 18. Jahrhundert,* edited by Wolfram Mauser and Barbara Becker-Cantarino. Tübingen: Niemeyer, 1991.

Kenkel, Karen. "The Personal and the Philosophical in Fichte's Theory of Sexual Difference." In *Impure Reason: Dialectic of Enlightenment in German,* edited W. Daniel Wilson and Robert C. Holub, 278–300. Detroit: Wayne State University Press, 1993.

Keppel-Kriems, Karin. *Mignon und Harfner in Goethes "Wilhelm Meister": Eine geschichtsphilosophische und kunsttheoretische Untersuchung zu Begriff und Gestaltung der Naiven.* Marburger Germanistische Studien, 7. Frankfurt a/M, Bern, and New York: Peter Lang, 1986.

Kimmel, Michael S. "'Greedy Kisses' and 'Melting Extasy.'" In *Love Letters Between a Certain Late Nobleman and the Famous Mr. Wilson,* edited by Michael S. Kimmel. New York: Harrington Park, 1990.

King, Lester. *The Medical World of the Eighteenth Century.* Chicago: University of Chicago Press, 1958.

———. *The Philosophy of Medicine: The Early Eighteenth Century.* Cambridge: Harvard University Press, 1978.

Kittler, Friedrich A. "Über die Sozialisation Wilhelm Meisters." In *Dichtung als Sozialisationsspiel,* edited by Friedrich A. Kittler and Gerhard Kaiser. Göttingen: Vandenhoeck & Ruprecht, 1978.

Klages, Ludwig. *Goethe als Seelenforscher.* 3d ed. Zürich: Hirzel, 1949.

Knigge, Adolph Freiherr von. *Ueber den Umgang mit Menschen.* 5th ed. 3 vols. Frankfurt and Leipzig, 1796.

Kontje, Todd. *The German Bildungsroman: A History of a National Genre.* Columbia, S.C.: Camden, 1993.

———. *Private Lives in the Public Sphere: The German "Bildungsroman" as Metafiction.* University Park: Pennsylvania State University Press, 1992.

Koopmann, Helmut. "Wilhelm Meisters Lehrjahre (1795/96)." In *Goethes Erzählwerk: Interpretationen,* edited by Paul Michael Lützeler and James E. McLeod, 168–191. Stuttgart: Reclam, 1985.

Koranyi, Stephan. *Autobiographik und Wissenschaft im Denken Goethes.* Abhandlungen zur Kunst-, Musik- und Literaturwissenschaft 352. Bonn: Bouvier, 1984.

Korff, H. A. *Geist der Goethezeit.* 4th ed. 4 vols. Leipzig: Koehler and Amelang, 1958.

Kowalik, Jill Anne. "Feminine Identity Formation in *Wilhelm Meisters Lehrjahre.*" *MLQ* 53, no. 2 (June 1992): 149–72.

Krauß, Paul. "Mignon, der Harfner, Sperata: Die Psychopathologie einer Sippe in *Wilhelm Meisters Lehrjahren.*" *Deutsche Vierteljahresschrift* 22 (1944): 327–54.

Kries, Johannes von. "Goethe als Psycholog," *Philosophie und Geschichte.* Eine Sammlung von Vorträgen und Schriften aus dem Gebiet der Philosophie und Geschichte 5. Tübingen: J.C.B. Mohr, 1924.

Krüger, Johann Gottlob. *Diät oder Lebensordnung.* 2d ed. Halle: Hemmerde, 1763.

La Mettrie, Julien Offray de. *Der Mensch als Maschine* (1748). Edited and translated into German, with an essay, by Bernd A. Laska. LSR-Quellen; 1. Nürnberg: LSR-Verlag, 1985.

Lacan, Jacques. "The Mirror Stage." In *Ecrits,* translated by Alan Sheridan. New York: Norton, 1977.

Lämmert, Eberhard. "Goethe als Novellist." In *Goethe's Narrative Fiction: The Irvine Goethe Symposium,* edited by William J. Lillyman. Berlin and New York: Walter de Gruyter, 1983.

———. "Goethes empirischer Beitrag zur Romantheorie." In *Goethes Erzählwerk. Interpretationen,* edited by Paul Michael Lützeler and James E. McLeod, 9–36. U.B. Nr. 8081. Stuttgart: Reclam, 1985.

Langendorff, Erich. *Zur Entstehung des bürgerlichen Familienglücks: Exemplarishce Studien anhand literarischer Texte.* Eurpäische Hochschulschriften, Reihe I, 672. Frankfurt a/ M, Bern, and New York: Peter Lang, 1983.

Laplanche, Jean, and J. P. Pontalis. *The Language of Psycho-Analysis.* Translated by Donald Nicholson-Smith. New York: Norton, 1974.

Laqueur, Thomas. *Making Sex: Body and Gender from the Greeks to Freud.* Cambridge: Harvard University Press, 1990.

Laska, Bernd A. "Julien Offray de la Mettrie." In *Der Mensch als Maschine,* by Julien Offray de La Mettrie. Nürnberg: LSR-Verlag, 1985.

Lawätz, Heinrich Wilhelm. *Ueber die Tugenden und Laster, so wie überhaupt über die Neigungen und Leidenschaften des Menschen,* part 1. Flensburg, Schleswig and Leipzig, 1789.

Lee, W. Robert. "The German Family: A Critical Survey of the Current State of Historical Research." In *The German Family: Essays on the Social History of the Family in Nine-teenth- and Twentieth-Century Germany,* edited by Richard J. Evans and W. Robert Lee, 19–51. Totowa, N.J.: Barnes and Noble, 1981.

Leibbrand, Werner, and Annemarie Wettley. *Der Wahnsinn: Geschichte der abendländischen Psychopathologie.* Orbis Academicus, II-12. Freiburg and München: Karl Alber, 1961.

Leibniz, Gottfried Wilhelm. *Leibniz: Selections.* Edited by Philip P. Wiener. New York: Scribner, 1951.

Lepenies, Wolf. *Melancholie und Gesellschaft.* Frankfurt a/M: Suhrkamp, 1969.

Lichtenberg, G. C. *Südelbücher.* Edited by Franz H. Mautner. Frankfurt a/M: Insel, 1983.

Loquai, Franz. *Künstler und Melancholie in der Romantik.* Helican, 4. Frankfurt a/M, Bern, and New York: Peter Lang, 1984.

MacLeod, Catriona. "Pedagogy and Androgyny in *Wilhelm Meisters Lehrjahre.*" *MLN* 108 (1993): 389–426.

Mahoney, Dennis. "The Apprenticeship of the Reader: The Bildungsroman of the 'Age of Goethe.'" In *Reflection and Action: Essays on the Bildungsroman,* edited by James Hardin, 97-117. Columbia: University of South Carolina Press, 1991.

Martini, Fritz. "Der Bildungsroman: Zur Geschichte des Wortes und der Theorie." *Deutsche Vierteljahresschrift* 35 (1961): 44–64.

Matt, Peter von. "Anwendung psychoanalytischer Erkenntnisse in der Interpretation: 'Das psychodramatische Substrat.'" In *Psychoanalytische Textinterpretation,* edited by Johannes Cremerius, 29–45. Hamburg: Hoffmann u. Campe, 1974.

Mattenklott, Gerd. *Melancholie in der Dramatik des Sturm und Drang.* Stuttgart: Metzler, 1968; reprint, Königstein/Ts: Athenäum, 1985.

Mauser, Wolfram. "Johann Gottlieb Krügers 'Träume.' Zu einer wenig beachteten literarischen Gattung des 18. Jahrhunderts." In *Goethe aus interkulturellen Perspektive, en hommage à Gonthier-Louis Fink,* edited by Adrian Fink and Gertrud Gréciano. Strasbourg: Institut d'études allemandes, Université de Sciences Humaines de Strasbourg, 1988.

———. "Melancholieforschung des 18. Jahrhunderts zwischen Ikongraphie und Ideologie-kritik: Auseindersetzung mit den bisherigen Ergebnissen und Thesen zu einem Neuansatz." *Lessing Yearbook* 13 (1981): 253–77.

May, Kurt. *"Wilhelm Meisters Lehrjahre, ein Bildungsroman?" Deutsche Vierteljahresschrift* 31 (1957): 1–37.

Mayer, Hans. *Goethe. Ein Versuch über den Erfolg.* Frankfurt a/M: Suhrkamp, 1973.

Meiners, Christoph. *Vermischte philosophische Schriften.* 3 vols. Leipzig, 1775.

Metzger, Johann Daniel. *Grundsätze der allgemeinen Semiotik.* Königsberg, 1785.

———. *Vermischte medicinische Schriften.* 2d ed. 2 vols. Königsberg: Dengel, 1784.

Miller, J. Hillis. *The Ethics of Reading: Kant, de Man, Eliot, Trollope, James, and Benjamin.* Wellek Literary Lectures at the University of California, Irvine. New York: Columbia University Press, 1987.

Mitterauer, Michael, and Reinhard Sieder, eds. *Historische Familienforschung.* Frankfurt a/M: Suhrkamp, 1982.

Mocek, Reinhard. "Zum Mechanismus-Vitalismus-Pardigma der Stahl-Ära." In *Georg Ernst Stahl (1659–1734): Hallesches Symposium 1984,* edited by Wolfram Kaiser and Arina Völker, 31–40. Halle: Martin-Luther-Universität Halle-Wittenberg, 1985.

Model, Anselm. *Metaphysik und reflektierende Urteilskraft bei Kant: Untersuchungen zur Transformierungen des leibnizischen Monadenbegriffes in der "Kritik der Urteilskraft."* Monographien zur philosophischen Forschung, 247. Frankfurt a/M: Athenäum, 1987.

Möbius, P. J. *Über das Pathologische bei Goethe.* 2d ed. 1898. Reprint, Munich: Matthes and Seitz, 1982.

Montegut, Emile. *La Revue des deux mondes,* 1863, 194–95.

Morgenstern, Karl. "Über das Wesen des Bildungsromans," *Inländisches Museum* 1, no. 3 (1820). Reprinted in *Zur Geschichte des deutschen Bildungsromans,* ed. Rolf Selbmann, Wege der Forschung 640 (Darmstadt: Wissenschaftliche Buchgesellschaft, 1988).

Müller, Carl. *Jeremias Gotthelf und die Ärzte.* Bern: Paul Haupt, 1959.

Müller, Lothar. *Die kranke Seele und das Licht der Erkenntnis: Karl Philipp Moritz' "Anton Reiser."* Frankfurt a/M: Athenäum, 1987.

Muenzer, Clark S. *Figures of Identity: Goethe's Novels and the Enigmatic Self.* University Park: Pennsylvania State University Press, 1984.

Nager, Frank. *Der heilkundige Dichter: Goethe und die Medizin.* 3d ed. Zürich: Artemis, 1992.

Nassen, Ulrich. "Trübsinn und Indigestion—Zum medizinischen und literarischen Diskurs über Hypochondrie im 18. Jahrhundert." In *Fugen: Deutsch-Französisches Jahrbuch für Text-Analytik,* 171–86. Olten and Freiburg im Breisgau: Walter, 1980.

Neubauer, John. *Bifocal Vision. Novalis' Philosophy of Nature and Disease.* University of North Carolina Studies in the Germanic Languages and Literatures, 68. Chapel Hill: University of North Carolina Press, 1971.

———. *The Fin-de-Siècle Culture of Adolescence.* New Haven: Yale University Press, 1992.

Neumann, Gerhard. "'Ich bin gebildet genug, um zu lieben und zu trauern': Die Erziehung zu Liebe in Goethes 'Wilhelm Meister.'" In *Liebesroman—Liebe im Roman: Eine Erlanger Ringvorlesung,* edited by Titus Heydenreich with Egert Pöhlmann, 41–82. Erlanger Forschungen, Reihe A, Geisteswissenschaften, 41. Erlangen: Universitätsbibliothek, 1982.

———. "Wissen und Liebe: Der auratische Augenblick im Werk Goethes." In *Augenblick und Zeitpunkt: Studien zur Zeitstruktur und Zeitmetaphorik in Kunst und Wissenschaften*, edited by Christian W. Thomsen and Hans Holländer, 282–305. Darmstadt: Wissenschaftliche Buchgesellschaft, 1984.

Nicolai, Ernst Anton. *Gedancken von den Würkungen der Einbildungskraft in den menschlichen Körper.* 2d ed. Halle: Hemmerde, 1751.

Nitzschke, Bernd. "Goethe ist tot, es lebe die Kultur." Introduction to *Über das Pathologische bei Goethe*, by P. J. Möbius. Munich: Matthes and Seitz, 1982.

Novalis (Friedrich von Hardenberg). *Werke.* Edited by Gerhard Schulz. Munich: Beck, 1969.

———. *Schriften.* Edited by Richard Samuel. 2d ed. 4 vols. Stuttgart: Kohlhammer, 1960.

Obermeit, Werner. *"Das unsichtbare Ding, das Seele heißt": Die Entdeckung der Psyche im bürgerlichen Zeitalter.* Frankfurt a/M: Syndikat, 1980.

Öhrgaard, Per. *Die Genesung des Narcissus: Eine Studie zu Goethe: "Wilhelm Meisters Lehrjahre."* Translated by Monika Wesemann. Kopenhagener Germanistische Studien, 7. Copenhagen: Koebenhavns Universität, Institut for Germansk Filologi, 1978.

Osinski, Jutta. *Über Vernunft und Wahnsinn: Studien zur literarischen Aufklärung in der Gegenwart und im 18. Jahrhundert.* Bonner Arbeiten zur deutschen Literatur, 41. Bonn: Bouvier, 1983.

Pickett, T. H. "K. A. Varnhagen von Ense: The Original Goethianer." *Colloquia Germanica* 19, no. 2 (1986): 138–44.

Pietzcker, Carl. *Einführung in die Psychoanalyse des literarischen Kunstwerkes am Beispiel von Jean Pauls "Rede des toten Christus."* Würzburg: Königshausen und Neumann, 1983.

Pinkernel, Beate. See Berghahn, Klaus L.

Platner, Ernst. *Vermischte Aufsätze über medicinische Gegenstände.* Leipzig, 1796.

Platner, Johann Zachariä. *Gründliche Einleitung in die Chirurgie oder kurze Anweisung alle Krankheiten, so denen Chirugis vorkommen.* 2 parts. Leipzig: Caspar Fritsch, 1757.

Pontalis, J. P., and Jean Laplanche. See Laplanche, Jean.

Popkin, Richard H. "Medicine, Racism, Anti-Semitism: A Dimension of Enlightenment Culture." In *The Languages of Psyche: Mind and Body in Enlightenment Thought: Clark Library Lectures, 1985–1986,* edited by G. S. Rousseau, 405–42. Berkeley: University of California Press, 1990.

Potter, Edith, and Max L. Baeumer. See Bauemer, Max L.

Probst, Christian. "Das Menschenbild der praktischen Medizin im 18. Jahrhundert, gezeigt an den Beispielen der Iatromechanik und des Epidemismus." In *Deutschlands kulturelle Entfaltung: Die Neubestimmung des Menschen*, edited by Berhard Fabian, Wilhelm Schmidt-Biggermann, and Rudolf Vierhaus, 156–58. Studien zum 18en. Jahrhundert, 2–3. München: Kraus, 1980.

———. *Der Weg des ärztlichen Erkennens am Krankenbett: Herman Boerhaave und die ältere Wiener medizinische Schule.* Vol. 1, *1701–1787.* Sudhoffs Archiv. Zeitschrift für Wissenschaftsgeschichte, 15. Wiesbaden: Franz Steiner, 1972.

Pröhle, Heinrich. *Lessing, Wieland, Heinse: Nach den handschriftlichen Quellen in Gleims Nachlasse dargestellt.* 2d ed. Berlin: Liebel, 1879.

Promies, Wolfgang. *Die Bürger und der Narr, oder das Risiko der Phantasie: Sechs Kapitel über das Irrationale in der Literatur des Rationalismus.* München: Carl Hanser, 1966.

Rather, L. J. *Mind and Body in Eighteenth-Century Medicine: A Study Based on Jerome Gaub's "De regimine mentis."* London: Wellcome Historical Medical Library, 1965.

Reil, Johann Christian. *Rhapsodieen über die Anwendung der psychischen Curmethode auf Geisteszerrüttungen.* Halle: Curt, 1803; reprint, Amsterdam: E. J. Bonset, 1968.

Reuchlein, Georg. *Bürgerliche Gesellschaft, Psychiatrie, und Literatur. Zur Entwicklung der Wahnsinnsthematik in der deutschen Literatur des späten 18. und frühen 19. Jahrhunderts.* Münchner Germanistische Beiträge 35. Munich: Wilhelm Fink, 1986.

————. *Die Heilung des Wahnsinns bei Goethe: Orest, Lila, der Harfner, und Sperate: Zum Verhältnis von Literatur, Seelenkunde, und Moral im späten 18. Jahrhundert.* Literatur & Psychologie, 13. Frankfurt a/M, Bern, and New York: Peter Lang, 1983.

Rey, Michel. "Police and Sodomy in Eighteenth-Century Paris: From Sin to Disorder." In *The Pursuit of Sodomy: Male Homosexuality in Renaissance and Enlightenment Europe,* edited by Kent Gerard and Gert Hekma, 129–46. New York: Harrington Park, 1989.

Richter, Simon. *Laocoon's Body and the Aesthetics of Pain: Winckelmann, Lessing, Herder, Moritz, Goethe.* Detroit: Wayne State University Press, 1992.

Rickels, Laurence. *The Case of California.* Baltimore: Johns Hopkins University Press, 1991.

Riedel, Wolfgang. *Die Anthropologie des jungen Schiller: Zur Ideengeschichte der medizinischen Schriften und der "Philosophischen Briefe."* Würzburg: Königshaus und Neumann, 1985.

Roberts, David. *The Indirections of Desire: Hamlet in Goethe's "Wilhelm Meister."* Reihe Siegen, Beiträge zur Literatur und Sprachwissenschaft, 14, Germanistische Abteilung. Heidelberg: Carl Winter Universitätsverlag, 1980.

Roberts, Marie Mulvey, and Roy Porter. Introduction to *Literature and Medicine in the Eighteenth Century,* edited by Marie Mulvey Roberts and Roy Porter. New York: Routledge, 1993.

Röder, Gerda. *Glück und glückliches Ende im deutschen Bildungsroman: Eine Studie zu Goethes "Wilhelm Meister."* Munich: Max Heuber, 1968.

Romanell, Patrick. *John Locke and Medicine.* New York: Prometheus, 1984.

Rothschuh, Karl Eduard. "Leibniz, die prästabilisierte Harmonie und die Ärzte seiner Zeit." In *Mathematik-Naturwissenschaften,* vol. 2 of *Akten des internationalen Leibniz-Kongresses Hannover, 14–19 November 1966.* 5 vols. Studia Leibnitziana Supplementa, II. Wiesbaden: Franz Steiner, 1969.

Rousseau, George S. "Cultural History in a New Key: Towards a Semiotics of the Nerve." In *Interpretation and Cultural History,* edited by Joan H. Pittock and Andrew Wear. London: Macmillan, 1991.

————. *Perilous Enlightenment: Pre- and Post-modern Discourses: Sexual, Historical.* Manchester: Manchester University Press, 1991.

Rousseau, George S., and Roy Porter, eds. *Sexual Underworlds of the Enlightenment.* Manchester: Manchester University Press, 1987.

Rüdiger, Andreas. *Herrn Christian Wolffens Meinung von dem Wesen der Seele und eines Geistes überhaupt; und D. Andreas Rüdigers Gegen-Meinung.* Leipzig: J. S. Heinsii, 1727.

Saine, Thomas P. "Über Wilhelm Meisters 'Bildung.'" In *Lebendige Form: Interpretationen zur deutschen Literatur. Festschrift für Heinrich E. K. Henel,* edited by Jeffrey L. Sammons and Ernst Schürer, 63–81. Munich: Wilhelm Fink, 1970.

Saße, Günther. *Die aufgeklärte Familie: Untersuchungen zur Genese, Funktion, und Realitätsbezogenheit des familialen Wertsystems im Drama der Aufklärung.* Studien zur deutschen Literatur, 95. Tübingen: Niemeyer, 1988.

Sauder, Gerhard. "Popularphilosophie und Kant-Exegese: Daniel Jenisch." In *Idealismus und Aufklärung: Kontinuität und Kritik der Aufklärung in Philosophie und Poesie um 1800,* edited by Christoph Jamme and Gerhard Kurz, 162–78. Deutscher Idealismus, 14. Stuttgart: Klett-Cotta, 1988.

Schiebinger, Londa. *The Mind Has No Sex? Women in the Origins of Modern Science.* Cambridge: Harvard University Press, 1989.

Schiller, Friedrich. *Schillers Briefwechsel mit Körner von 1784 bis zum Tode Schillers.* Edited by Karl Goedeke. 2d ed. Leipzig: Veit & Co., 1878.

———. *Schillers Werke: Nationalausgabe.* Edited by Benno von Wiese. Weimar: Böhlhaus, 1962.

Schings, Hans-Jürgen. "Agathon–Anton Reiser–Wilhelm Meister: Zur Pathogenese des modernen Subjekts im Bildungsroman." In *Goethe im Kontext,* edited by Wolfgang Wittkowski, 42–68. Tübingen: Max Niemeyer, 1984.

———. "Der anthropologische Roman: Seine Entstehung und Krise im Zeitalter der Spätaufklärung." In *Deutschlands kulturelle Entfaltung: Die Neubestimmung des Menschen,* edited by Bernhard Fabian, Wilhelm Schmidt-Biggemann, and Rudolf Vierhaus, 247–75. Studien zum 18en. Jahrhundert, vols. 2/3. Munich: Kraus, 1983.

———. *Melancholie und Aufklarung.* Stuttgart: Metzler, 1977.

———. "Natalie und die Lehre des †††: Zur Rezeption Spinozas in 'Wilhelm Meisters Lehrjahren.'" *Jahrbuch des Wiener Goethe-Vereins* 89–91 (1985–87): 37–88.

———. "Symbolik des Glücks: Zu Wilhelm Meisters Bildergeschichte." In *Johann Wolfgang von Goethe: One Hundred and Fifty Years of Continuing Vitality,* edited by Ulrich Goebel and Wolodymyr T. Zyla, 155–77. Annual Comparative Literature Symposium 15. Lubbock: Texas Tech Press, 1984.

———. "Wilhelm Meisters Geselle Laertes." *Euphorion* 77, no. 4 (1983): 419–37.

———. "Wilhelm Meisters schöne Amazone." *Jahrbuch der deutschen Schillergesellschaft* 29 (1985): 141–206.

Schipperges, Heinrich. "Der Medicus Schiller und das Konzept seiner Heilkunde." In *Schiller und die höfische Welt,* edited Achim Aurnhammer, 134–47. Tübingen: Niemeyer, 1990.

Schlaffer, Hannelore. *Wilhelm Meister: Das Ende der Kunst und die Wiederkehr des Mythos.* Stuttgart: Metzler, 1980.

Schlaffer, Heinz. "Exoterik und Esoterik in Goethes Romanen." *Goethe-Jahrbuch* 15 (1978): 212–26.

Schlechta, Karl. *Goethes Wilhelm Meister.* Frankfurt a/M: Vittorio Klostermann, 1953.

Schlegel, Friedrich. *Schriften zur Literatur.* Edited by Wolfdietrich Rasch. 2d ed. Munich: DTV, 1985.

Schöne, Albrecht. "Interpretationen zur dichterischen Gestaltung des Wahnsinns in der deutschen Literatur." Diss., University of Münster, 1951.

Schrenk, Martin. "Der Umgang mit dem Geisteskranken in der beginnenden deutschen Psychiatrie." "Habilitationsschrift," Albert-Ludwigs Universität zu Freiburg i. Br., 1968.

———. *Über den Umgang mit Geisteskranken: Die Entwicklung der psychiatrischen Therapie vom "moralischen Regime" in England und Frankreich zu den "psychischen Curmethoden" in Deutschland.* Monographien aus dem Gesamtgebiete der Psychiatrie. Psychiatry Series, 10. Berlin, Heidelberg, and New York: Springer Verlag, 1973.

Schwab, Dieter. "Familie." In *Geschichtliche Grundbegriffe. Historisches Lexikon zur politisch-sozialen Sprache in Deutschland,* edited by Otto Brunner, Werner Conze, and Reinhart Kosselek. 8 vols. Stuttgart: Klett, 1975.

Schwanitz, Hans Joachim. *Homöopathie und Brownianismus, 1795–1844: Zwei wissenschaftstheoretische Fallstudien aus der praktischen Medizin.* Stuttgart: Fischer, 1983.

Sedgwick, Eva Kosofsky. *Between Men: English Literature and Male Homosocial Desire.* New York: Columbia University Press, 1985.

Selbmann, Rolf, ed. *Zur Geschichte des deutschen Bildungsromans*. Wege der Forschung 640. Darmstadt: Wissenschaftliche Buchgesellschaft, 1988.

Showalter, Elaine. *The Female Malady: Women, Madness, and English Culture, 1830– 1980*. New York: Penguin, 1985.

Shryock, Richard Harrison. *The Development of Modern Medicine: An Interpretation of the Social and Scientific Factors Involved*. London: Gollancz, 1948.

Sloterdijk, Peter. *Der Zauberbaum: Die Entstehung der Psychoanalyse im Jahr 1785: Ein epischer Versuch zur Philosophie der Psychologie*. Frankfurt a/M: Suhrkamp, 1985.

Smollett, Tobias. *The Adventures of Roderick Random* (1748). Edited Paul-Gabriel Boucé. New York: Oxford University Press, 1979.

Sontag, Susan. *AIDS and its Metaphors*. New York: Farrar, Straus, Giroux, 1989.

———. *Illness as Metaphor*. New York: Vintage: 1979.

Spieß, Christian Heinrich. *Biographien der Wahnsinnigen*. Edited, with an afterword, by Wolfgang Promies. Neuwied and Berlin: Luchterhand, 1966.

Stahl, Georg Ernst. *Über den mannigfaltigen Einfluß von Gemütsbewegungen auf den menschlichen Körper (Halle 1695). Über die Bedeutung des synergischen Prinzips für die Heilkunde (Halle 1695). Über den Untershied zwischen Organismus und Mechanismus (1714). Überlegungen zum ärztlichen Hausbesuch (Halle 1703)*. Translated and annotated, with introduction, by B. Josef Gottlieb. Sudhoffs Klassiker der Medizin, 36. Leipzig: J. A. Barth, 1961.

Staiger, Emil. *Goethe*. 3d ed. 3 vols. Zürich: Atlantis, 1962.

Stanitzek, Georg. "Bildung und Roman als Momente bürgerlicher Kultur: Zur Frühgeschichte des deutschen 'Bildungsromans.'" *Deutsche Vierteljahresschrift* 62, no. 3 (September 1988): 416–50.

Starobinsky, Jean. *Geschichte der Melancholiebehandlung von den Anfängen bis 1900*. Documenta Geigy, Acta psychosomatica, 4. Basel: n.p., 1960.

Steakley, James. "Sodomy in Enlightenment Prussia: From Execution to Suicide." In *The Pursuit of Sodomy*, edited by Kent Gerard and Gert Hekma, 163–76. New York: Harrington Park, 1989.

Steer, A. G. "The Wound and the Physician in Goethe's *Wilhelm Meister*." In *Studies in German Literature of the Nineteenth and Twentieth Centuries: Festschrift for Frederic E. Coenen*, edited by Siegfried Mews, 11–23. Chapel Hill: University of North Carolina Press, 1970.

Steudel, Johannes. "Leibniz fordert eine neue Medizin." In vol. 2 of *Akten des internationalen Leibniz-Kongresses. Hannover, 14–19 November, 1966*. Studia Leibnitiana Supplementa, 2. Wiesbaden: Franz Steiner, 1969.

———. *Leibniz und die Medizin: Rede bei Übernahme des Rektoramtes der Rheinischen Friedrich-Wilhelms-Universität zu Bonn am 15. November 1958*. Bonner Akademische Reden, 20. Bonn: Peter Hanstein, 1960.

Straub, Katrina. "The Guilty Pleasures of Female Theatrical Cross-Dressing and the Autobiography of Charlotte Clarke." In *Body Guards: The Cultural Politics of Gender Ambiguity*, edited Julia Epstein and Kristina Straub, 142–66. New York: Routledge, 1991.

Sulzer, Johann Georg. *Kurzer Begriff aller Wißenschaften und andere Theile der Gelehrsamkeit, worin jeder nach seinem Inhalt, Nuzen, und Vollkommenheit kürzlich beschrieben wird*. 2d ed. Leipzig: J. Chr. Langenheim, 1759.

Thomé, Horst. *Roman und Naturwissenschaft: Eine Studie zur Vorgeschichte der deutschen Klassik*. Frankfurt a/M, Bern, and Las Vegas: Peter Lang, 1978.

Tieck, Ludwig. *Schriften.* Vol. 15, *Erzählungen.* Berlin: Reimer, 1829.

Tissot, Samuel. *Abhandlung über die Nerven und deren Krankheiten.* Translated by J. C. G. Ackermann. 2 vols. Frankfurt and Leipzig, 1782.

———. *Versuch von denen Krankheiten, welche aus der Selbstbefleckung entstehen.* Frankfurt a/M, 1771.

———. *Von der Gesundheit der Gelehrten.* Translated from the French. Leipzig: J. G. Müller, 1775.

Tobin, Robert. "The Medicinalization of Mignon." In *Goethes Mignon und ihre Schwestern: Interpretationen und Rezeption.* New York: Peter Lang, 1993.

———. "Prescriptions: The Semiotics of Medicine and Literature." *Mosaic* 33, no. 4 (December 2000): 179–92.

———. *Warm Brothers: Queer Theory and the Age of Goethe.* Philadelphia: University of Pennsylvania Press, 2000.

Toellner, Richard. "Medicina Theoretica—Medicina Practica: Das Problem des Verhältnisses von Theorie und Praxis in der Medizin des 17. und 18. Jahrhunderts." In *Theorie cum Praxi: Zur Verhältnis von Theorie und Praxis im 17. und 18. Jahrhundert: Akten des IV. Internationalen Leibniz Kongresses.* 4 vols. Studia Leibnitiana Supplementa, 22. Wiesbaden: Franz Steiner, 1982.

Trumbach, Randolph. "The Birth of the Queen: Sodomy and the Emergence of Gender Equality in Modern Culture, 1660–1750." In *Hidden from History: Reclaiming the Gay and Lesbian Past,* edited Martin Duberman, Martha Vicinus, and George Chauncey Jr., 129–40. New York: Meridian, 1990.

———. "London's Sapphists: From Three Sexes to Four Genders in the Making of Modern Culture." In *Body Guards: The Cultural Politics of Gender Ambiguity*, edited by Julia Epstein and Kristina Straub, 112–41. New York: Routledge, 1991.

Unzer, Johann August. *Medicinisches Handbuch.* Lüneberg and Hamburg: Berth, 1770.

Vaget, Hans Rudolf. "Goethe the Novelist: On the Coherence of His Fiction." In *Goethe's Narrative Fiction. The Irvine Goethe Symposium,* edited by William J. Lillyman, 1–20. Berlin and New York: Walter de Gruyter, 1983.

Veil, Wolfgang H. *Goethe als Patient.* 3d ed. Medizin in Geschichte und Kultur, 3. Stuttgart: G. Fischer, 1963.

Vicinus, Martha. "'They Wonder to Which Sex I Belong': The Historical Roots of Modern Lesbian Identity." In *The Lesbian and Gay Studies Reader,* edited by Henry Abelove, Michèle Aina Barale, and David Halperin, 432–52. New York: Routledge, 1993.

Wagnitz, Heinrich. *Historische Nachrichten und Bemerkung über die merkwürdigsten Zuchthäuser in Deutschland: Nebst einem Anhang über die zweckmäßigste Einrichtung der Gefängnisse und Irrenanstalten.* Halle: Gebauer, 1791–94.

Wall, Richard. *Family Forms in Historic Europe.* Cambridge: Cambridge University Press, 1983.

Watt, Ian. *The Rise of the Novel: Studies in Defoe, Richardson, and Fielding.* Berkeley: University of California Press, 1964.

Weber-Kellermann, Ingebord. *Die deutsche Familie: Versuch einer Sozialgeschichte.* Frankfurt a/M: Suhrkamp, 1974.

Weickard, Melchior Adam. *Entwurf einer einfachern Arzeneykunst oder Erläuterung und Bestätigung der Brownischen Arzneylehre.* Frankfurt a/M: Andrea, 1795.

———. *Der philosophische Arzt.* 2d ed. 4 vols. Frankfurt, Hanau, and Leipzig, 1782–85.

Weissberg, Liliane. *Geistersprache: Philosophischer und literarischer Diskurs im späten achtzehnten Jahrhundert.* Würzburg: Königshaus & Neumann, 1990.

Wenzel, Manfred. *Goethe und die Medizin: Selbstzeugnisse und Dokumenta.* Frankfurt a/M: Insel, 1992.

Wettley, Annemarie, and Werner Leibbrand. See Leibbrand, Werner.

Wezel, Johann Karl. *Versuch über die Kenntniß des Menschen.* 2 vols. 1784–85. Reprint, Frankfurt a/M: Athenäum, 1971.

Wieland, Christoph Martin. *Werke.* Edited by Fritz Martini and H. W. Seiffert. 5 vols. Munich: Hanser, 1964–68.

Wilson, W. Daniel. "Science, Natural Law, and Unwitting Sibling Incest in Eighteenth-Century Literature." *Studies in Eighteenth-Century Culture* 13 (1984): 249–70

———. "Weimar Politics in the Age of the French Revolution: Goethe and the Spectre of Illuminati Conspiracy." *Goethe Yearbook* 5 (1990): 163–86.

Witzleben, Henry von. "Goethe und Freud." *Studium Generale* 19 (1960): 606–27.

Wolff, Christian. *Gedancken von Gott, der Welt, und der Seele des Menschen, auch allen Dingen überhaupt.* 3d ed. 2 vols. Halle: Renger, 1725.

Wolff, Eugen. *Mignon: Ein Beitrag zur Geschichte des Wilhelm Meister.* Munich: Beck, 1909.

Wunderlich, Gesa. *Krankheits- und Therapiekonzepte am Anfang der deutschen Psychiatrie (Haindorf, Heinroth, Ideler).* Abhandlungen zur Geschichte der Medizin und der Naturwissenschaften, 41. Husum: Matthiesen, 1981.

Wundt, Max. *Goethes Wilhelm Meister und die Entwicklung des modernen Lebesideals.* Berlin and Leipzig: G. J. Göschen, 1913.

Zedler, Johann Heinrich. *Großes Universal-Lexikon aller Wissenschaften und Künste.* 64 vols. Leipzig and Halle: Zedler, 1735.

Zimmermann, Johann Georg. *Fragmente über Friedrich den Großen: Zur Geschichte seines Lebens, seiner Regierung, und seines Charakters.* 3 vols. Leipzig, 1790.

———. *Ueber die Einsamkeit.* 4 vols. Frankfurt and Leipzig, 1785.

———. *Von der Erfahrung in der Arzneykunst.* New edition. Zürich: Orell, Geßner, Füeßlin, und Co., 1777.

———. *Von der Einsamkeit.* Frankfurt and Leipzig, 1777.

Ziolkowski, Theodore. *German Romanticism and Its Institutions.* Princeton: Princeton University Press, 1990.

Zückert, Johann Friedrich. *Medicinisches Tischbuch, oder Cur und Präservation der Krankheiten durch diätetische Mittel.* 2d ed. Berlin: Mylius, 1775.

Index